INTERGOVERNMENTAL
MANAGEMENT *for the*
TWENTY-FIRST CENTURY

Intergovernmental Management *for the* Twenty-First Century

Timothy J. Conlan

Paul L. Posner

editors

Sponsored by
National Academy of Public Administration

BROOKINGS INSTITUTION PRESS
Washington, D.C.

ABOUT BROOKINGS
The Brookings Institution is a private nonprofit organization devoted to research, education, and publication on important issues of domestic and foreign policy. Its principal purpose is to bring the highest quality independent research and analysis to bear on current and emerging policy problems. Interpretations or conclusions in Brookings publications should be understood to be solely those of the authors.

Library of Congress Cataloging-in-Publication data

Intergovernmental management for the twenty-first century / Timothy J. Conlan and Paul L. Posner, editors.
   p. cm.
   Summary: "Defines an agenda for improving the performance of America's intergovernmental system. Looks at the current state of intergovernmental relations, analyzes the system's fiscal underpinnings, and identifies principal tools to define intergovernmental management. Applies these themes to critical policy areas such as homeland security, education, welfare, health care, and the environment"—Provided by publisher.
   Includes bibliographical references and index.
   ISBN 978-0-8157-1542-9 (cloth : alk. paper)
   ISBN 978-0-8157-1541-2 (pbk. : alk. paper)
   1. Federal government—United States. 2. Central-local government relations—United States. 3. Decentralization in government—United States. 4. Intergovernmental fiscal relations—United States. I. Conlan, Timothy J. II. Posner, Paul L. III. Title.

JK325.I55 2008
352.140973—dc22   2008015705

9 8 7 6 5 4 3 2 1

The paper used in this publication meets minimum requirements of the American National Standard for Information Sciences—Permanence of Paper for Printed Library Materials: ANSI Z39.48-1992.

Typeset in Adobe Garamond

Composition by Cynthia Stock
Silver Spring, Maryland

Printed by R. R. Donnelley
Harrisonburg, Virginia

To Sam Beer
Teacher, Scholar, Friend

CONTENTS

Foreword   ix
ALICE M. RIVLIN

Acknowledgments   xiii

1   *Introduction: Intergovernmental Management
    and the Challenges Ahead*   1
    TIMOTHY J. CONLAN AND PAUL L. POSNER

PART I
FRAMING THE INTERGOVERNMENTAL DEBATE

2   *Updating Theories of American Federalism*   13
    RICHARD P. NATHAN

3   *Between a Rock and a Hard Place:
    The Evolution of American Federalism*   26
    TIMOTHY J. CONLAN

4   *Intergovernmental Finance in the New Global Economy:
    An Integrated Approach*   42
    RAYMOND C. SCHEPPACH AND FRANK SHAFROTH

PART II
TESTING THE INTERGOVERNMENTAL SYSTEM:
ISSUES AND CHALLENGES

5 *Developing a National Homeland Security System:
   An Urgent and Complex Task in Intergovernmental Relations*   77
   CHARLES R. WISE AND RANIA NADER

6 *Accountability and Innovation: New Directions
   in Education Policy and Management*   102
   KENNETH K. WONG

7 *Welfare Reform: A Devolutionary Success?*   124
   JOCELYN M. JOHNSTON

8 *Medicaid Waivers: License to Shape the Future
   of Fiscal Federalism*   157
   CAROL S. WEISSERT AND WILLIAM G. WEISSERT

9 *Regionalism and Global Climate Change Policy:
   Revisiting Multistate Collaboration as an
   Intergovernmental Management Tool*   176
   BARRY G. RABE

PART III
ISSUES OF GOVERNANCE IN THE INTERGOVERNMENTAL SYSTEM

10 *From Oversight to Insight: Federal Agencies
    as Learning Leaders in the Information Age*   209
    SHELLEY H. METZENBAUM

11 *Performance Management and Intergovernmental Relations*   243
    BERYL A. RADIN

12 *Block Grants and Devolution: A Future Tool?*   263
    CARL W. STENBERG

13 *Mandates: The Politics of Coercive Federalism*   286
    PAUL L. POSNER

14 *Intergovernmental Lobbying: How Opportunistic Actors
    Create a Less Structured and Balanced Federal System*   310
    TROY E. SMITH

15 *Conclusion: Managing Complex Problems
    in a Compound Republic*   338
    PAUL L. POSNER AND TIMOTHY J. CONLAN

Contributors   353
Index   355

Foreword

In presidential campaigns, candidates of both parties wax eloquent about what they will do, if elected, to improve the public services that citizens most care about. They confidently assure voters that they will improve the performance of local schools, repair dangerous bridges, ensure low-income families access to effective health services, clean up pollution, reduce street crime, and respond rapidly to natural disasters and terrorist attacks. A listening voter might be forgiven for believing that, with the consent of Congress, a president has the power to deliver on these promises and implement the policies for which the voters have chosen him or her over other candidates. In fact, however, this voter would be wrong. With respect to all these issues so close to voters' hearts, a new president, even with a cooperative Congress, has at best a mandate to negotiate policy changes with fifty states and even less direct responsibility for implementing new policies once they have been decided.

In national defense, foreign affairs, and a few domestic programs (notably, Social Security and Medicare), the federal government calls the shots. Most domestic policy, however, involves multiple layers of government in complex and often obscure ways. The federal government uses an incredible array of policy tools, including regulations, mandates, incentive grants, partnerships, and persuasion, to exert its influence on policies and relies heavily on states and their localities to carry them out. This complicated federal system has many benefits in a huge and diverse country with a strong tradition of resisting central authority. It permits flexibility and innovation in public services and allows for differences in priorities in different parts of the country. But it also has potential for stress, mismanagement, wasteful infighting, and undesired outcomes when policymakers at all levels lose sight of the importance of keeping the intergovernmental machinery in repair and operating smoothly.

This book brings together the wisdom and ideas of a group of thoughtful, knowledgeable experts on our federal system. It deals both with the overall state of intergovernmental interaction and with particular areas of difficulty or innovation. Collectively, the authors shout loud and clear, "Pay attention to our federal system! It is changing; it is stressed, and the stresses are about to get much worse. If you care about improving public services in the United States, work hard now to understand and improve the functioning of our federal system." This warning could hardly be timelier, and this book backs it up with solid research on the state of our federal system.

There are cogent reasons for refocusing on federalism right now. The grim outlook for the federal budget makes it inevitable that in the near future, strains between the federal government and the states over funding domestic programs will escalate into a crisis. Promises made to seniors under Social Security and Medicare, combined with dramatic prospective increases in the number of older people and the rising cost of medical care, mean that federal spending will far outrun federal revenues over the next couple of decades. Federal decisionmakers will be forced to choose among extremely unpopular options—raising taxes, reneging on promises to the elderly, and drastic cuts in other spending, including money for state and local governments. These tough choices will have to be made in the context of strong antitax sentiment at all levels of government and escalating demand for exactly the services that involve maximum interaction between Washington and the states. Citizen concern about education, affordable health care, safe infrastructure, environmental protection, reduction in crime, and rapid response to threats and disasters is sure to keep on growing. Responding adequately to these widely felt needs will take constant attention to improving the functioning of our federal system.

Making federal-state interactions work smoothly is neither easy nor glamorous. As the authors of this volume point out, the few institutions historically charged with improving intergovernmental communications—or even keeping track of what is happening—have been seriously neglected in recent years and in some cases abolished. We need to reverse course quickly. Improving the machinery of federalism is essential to making government services more responsive and effective at all levels and dealing with the looming choices posed by the demographic and economic pressures that face the United States in the years immediately ahead. The authors of this book have made a major contribution to the cause of public understanding of the importance of intergovernmental interaction in our federal system and how to improve it.

ALICE M. RIVLIN

Acknowledgments

This book had its origins in our years of working in and around the U.S. Congress. From that vantage point, it was apparent that issues of intergovernmental management were absolutely central to the design and effective implementation of federal policy, yet relatively little in-depth analysis was available to inform and help shape legislative decisionmaking. Given the demise of analytical institutions such as the Advisory Commission on Intergovernmental Relations, it was high time for some fresh thinking about the design and management of federal intergovernmental policy. This book represents an attempt to begin addressing that need, and it could not have been conceived, written, or edited without the assistance of a great many people.

Our thanks go first to the authors of our various chapters, each of whom kindly agreed to depart from his or her own research agenda and professional demands to contribute to this volume. We have benefited greatly from their insights and expertise, as expressed both in their written chapters and in our discussions and conversations with them. Whatever contributions this volume makes to understanding and dealing with the challenges of intergovernmental management in the years ahead rests principally on their shoulders.

We would also like to thank the National Academy of Public Administration, which is the cosponsor of this volume. The book project itself was launched in conjunction with a research conference at George Mason University in 2005, which was cosponsored with NAPA's Standing Panel on the Federal System. In addition to those in this volume, a number of other scholars and NAPA Fellows contributed papers and participated in the conference, including Deil Wright, Enid Beaumont, Bruce McDowell, Costas Toregas, and William Jenkins. Several others served as discussants at the conference, providing very valuable advice on the direction of the book as a whole and on the content of individual chapters. We owe a special thanks to these participants, especially Tom Stanton, Sheldon Edner, Jim Frech, and Scott Fosler.

More broadly, we owe an intellectual debt to many outstanding scholars in the fields of federalism, intergovernmental relations, and intergovernmental management. Foremost among these are Samuel H. Beer, to whom this volume is dedicated; Alice Rivlin, who wrote the foreword for this book; David B. Walker; and David R. Beam.

We also would like to thank all of those at the Brookings Institution and the Brookings Institution Press who helped to support this book, especially Robert Faherty, Christopher Kelaher, and Pietro Nivola, all of whom saw potential in this project from the very beginning, and Mary Kwak and our editor, Katherine Kimball, who helped to bring the book to fruition. Finally, we thank three anonymous external reviewers for Brookings, who supported its publication and gave us excellent advice and feedback on its content.

Finally, but most important, we owe a special debt of gratitude to our wives, Arlene Posner and Marge Wieners, and to our children, who tolerated our absences and provided love and support throughout the process. They taught us the true meaning of the terms *partnership* and *collaboration,* which are used so widely throughout this book.

1

INTRODUCTION

Intergovernmental Management and the Challenges Ahead

TIMOTHY J. CONLAN AND PAUL L. POSNER

The intergovernmental system in the United States faces emerging challenges ushered in by economic, technological, and demographic trends of the twenty-first-century. As the nation's population ages, all levels of government will face new and more difficult fiscal choices that will test the capacity of our system to respond to emerging needs. At the same time, our institutional capacity to analyze these changes, to assess their implications for the intergovernmental system, and to craft sensible and effective policy responses has been diminishing. Particularly at the national level, an analytical infrastructure of executive branch entities, legislative subcommittees, and independent federal agencies that was gradually constructed over many years has been pruned and allowed to erode, thus undermining our institutional capacity to respond as new problems emerge. In a modest way, this book is intended to help address this knowledge gap.

New Challenges

Demographic, technological, and social changes are reshaping the nation's economy and creating new challenges for governments at all levels. An aging society and new health care technologies are driving health care costs to ever

1

higher levels. By some estimates, total health care expenditures are projected to reach 20 percent of gross domestic product by 2016. Spending for Medicare and Medicaid alone is projected to make up more than 31 percent of the total federal budget by 2017 and, without policy changes, will continue to grow further in subsequent years.[1] State budgets are also projected to become increasingly dominated by health care expenditures, squeezing the fiscal capacity needed to address infrastructure, education, and other emerging demands. State and local revenue systems face new challenges from a more globalized and technocratic economy with more mobile sources of commerce and income that can elude the grasp of taxing authorities at subnational, and even national, levels of government.[2]

Fiscal limits and constraints, however, have not translated into downsized public expectations for government. Quite the contrary: public expectations for governmental responses to a wider range of public and private problems have prompted growth in the number, size, and complexity of governmental initiatives and programs. Most important, the major public problems and policy responses of recent years are overwhelmingly intergovernmental in nature. The nature of policy challenges and the resources needed to address them are not the preserve of a single level of government; rather, the problems and the solutions to emerging challenges are widely distributed throughout our intergovernmental system.

Accordingly, the programmatic and fiscal fortunes of all levels of government have become more intertwined and interdependent than ever before. From the federal perspective, state and local program priorities, management capacity, and fiscal resources have become more essential to the success of national initiatives in such areas as health care, education, homeland security, and environmental management. As the range of federal initiatives has grown, so has the reach of federal programs, resources, and mandates into an ever wider range of state and local activities heretofore largely untouched by intergovernmental systems, from fire departments to sales tax regimes to elections administration.

The spending priorities, programmatic choices, and management practices of state and local government have increasingly come to reflect the initiatives of numerous national and even international actors and influences. On the spending side, Medicaid has nearly doubled as a share of state budgets over the past ten years and is expected to constitute one-third of state budgets over the next ten years. On the revenue side, state and local governments' revenue policies and administration have increasingly become constrained by federal preemptions, national and global business pressures, and emerging technological changes.

Adding complexity to these fiscal, demographic, and administrative challenges are correlated changes in our political system. Political processes, access, and communications have all been affected by changes in technology, finance, and organization. These changes have, in turn, altered the distribution of power within the intergovernmental system, often to the detriment of state and local governments. The explosion of interest groups and lobbyists in Washington, the proliferation of new forms of media, and changes in the political party system all affect the national policy process. They have also contributed to the rise of more self-interested, opportunistic behavior among actors in the intergovernmental system, as witnessed by the continued growth of categorical grants and the explosion of earmarks in the past ten years.

In some respects, these changes are a continuation of long-standing trends in the federal system that have been noted for more than forty years. What is new is the range of program areas that are touched by these issues and the growing stakes associated with intergovernmental programs. These trends are epitomized by the emergence of local fire departments—one of the last bastions of purely localized services—as a critical front line in the national homeland security initiative. Similarly, local schools have become a target in the national bull's-eye on education reform. Performance failures by these quintessentially local institutions now have come to be seen as having major national consequences, whether it be for national security or for the nation's educational and economic future.

These challenges will test the capacity, flexibility, and adaptability of our intergovernmental system. The design and management of intergovernmental programs have become more critical to the achievement of national goals across many areas. The emergence of new federal models of accountability for national performance goals in education, welfare, and environmental protection will test the capacity of the system to address national performance outcomes while also adapting these programs to the unique priorities, needs, and capacities of state and local systems. Emerging state and local forms of collective action will also have an impact on national goals—whether from states that have organized to achieve common objectives in such areas as streamlining sales tax policy and administration or from local areas that have reinvigorated regionalism to address spillovers and achieve more uniform policy outcomes across a regional area.

Eroding Institutional Capacity

As these changes unfold, the capacity of our intergovernmental system to systematically assess and respond to these developments will be tested as well.

Monitoring the performance and capacity of a diverse system of intergovernmental partners has always been a challenge. As the importance and relevance of intergovernmental management become more central to more policy areas, gaining a systematic and credible understanding of trends in the fiscal, programmatic, and administrative capacity of the system has become more critical.

At the same time that our need for understanding complex intergovernmental relationships is growing, our institutional capacity for intergovernmental monitoring and analysis has been weakened. Over the past quarter century, the small but invaluable network of federal offices and agencies established to help improve and rationalize intergovernmental management has been diminished, disbanded, or transformed into instruments of advocacy. At the same time, congressional attention to issues of intergovernmental relations and public administration has also eroded as intergovernmental subcommittees have been abolished or diminished in stature.

Organizational changes in the federal executive branch have been particularly striking. The White House Office of Intergovernmental Affairs, which traces its origins back to the Kestnbaum Commission of the 1950s, has gradually lost analytic capacity and policy influence. Since the mid-1980s its role has rarely extended beyond political outreach and liaison activities with state and local officials. Indeed, the office is hardly visible in the Bush White House, having been eclipsed by the president's faith-based initiative and political operations.

The Office of Management and Budget, a once-robust presence in intergovernmental management in the late 1960s and early 1970s, also dwindled over time. The intergovernmental relations office was formally abolished in 1983, and its responsibilities were divided or disbanded over time. "There is no crosscutting intergovernmental management institution any more," observes Dwight Ink, a former OMB assistant director.[3] Similarly, the Treasury Department's Office of State and Local Finance, once an important source of information and expertise on intergovernmental financial issues, was eliminated in 1988 and never replaced.

Nowhere has the decline in federal intergovernmental expertise been more dramatic than in the elimination of the Advisory Commission on Intergovernmental Relations (ACIR) in 1996. As the "permanent" successor to the Kestnbaum Commission, the ACIR was once a major source of data, policy analysis, and intergovernmental management expertise in the federal government. It played an important role in the design and creation of a host of intergovernmental policy initiatives, including General Revenue Sharing, block grants, and unfunded mandates reform. It also produced landmark research on public finance, intergovernmental regulation, substate and multistate regionalism, and the grant-in-aid system. Yet a slow period of decline beginning in the 1980s culminated in drastic budget cuts and the agency's ultimate termination by the 104th Congress.

Legislative indifference to the infrastructure of intergovernmental management was exhibited within Congress as well. Legislative subcommittees on intergovernmental relations, which were established in both the House and the Senate in the 1950s and early 1960s, became active centers of legislative initiatives and oversight from the 1960s through the mid-1980s. In 1987, however, the Senate abolished its stand-alone subcommittee on intergovernmental relations, merging it with the former subcommittee on the District of Columbia. Since 1995 there has been no Senate subcommittee with "intergovernmental relations" in its title. In the House, the Subcommittee on Human Resources and Intergovernmental Relations became the Subcommittee on Human Resources in 1997. "Intergovernmental relations" was temporarily restored to the title of a minor House subcommittee in 2001,[4] but that too was abolished in the 109th Congress. Today, only the Government Accountability Office and the Congressional Budget Office have small organized units dedicated to intergovernmental management and policy issues.

Consequently, the capacity of our policymaking institutions to oversee the performance of the system and to take concerted action to strengthen that system has become a defining issue for effective governance in the twenty-first century. Although in recent years each level of government has fortified its capacity to measure its costs and performance, the management of programs and policies across boundaries has yet to become a focus for concerted attention, analysis, and reform.

The Outline of this Book

This volume is intended to chart potential pathways for improving governance in our intergovernmental system. The chapters in the first section provide an analysis of trends that are shaping current practice in the intergovernmental system as well as analytical frameworks for interpreting those trends. Later chapters examine in more detail specific policy arenas in which intergovernmental management is central to policy outcomes and debates—homeland security, education, welfare reform, environmental policy, and health care. The book concludes with chapters addressing the capacity of the system to govern, oversee, and reform the intergovernmental system.

Framing the Intergovernmental Debate

Part 1 presents analyses designed to help illuminate the evolution of contemporary federalism as well as fiscal, regulatory, and political trends that are shaping the context of intergovernmental management. In chapter 2, Richard Nathan argues that the federal system has been a powerful driver of governmental growth in the United States. This argument builds upon his earlier proposition that American federalism has evolved in cycles of federal-state activism. Specifically, Nathan has argued that during past periods of national conservative dominance states served as the centers of progressive policy experimentation, though during eras of national liberalism they have often seemed to be conservative bulwarks.[5] Here he takes the argument further, suggesting that over time this process has the effect of ratcheting up governmental growth and activism, as expansive innovations at one level become the foundation for expanded programs at the other, once political conditions turn favorable.

In chapter 3, Timothy Conlan takes up the topic of federal evolution from another perspective. Conlan suggests that we have exhausted our insights from the Betty Crocker school of intergovernmental analysis, with its proliferation of federalism cake metaphors, and recommends turning to paradigms drawn from the natural sciences to help interpret developmental processes in the federal system. In particular, he suggests that geology can provide a rich vein of analogies for understanding both periods of change in the federal system and major continuities from one era to the next.

Fiscal and economic trends shaping the future of intergovernmental relations are analyzed by Ray Scheppach and Frank Shafroth in chapter 4. The authors outline the forces driving the emerging economy—globalization, technology, deregulation, and demographic change—and sketch their implications for federal and state expenditure and revenue systems. They suggest a series of budgetary reforms and changes in taxation to help the intergovernmental system cope with the challenges ahead.

Major Policy Issues Testing the Intergovernmental System

Part 2 focuses on specific policy domains in which the intergovernmental system is facing contemporary challenges. In chapter 5, Charles Wise and Rania Nader examine the post-9/11 expansion of federal involvement in homeland security and national efforts to create an integrated intergovernmental system in this policy field. They explore the challenges of designing, funding, and implementing a coordinated system of emergency planning, intelligence, preparedness, and response in a domain characterized by conflicting federal, state, and local roles, resources, and capabilities.

A similar theme of intergovernmental tension is developed by Kenneth Wong in chapter 6, which examines the Bush administration's efforts to shape education standards and services in the traditionally decentralized field of public education. Wong places the No Child Left Behind program in the context of earlier state and federal efforts to improve performance standards in education and to increase public education services to poor children. He also analyzes the challenges of policy design and implementation in this field and the intergovernmental intersection of education initiatives at multiple levels of government, from voucher initiatives to state takeovers of failing local schools.

In contrast to nationalizing trends in homeland security and education, welfare policy was the focus of a widely heralded attempt at policy devolution in 1996, when Congress replaced Aid to Families with Dependent Children with the Temporary Assistance for Needy Families (TANF) block grant. In chapter 7, Jocelyn Johnston seeks to gauge the success of this effort by exploring the implementation of welfare reform and its policy consequences. She examines new areas of state discretion provided by welfare reform as well as the impact of tightened federal standards for welfare eligibility and job placement. Finally, she assesses the intergovernmental effects of welfare reform's reauthorization in 2006.

Another technique of policy decentralization is explored by Carol and William Weissert in chapter 8, which analyzes the effects of federal waivers in the administration of state Medicaid programs. Just as waivers were used to experiment with welfare reform before the enactment of TANF, administrative waivers of federal rules and standards in the Medicaid program are allowing new approaches to the delivery of health services to the poor in several states. The Weisserts examine the political and administrative strengths and weaknesses of waivers as a tool of intergovernmental management. They also examine programs being developed and implemented in states such as Florida and Massachusetts, seeking to uncover emerging trends in health care finance and service delivery.

A final chapter in part 2 explores decentralized policy innovation at the state level in the absence of explicit federal policy initiatives. In chapter 9, Barry Rabe examines the proliferation of state global warming initiatives. He pays particular attention to "bottom-up" regional efforts, seeking to discover whether this form of decentralized regionalism can represent a new model for environmental policymaking.

Issues of Governance in the Intergovernmental System

A final set of chapters in this book looks at crosscutting issues of governance, management, and reform in intergovernmental programs. Chapters 10 and 11 constitute a dialogue on the strengths and weaknesses of performance management in the intergovernmental system. In chapter 10, Shelley Metzenbaum proposes that federal agencies administering intergovernmental programs focus less on enforcing accountability and more on stimulating experimentation, learning, and diffusion of best practices among state and local implementers. To this end, she urges agencies to focus their energies on devising appropriate policy goals and performance measures, backed by appropriately structured incentives and penalties. In chapter 11, Beryl Radin also examines performance management in federal grant programs, but she stresses that caution is necessary to avoid negative and unanticipated consequences. Most important from an intergovernmental standpoint, Radin notes that performance management approaches have the potential to encourage unexpected and often excessive centralization in federal programs.

In various ways, issues of centralization and decentralization also emerge as critical issues in the final three chapters. In chapter 12, Carl Stenberg considers the future of block grants as a tool of devolution, based on experience with earlier block grants. He suggests that, by some measures, block grants can contribute a greater degree of flexibility to the intergovernmental system, but their potential is often overstated and difficult to realize.

Whereas block grants and other techniques of devolution are often constrained in their impact, Paul Posner finds in chapter 13 that the velocity of federal mandating has continued apace during the Bush administration. Although some anticipated a retreat—or at least a respite—from intergovernmental regulation during the first era of unified Republican control in Washington since the early Eisenhower administration, Posner documents the continued growth of federal mandates, including areas like education standards and fire protection that have traditionally been the preserves of state and local government. To explain this growth, Posner develops a model of mandate politics that focuses on the behavior of policymakers at both the national and subnational levels.

The theme of intergovernmental politics is continued in chapter 14, by Troy Smith. Smith examines the influence of intergovernmental lobbying on federal policymaking. Changes in judicial doctrines and in American politics have relaxed traditional constraints on intergovernmental policies, he argues, placing a premium on lobbying efforts by state and local officials. He explores collective action problems that limit the ability of state and local government associations to work effectively on certain issues and examines the conditional strengths and weaknesses of individual state lobbying to influence federal policy decisions.

Finally, in chapter 15, Paul Posner and Tim Conlan take stock of the findings of previous chapters and consider options for policy responses and reform. They discuss the political roots of policy nationalization and the increasing velocity with which policy innovations at the state level are emulated by Washington and often reimposed as mandates on the states. They also discuss the erosion of cooperative federalism and the transition to more coercive and opportunistic forms of intergovernmental relations. Although the federal government continues to "borrow strength" from states and localities for the administration and partial financing of federal policy initiatives, Posner and Conlan also note that such strength cannot merely be assumed in the future, given the expected economic and demographic challenges in the years ahead. Finally, they consider the enduring strengths of the federal system, strengths that may help it meet the policy and managerial challenges in the years ahead.

Notes

1. U.S. Department of Health and Human Services, Office of Assistant Secretary for Planning and Evaluation, *An Overview of the U.S. Health Care System* (Centers for Medicaid and Medicare Services, 2007); Congressional Budget Office, *The Budget and Economic Outlook: Fiscal Years 2008–2017* (2007), p. 50.

2. Center for Intergovernmental Relations, *Financing Governments in the 21st Century: Intergovernmental Collaboration Can Promote Fiscal and Economic Goals* (Washington: National Academy of Public Administration, 2006).

3. Quoted in Tim Conlan, "From Cooperative to Opportunistic Federalism: Reflections on the Half-Century Anniversary of the Commission on Intergovernmental Relations," *Public Administration Review* 66 (September–October 2006): 663–76, p. 669.

4. The House Subcommittee on Technology, Information Policy, Intergovernmental Relations, and Census.

5. Richard P. Nathan, "Federalism: The Great 'Composition,'" in *The New American Political System,* edited by Anthony King, 2d ed. (Washington: American Enterprise Institute, 1990), pp. 241–45.

PART I

FRAMING THE
INTERGOVERNMENTAL DEBATE

2

Updating Theories of American Federalism

RICHARD P. NATHAN

Modern federalism was born in America.[1] Arguably, it was born of political necessity. It was not a bold new invention so much as what James Madison called a "composition," taking into account the existence of thirteen colonies (now states) that were unlikely to look kindly at their abolition and replacement with a national government.[2] We cannot know what the founders' motives were. Perhaps they liked this new blend whereby citizens are citizens of two governments, national and state. We can be pretty sure, however, that James Madison and Alexander Hamilton were more interested in unification than preservation—that is, more interested in the establishment of a national government than in the preservation of the powers and perquisites of the colonial governments, some of which (Virginia most of all) had a vast expanse of land and a strong standing army, while others were small and sparsely populated. Later, in 1798, outraged by John Adams' alien and sedition laws, Madison turned against his own invention when he authored the Virginia Resolutions, arguing for the state's right to secede from the new union.

The earliest justifications for the federal form were grounded in a central premise of James Madison (although not original) about the need for countervailing mechanisms to prevent the rise of overreaching power holders, surely a worthy concern. *The Federalist Papers,* which he wrote with Alexander Hamilton and John Jay (like modern op-ed articles) to advance the ratification of the U.S. Constitution, emphasized the idea that the three branches of the national government and the division of power between it and the states would prevent such excesses. States would check and balance out the authority of the national government. But they have done more than this. The activist role of the states over time has ratcheted up governmental power and responsibility in the society and the economy. In examining this proposition, the perspective of this chapter is historical.

Historical Perspective

In the nineteenth century, the role of government in the society and economy of the United States was limited except in wartime and for some, but not extensive, internal improvements. The dominant view of the relationship between the nation and the states was that of dual federalism, stipulating a discrete division of power and responsibilities between them. This division was seen in presidential actions (vetoes in some instances, and a lack of initiative in others) and in Supreme Court decisions that prohibited national government incursions into domestic policy domains on the grounds that such actions would invade state sovereignty. John Tyler was the first president to use the veto for the purpose of "maintaining the structural division of authority between the states and the federal government."[3] Tyler vetoed two national bank bills (1841) and two provisional tariff bills (1842) because he believed each would produce a chain reaction that would obscure the line between state and federal power. He also vetoed a bill to appropriate $340,000 for improvements to eastern harbors (1844), a proposal he viewed as outside the bounds of congressional commerce power and thus a threat to state sovereignty.[4] But that was then. What about now?

In the mid-twentieth century, lines became blurred. Practice, as well as academic theories of American federalism, moved from dualism to a dynamic concept as advanced in the writing of the political scientist Morton Grodzins, who emphasized the complexity of federalism, not as a layer cake but as a marble cake with "an inseparable mixture of different colored ingredients."[5] This viewpoint was advanced by some scholars in terms that depicted American federalism as inchoate and complicated—one account describes it as "bankrupt" and another as indecipherable.[6] Scholars in this camp saw the federal-state relationship as weakening over time and viewed American federalism as a way station on the road to a unitary form. The political scientist Luther Gulick said in the Great Depression years, "The American state is finished. I do not predict that the states will go, but affirm they have gone," and Harold Laski wrote about "the obsolescence of federalism." Jon C. Teaford in his excellent book *The Rise of the States* quotes former U.S. senator Everett Dirksen of Illinois (a noted phrasemaker), saying he was concerned that if prevailing trends continued, "the only people interested in state boundaries [would] be Rand-McNally."[7]

Not everyone shares this view now—or did then. Other scholars challenge the characterization of U.S. federalism that highlights its constant changeability and the resulting problem that nothing is clear, along with the prognosis that federalism is on the way out.

Writing at the same time as Grodzins, in the 1960s, the British political scientist K. C. Wheare said, "The test which I apply for federal government is simply this. Does a system of government embody predominantly a division of powers between general and regional authorities, each of which, in its own sphere, is co-ordinate with the others and independent of them?" In addition, the central and regional governments must have "exclusive control" in some areas of activity.[8] The view of the American political scientist Arthur W. Macmahon is similar: "The matters entrusted to the constituent governments in a federal system (whether their powers are residual or delegated) must be substantial and not trivial."[9]

My position is that states have played a strong and leading role in responding to domestic needs, that they still do, and that their role has been crucial for the development of national domestic policies and programs. My view is less legalistic and more nuanced than Wheare's and Macmahon's and at the same time more positive about the importance of the state role in American federalism than those of Morton Grodzins, Luther Gulick, and Harold Laski.

A useful insight as the starting point for this interpretation is found in the writing of Richard Neustadt on the horizontal dimension of American government, as opposed to its vertical federalism dimension.[10] Neustadt portrays the U.S. national government, with its three branches, as based not so much on the separation of powers as on the concept of separate institutions sharing power.[11] In the same way, the national government and the states share power. Indeed, they share power in complex ways. There is no getting around this.

Responsibilities for governmental functions can be shared in three major ways, through policymaking, finance, and administration.[12] Typical of many major functional areas of U.S. domestic public affairs are intergovernmental arrangements whereby the national government has a role in making policy and financing it but administrative responsibility is lodged with the states, which also share in policymaking and financing. Over time, the process by which these sharing arrangements are shifted and shaped has expanded the role of government in the U.S. economy and society. This is because the American brand of federalism has produced surges of governmental growth and activism on the part of both the national government and the states. Historically, these surges have had a pro-government, growth-inducing effect.

The historical approach to the study of American federalism taken in this chapter emphasizes assessments of the impact and sustainability of major changes in the functions of the national government and state governments. This approach can be contrasted with approaches that are more legalistic, emphasizing changes in laws and regulations within major functional areas of government. The challenge for scholars of American federalism is to evaluate both types of data—broad gauged and more specific—in terms of their degree of influence on the development of governmental powers and responsibilities over time.

The United States is not alone among Western democracies in having expanded the role of government. Modern industrial democracies have mixed economies; citizens have become increasingly dependent on a wide range of public institutions for the provision of services—education, poverty relief, public health and the provision of health care, workplace protections and supports, the regulation of markets, transportation, environmental protection, parks and recreation—the list goes on, encompassing many and diverse services that are heavily influenced by state governments and the local governments they charter and can oversee.

In periods when support for governmental activism was on the wane in Washington and in the country as a whole, the existence of a state-level counterforce kept the pressure on for public sector growth. Innovations, particularly those of progressive states, have been tested, refined, debugged, and often diffused across the country. In some cases, they have morphed into national policies and programs. The oscillation of surges of governmental activism, sometimes from the center and sometimes from the periphery, has impelled the growth of governmental power in a way that would not otherwise have occurred in the individualistic political culture of America.

The European pattern of a generally steadier growth path for public services and the welfare state differs from the choppier pattern of growth in the American setting. Social policies and programs in the United States have grown in ways that, according to Theda Skocpol, are often overlooked and misunderstood in characterizing the nation as the Wild West of free enterprise and limited government. Skocpol points out that from 1880 to 1929, forty-four states adopted workers' compensation laws, six adopted old-age pensions, and forty-four adopted mothers' pensions.[13] The same is true for the regulatory role and activities of state governments in the nation's industrializing economy. Regulation of railroads, public utilities, insurance, and securities corporations were developed over time by leading states, often diffused to other states, and in some cases morphing into national government responsibilities as interconnectedness in the economy increased.[14] Referring to roughly the same period as Skocpol, Allan Nevins and Henry Steele Commager write that "the first great battles of the reform movement were fought out in the states."[15] Examples of state initiatives in areas of domestic policy at the turn of the century include compulsory school attendance, vaccination laws, the creation of state boards of education, reforms of political processes, a growing role for state boards of charity, child labor laws, and state regulatory policies in licensing and zoning.

In the 1920s, when the country was "keeping cool with Coolidge," states were the source of progressive initiatives like mothers' pensions (which Skocpol highlights), unemployment insurance, public assistance, and workmen's compensation. James T. Patterson notes that states "preceded the federal government in regulating large corporations, establishing minimum labor standards, and stimulating economic development." He adds that "the most remarkable development in state government in the 1920s was the increase in spending."[16] In this way and others, state initiatives planted the seeds of Franklin D. Roosevelt's New Deal.

Fast-forward to the 1980s, when the pendulum of national social policy swung away from Lyndon Johnson's Great Society. Again, there was a surge in state-level activism, in this case in response to President Ronald Reagan's 1981–82 cuts in federal domestic spending. States reshaped their counterpart programs to reflect their priorities, increased the funding of programs in areas in which the federal government became less active, and assumed more control over the activities of local governments. In doing so, states expanded their influence, both vis-à-vis the federal government and in their relationships with local governments and nonprofit organizations.[17] In much the same way, Barry Rabe has documented how state governments developed—and continue to advance—innovative environmental policies, forming coalitions that cut across regions and partisan divides to combat global warming. In doing so, they have assumed a leadership role in a field that conventionally has been regarded as assigned to the federal government.[18]

The New, New Federalism

At the present time, liberals are on the march at the state level. Federalism is being discovered—some would say rediscovered—by liberals. Representative Barney Frank (D.-Mass.) was compared to states' righter and former U.S. senator Strom Thurmond when he argued that the states (with Massachusetts out front) should be the arbiters of same-sex marriage.[19] Frank is not alone. Other liberals see the states, particularly those with liberal leaders, as the appropriate governments to deal with domestic hard challenges. Following are some examples.

On several occasions the federal government has tried strategies to halt the growth of the Medicaid program, which aids the elderly, the disabled, and poor families. But since the program has such a broad constituency of recipient groups (not just the poor) and multiple provider interests, state governments have fought back (so far quite successfully) to shield Medicaid from Washington's retrenchment efforts.

On a broader canvas, state governments are actively reforming health policy to expand coverage, control costs, advance preventive strategies, rationalize decisionmaking about facilities, and institutionalize new information and management systems. This quiet revolution is not unusual in American public policymaking: Health reform is happening while we are talking about it. Whatever national reforms are adopted in the future, there is much to be learned from what states have been doing for the past five years.

Cleaning up the environment is a policy area in which many states are ahead of the curve compared with the federal government. This is demonstrated, for example, by the nine-state northeastern accord to freeze power plant emissions and similar regional efforts under way in California, Washington, and Oregon.[20]

Activists in many states are pulling every lever—on the part of the courts, the executive branch, and the legislature—to distribute school funding in ways that provide more aid to poor core-city and rural communities. States are also leading the way in setting up preschool programs.

States have also intervened in the provision of public infrastructure. Although the federal highway act is a big factor in the transportation field, economic development interests at the state level on a general basis view state governments as their best avenues and instruments for providing public facilities. Some of the activism to do this is old-fashioned pork barreling, but this does not diminish its importance. States often play a strong role in providing facilities for economic development as well as for other public services, as advocated, for example, by supporters of K–12 and higher education, social services, libraries, the arts, outdoor recreation, parks, and the like.

The same point applies to regulatory matters. The minimum wage is an example of an area in which states are out front nationally. According to a *USA Today* survey, seventeen states covering 45 percent of the national population have set minimum wages above the federal rate of $5.15 an hour.[21] Following California's lead in adopting a $3 billion bond issue to support stem cell research, other states have joined in, notably Illinois, Connecticut, and New Jersey.[22]

Some policy domains are not good issues for liberals to pursue nationally. Sex education is one of these—the expectation being that currently national action would cater to the intense concerns of religious fundamentalists and other conservative groups. The debate in 2005 on the Terri Schiavo case in Florida is one example of a state favoring a more liberal policy than that of President George W. Bush—and, in this case, also of its governor, the president's brother Jeb Bush. Although not a likely area for federal policymaking, teaching about evolution is yet another example of a sensitive subject that from a liberal point of view is best left to the states. In this way, large and small policies move around in American federalism. There is the case, for example, of a bill in Congress to combat the use of ingredients in cold medicines that can be used to make methamphetamine. Congressional sponsors of the legislation sided with Oregon, which "wanted to be tougher than the federal law."[23] Similarly, in an Oregon case argued before the U.S. Supreme Court, the question was whether the U.S. attorney general (John Ashcroft in 2001) could abrogate a state law permitting the administration of drugs to assist suicides. Somewhat surprisingly, the *Wall Street Journal* sided with the state on this issue in an editorial headlined, "The New, New Federalism."[24]

There also has been debate in the courts to rein in state policies permitting the use of marijuana by patients suffering from cancer and other illnesses. Similar essentially liberal issues involving state policies have arisen in the field of bioethics and on matters concerning the efforts of federal agencies to weaken state constitutional restrictions on the use of public funds to support faith-based social programs.[25] Although it is not so much a liberal versus conservative issue, the earnestness of state opposition to federal rules and requirements under the No Child Left Behind Act is evidence of state governments' feistiness in recent years in asserting their prerogatives.[26]

Franklin Foer, in the *New York Times Book Review,* said recently that this liberal version of new federalism "may look like a desperate reaction on the part of some liberals to the conservatives' grip on Washington. But in fact the well-known liberal liking for programs at the national level has long coexisted alongside a quieter tradition of principled federalism—skeptical of distant bureaucracies and celebratory of local policy experimentation."[27] In similar terms, Andrew Sullivan notes that "the U.S. Constitution was devised not as a means to avoid social and cultural polarization, but as a way to manage it without splitting the country apart." He adds, "And it says a huge amount about our contemporary amnesia with regard to the benefits of federalism that this should now be seen as some sort of revelation."[28] Summing up this literature, Paul Glastris in the *Washington Monthly* asks, "Why shouldn't the Democrats become the party of federalism?"[29]

Observations by liberals on the benefits of the federal form have their counterpart in contemporary writings from the right. Michael Greve, of the American Enterprise Institute, has advanced a strident theory of American federalism as "inverted" in the way it has produced governmental growth and the accretion of governmental powers and responsibilities: "In short, we have not one but two federalism problems. The first, well-known problem is federal overreach and meddling in local affairs that 'can never be desirable cares of general jurisdiction.' The second, poorly understood but increasingly virulent federalism problem is state interference with sister-states in national affairs. My shorthand for the concurrent emergence of those problems is 'constitutional inversion.'" Greve lambastes the rise of what he characterizes as "intergovernmental cartels," consisting of public agencies and unions, interest groups, and the providers of public service, that in his view have powered this constitutional inversion. He goes so far as to say that because federalism is a Leviathan force (his terminology), "we might be better off with a wholly national government."[30]

Similarly, Steven Malanga of the Manhattan Institute sees a problem for American government in the role and activities of "coalitions of tax eaters."[31]

> One group stands out as increasingly powerful and not quite in step with the old politics on the Left: those who benefit from an expanding government, including public-sector employees, workers at organizations that survive off government money, and those who receive government benefits. In cities, especially, this group has seized power from the taxpayers, as the vast expansion of the public sector that has taken place since the beginning of the War on Poverty has finally reached a tipping point.[32]

Malanga's diagnosis should be familiar to readers of this book. In the literature of political science, the concept of "iron triangles" has had salience for a long time. The term refers to coalitions of legislators, interest groups, and public agencies that pressure for and advance their governmental interests. President Dwight Eisenhower, in his farewell speech, spoke in similar terms about the dangers of the "military industrial complex."[33] This characterization resembles both Greve's intergovernmental cartels and Malanga's coalitions of tax eaters.

It is an oversimplification to depict such functional-area power wielders as operating at the state or national levels and either pulling for more governmental action from the center or pushing for it from the states. Such actors are better viewed as intergovernmental. They operate at both the federal and state level, and in many large local governments as well. They combine national, state, and local governmental and nongovernmental actors. Their strongest influence, whether it is exercised in Washington or at the state and local levels, depends on the values of the times. In liberal periods, liberal activists are likely to view the center as their best bet for getting things done—as do conservative groups in conservative times. It is not federalism these coalitions care about. It is advancing their interests. A commenter on an earlier paper referred to this as "venue shopping."[34] Mathematically, it is easier to advance one's purpose from the center rather than from fifty or more places as venues for political action, but it is not always possible to do so.

In the field of social policy, the result of this pattern of periodic surges is that programs have grown. The wide-ranging pluralism of actors and interest produces governmental untidiness, fragmentation, and inefficiencies. But, as James K. Galbraith has observed, the cumulative effect is that for many areas of social government (health, housing, child care, education, aid for the aged and disabled, drug treatment, and other social services), the American social safety net is now much more extensive than it is perceived to be.[35] It is a common mistake for observers to focus so heavily on the pulling and hauling of interests in the political process in Washington that they fail to appreciate the size and scope of these institutional structures.[36] Conservative actions by states can hold back social policy. For example, states in which antiabortion forces are powerful, or where there is a strong resistance to clamping down on immigration or advancing affirmative action or aiding the poor, can constrain national policy activism. The Sagebrush Rebellion in the American West is an example in the conservation field of one way resistance to central government policymaking can be a strong force on the part of state governments.[37] But over time this has not been the predominant effect of the state government role in American federalism. The unabashedly opportunistic and dynamic character of American federalism has abetted governmental growth.

Concluding Comment

The theory of this chapter, that American federalism has had a strong and lasting influence in ratcheting up governmental power and influence, focuses on substantive policy actions as the units of analysis. This theory can be contrasted to the more nationally centered theory of coercive federalism, which places relatively more emphasis on laws and regulations, particularly legal preemptions of the states by the national government.[38] It is generally less bullish than the theory advanced here, which emphasizes the activist, pro-government role of the American states. Such differences of interpretation in the academic literature can never be fully and definitively resolved. The ratcheting-up theory of U.S. federalism advanced here is decidedly state focused. It reverses the conventional politics that conservatives (often applying to Republicans) should like and support American federalism and liberals (represented by pro-government Democrats) should look more kindly on it than they typically do. This is not to deny that when expansionist views about government prevail in the society, liberals can feast at the federal government table. But over time and on the whole, I conclude that it is not unreasonable for liberals to champion federalism and conservatives to regard it as a Leviathan force.

Notes

1. This chapter is inspired by the work of Samuel H. Beer, a teacher to many of the contributors to this volume, to whom this book is dedicated. See Samuel H. Beer, "The Modernization of American Federalism," *Publius: The Journal of Federalism* 3 (Fall 1973): 49–95; Samuel H. Beer, "Federalism, Nationalism, and Democracy in America," *American Political Science Review* 72 (March 1978): 9–21; and Samuel H. Beer, *To Make a Nation: The Rediscovery of American Federalism* (Harvard University Press, 1993).

2. James Madison, *Federalist* No. 39, in *The Federalist Papers,* by Alexander Hamilton, James Madison, and John Jay (New York: New American Library, 1961), p. 246.

3. J. Richard Broughton, "Rethinking the Presidential Veto," *Harvard Journal on Legislation* 42 (Winter 2005): 123–24 (www.law.harvard.edu/students/orgs/jol/vol42_1/broughton.php).

4. Ibid.

5. Morton Grodzins, "The Federal System," in *Goals for Americans: The Report of the President's Commission on National Goals* (Columbia University Press, 1960), pp. 265–82, 265.

6. Michael D. Reagan and John G. Sanzone, *The New Federalism* (Oxford University Press, 1981), p. 19; Richard H. Leach, *American Federalism* (New York: W. W. Norton, 1970), p. 17 ("Precisely what 'federalism' means is now and never has been clear").

7. Gulick, Laski, and Dirksen quoted in Jon C. Teaford, *The Rise of the States* (Johns Hopkins University Press, 2002), p. 1. Although Teaford is cited here, his view of the role of the states is not consonant with that of other scholars cited in this chapter. Rather than slumbering, he says, in the twentieth century the states "sprang to life under a new breed of bright and vigorous governors," and they have been "vital actors" from the 1890s onward (p. 5).

8. K. C. Wheare, *Federal Government,* 4th ed. (Oxford University Press, 1964), pp. 33, 4–5.

9. Arthur W. Macmahon, "The Problem of Federalism: Survey," in *Federalism Mature and Emergent,* edited by Arthur W. Macmahon (New York: Doubleday, 1955), pp. 3–27, 4.

10. This point was suggested by Samuel H. Beer.

11. Richard E. Neustadt, *Presidential Power and the Modern President: The Politics of Leadership from Roosevelt to Reagan* (New York: Free Press, 1990).

12. Richard P. Nathan, "State and Local Governments under Federal Grants: Toward a Predictive Theory," *Political Science Quarterly* 98 (Spring 1983): 47–57.

13. Theda Skocpol, *Protecting Soldiers and Mothers: The Political Origins of Social Policy in the United States* (Harvard University Press, 1992), p. 9, table 1.

14. Thomas K. McGraw, *Prophets of Regulation* (Harvard University Press, 1984).

15. Allan Nevins and Henry Steele Commager, *A Pocket History of the United States* (New York: Washington Square Press, 1981), pp. 346–47.

16. James T. Patterson, *The New Deal and the States: Federalism in Transition* (Princeton University Press, 1969), pp. 4, 7.

17. Richard P. Nathan and Fred C. Doolittle, "The Untold Story of Reagan's New Federalism," *Public Interest,* no. 77 (Fall 1984): 96–106. See also Richard P. Nathan and others, *Reagan and the States* (Princeton University Press, 1987).

18. Barry G. Rabe, *Statehouse and Greenhouse: The Emerging Politics of American Climate Change* (Brookings, 2004). See also Ronald Brownstein, "A Wave of Activism in States May Signal a Surge Nationwide," *Los Angeles Times,* December 5, 2005, p. A9.

19. Franklin Foer, "The Joy of Federalism," *New York Times Book Review,* March 6, 2005, pp. 12–13.

20. Anthony DePalma, "9 States in Plan to Cut Emissions by Power Plants," *New York Times,* August 24, 2005, p. A1.

21. Dennis Cauchan, "States Say $5.15 an Hour Too Little," *USA Today,* May 30, 2005, p. A1.

22. James W. Fossett, "Federalism by Necessity: State and Private Support for Human Embryonic Stem Cell Research," policy brief (Albany, N.Y.: Rockefeller Institute of Government, August 9, 2007).

23. Jim Barnett, "Federal Meth," *Oregonian,* July 29, 2005, p. 1.

24. "The New, New Federalism," *Wall Street Journal,* October 5, 2005, p. A20. See also Linda Greenhouse, "Justices Explore U.S. Authority over States on Assisted Suicide," *New York Times,* October 6, 2005, p. A1.

25. Glenn McGee, *Beyond Genetics: Putting the Power of DNA to Work in Your Life*

(New York: HarperCollins, 2003); Anne Farris, Richard P. Nathan, and David J. Wright, *The Expanding Administrative Presidency: George W. Bush and the Faith-Based Initiative* (Albany, N.Y.: Rockefeller Institute Press, 2004).

26. Richard P. Nathan, Thomas L. Gais, and James W. Fossett, "Bush Federalism: Is There One, What Is It, and How Does It Differ?" paper prepared for the Association for Public Policy Analysis and Management annual research conference, Washington, D.C., November 7, 2003. It is worth noting of federal preemptory actions that it is one thing to take them, another to make them stick.

27. Foer, "Joy of Federalism."

28. Andrew Sullivan, "Federal Express," *New Republic* 231 (December 12, 2004): 6.

29. Paul Glastris, "What Now? A Discussion on the Way Forward for the Democrats," *Washington Monthly* 36 (December 2004): 20–24.

30. Michael S. Greve, "Madison with a Minus Sign," American Enterprise Institute (http://federalismproject.org/depository/Madisonminussign.pdf), pp. 1–2, 3; Greve cites the quote, "can never be desirable cares of general jurisdiction," to Alexander Hamilton, *Federalist* No. 17, in *The Federalist Papers,* by Alexander Hamilton, James Madison, and John Jay, edited by George W. Carey and James McClellan (Indianapolis: Liberty Fund, 2001), p. 81.

31. Steven Malanga, "The Real Engine of Blue America," *City Journal* 15 (Winter 2005): 66–73 (www.freerepublic.com/focus/f-news/1319836/posts), p. 67.

32. Ibid., p. 1.

33. Dwight D. Eisenhower, "Farewell Speech," January 17, 1961 (www.eisenhower.archives.gov/speeches/farewell_address.html).

34. Donald W. Moran, e-mail message, November 28, 2005, in response to Richard P. Nathan, "There Will Always Be a New Federalism," paper prepared for the American Enterprise Institute Federalism Project, December 14, 2005. On this subject, see E. E. Schattschneider, *The Semisovereign People: A Realist's View of Democracy in America* (New York: Holt, Rinehart, and Winston, 1960).

35. James K. Galbraith, "What Is the American Model Really About? Soft Budgets and the Keynesian Devolution," Public Policy Brief 72 (Levy Economics Institute of Bard College, June 2003).

36. Ron Haskins, "The Governors and the Development of American Social Policy," in *A Legacy of Innovation: Governors and Public Policy,* edited by Ethan G. Sribnick (University of Pennsylvania Press, 2008, forthcoming), emphasizes the multiplicity of policies and programs that aid the poor and needy.

37. This movement originated in western states, especially Nevada, and gained momentum beginning in the 1960s. Nevada Assembly Bill 413, entitled the Sagebrush Rebellion, passed the legislature in 1979. It called for the establishment of a review board and state control of lands within the state managed by the U.S. Bureau of Land Management. Other western states passed similar bills. The movement became prominent nationally during Ronald Reagan's presidential campaign in 1980: once elected, he pledged, he would work toward a "sagebrush solution."

38. This theory is highlighted in Paul Posner, "The Politics of Coercive Federalism in the Bush Era," *Publius: The Journal of Federalism* 37 (Summer 2007): 390–411; and Joseph F. Zimmerman, "Congressional Preemption during the George W. Bush Administration," *Publius: The Journal of Federalism* 37 (Summer 2007): 432–52. Both articles are based on a symposium on federalism developments during the George W. Bush presidency. See also John Kincaid, "From Cooperative to Coercive Federalism," *Annals of the American Academy of Political and Social Science* 509 (May 1990): 139–52.

3

BETWEEN A ROCK AND A HARD PLACE

The Evolution of American Federalism

TIMOTHY J. CONLAN

M etaphors have long been used as tools to help us think about the nature and evolution of federal systems.[1] Cake metaphors have been especially prominent, beginning with Morton Grodzins' well-known comparisons of dual federalism to a layer cake and cooperative federalism to a marble cake.[2] Other varieties of baked goodies inevitably followed: fruitcake federalism in the 1970s, crumb-cake federalism in an era of declining federal aid, and upside-down-cake federalism in the era of No Child Left Behind.

This smorgasbord of dessert metaphors has been inspired by the continuing evolution of the American federal system. Although many of these seem to be rather half baked, they have sought to capture intergovernmental change within a common framework. Alternative efforts to illustrate trends in the system with a disparate mix of metaphors have typically lacked a unifying theme. For example, in *Understanding Intergovernmental Relations*, Deil Wright suggests seven different metaphors to describe the phases of American federalism during its first two hundred years (see table 3-1).[3]

This framework captures much of the prevailing wisdom about each period: new metaphors help to capture emergent features or dynamics within the U.S. federal system as it evolved from one with a substantial degree of autonomy between federal and state governments to dense networks of

Table 3-1. *Phases of Federalism and Associated Metaphors*

Phase	Metaphor	Time period
Conflictual	Layer cake	1800s–1930s
Cooperative	Marble cake	1930s–50s
Concentrated	Water taps	1940s–60s
Creative	Flowering	1950s–60s
Competitive	Picket fence	1960s–70s
Calculative	Facade	1970s–80s
Contractive	De Facto	1980s–90s

Source: Deil Wright, *Understanding Intergovernmental Relations,* 3d ed. (Pacific Grove, Calif.: Brooks-Cole, 1988).

interaction under cooperative federalism and on to more contentious and coercive relationships in subsequent years.[4] But this effort, and others like it, suffers from vague boundaries and period overlap. If three phases—and three metaphors—apply to the 1950s and three cover the 1960s, how well can one "phase" be distinguished from another? Even if different stages gradually phase in and out, what do we do about "relics" of earlier stages that continue to persist? The cooperative extension service is still cooperative, just as it was in the 1920s or the 1950s, even though we have also seen the development of more coercive regulatory models of federal-state interaction elsewhere in agriculture, such as pesticide regulation and wetlands protections.

Thus one problem in describing the stages of American federal development is that prominent examples of previous stages persist in each new era. Broad sectors of public policy, such as family law and foreign affairs, are still characterized by a substantial—though not exclusive—dose of dual federalism, with the states predominating in one arena and the national government the other. Public health, trade and export promotion, and highway construction still provide prominent examples of cooperative federalism in practice, whereas environmental protection and civil rights have been characterized often, though not exclusively, by coercive regulatory tools of intergovernmental relations. Finally, fields like education and homeland security are moving away from deferential and cooperative modes of interaction toward more co-optive models of intergovernmental relations.

How are we to make sense of this complexity? Metaphors can still assist us with this task, graphically highlighting critical variables and illustrating key relationships.[5] But this chapter suggests that it is time to close down the intergovernmental bakery and turn to other sources of metaphors, drawn from the natural sciences.

Intergovernmental Metaphors from the Natural Sciences

The social sciences have borrowed a variety of metaphors and paradigms from the natural sciences, some of which have potential for enhancing our understanding of intergovernmental relations. Biological theories have been used to explore the growth of government programs, the development of interest group communities, and the evolution of social norms.[6] Such paradigms might usefully be adapted to describe the evolution of the federal system and the "ecology" of intergovernmental programs. Similarly, chaos theory has been used to advance our understanding of developments in public administration, and it might help describe complexity and path dependency in the intergovernmental system.[7] Geology can serve as another systematic source of intergovernmental insights, and it is the metaphor I would like to explore here.

Evolutionary Theory

Evolutionary theory is an appealing source of metaphors for intergovernmental relations, and it has been widely used in other areas of political science. The concept of punctuated equilibrium, for example, has been used to describe and analyze the development of public policy agendas.[8] A similar framework might be adapted to explain developmental patterns in American federalism, marked by periods of dramatic change, such as the New Deal or the Great Society, followed by longer periods of relative stability and incremental change.

Population ecology models have been adapted by political scientists to explain patterns of interest group development and density among the different states.[9] Such a concept might similarly be adapted to explain the varying densities of grant programs or other intergovernmental relationships in different functional areas. The ecological concept of islandness, which explains unique patterns of species evolution in isolated niches, has been used in sociology and geography, and it might be adapted to help explain distinctive clusters of intergovernmental relationships in different policy communities.

One area that needs more attention in the adaptation of biological theories to the evolution and development of the intergovernmental system is the mechanism causing observed patterns of change. That the intergovernmental system evolves is not a novel or controversial observation. Explaining the causes and direction of change, however, presents a challenge. In evolutionary biology, the causal mechanism is natural selection. Perhaps such a concept could be adapted to political evolution as well: In this case, the driving force of political ambition is constrained and shaped by the changing context of fiscal, administrative, and sociological habitats; thus a heightening of fiscal constraints restricts the growth of discretionary grants and favors greater use of regulatory tools or tax expenditures to satisfy the political ambitions of national politicians. Such concepts have at least superficial appeal, but they require more careful and systematic development for evolutionary theory to reach its potential in explaining intergovernmental relations.

Chaos Theory

Chaos theory offers another paradigm with potential for illuminating important elements of the intergovernmental system. Chaos, in fact, was one of the defining characteristics of American federalism, according to Morton Grodzins, and one of the "virtues" of our governmental system, contributing to its energy, responsiveness, and openness.[10]

As a mathematical concept, however, chaos has a more precise meaning than the tumultuous blending of public-private and federal-state-local roles that Grodzins celebrates. Chaos theory was developed to explain the behavior of nonlinear dynamical systems, such as turbulence and weather. Such systems are highly sensitive to initial conditions and unpredictable over time. Very small changes in initial conditions can generate quite different outcomes in the system (the so-called butterfly effect). Despite this unpredictability and appearance of randomness, chaotic systems create a form of order by repeating patterns at different scales or levels of measurement.

In the social sciences, chaos theory has been used to describe the behavior of markets in economics and organizational behavior in public administration.[11] Its characteristics may also be helpful in understanding intergovernmental relations. Sensitivity to initial conditions has been apparent in the path-dependent evolution of the federal system: modest policy decisions in the past have structured the course of future developments. Contending forces of centralization and decentralization parallel the competing negative and positive feedback loops that generate chaotic behavior, as well. Finally, the characteristic of scale invariability is often apparent in the federal system, whereby similar problems and challenges—monitoring accountability in grants and contracts, tensions between elected and career officials, substituting fees for taxes—are frequently replicated at different levels and scales of government. On the other hand, pure chaotic systems are ultimately deterministic in ways that human interactions in complex systems are not.

Geological Concepts

A third but as yet untapped source of descriptive metaphors for intergovernmental relations is geology. Like evolution and chaos theory, geological analogies have the advantage of capturing time, the critical variable in historical development. Geology also captures the duality of dynamism and stability of the intergovernmental system, with its convoluted patterns of continuity amid change. Finally, geology provides a variety of useful metaphors that allow one to capture the complexity of our evolving intergovernmental system within a single theoretical framework rather than seek out unique and unrelated images for every new development.

Like any metaphor, geology does not permit perfect analogies in all cases. In particular, it may give the impression of greater permanence and stability in the intergovernmental system than actually exists. "Solid as a rock" and "you can't move mountains" are common phrases that suggest the immutable character of geological formations. But mountains do, in fact, move—entire continents drift—and rocks are made and unmade over the course of earth history. What appears to be stable and unchanging in a human lifespan is a highly dynamic and changing system over geologic time.

Three Geological Perspectives on the Federal System

Geologists classify rocks into three different types: sedimentary, metamorphic, and igneous. Sedimentary rocks develop from deposits of clay, sand, and calcite that accumulate gradually at the bottom of oceans. The resulting rocks are built up gradually over time, often in distinctive layers like those visible in the Grand Canyon. Metamorphic rocks are formed out of sedimentary or other rocks that have been transformed by extreme heat and pressure. Thus marble is formed from sedimentary limestone that is subjected to the enormous weight and heat of subduction. Igneous rocks are formed out of molten magma that cools to form granite or basalt. Each of these major rock types provides a useful metaphor for aspects of our evolving federal system.

Sedimentary Federalism

A sedimentary model of the federal system highlights the different patterns of intergovernmental interaction that have evolved over time. This metaphor suggests both change and continuity—illustrating how new patterns of intergovernmental relations are often layered atop existing ones, just as new layers of sediment get deposited on top of earlier ones. Thus though new forms of intergovernmental relations have developed historically, these new patterns of

Figure 3-1. *State and Local Expenditures, 2001*

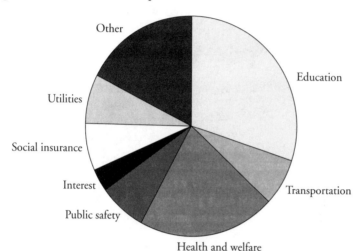

Source: U.S. Census Bureau, Governments Division, *2002 Census of Governments,* table 1, "State and Local Government Finances, by Level of Government and by State, 2001–2002," October 2005 (www.census.gov/govs/estimate/0200ussl_1.html).

intergovernmental relations often supplement earlier patterns rather than wholly supplant them. This contrasts with metaphors that focus on substitution—the replacing of layer-cake federalism with marble-cake federalism, for example, as patterns evolve over time.[12]

From the perspective of sedimentary federalism, then, the current intergovernmental system is best captured not by a single framework, such as dual, cooperative, or coercive federalism, but by all of the above. For example, our intergovernmental system still retains notable attributes of dual federalism, evident in public law, policy agendas, and public finance. Figures 3-1 and 3-2 show the major expenditure categories of the federal and combined state and local levels of government. Although there are substantial areas of comparability and overlap—both levels spend a considerable portion of their budgets on health and welfare, for example—the differences in spending priorities are even more striking. As one would expect, the federal government expends a substantial portion of its budget on defense and international affairs—items that are largely missing from the major accounts of state and local governments. Social insurance spending is far more significant at the national level, as is interest on the debt. In contrast, education is the largest single item of state and local expenditures but only a modest portion of the federal budget.

Figure 3-2. *Federal Expenditures, 2001*

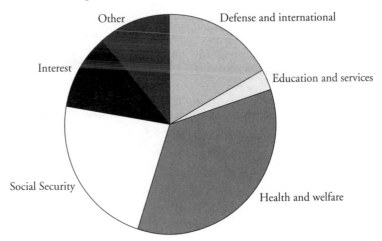

Source: Budget of the U.S. Government, Fiscal Year 2002, historical tables.

Public safety looms large in subnational accounts but is melded into the "other" category of federal expenditures.

A similar legacy of differentiation persists on the revenue side. The federal government relies overwhelmingly on the personal income tax, social insurance taxes, and borrowing for its revenues. State and local governments rely heavily on property and sales taxes, respectively, as well as intergovernmental grants-in-aid.

Substantial vestiges of dual federalism persist outside of public finance, as well. To this day, broad swathes of public policy and law remain within the principal jurisdiction of state government authority, with only modest or sharply circumscribed federal involvement. Family law, corporate law, land-use regulation, and fire protection are all examples of this pattern. By the same token, the Supreme Court has reaffirmed the national government's supremacy over defense and foreign affairs.[13]

Although important legacies of dual federalism persist, no one would claim that it characterizes the whole or even the principal dimension of American federalism today. Whatever the extent to which dual federalism once described our intergovernmental system as a whole—and this has long been debated—its influence has been diminishing for the past 150 years. The growth of federal grants-in-aid is a case in point: grants constituted the principal tool of cooperative federalism, and their expanded use and dramatic growth in the twentieth century were the most prominent harbingers of a new era in federalism.[14] As Deil Wright notes, cooperative federalism is generally considered to have characterized the intergovernmental system from the 1930s to the 1960s. The federal government became involved in a host of traditional state and local responsibilities, giving rise to an unprecedented degree of mixing and sharing of functions and responsibilities. There also developed a more cooperative approach to dealing with shared responsibilities. Joint action was lubricated by federal fiscal incentives, accompanied by a generally deferential attitude toward states and the cultivation of shared goals.[15]

The intergovernmental system today is widely perceived to be more coercive and conflictual than it was in the heyday of cooperative federalism. But just as elements of dual federalism have persisted over time, the post-1960 rise of regulatory federalism did not eviscerate cooperative modes of intergovernmental interaction everywhere or overnight. Many governmental functions and activities are still largely characterized by patterns of cooperative federalism, with a heavy emphasis on intergovernmental grants and subsidies, shared responsibilities, common professional beliefs that cut across the vertical levels of government, and considerable intergovernmental comity and trust. This model continues to describe much of the public health world, for example, just as it did in Grodzins' day; his archetypical example of cooperative federalism, after all, was the county "sanitarian." Cooperative federalism is also in evidence in the generally collaborative world of highway programs, as well as in many functions of economic development, such as export promotion. In the latter instance, one study of state and federal trade programs has found "impressive patterns of close and pervasive federal-state cooperation on a variety of international issues where both levels of government share common or complementary policy goals. Close cooperation was particularly evident on trade promotion and agricultural issues, where federal and state officials commonly shared information, office space, support services, and financial responsibility for program operations. Cooperative support for educational exchange programs and environmental assistance programs was also widespread."[16]

Since the 1960s and 1970s, more co-optive and coercive models of federalism have been layered on top of these earlier patterns. Indeed, one of the most profound changes in American federalism has been the changing mix of policy instruments employed in federal-state-local relations, moving the system away from an almost total reliance on grants and incentives and toward instruments that impose sanctions on, preempt, or co-opt state and local authority. There was an enormous expansion of federal mandates from the

1960s to the 1990s—both in absolute numbers and in the creation of new and more intrusive forms of federal regulation. Between 1960 and 1993, according to U.S. Advisory Committee on Intergovernmental Relations estimates, more than sixty new federal mandates were enacted, primarily in the fields of consumer and environmental protection, civil rights, and transportation. Only two such mandates existed before 1960.[17] Similarly, there was a doubling of federal preemptions of state and local authority in the 1970s and 1980s. According to Joseph Zimmerman, 348 of the 513 federal preemption statutes enacted by Congress since 1790 were adopted after 1965.[18]

These developments have led some to characterize the current era as one of coercive federalism.[19] There are clearly coercive elements in the growth of federal mandates, but overall, co-optive federalism seems the more apt term. Federal preemption, prescriptive but voluntary federal grant programs, and the stimulation of vertical functional relations are directed more at co-opting state and local governments and substituting federal policy priorities than coercing them directly.

From the perspective of sedimentary federalism, the development of newer modes of intergovernmental relations does not mean that old forms disappear altogether. They persist, often below the surface, and provide a foundation for more recent patterns of interaction. The relative "thickness" of the different layers of intergovernmental relations varies as well. As suggested earlier in this chapter, the cooperative layer is relatively thick or prevalent in public health services but less so in other areas. Overall, however, the character of intergovernmental relations changes over time as new relationships evolve and older patterns shrink and undergo metamorphic changes.

Metamorphic Federalism

Because of the accumulating and deepening layers of intergovernmental interaction, the system today is clearly different from what it was in the past. As with metamorphic rock, in which heat and pressure change mineral and crystalline structures from one form to another, so the political and institutional pressures of new forms of interaction alter some of the older patterns in the system. There has been a metamorphosis in the character of intergovernmental relations within specific policy realms. But the pattern is uneven because "deposits" of newer, more co-optive forms of federalism have been prevalent in some policy fields but rare in others.

Environmental protection is an example of a policy realm that has taken shape mainly in the post-1960s era, and its patterns of intergovernmental relations reflect its development in an era of regulatory federalism. Policy responses to environmental problems moved up the system from local to state to federal as the geographic extent of pollution problems expanded. Initial federal responses were largely collaborative and focused on research and incentives. But federal involvement expanded and deepened with the adoption of new, more intrusive techniques of intergovernmental regulation. Thus partial preemption programs—in which the national government establishes minimum standards but permits state implementation of these or more stringent state pollution standards—became common in the environmental arena, in programs like the Clean Air Act of 1970, the Clean Water Act of 1972, and the Surface Mining Control and Reclamation Act of 1977.[20] Direct order mandates and crosscutting federal requirements have been employed in this field as well. The conflictual character of intergovernmental relations in environmental policy became so prevalent that it was a key motivation behind the movement for unfunded mandates reform. It also spurred the search for more collaborative forms of federal-state-local relations, such as the performance partnership approach developed in the National Environmental Performance Partnership System program in the mid-1990s. Since that time, there has been some relaxation in the most stringent and costly national approaches, but the field remains characterized by a strong framework of national policy direction.

In contrast, intergovernmental relations in education were historically cooperative and deferential in nature but have undergone a metamorphosis in recent years. Traditionally, the federal government has assumed a supportive but deferential stance in elementary and secondary education, viewing the federal role as one of assisting the states with advancing their own policy visions in the field.[21] In recent decades, however, in response to growing federal attention to issues of education reform and the needs of disadvantaged groups, the federal role has become increasingly assertive and less deferential. In many respects, this process began with the National Defense Education Act in 1958, when the Soviet launch of Sputnik raised national concerns about the state of American education. The act sought to reform math, science, and language education through the use of grants and subsidies. The federal role became more assertive in the mid-1960s, when the focus shifted to assisting the educationally disadvantaged through programs such as Title I, bilingual education, and, in 1975, the Education for All Handicapped Children Act. This latter program continued to provide funds but was principally regulatory, mandating individualized education plans for all eligible students, broader access to education, and changes in instruction. The federal government's share of funding for these requirements provided only a fraction of the cost of the program, rather than the 40 percent originally promised.

This increasingly directive national approach to education reached a new plateau in the No Child Left Behind Act signed into law in 2002. This legislation institutionalized federal leadership in education reform and accountability, establishing strict timetables for the achievement of student progress goals, rigid and demanding annual testing requirements, mandated services for students attending schools failing to meet requirements, and significant potential for restructuring local public education in the future if standards are not met. Given the program's implications for local control of education and curriculum, the federal role in education has been truly transformed, and little is left of the traditional stance of federal deference in elementary and secondary education.

Homeland security is another policy field that is undergoing a clear metamorphosis. The federal role in homeland security–related fields was traditionally quite modest. In fire protection, for example, there was little history of federal support before September 11, 2001, apart from modest expenditures for fire research, small grant programs supporting local responders, and a cooperative approach to implementing federal responsibility for fires on federal lands. Federal involvement in law enforcement has a longer and more substantial history but has traditionally been secondary and deferential. There is a long history of cooperative intergovernmental relations in the law enforcement field, both vertically and horizontally with neighboring jurisdictions. The first major federal financial role came in 1968 with adoption of the Law Enforcement Assistance Act—a block grant with few federal controls and diverse (and sometimes wasteful) local responses. The program's funding terminated in 1980, and no comparably large federal program in local law enforcement was adopted until the 1990s, when the federal Community Oriented Policing Services program was adopted to promote community policing.

The real metamorphosis in the federal role occurred in the aftermath of the terrorism events of September 11, 2001. Again, substantial new federal funds were provided, accompanied by a much more assertive federal role. The newly created Department of Homeland Security began acting at times more like a national ministry of the interior than as a cooperative partner in a system in which state and local first responders play a central role, making large demands with too little consultation. The depth of the transformation was symbolized by the Federal Emergency Management Agency's 2005 requirement that local police stop using "ten-codes" (such as 10-4 for "message understood") and begin using plain language in their radio transmissions. Future federal funding would be contingent on this and other requirements of the National Incident Management System.[22]

Thus the potential for metamorphic change in intergovernmental relations, brought about in part by the accumulating weight and density of tasks and interrelationships, offers an illuminating perspective on the evolution of the federal system. Moreover, such metamorphic changes appear to develop in a predictable manner across policy domains. Paul Peterson, Barry Rabe, and Kenneth Wong have argued, for example, that federal redistributive programs have shown predictable patterns of development in areas as diverse as education, health care, and housing. Initial local noncompliance with ambitious federal redistributive aims is often followed by a regime of ever stronger federal regulations, restrictions, and mandates. The resultant conflict often leads either to the abandonment of redistributive aims or the gradual co-option of state and local governments, through the development of standard routines and practices, new professional commitments from within, and new or stronger interest group pressures from without.[23]

Igneous Federalism

Igneous rock is formed by the cooling of molten rock from the earth's mantle when it encounters air or water. One way in which this happens is volcanic eruptions on land and under water associated with subduction zones. Such zones occur at the edges of tectonic plates and are often areas of intense geologic activity—earthquakes, volcanic eruptions, and other seismic activity. Igneous processes are the most dramatic and dynamic forms of rock creation and thus provide a good metaphor for periods of dramatic change in American intergovernmental relations.

The federal system has occasionally been subject to what can be thought of as seismic events—large, rapid changes in patterns of intergovernmental interaction and in the scope and scale of federal power relationships that are quite distinct from the slow and steady changes of metamorphic federalism. The Civil War is the most dramatic example, not only because of its horrendous bloodshed but also because it determined whether the country would remain united or would fragment into two or more separate and competing nations. The Union victory not only settled the question of an indestructible union, it also laid the political and constitutional foundation for a much more centralized federal system. Such potential was only partially realized until the New Deal era of the 1930s. Then, in less than a decade, American federalism was transformed, as the national government assumed a clearly preeminent fiscal and political role. Not only did the public sector share of GDP double between 1929 and 1939, but the federal fiscal role was transformed from junior to senior partner in the intergovernmental system relative to the state and local sectors.

There have been more recent transformations, as well. The Great Society era certainly qualifies, given the creation of landmark legislation like the Civil Rights and Voting Rights Acts, Medicaid and Medicare, federal aid to education, a tripling of federal aid programs overall, and the nationalization of the Bill of Rights by the Supreme Court under Earl Warren. The sharp reductions in federal tax rates and in federal grants-in-aid in the 1980s qualify as well. Collectively, such changes demonstrate the system's capacity for large-scale rapid change under favorable circumstances. Moreover, just as the movement of large tectonic plates serves as an engine of igneous processes in geology, so large-scale demographic and sociological shifts in American politics provide energy for large policy shifts in intergovernmental relations. The growth of class-oriented industrial society before the New Deal, the civil rights movement and economic affluence in the 1960s, and the partisan realignment of southern politics all constitute underlying engines of political plate tectonics that have driven subsequent events in American federalism.

Implications for Intergovernmental Management

The richness of geologic metaphors for American federalism has useful implications for thinking about intergovernmental management. The first is that different patterns of intergovernmental relations require different approaches to intergovernmental management. Managing in the context of dual federalism, for example, requires an emphasis on classic features of public administration in order to effectively manage one's own staff, budgets, and activities. Cooperative federalism demands greater emphasis on the skills of indirect governance: understanding and mobilizing diffuse networks, placing a premium on bargaining skills and employing incentives, nurturing professional relationships. Regulatory federalism tends to be more conflictual and places greater emphasis on technical knowledge and legal authority. Mastering any one set of management skills is complex in its own right, but the insight of sedimentary federalism, with its spotty and uneven layers of intergovernmental relations, suggests that different skill sets may be needed for effective management in different fields of endeavor. Moreover, many functional fields are now characterized by multiple styles of intergovernmental relations and thus require a combination of management skill sets to accommodate the intergovernmental geology of the field.

Given the change-oriented character of metamorphic and igneous federalism, the geologic model also suggests the need for adaptability on the part of public sector managers. Because programs and policies are subject to change over time, sometimes gradually and other times as part of dramatic waves of change and reform, intergovernmental managers must be able to adapt with changing managerial skill sets as the needs arise.

Notes

1. William Stewart, *Concepts of Federalism* (Lanham, Md.: University Press of America, 1984).

2. Morton Grodzins, *The American System: A New View of Government in the United States* (Chicago: Rand McNally, 1966), p. 8.

3. Deil Wright, *Understanding Intergovernmental Relations,* 3d ed. (Pacific Grove, Calif.: Brooks-Cole, 1988), p. 67.

4. David R. Beam, Timothy J. Conlan, and David B. Walker, "Federalism: The Challenge of Conflicting Theories and Contemporary Practice," in *Political Science: The State of the Discipline,* edited by Ada Finifter (Washington: American Political Science Association, 1983), pp. 247–79; John Kincaid, "From Cooperative to Coercive Federalism," *Annals of the American Academy of Political and Social Science* 509 (May 1990): 139–52.

5. See, for instance, Mark Schlesinger and Richard Lau, "The Meaning and Measure of Policy Metaphors," *American Political Science Review* 94 (September 2000): 611–26; Keith L. Shimko, "Metaphors and Foreign Policy Decision Making," *Political Psychology* 15 (December 1994): 655–71; and Michael Barzelay and Linda Kaboolian, "Structural Metaphors and Public Management Education," *Journal of Policy Analysis and Management* 9 (Autumn 1990): 599–610.

6. See, for example, Virginia Gray and David Lowery, *The Population Ecology of Interest Representation: Lobbying Communities in the American States* (University of Michigan Press, 1996); Cynthia Cates Colella and David R. Beam, "The Political Dynamics of Intergovernmental Policymaking," in *The Nationalization of State Government,* edited by Jerome J. Hanus (Lexington, Mass.: D. C. Heath, 1981), pp. 134–56; and Elinor Ostrom, "Collective Action and the Evolution of Social Norms," *Journal of Economic Perspectives* 14 (Summer 2000): 137–58.

7. See, for example, R. A. Thiétart and Bernard Forgues, "Chaos Theory and Organization," *Organization Science* 6 (January–February 1995): 19–31; and L. Douglas Kiel and Euel Elliott, eds., *Chaos Theory in the Social Sciences* (University of Michigan Press, 1996). Complexity and chaos were favorite themes of Morton Grodzins, as well; see Grodzins, *American System,* chaps. 1, 5, and 13.

8. Frank Baumgartner and Bryan Jones, *Agendas and Instability in American Politics* (University of Chicago Press, 1993). The concept is derived from the paleontologist Stephen J. Gould's framework for reconciling normal patterns of incremental evolution with the record of periodic mass extinctions and the efflorescence of new species.

9. Gray and Lowery, *Population Ecology of Interest Representation.*

10. Grodzins, *American System,* pp. 125–36, 334.

11. See, for example, Thiétart and Forgues, "Chaos Theory and Organization"; and Gene A. Brewer, Bruce J. Neubauer, and Karin Geiselhart, "E-Government Systems: Critical Implications for Public Administration and Democracy," *Administration and Society* 38 (September 2006): 472–99.

12. In seeking to make sense of the overlapping phases of intergovernmental relations, Deil Wright (*Understanding Intergovernmental Relations,* p. 66) also draws on a geological analogy, writing that "the present state of IGR [intergovernmental relations] results from multiple overlays of each of the seven phases. The task of an IGR analyst is like that of a geologist: to drill or probe the several strata and from the samples make inferences about the surface as well as the substructure of the terrain."

13. See, for example, two recent Supreme Court cases upholding federal authority over international trade and the national guard: *Crosby* v. *National Foreign Trade Council,* 530 U.S. 363 (2000), and *Perpich* v. *Dept. of Defense,* 496 U.S. 334 (1990).

14. Jane Perry Clark, *The Rise of a New Federalism* (Columbia University Press, 1938).

15. See Grodzins, *American System;* and Stephen K. Bailey and Edith K. Mosher, *ESEA: The Office of Education Administers a Law* (Syracuse University Press, 1968).

16. Timothy J. Conlan and Michelle A. Sager, *International Dimensions of American Federalism: State Policy Responses to a Changing Global Environment* (Washington: U.S.-Asia Environmental Partnership and Council of State Governments, 1997), p. 65.

17. Exact numbers of federal mandates are difficult to estimate, depending on the definitions used and the treatment of major reauthorizations and expansions. Estimates given by the U.S. Advisory Commission on Intergovernmental Relations can be taken as conservative, however; the National Conference of State Legislatures put the total estimate at 185 during this same period; see U.S. Advisory Commission on Intergovernmental Relations, *Federal Regulation of State and Local Governments: The Mixed Record of the 1980s,* A-126 (Washington: Advisory Commission on Intergovernmental Relations, July 1993), for more details. Although the commission estimates are now more than ten years old, few of the regulations involved have been rescinded, relaxed, or terminated (reauthorization of the Safe Drinking Water Act in 1996 is an exception). Passage of the Unfunded Mandates Reform Act in 1995 appears to have slowed the rate of adoption for certain kinds of new mandates but did not rescind or relax existing ones.

18. Joseph Zimmerman, "The Nature and Political Significance of Preemption," *PS: Political Science and Politics* 38 (July 2005): 359–62. See also Pietro S. Nivola, *Tense Commandments: Federal Prescriptions and City Problems* (Brookings, 2002).

19. See, for example, Kincaid, "From Cooperative to Coercive Federalism."

20. See U.S. Advisory Commission on Intergovernmental Relations, *Regulatory Federalism: Policy, Process, Impact and Reform,* A-95 (Government Printing Office, 1984); and David M. Welborn, "Conjoint Federalism and Environmental Regulation in the United States," *Publius: The Journal of Federalism* 18 (Winter 1988): 27–43.

21. Bailey and Mosher, *ESEA: The Office of Education Administers a Law.*

22. Joe Fiorill, "Local Emergency Teams Resist Plain-Language Radio Rules," Government Executive, August 26, 2005 (http://govexec.com/story_page.cfm?filepath=/dailyfed/0805/082605gsn1.htm).

23. Paul E. Peterson, Barry Rabe, and Kenneth Wong, *When Federalism Works* (Brookings, 1986).

4

INTERGOVERNMENTAL FINANCE IN THE NEW GLOBAL ECONOMY

An Integrated Approach

RAYMOND C. SCHEPPACH AND FRANK SHAFROTH

Technology, globalization, and demographic changes are all powerful forces that are driving major economic and social change in the United States. The nation has adapted to numerous changes over its more than 200-year history, but these three simultaneous changes will clearly challenge the nation. The current and future impacts on individuals and firms, as well as on sectors and regions, will be dramatic. The key question for U.S. governments at all levels is whether they will adapt quickly enough or will instead become a major impediment to economic growth and social justice.

This chapter focuses primarily on the U.S. federal-state intergovernmental system, particularly spending and revenue systems. Although the role of local government is not a major focus, many of the implications are also relevant for that level of government. A number of structural changes will accompany the changes in technology, globalization, and demographics, each of which will create problems for government and require modifications, particularly in the arena of state-federal spending and tax systems. The focus here is on the performance and efficiency of the system, as well as on equity.

Forces Driving Change

Together, technology and globalization have brought about a new economy characterized by different sources of wealth and income, consumer choices, and capital investment needs. The major technology change is the convergence of information and telecommunications. Essentially, the very basis of economic value has changed: Transactions no longer just combine natural resources with labor to create value; now, value is created by combining knowledge with technology.[1] Similarly, the expansion of bilateral and multilateral trade agreements and the entry of more countries like China into the World Trade Organization have substantially reduced trade barriers. The combination of expanded trade agreements and technology is creating a world without borders.

At the same time, the world economy is becoming more service oriented as goods become a smaller proportion of final demand. Even those goods that continue to be produced are becoming weightless as the ratio of weight to value is dropping each year. In addition, intangibles are becoming more important than tangibles, which creates problems in defining when and where economic transactions take place, particularly from a tax and revenue standpoint.

Markets also are becoming more dynamic. Markets in the old economy were stable, but real competition was often limited. In the new economy, a larger number of global buyers and sellers set prices. The rate of innovation, product quality, and time to market are becoming more important than costs and prices.

New partnerships are the wave. Today, companies partner on some products and compete on others. This new mix of cooperation and competition creates a very flexible economy. Entrepreneurs are spurring economic growth, and the gazelles—the small, rapidly growing venture capital–based companies that capture new markets—are the new drivers of the economy. The organization of production is also changing rapidly. The old economy had mass production, whereas the new economy has flexible production, allowing products to be tailored to consumer needs.

Although this new economy is dramatically altering the economic landscape, there also are tectonic demographic shifts as the population ages. The fastest growing population cohort is that over the age of sixty-five. The growth rate of this cohort increased from 11.1 percent in the 1980s to 12.3 percent in 2000 and is projected to grow 15.8 percent in 2020 and 20.5 percent in

2040. The cohort over age eighty-five is growing even faster as individuals live longer.[2] This also means that the rate of entry of new workers into the labor force is growing more slowly, which changes the share of individuals working and not working. Finally, a large percentage of the population growth is in minority populations, particularly immigrants, who traditionally have lower educational attainment and skill levels.

The Implications of Change on the Intergovernmental System

This combination of technology, globalization, and demographic change will create numerous challenges for the intergovernmental system. First, the demographic changes will create a teeter-totter effect: as the growth in the elderly population soars, state and federal tax revenues will erode, and state and federal expenditures will mushroom. Already, Medicaid, the state-federal health care program for low-income individuals, has surpassed all elementary and secondary education as the most expensive part of state budgets (measured as a percentage of spending from all sources)—driven by the enormous and growing costs of nursing home care.[3] Medicaid and Medicare are the fastest-growing components of the federal budget, with Social Security not far behind.

Most of these elderly taxpayers will derive their income from sources other than wages (Social Security, pensions, capital gains, and dividends, for example—income generally taxed by both federal and state governments at lower rates than earned income). Exemptions from state sales and use taxes for medical expenditures such as pharmaceuticals and medical devices—two items of disproportionate use by the elderly—are likely to result in additional tax revenue erosion for state and local governments, even as expenditures are expected to swell, not just because of the growing proportion of elderly but even more so because of the rapid aging of the elderly.

Second, the private sector will be required to respond quickly to changing world markets. Given that governments are major investors in both human and physical capital and have a major role in regulation, they should partner with the private sector in responding to this new world competition. Government, however, is inherently slow in accommodating change and adapting to new priorities, new functions, and new institutions. State and federal governments must first adopt clear lines of responsibility regarding which level of government should administer and fund which programs. In other words, the duplication and overlapping of responsibilities must be dramatically reduced. Then, in delivering all services, both levels of government must become more flexible, adaptable, timely, citizen friendly, accountable, innovative, and performance driven. This is critical not only in responding to the new economy but also in maintaining citizens' faith in government.

Third, the movement toward a services and intangibles economy will dramatically reduce state revenues, since most state sales and use taxes apply only to goods. States generally do not tax services, the fastest-growing component of demand, and many items (for example, CDs and DVDs) that used to be sold in stores as goods and were subject to sales tax are now digitized, downloaded, and untaxed.[4] This digitalization of products will only accelerate in the future. Furthermore, states' inability to tax many goods sold over the Internet as well as content such as video, which comes into individual households through the Internet, cable, satellite, or telephone, will further erode state tax revenues.

The implication of this erosion is higher and higher sales tax rates on shrinking tax bases, which contradicts a basic tenet of good tax policy—that taxes should have a broad base and a low rate. Taxing goods at a high rate and services and Internet-related services at a rate of zero distorts prices and creates economic distortions throughout the economy, particularly in investments. It also creates major equity issues between types of sellers and consumers.

Fourth, as a result of the expansion of trade agreements and technology, the acceleration of international trade as a percentage of world output will lead to continued preemption of state regulatory and tax authority and also change the responsibilities of federal and state governments. Over time, more and more standards will be set in the international marketplace by private sector groups and by centralized governments. This has already happened in the negotiation of various U.S. trade agreements, such as the North American Free Trade Agreement,[5] and will only accelerate over time. State functions also will change as states take on additional responsibilities to assist workers during transition when a region quickly loses jobs to trade. The cumulative impact of these and other federal preemptions may eventually make states mere administrative extensions of the federal government rather than sovereign entities.

The Existing Intergovernmental Budget Framework

The existing budget framework starts with the U.S. Constitution, which states that both the federal government and the states are sovereign. The Constitution further delineates federal and state responsibilities, assigning jurisdiction over national defense and relations with other nations to the federal government while giving states jurisdiction over other governmental functions. The federal government has retained its authority over national defense and international relations over the past two centuries, but the powers reserved for the states have dramatically eroded over time as the federal government has preempted states' authority, primarily under the interstate commerce clause of the Constitution. During this same period, a significant shift has occurred in governmental roles, with the federal government focusing more and more of its resources on aid to individuals through entitlement spending—leaving greater and greater responsibility for the nation's physical infrastructure to states and local governments. In 1960 the federal government financed 47.3 percent of physical capital in the nation; by 2005 that percentage had declined to 14.3 percent.[6]

Financing wars, entitlement spending, and interest on the national debt has begun to overwhelm the federal budget and crowd out federal investment in the infrastructure of ports, airports, and highways so vital to competitiveness in the global economy.[7] The ebbing of the federal role in financing infrastructure has become a gnawing tax issue for states, faced with the task of financing the national infrastructure for a growing economy at a time of growing congestion, reduced gas tax revenues, higher interest rates, increased federal interference with state capital financing, and decreasing federal funding.

State and local budgets are remarkably unlike the federal budget, not only because they must be balanced each year but also because of the tax-financing distinctions between operating and capital budgets. The two, however, are closely linked as the operating budgets that fund the day-to-day operations of government include maintenance of capital as well as depreciation and interest on the bonds for that capital. Generally, states and local governments issue tax-exempt bonds with a useful life in excess of five years to finance public infrastructure. The bonds, whose interest is exempt from federal individual income taxes, are secured either by a state's full faith and credit of its taxing authority or, if it is a revenue rather than a general obligation bond, by a secured pledge of tax revenue, fees, or tolls to meet the interest payments to the bondholders and repay the principal at maturity. The purpose of the borrowing is to spread the taxes or user fees over the useful life of the infrastructure so that today's taxpayers do not have to pay for the benefit of tomorrow's.

Federal outlays in 2005 were $2.47 trillion, or about 20 percent of gross domestic product. State and local spending from their own sources was about $1.39 trillion in 2005, about 11 percent of GDP. Most federal spending was for national defense (about 20 percent of federal spending) and for direct payments to individuals, primarily Social Security, Medicaid, and Medicare (about $1.21 trillion, or 49 percent of federal spending in 2005). Net interest was about $184 billion, leaving $220 billion for the operation of all other domestic programs.[8]

Perhaps the greatest changes in federal responsibility occurred in 1935, when the federal government created Social Security, and in 1965, when it created the Medicaid and Medicare programs. Both Medicare and Social Security are programs for people over the age of sixty-five, and they are financed and administered entirely by the federal government. On the other hand, Medicaid, which provides health care for low-income individuals, is funded by federal and state governments and is administered by states.

These three major programs were created as entitlement programs, whereby individuals who meet the eligibility criteria receive benefits automatically. The creation of these programs was a major departure from earlier programs, which were given specific yearly appropriations. These entitlement programs grew dramatically over time owing to inflation and to expansion in benefits and eligible populations.[9] Although entitlements have provided security for individuals, from a fiscal standpoint they have become uncontrollable. This in turn has created major tensions between the federal government and states, particularly around funding for Medicaid.

Medicaid originally provided health care for low-income single women and children but has grown dramatically over time to include care for the disabled as well as nursing home care for the elderly. This federal-state program is funded, on average, 55 percent by the federal government and 45 percent by the states. However, the state share differs substantially by state because state contributions are based on a formula that provides a heavy weight to the per capita income of individual states. Currently, poorer states, such as Mississippi, receive 76 percent federal funding, whereas wealthier states, New York, for example, receive a 50 percent federal share. The federal government requires all states to provide certain mandatory benefits to eligible populations but also allows states to add optional benefits and eligible populations, which do receive the federal match.[10] This program now spends about $350 billion a year in state and federal money and has seen annual growth of 11 percent over the past twenty-five years.[11] Given the different shares paid by states, Medicaid is the major federal program that de facto reallocates funding to poor states. The food stamp program is the only other such entitlement program. It provides food credits for low-income individuals and is funded entirely by the federal government, but it is administered by the states. Welfare (Temporary Assistance for Needy Families—TANF), which historically had been an individual entitlement, was converted to a block grant to the states in 1996.

In 2005 federal grants to state and local governments amounted to $426 billion, about 17 percent of federal spending. However, about $182 billion of that total went to Medicaid, which states must match. This leaves a total of about $244 billion that from the federal standpoint would be classified mostly as discretionary grants. Of the total amount of discretionary grants, the major programs include Title I education, special education, and Pell grants, amounting to $12.7 billion, $10.6 billion, and $13.0 billion, respectively, in 2005. It also includes about $45 billion in transportation funding, $17.3 billion for TANF, $11.8 billion for child nutrition, and $14.7 billion for tenant-based rental assistance (2005 figures).[12] Although these represent some of the larger programs, approximately eight hundred other grants to state and local governments fund narrowly defined purposes. Both the employment and training and health care areas contain a large number of narrowly targeted programs. Many of these programs require state matches, and some have maintenance-of-effort requirements forbidding states to withdraw the state funding. Approximately 85 percent of the grant funds are distributed by formulas, each grant having a different formula.

To understand total state funding, it is important to differentiate between spending from broad-based state taxes and from other state funds that are restricted by state law for particular functions or activities; the best example of this is gasoline taxes, which are dedicated to transportation funding. The federal government funding that is provided to states or through states to individuals must then be added. Total state funding for 2005 was about $1.2 trillion, including both operating and capital expenditures. Of this total, 43.1 percent came from state general funds, 24.8 percent from other state dedicated funds, 29.5 percent from federal grants to states, and 2.5 percent from bond financing. Of the total state spending, 22.3 percent went for Medicaid, 21.4 percent for elementary and secondary education, 10.9 percent for higher education, 8.0 percent for transportation, and 28.4 percent for all other functions of state government.[13] Over the past twenty years the dramatic growth in Medicaid has forced states to cut spending in all the other areas except elementary and secondary education.

Rethinking Budget Federalism

The concept of networked state government is beginning to emerge in these early years of the twenty-first century. Just as the information economy is shifting from a reliance on mainframe computers to the use of personal computers, palm pilots, and other wireless handheld instruments, so too must networked governments evolve to stimulate responsiveness, innovation, and efficiency. As the nation tries to adjust to change, and change occurring on Internet time, it has to redefine the roles and responsibilities of governments. The resolution of many policy issues—ranging from the need for adequate physical and human capital to the effective delivery of services to defining citizen needs—cannot be left to the free market or a centralized bureaucracy. As the United States enters this uncharted territory, it must radically recast government to ensure citizen support and pioneer new approaches to governance that disaggregate decisionmaking.

Viewed through the prism of federalism, technology and globalization are competing forces. On one hand, they press to eliminate borders, threaten sovereignty, and mandate one-size-fits-all standards. On the other hand, they offer the promise of vastly increasing the ability of state and local governments to respond more quickly and effectively to the needs and demands of businesses and citizens. So, for instance, Arlington County, Virginia, has developed a contractual relationship with Oracle On Demand in Austin, Texas, to manage its information applications. All Arlington payroll, financial, budget, and human resources data reside in Austin. County employees access Oracle On Demand services from their desktops. Response to a query from Arlington arrives in a fraction of a second. Files are moved locally and printed on Arlington printers in seconds. The Austin facility is backed up instantaneously by three sites located in New Jersey, California, and overseas. Should a system crash or a natural disaster occur, the Arlington queries will be instantaneously redirected to one of these sites without notice or delay to the user in Arlington. Should a disaster or other event occur in Arlington, the entire system could be accessed from somewhere else.

Technology is creating opportunities that, in turn, are critical to development of a new federal-state partnership that parallels the types of changes taking place in the new economy. The existing intergovernmental system is antiquated owing to the overlapping responsibility between levels of government and the lack of accountability, responsiveness, and customer focus. The current system contributes to ad hoc and narrow decisionmaking.[14] It not only distorts spending priorities but also creates significant inefficiencies in delivering services. This is to say nothing about the timeliness of decisions. Our current intergovernmental system has evolved slowly over time, but the structure has essentially been the same since the early 1960s. It must be replaced with a new broad vision of federalism.

New Strategies for Discretionary Spending

The almost eight hundred federal individual discretionary programs with narrow purposes, different state matches, and different allocation formulas should be collapsed into fifteen to twenty broad consolidation grants. These grants should have new negotiated performance standards, offering bonuses for high performance and sanctions for low performance. Essentially, three types of grant consolidation strategies could be implemented: consolidating similar grant programs at the federal level, consolidating diverse grant programs under a single grant, and consolidating state and local grants. Pilot projects should start with a few states in each category, then expand over time as procedures and processes are perfected.

Part of rethinking discretionary grants must involve thinking about flexibility, incentives, and sanctions. Discretionary grants should recognize differences in places and people and in needs and priorities. They also should recognize the validity of experimenting with different approaches. The tension is between federal goals and state and local goals. Should the federal government allocate only 95 percent of the discretionary grant, holding back the remainder in a bonus pool, so states that eventually meet the goals would receive their full amount and those that significantly exceed them would receive a bonus? Bonuses could be monetary, or they could take the form of greater flexibility to meet the needs of a similar population.

CONSOLIDATE SIMILAR STATE GRANT PROGRAMS. One approach the federal government could take to respond to the challenges of the new economy is to collapse similar federal grant programs of different federal agencies into simplified programs that permit states to draw down funds after negotiating performance measures with the federal government. Such consolidation would allow a state to tailor the program to the needs of its citizens. Performance measures would ensure that states know what has to be achieved in spending the funds and permit federal agencies and Congress to provide oversight based on performance.

In this approach, states would be responsible for developing performance measures to meet the needs of their population and then negotiate an agreement with the lead federal agency that would ensure program responsiveness. This would stimulate solutions based on states' capacity and infrastructure and promote results-driven, performance-oriented projects. The federal government's oversight role would be to evaluate whether the desired outcomes were achieved. The adoption of each consolidated grant would streamline federal-state communications and shift the focus from separate programmatic procedures to comprehensive outcomes.

This approach could be implemented in several broad policy areas such as health, employment and training, economic development, and education, where there are presently a large number of narrowly targeted grants across several agencies. For example, the twenty-one economic development programs from the Departments of Agriculture, Housing and Urban Development, and Commerce could be collapsed into one grant, the Department of Commerce serving as the lead agency responsible for negotiation and oversight.

CREATE STATE PERFORMANCE PARTNERSHIP AGREEMENTS WITH SUPER WAIVERS. Another approach is to allow states to combine funds from disparate federal programs into a single grant through a waiver procedure.[15] This model would allow state grants with very different purposes to be combined on a time-limited basis (for example, five years under a waiver agreement). For example, by combining transportation, environmental, housing, and economic development grants into a single grant, a state could address high-priority transportation and housing density needs with creative solutions that better respond to citizens needs.

This model would promote efficiency and flexibility because states could experiment with different strategies to serve customers and achieve the desired outcomes. States could adapt their programs and services to changing needs, and they would have the necessary federal funding to accommodate a shift in priorities. As employment or housing markets change so, too, could state programs change. Similarly, the model has the potential to be more market oriented and consumer friendly; resources could be reallocated to provide more choices to the customer, whether it be longer hours of service or increased use of interactive technologies. As program managers are freed from requirements to design services based on a federal template, innovation would also be encouraged.

By focusing on outcomes, states would be freed from measuring success based on inputs. They could use performance measures, indicators, and customer feedback as measures of progress. Accountability to the federal government could be addressed by requiring initial federal approval of the performance measures, after consultation and negotiation of the waiver with the state. A joint evaluation by the state and the lead federal agency would enable mutual understanding of successes and failures. If a state successfully meets the outputs established by the agreement, it could be rewarded with additional bonuses. Similarly, failure to meet minimum performance measures could result in sanctions, such as loss of funding.

This model would enhance efficiency by reducing administrative overhead costs and the paperwork states must provide to the federal government to receive annual grants. More important, it would defer to state governments selection of the highest priorities for spending federal dollars while ensuring the federal government and the public that programs are delivered in an accountable manner.

CONSOLIDATE STATE AND LOCAL GRANTS. As regional economies become more important, federal, state, and local leaders must rethink discretionary programs along multi-issue, multiagency, and multijurisdictional lines. For example, in virtually every high-technology corridor, traffic congestion is an overwhelming problem. Traffic connects jurisdictions and is related to zoning and land-use decisions. Consequently, traffic congestion can only be addressed by local, state, and federal agencies working together. Similarly, these high-technology corridors compete with one another and similar corridors in the global marketplace. For example, firms from Bangalore, India, compete with firms from Silicon Valley, California. The federal government, the state of California, and the regional governments in Silicon Valley may want to assist these Silicon Valley firms by reshaping state-federal employee training and transportation programs.

Allowing a state and various local governments to aggregate federal dollars from a variety of grant programs and focus them on a particular underdeveloped region would be an important option. A state could designate a low-income rural region for an intensive economic development effort, for example. Federal housing, transportation, workforce development, and rural economic development funds could be consolidated into a package and directed to several communities within the targeted region. The state and various local governments would need flexibility in how they use the funds to address the region's needs most effectively. To minimize the overlapping of responsibilities and clarify lines of accountability, the state could designate a specific agency to lead the effort.

A state and local consolidation model would be accountable not only to its recipients and customers but also to a lead federal agency. Measurable outcomes would be negotiated by all three levels of government. Focusing on a particular region of the state gives the model the ability to seek input from the citizens and businesses that would be directly impacted by the assistance. Cooperative planning could occur in the region, and the process could seek direct participation from the communities. Local governments in the region would need to be intimately involved in determining the shape and scope of the development. State efforts would have to be consistent with local plans and institutions. Bonuses and sanctions for meeting or not meeting critical performance measures could also be part of this model. The best way to implement such a model, like the previous one, would be through a five-year time-limited waiver that, if deemed successful, would be renewable for another five years.

A New Strategy for Entitlement Programs

Historically, providing for the health and welfare of the nation's citizens has been a shared responsibility of the federal and state governments. Medicare, Medicaid, the food stamp program, TANF, and Social Security are the largest federal entitlement programs serving low-income families, the elderly, and the disabled. In the past, the division of responsibility has been fairly straightforward. The federal government has been primarily responsible, through Medicare, Social Security, and Supplemental Security Income programs, for payments and other targeted assistance to elderly people (that is, those over the age of sixty-five) and individuals with disabilities. States, through the food stamp program, Medicaid, and TANF (and, before TANF, Aid to Families with Dependent Children), have been responsible for administering federal programs for children and families. Although this is an oversimplification, the federal government has been responsible for populations that have left the workforce entirely—generally, those over the age of sixty-five—and states have been responsible for populations that are in, will soon be in, or may return to the workforce.

In the twenty-first century world of health and human services, one of the major policy challenges is deciding whether the current division of federal and state program responsibility is appropriate. There exists sound rationale for much of the current system, particularly around the federal government's continuing responsibility to both fund and administer Social Security and Medicare. Both of these programs are for the elderly, primarily the retired population. Since the elderly often retire in southern and western states because of lower costs and milder climates, there is a strong case for federal funding so that there is not a differential impact on those states with a significant share of the elderly. Similarly, a strong case can be made to continue state administration of TANF and the food stamp program because states are better positioned to coordinate these federal programs with other state programs for these populations.

However, Medicaid, as it is currently administered, and its relationship to Medicare is a major problem.[16] Under the current system, an individual who has adequate income, is in decent health, and is over the age of sixty-five will obtain most of his or her health care needs through Medicare. However, an individual whose health fails, requiring nursing home assistance, and who no longer has adequate income becomes dually eligible for both Medicaid and Medicare. For example, physician and pharmaceutical services may still be funded from Medicare, while payment of nursing home care will be paid through Medicaid. This dual responsibility, which represents about 42 percent of the total cost of Medicaid, causes substantial confusion for the eligible person in knowing which level of government is responsible. It is also true that neither the federal government nor the states have appropriate incentives for efficiency, since any potential savings must be shared with the other level of government.[17] Given that Medicare and Medicaid are two of the largest federal programs, this overlap creates huge inefficiency in both programs.

Two overarching goals must guide the restructuring of Medicaid. First, it is critical to eliminate the shared responsibility for the dually eligible population. Specifically, one level of government must be responsible for administering each specific population. Second, there should be a continuum of services for individuals once they enter Medicare at age sixty-five, regardless of income.

Given these two goals, the Medicaid program would be restructured along the following lines: The acute care program for relatively healthy women and children would be 100 percent funded and administered by states. Because they administer all other low-income programs such as TANF and the food stamp program, as well as education and training, the states have an advantage in coordinating all these programs through individual caseworkers who work with these populations. Similarly, states would administer programs for the disabled populations for similar reasons, but such programs would be funded by both the federal and state governments. The federal Medicare program would start when an individual turned sixty-five and would continue until death, providing all services as a continuum. The federal government could contract with health care providers or states to administer this program. Given the additional cost to the federal government, Medicare will most likely have to become either a needs-based program or have an additional revenue stream—or both.

Political Obstacles

Although the restructuring of the Medicaid and Medicare programs and the collapsing of eight hundred narrow categorical grants into fifteen to twenty broad consolidated grants will become more critical over time, there will be a real uphill battle in Congress. Historically, numerous attempts have been made to streamline programs, but most have failed because passage would have required various committees to give up their jurisdiction over programs.[18]

The states themselves are often an obstacle, as consolidation would create a reallocation of funding to state and local governments and therefore create winners and losers. For this reason, finding a consensus among the states also presents a problem.

The only real possibility for change would be if a presidential candidate were to make reform of the current system a key campaign issue—and were actually elected. Even then, there would be numerous compromises throughout the legislative process, which would most likely end in only incremental changes.

Rethinking Tax Federalism

In 2005 the federal government received tax revenues of about $2.15 trillion, of which about 43 percent came from individual income taxes and 13 percent from corporate income taxes. Both corporations and individuals paid jointly about 37 percent of total tax revenues for social insurance and retirement. Finally, about 7 percent came from excise taxes and other miscellaneous receipts. All of these taxes are collected directly by the federal government; they are not collected by lower levels of government and then remitted to the federal government. State and local governments had receipts of $1.04 trillion in 2004, of which 22 percent was from income taxes, 35 percent sales taxes, and 31 percent from property taxes, with the remainder, including business activity taxes, providing a little more than 12 percent. To this total, which states and local governments collect, federal grants-in-aid for another $350 billion must be added. This, with various other adjustments for other transfers, brings the total revenue for state and local governments to $1.6 trillion.[19] This does, however, double count federal grants-in-aid (that is, they have been specified in both the spending and revenues of state and local governments).

Even if intergovernmental expenditures can be restructured, it will be critical to also rationalize federal, state, and local tax systems. Technology and the rapid change from a tangibles to an intangibles economy have undercut tax borders and eroded state and local tax bases. For instance, more and more forms of software, information, and entertainment that are taxed in their tangible state are now capable of being distributed digitally and widely sold and delivered over the Internet. Consumption of such services will grow as the high-speed connections needed to access multimedia content proliferate and the industry develops simpler technologies for viewing such content on television screens, creating the potential for an increasing erosion of state and local revenues.[20] Similarly, the threat of global warming will require a federal-state rethinking of current gas taxes to finance the federal and state highway trust funds; for as demand increases—more Americans are buying more, and more fuel-efficient, cars, and Congress itself has mandated greater fuel efficiency—there has been a steady and growing erosion of federal and state tax revenues into transportation trust funds, even as an aging infrastructure increasingly crumbles.[21] Therefore, a restructuring will be necessary to enable citizens and businesses to understand which level of government is taxing and which is providing services.

It also is important to craft a more simplified tax structure that is fair and equitable. A public finance system for the twenty-first century must overcome the systemic and institutional shortcomings that handicap the current system. This will clearly require greater interstate and federal-state cooperation. Rethinking the nation's tax and revenue systems will also require finding ways to avoid tax competition among the different levels of government. New models should strive to meet several objectives, including simplicity, equity, neutrality, transparency, and sovereignty. The difficulty of reconciling the conflicts between the Constitution's supremacy clause and the Tenth Amendment should not divert policymakers from the task of restoring accountability and jointly shouldering the responsibility to shape the future and frame the questions that must be answered.

Coordination also is necessary as federal, state, and local revenue systems face new challenges from an aging U.S. population and a more global and technology-based economy, which is suffused with more mobile sources of commerce and income that can easily elude the grasp of taxing authorities at subnational—and even national—levels of government. Borders are disappearing with advances in transportation and telecommunication systems, so that intergovernmental tax systems constructed on a foundation of physical borders and physical presence are rapidly becoming antiquated. The problem is exacerbated by the fact that capital mobility has become instantaneous. In world money markets, $3.2 trillion moves across international boundaries every day.[22] Yet the intergovernmental tax system remains characterized by stovepipe workings and by relative autonomies, where all three levels of government can and do tax the same resources. All three levels have income taxes—with state and local individual and corporate systems generally piggybacked on the federal system. All three levels levy sales and excise taxes, but this revenue source is dominated by state and local governments. The third leg of the stool—the property tax—remains largely restricted to local governments. Social insurance and retirement taxes, which make up 35 percent of federal tax revenues, are unique to the federal level.[23]

Part of the genius of America's founders was the creation of tax federalism, which was perhaps spawned by the unique way in which local communities formed to create the colonies that later became states. The states, in turn, created a federal government, but one in which, as Alexander Hamilton wrote, "the individual States should possess an independent and uncontrollable authority to raise their own revenues for support of their own wants."[24] Charles McLure and Walter Hellerstein, more than two centuries later, express a similar sentiment with regard to the traditional congressional reluctance to intervene in matters of state taxation: "We believe the answer lies in the strong tradition of state tax sovereignty, which is reflected in long-standing political and constitutional understandings. The states' sovereign power of taxation has always been regarded as essential to their independent existence and thus to the scheme that the Framers created."[25] In the most recent decade, that reluctance appears to have dissipated.

Restoring that original concept should be an important goal of national— as opposed to federal—tax reform. Mark Weinberger, a former assistant secretary of tax policy for the Treasury Department, said that federal policymakers will significantly revise the tax code after 2008, when major budget pressures are likely to force the otherwise politically thorny issue of tax reform: "You need a precipitating event to force big policy changes in Washington. I believe the demographic changes and the fiscal challenges we face in the country will, by necessity, include changes to the structure and level of taxes in this country." The demographic changes have already led the President's Advisory Panel on Federal Tax Reform to recommend major changes and streamlining in a state-preemptive way to the current plethora of federal tax-deferred savings plans in 2005.[26]

How do the three levels of government move to a new system of taxation that does not limit economic growth but ensures that the economy contributes a fair share for governance and investment? Is the federal role to provide incentives for states to adopt a consistent sales tax that applies to all goods and services and is destination based, whether or not there is "nexus," provided the system does not impose unreasonable burdens? Should revenues from a federal sales tax be pooled in a trust fund and distributed to state and local governments?

Most assessments of federal, state, and local tax and revenue systems identify four shortcomings that must be addressed before those systems can adequately finance government services in the new economy of the twenty-first century:

—Taxes that were designed for a manufacturing economy and have not kept pace with changes in economic activity must be restructured. These taxes are not as responsive as they should be and create artificial differences among similar activities, enterprises, and transactions.

—The increasing globalization of economic activity creates increased opportunities for income shifting and tax planning; it requires a rethinking of certain tax principles so certain taxes can remain vibrant and distortions in the marketplace can be minimized.

—The deregulation of various economic sectors has had profound impacts on certain types of taxes. These taxes must be updated to reflect the new role of markets in establishing priorities. (The best example here is the telecommunications industry, which has been deregulated but is still taxed as if it were a monopoly. See box 4-1).

—Taxes at the federal, state, and local levels have generally been administered independently of one another. The result is increased complexity and burden imposed on businesses and individuals making a good-faith effort to comply with tax laws.

The increasingly global nature of business, crossing not only state and local but also international borders, presents unique challenges for federal and state tax writers. Large firms can shift income across these borders for tax purposes, so the taxable income of these enterprises in the United States and within each state may sum to less than the total accounted for on all tax returns. The corporate tax base is becoming increasingly more unpredictable, and serious inequities may be introduced between large multistate or multinational firms and smaller in-state businesses. As an increasing number of electronic commerce, other technology, health care, natural resource, financial, and telecommunication firms become international or simply move offshore, the federal government and states will have to work together to eliminate these inequities.

Moreover, policymakers will have to address the way in which the revenue policies and administration of states and local governments have increasingly become constrained by federal preemptions. Emerging state and local forms of collective action will also have an impact on national goals—whether from states that have organized to achieve common objectives in such areas as streamlining sales tax policy and administration or from local areas that have

Box 4-1. *Communications: A Special Case*

As innovation and convergence of existing networks and technologies rapidly evis-cerate existing telecommunications companies and networks, what are the implica-tions for state and local governments? The Federal Communications Commission (FCC) indicates that 104 million households in this country had telephone service in 2002, representing 95.3 percent of total households in the United States. The FCC breaks this down into incumbent local exchange carriers—127 million residen-tial and small-business access lines—and competitive local exchange carriers—14.4 million access lines. According to the FCC, there were more than 136 million wire-less telephone subscribers—more than the total of all access lines provided by all the Regional Bell Operating Companies.[1] The networks that stemmed from the original string connection—from one tin can to another—before the beginning of the last century are entering their own magical mystery tour. The business models that have worked for decades for local telecommunications providers and networks are begin-ning to appear obsolete. It is not just the challenge of cable, with its aggressive fiber optic challenge, nor e-mail and its progeny, like instant messaging, but the revolu-tion of innovations like voice over Internet protocol and advanced wireless technolo-gy that are undermining the foundations of the nation's $300 billion telecommuni-cations industry. Over the past century, telephone companies invested $200 billion to build networks that give each call a unique path.[2] The vibrations of voices over lines are beginning to turn into pulsars of light and networks or ganglia of atoms and light waves that move in ways never contemplated and in volumes that even teenagers can barely grasp.

States and local governments, to an extent, were able to construct significant reliance on utility monopolies. In return for a guaranteed rate of return, govern-ments were able to ensure a big employer, a high degree of regulation, and a reliable base of tax revenues. The transformation of telecommunications monopolies, how-ever, is taking states and local governments to a planet they have never known. Although the advent of networks of new communications technologies is providing great efficiencies and savings on one side, the transformation is leading to nearly uncontrollable erosion on the other. Even without federal intrusion and preemption, the existing state and local regiment cannot persist. Patterns of state discriminatory tax systems will simply accelerate transformations.

Notes

1. Federal Communications Commission, *Eighth Annual CMRS Competition Report,* FCC 03-150 (June 26, 2003).

2. Ken Brown and Almar Latour, "Heavy Toll: Phone Industry Faces Upheaval as Ways of Calling Change Fast; Cable, Wireless Hurt the Value of Old Networks, Threaten a Business Model; Echoes of Railroads' Ordeal," *Wall Street Journal,* August 25, 2004, p. A1.

reinvigorated regionalism to address spillovers and achieve more-uniform policy outcomes across a regional area.

With three government hands in every taxpayer's pocket, how will the taxes collected be used?[27] The difficult question is whether the federal, state, and local governments should "disentangle." This question raises issues of accountability, sovereignty, and equity. Disentangling requires a revitalization of the doctrine of reciprocal immunity, meaning that states and the federal government may not tax one another. For example, should the federal government turn over to states the more than $70 billion it collects through excise taxes each year? Should the federal government confirm state authority to require the collection and remittance of sales and use taxes on remote vendors in return for states' conceding corporate income tax revenues and granting all property and personal property tax revenues to local governments? Should the federal government adopt a tax and set aside fixed percentages of the revenues raised for each level of government so that all will have a greater stake in coordinating infrastructure investment and service delivery?

Adapting to the New Economy

A significant surprise is the resiliency of state tax systems over the past decade, given the limited adjustments in tax policy that have been enacted to accommodate the fundamental economic, demographic, and technological changes that have taken place. State revenues have gone from running at record levels in the late 1990s to two or three years of negative or anemic growth and then to another period of record growth during 2005 and 2006.[28] All this has been accomplished without any fundamental reform of state tax structures. Instead, by working around the margins on such things as pressing the envelope on jurisdiction for sales and corporation income taxes, various approaches to shoring up the corporate income tax through add-back statutes and alternative tax bases, greater reliance on cigarette taxes, one-shot revenues from amnesties, and some stepped-up enforcement with respect to tax shelters and other areas, states have been able to get by with aging, outdated tax structures and at the same time maintain balanced budgets and deliver an acceptable level of service.

Over the past score of years, while the U.S. economy has continued its rapid evolution from a manufacturing to a knowledge-service economy, no state has begun to tax a wide range of service transactions. Corporate income taxes are relatively unchanged, and property taxes have changed little. Where states have undertaken reform, it has usually been driven by an exogenous factor, such as school finance litigation or other public education needs.[29]

Threats to Dual-Tax Sovereignty

There is a growing lack of coordination among governmental tax and revenue systems at all three levels that is causing burdens and complexity for industry. There also is an increasing lack of accountability and a growing tendency to preempt the revenues of another level of government. These factors threaten our system and the ability to maintain dual-tax sovereignty. Three threats are particularly strong: increased federal propensity to intervene in state tax matters with a point of view that says it is a federal obligation to correct what it perceives as injustices perpetrated by states or local governments without any showing of need, harm, or impact on interstate commerce; federal actions to meet federal—as opposed to national—policy objectives in ways that shrink the state and local income tax base; and insufficient compatibility and willingness of states and local governments to coordinate their activities to achieve uniformity or consistency in tax policies, which has led to increasing calls for federal intervention.

Such developments require that policymakers carefully examine the implications of the new economy, identify objectives for an intergovernmental tax and revenue system, and craft new, more streamlined models of taxation. Some of this intergovernmental challenge is driven by the simple fact that over the past few years, the number of congressional threats that directly affect state and local tax authority has increased dramatically. In the spring of 2006, at least three bills affecting individual state and local income taxes, and two dealing with property taxes, were introduced. An extension of the Internet Tax Freedom Act that preempts state and local tax authority was passed in November 2007. During the 2006–08 period, a number of bills to preempt state corporate income taxes (that is, business activity taxes) were introduced and passed by the U.S. House of Representatives.[30]

In the summer of 2007, a Treasury Department study questioned state and local authority to issue tax-exempt debt, suggesting that eliminating this tax break could provide revenues to help finance a reduction in federal corporate income taxes—yet it ignored entirely both the state and local revenue consequences and the impact on national infrastructure financing.[31] The same study expressed apprehension at the "disparate treatment between physical and human capital," noting that the current federal tax code "discourages investment in physical capital relative to human capital."[32] Yet again the suggested means to reduce the disparity was the imposition of federal corporate income taxes on the interest earned by corporations on state and local capital debt—in other words, increasing the cost of the levels of government responsible for the bulk of capital infrastructure financing.

Perhaps the best demonstration of the lack of cooperation and increasing federal ignorance of the nation's federalized or dual-sovereignty tax system was the portion of the new report noting the existence of "four different" tax systems affecting individuals and corporations in the United States, with no mention of state and local tax systems, as if they simply do not exist.[33] Whether inadvertent or simply unthinking, the increasing unwillingness to consider or be accountable for the total tax impact on taxpayers and on state and local governments is a sign of how far away this new century's federal tax policy has come from the likely intentions of the nation's founding fathers.

Such federal intervention could have increasingly harsh economic consequences. With consternation around the country over the proposed offshoring of ports management, the federal government must think far more strategically about state and local financing issues fundamental to the nation's economic foundations. It cannot and must not continue to establish various back-end-loaded savings plans while reducing the rate of tax on dividends and capital gains. These actions will increase the competition faced by state and local bonds in the tax-preferred savings market, thus increasing state and local costs and reducing competitiveness. Part of the legacy of the founding fathers is a federalism whereby almost all the vital services to both the old and new economies are provided by states and local governments—from water to highways to education. Thus federal tax preemption or ignorance can create a double whammy: insufficient resources to make the critical human and capital investments vital to competing in a global economy and increasing disparities between rich and poor. The United States is the only developed federal system on the planet that lacks some form of general fiscal assistance and fiscal equalization from the national to the subnational level of government. Canada has it, Germany has it, Switzerland has it, and India has it. Yet in this country, the state and local tax deduction is the only form of general fiscal assistance in the tax system. Although the economists may call it an inefficient form of assistance, it is all there is—and that poor remainder is under federal siege.

The Explosion of Intangibles

Beyond communications, the new century has seen a new world of nanotechnology and the ability to convert tangible products, from books and journals to stents, from a physical to a nonphysical presence—a state tax world of dynamic economic changes caused by deregulation, convergence, and acceleration of the ratio of intangible to tangible in the U.S. economy. Because states and local governments are so reliant on sales and use taxes[34]— taxes captured on the sale of tangible goods based on physical presence of the seller inside a state's border—the onrushing age of intangibility heralds some of the most difficult challenges ever to state taxing authority, at the same time creating countervailing, centrifugal forces that require the lowest level of government to deliver services and infrastructure investment uniquely packaged for a community's citizens and businesses.

Approaches for the Twenty-First Century

The greatest challenge in state tax policy over the next decade will be to reshape and modify state tax systems to accommodate the increasing pace of technological and economic change. The increased ability of economic activity to be directed and to take place remotely and the growing irrelevance of borders to how and where business is conducted present real issues for state tax systems and tax administrators. Responding to the challenges will require changes in state tax laws, greater cooperative and joint efforts among states and local governments, revised and improved relationships with the federal government, and greater cooperation with the business and taxpaying community. A failure to respond to these challenges will most likely result in a continued weakening of tax structures, less citizen and business compliance, and greater federal intervention in states' tax policies and matters.

Federal preemption, technology, growth in services, and convergence have caused substantial erosion of revenues for state and local governments. At the same time, the elimination of borders and tangibility is rendering antiquated the more than seventy-five hundred local tax systems within our federal system. Taken together, all of these limits have caused higher rates on a shrinking base and more biased and less equitable tax systems. Therefore, a new public finance system to overcome the shortcomings of the current system will require greater interstate and federal-state-local cooperation, new mechanisms to enhance mutual understanding, and more extensive partnerships. It also will require noninterference in tax or revenue systems exclusive to other levels of government. Where the income tax is a shared base between governments, for instance, there must be mutual engagement. In contrast, neither the sales nor property tax is shared with the federal government. Although the federal government might have a quasi-judicial role as a referee between the jurisdictions, there ought to be less federal interference or preemption, especially with regard to revenue systems from which it derives no revenue.

There is need for a new kind of model that is neither top-down nor just vertical, and states need to recognize that the requirements and challenges posed by the borderless, intangible, global economy will require adjusting federal and local relationships. The federal government, meanwhile, will have to recognize its role in assisting states to develop workable, viable tax systems, no longer arrogating to itself a role as a court of last resort to redress perceived grievances with state and local tax systems.

Similarly, rethinking the nation's tax and revenue systems will demand a renewed commitment to some sort of reciprocal immunity and to far better accountability vis-à-vis shared revenue bases and sources. Many states have income taxes, as does the federal government; the federal government also has excise taxes, which bring in almost $73.1 billion annually.[35] The federal government issues bonds, as do state and local governments. Federal bonds finance the operating debt of the government; the interest on these bonds is exempt from state and local taxation. State and local governments issue bonds largely to finance capital investment.

Tenets of Effective Tax Policy

The challenges to developing an intergovernmental tax system for the twenty-first century are much more overwhelming than challenges on the spending side. Unlike the federal and state budgets, a poor tax system will create more private sector distortions in key investment decisions, which could have a serious detrimental impact on long-run economic growth.

The basic tenets of effective tax policy have remained consistent over time. However, the current system—since it has not adjusted to economic, demographic, or technological changes—is obsolete. The system must be updated following these basic principles:

—Simplicity: In a borderless economy, the more complexity the nation can eliminate, the better it can serve the economy and the less governmental tax policy will create market distortions.

—Equity: Any new model should treat similar transactions and taxpayers similarly.

—Accountability: Each level of government should be accountable to its taxpayers, and no one level of government should interfere with, tax, or serve as the avenue of redress for any other level.

—Sovereignty: Any model must preserve taxpayers' ability to determine what level of revenues they want and need and how they prefer those revenues to be raised.

—Neutrality and transparency: Tax policy should not bias or create different outcomes for comparable transactions, and effective rates and revenues should be public.

—Adequacy: Tax and revenue systems need sufficient flexibility to ensure fiscal stability and resources.

—Administrability: New models must focus on ease of administration to facilitate fair enforcement and ensure taxpayer fairness and trust in the system.

Alternative Models

Virtually any model for greater coordination of federal, state, and local tax policy, as well as for greater simplification and uniformity in state tax policy and administration, implies some sacrifice or diminution of state sovereignty and local autonomy. Every step that states and localities take to conform their taxes to the federal tax or to make their taxes more uniform with one another reduces their flexibility and decisionmaking authority. These are actions that entail risks and sacrifice, as has been noted in the debate over a streamlined sales tax (see box 4-2). But the difficulties should not prevent movement toward a streamlined, intergovernmental tax system suited to the new economy. State officials need to weigh the effects of reform on sovereignty against the benefits to be realized from a twenty-first-century tax and finance system. State and federal leaders need to observe important tax principles and activities, including ensuring that federal actions or laws preserve states' sovereignty to choose which taxes they want to use and the extent to which they want to use them. Furthermore, it means being able to control, through tax rates and exemptions, the distribution of the tax burden among taxpayers.

A streamlined, intergovernmental tax system in which tax bases and tax administration are more integrated among states and with the federal government also requires increased interdependence among levels of government. In particular, decisions made at the federal level about the nature of certain tax bases may have a much greater impact on states and localities than under the present system. This interdependence requires a true partnership among levels of government in making revenue decisions. One level should not necessarily control what another may do, and there should be full consultation before making changes that affect other levels. There should also be institutional mechanisms to ensure that the impacts across levels of government are

Box 4-2. *Streamlined Sales Tax Project Model*

A version of the multistate model is the Streamlined Sales Tax Project, a unique partnership of states, local governments, and business to create a uniform sales and use tax system that sharply reduces collection burdens on vendors. In 2005 the states adopted the Streamlined Sales and Use Tax Agreement, a multistate agreement providing for simplification of the nation's more than seven thousand varying state and local sales tax laws,[1] marking the beginning of one of its key components, the amnesty program. The agreement is the culmination of a multiyear, nationwide effort by forty-four states, the District of Columbia, local governments, and members of the business community to develop measures to design, test, and implement a system that radically simplifies sales and use tax collection and administration by retailers and states. The adoption triggered a Web-based, centralized point-of-sale tax registration for the member states (www.sstregister.org/sellers); initiated an amnesty period for sellers that had not been contacted by member states for audit; and finalized the process for certification of software that will assist in the collection of sales tax. The simplified system reduces the number of sales tax rates, brings uniformity to definitions of items in the sales tax base, significantly reduces the paperwork burden on retailers, and incorporates new technology to modernize many administrative procedures. Full-member streamlined states are Indiana, Iowa, Kansas, Kentucky, Michigan, Minnesota, Nebraska, New Jersey, North Carolina, North Dakota, Oklahoma, South Dakota, Rhode Island, Vermont, West Virginia, and Wyoming. In addition, there are associate-member states, advisory states, and project states. Associate-member states are Arkansas, Ohio, Tennessee, and Utah.

Notes

1. The 2002 Census of Governors reports a total of 87,576 governmental units in the United States, of which 67,561 collected some kind of tax; however, state streamlined tax writers estimate that the number of state and local governments that levy and operate their own sales tax systems numbers about 7,500.

appropriately identified and assessed, much as the pioneering Unfunded Mandates Reform Act has worked. Consideration should also be given to allowing adequate time to adjust to and plan for changes before mandates become effective. In addition, new institutions or mechanisms may be needed to govern certain aspects of the tax system to ensure that states, by law or practice, function in a cooperative and uniform manner.

Accountability is not as clear cut in tax policy and administration as in other areas. Historically, there have been discussions of assigning certain revenue sources to one level of government or another, but it seems unlikely that the major taxes can be assigned to a particular level of government to administer and control alone. Remedies for an ailing public finance system revolve around more, not less, partnership and interdependence. Although there are relatively few intergovernmental—interstate or state-local-federal—tax coordination mechanisms, several models can help in considering future approaches. Some of these models are long-standing, others are relatively recent. They include the estate tax credit model, the federal-state income tax model, the multistate coordination model, hybrid approaches, and the investment model.

ESTATE TAX CREDIT MODEL. Without a doubt, the worst tax federalism policy change in the past decade was repealing the state estate tax credit over four years while phasing out the federal estate tax over a longer period. Not only did it deprive the states of several billion dollars (ultimately), but it also eliminated the estate tax in more than half of the states. The action was taken without consultation, and it treated a federal-state coordination mechanism as a form of revenue sharing that Congress felt was inappropriate. The real reason is, of course, that it increased the flow of revenue to the federal government (over what it would otherwise have been) so that Congress could reduce taxes further. The state estate tax credit, which had been a permanent feature of the federal estate tax since 1926, served as probably the most far-reaching model of intergovernmental tax coordination. Each taxable estate was allowed a 100 percent credit against the federal estate tax for state estate (or inheritance) taxes paid, up to a certain level. The model established a floor below which combined federal and state estate taxes could not fall. The goal was to ensure coordination of the federal and state estate tax bases and minimize interstate tax competition. (A similar mechanism exists for federal-state unemployment taxes.)

The estate tax credit model was effective in ensuring coordination, though it came at a cost of placing serious limits on state flexibility and autonomy because states had to conform to federal rules to take advantage of the credit. Yet the model could be considered for certain types of excise taxes where interstate price differentials are significant, promoting efforts to thwart tax evasion.

INCOME TAX MODEL. Federal, state, and local personal income taxes exhibit a reasonably high degree of coordination. The coordination results not from federal legal requirements but from practical considerations by states and local governments. All but five of the states with a broad-based personal income tax conform substantial parts of their tax base to the federal income tax base and start the computation of state income tax liability from a specified point on the federal return. Federal-state income tax conformity has several advantages for taxpayers and states. From a taxpayer perspective, it obviously eases the filing burden associated with income tax compliance because it promotes consistency in the definitions of income and expenses. From a state perspective, conformity enables the state to rely on federal information-reporting requirements, information exchange programs, and other audit and enforcement efforts in securing compliance with the state tax. These benefits can be enjoyed without sacrificing the ability to establish independent rates and exemptions that enable states to control and distribute the state income tax burden. Yet the conformity approach puts the state fiscal position somewhat at risk because substantial federal tax changes, generally taken without consultation or consideration of the state-level impact, affect state finances.

MULTISTATE COORDINATION MODEL. A third model for coordinating tax policy and administration involves state and local governments and sometimes the federal government, aiming to promote uniformity and cooperation on a multistate basis. The underlying rationale for such efforts is that it is in the best interests of the states and their taxpayers to jointly design their tax policy and administration because of the tax issues or taxpayers involved. Primary examples of this approach are the Multistate Tax Commission, the International Fuel Tax Agreement, and the Mobile Telecommunications Sourcing Act. The Multistate Tax Commission was formed in 1967 as part of a state response to proposed federal legislation that would have significantly constrained state taxation of interstate commerce and businesses. The commission operates programs to promote uniformity in the taxation of interstate commerce as well as several multistate compliance and taxpayer service efforts. More than forty states participate in one or more aspects of the commission's activities.

The International Fuel Tax Agreement seeks to reconcile the importance of borders in fuel taxation and transportation services with the requirements of an interstate economy. It provides a vehicle for apportioning the fuel tax paid by interstate motor carriers among the states in which the carriers operate but limits their filing, auditing, and other reporting obligations to interactions with a single base state. The agreement began as a voluntary, cooperative effort among states; later, federal law effectively mandated state participation.

The Mobile Telecommunications Sourcing Act resulted from the combination of telecommunications deregulation and the advent of the wireless industry, which made existing state and especially local tax systems more and more unworkable. This led to the creation of a coalition of industry, local governments, and states that focused simplification and administration efforts on areas where there could be agreement—or at least not polar opposition—as well as commitment to devise better and more equitable ways of taxing across borders, mutual respect, and a commitment to look for solution that benefits all parties.

Multistate cooperative approaches such as the Multistate Tax Commission and the International Fuel Tax Agreement provide maximum latitude and flexibility to participating states in designing approaches to resolve the issues they deem important. They also recognize the interdependence of states and can be effective in addressing the needs of the new economy. However, this model alone is unlikely to be sufficient to overcome the legal and institutional taxation hurdles that states will face in the twenty-first century.

NEW, HYBRID APPROACHES. A model that does not currently exist, but that merits exploration, would be one that combines and takes the best features of the other models. This model would most likely provide for a substantially greater federal role in establishing parameters or standards for state and local tax systems than has before been considered appropriate. Yet the nature of the issues confronting states requires that new approaches be considered. For example, the federal government, in consultation with states and localities, could establish minimum standards or definition for some types of state taxes so the taxes respond to the needs of the new economy for simplification, uniformity, certainty, and ease of administration. The federal government could also provide incentives to encourage states to meet such standards. These incentives could come in the form of financial incentives or in the form of removing certain legal and institutional impediments to sound tax policy. Alternatively, interstate compacts approved by Congress could achieve the same results but afford states and localities greater latitude in spelling out the details of tax policy.

The essential point is that an effective intergovernmental tax system and policy for the new economy will require that current legal and institutional barriers be overcome. These barriers can be removed, at least in part, by federal action. Consequently, it is reasonable to expect that the removal or reduction of these barriers be accompanied by state-local tax systems that meet certain standards of neutrality, simplicity, uniformity, and ease of administration. However, it is important that the federal government view its role in this endeavor as a partner in shaping an intergovernmental public finance system.

AN INVESTMENT MODEL. Although it would not constitute comprehensive reform, an alternative would be for the federal government or the states to enact specific solutions for specific problems. For example, as the nation has shifted from a manufacturing to a services and intangibles econ-omy—and as close to 25 percent of consumer sales have moved online—there has been significant erosion in state and local sales tax bases. A national sales tax that applied not just to goods but also to services would create an opportunity for states and local governments to piggyback—providing an opportunity to sharply reduce existing state sales tax rates yet benefit from a much more comprehensive base that better reflected the new economy. Lack-ing a federal intervention, states could broaden their own state and local sales tax systems to apply not just to all services but also to all goods—tangible and intangible. Although this would require a substantive investment in time, resources, and public education, it would address one of the more seri-ous tax problems on the state-local horizon. The piecemeal approach may be a way to both correct the most egregious problems and jumpstart more com-prehensive reform.

Preserving Dual-Tax Federalism

The real issue or challenge is how to maintain dual-tax sovereignty and improve coordination between state, local, and federal tax systems. There are three keys: First, there must be a recognition among federal policymakers that federal tax or finance actions affect states and local governments—not to mention all taxpayers and the national economy; that in our system states have independent taxing authority; and that states and local governments share (not that the federal government owns and states piggyback on) the income tax base. Second, there must be mutual respect between the three lev-els of government, so that actions taken at one level are done with an eye toward helping the other levels, or at least minimizing the disruption. Third, there must be consultation and dialogue between the levels of government so that the maximum coordination can be achieved, each level can fully meet its responsibilities, and a framework of how one level relates to another can be established.[36]

States and local governments need to move away from taxing regimes that have shades of a regulated monopoly and begin treating communications like other industries as well as strive to treat similar services similarly. This should be able to proceed on a state-by-state basis without a heavy federal hand. The federal government could play a constructive role by providing some mean-ingful, nonideological definitions of various types of services (that is, some buckets of services) around which states could then begin to build a taxing system or incentives. This set of definitions should help treat similar services similarly.

The former U.S. treasury secretary John Snow claimed that, as part of the Bush administration's federal tax reform efforts, he had solicited comments from the tax community and met with academic, business, and taxpayer groups to discuss federal tax reform. Noticeably absent was any mention of either states or local governments. It is difficult to imagine any circumstances under which a federal panel or administration would propose a federal tax reform approach that would address the most important goals and concerns of state and local governments; it is equally difficult to conceive of an actual federalism tax reform proposal emerging without the concerted, joint input of states and local governments. But long ago in the city of Philadelphia the three levels of government were created deliberately to be intertwined and mutually reinforcing. That ought to create a twenty-first-century taxing rule of federalism that would mandate state and local participation in and analysis of any proposed federal changes and a requirement that any federal or state preemption of tax revenues on any other level of government would automatically trigger offsetting dedicated tax revenues. The eighteenth-century promise of dual sovereignty, reciprocal immunity, and mutual reinforcement will be critical for the challenges of the twenty-first century—a century in which sorting out revenues will be decidedly challenging.

Debates over the propriety of federal intervention in state and local tax matters are intense and important. They are inherent in vibrant federalism because they touch one of the most sensitive nerves of our federal system— the tension between the states' right to exercise their sovereign tax powers and the nation's interest in a common market unfettered by burdensome state regulations. All three levels have a stake as stewards for the future in ensuring this tension is constructive.

A Concluding Comment

Historically, there has been a sound conceptual basis for both the intergovernmental budget framework and the intergovernmental revenue system of the United States. They have been relatively efficient, equitable, and simple to administer. However, globalization and technology changes as well as demographic shifts that emerged as we entered the twenty-first century are making both systems obsolete. Four critical issues are driving this change. First, the demographic effect of the aging of the population will be reflected in an erosion of state and federal revenues, while state and federal expenditures explode. Second, the private sector will have to respond more quickly to changing market conditions, and government will need to change accordingly.

This means a better definition of what level of government will administer what programs needs to be decided and that all levels of government must become more flexible, adaptable, timely, accountable, and performance driven. Third, the movement toward a services and intangibles economy will dramatically reduce state revenues, since most state sales and use taxes apply only to goods. It also creates efficiency and equity problems for the overall economy. Fourth, the acceleration of globalization and technology will lead to continued preemption of state regulatory and tax authority and also change the responsibilities of federal and state governments.

An obsolete intergovernmental budget and tax system will become an impediment to economic growth and social justice and similarly reduce citizen faith in government. For these reasons, it is essential for the United States to adopt a new blueprint. This blueprint would mean a better sorting out of intergovernmental responsibilities, especially in the critical area of health care, as our society rapidly ages. It also means collapsing the eight hundred individual categorical grants into fifteen to twenty consolidation grants. It must mean an end on the revenue side to blind and unaccountable federal preemption and interference, to be replaced by a much more strategic rethinking of how the three levels of revenue systems can enhance—rather than disrupt or interfere with—the others. For it is these revenues that will be required not just to pay down the most spectacular level of debt ever created by one nation but also to bridge the structural fiscal chasm and put the nation on a competitive path for the future.

A broad new blueprint is necessary, but it must be created by all three levels of government working closely together. The work should start now. Citizen alienation with government will only increase. A democracy needs the support of its citizens, and the system needs to adjust now, while intergovernmental tensions are positive, before there is a major crisis.

Notes

1. Michael Goodhart, "Democracy, Globalization, and the Problem of the State," *Polity* 33 (Summer 2001): 527–46.

2. "U.S. Interim Projections by Age, Sex, Race and Hispanic Origin," March 18, 2004, U.S. Census Bureau (www.census.gov/ipc/www/usinterimproj/).

3. National Association of State Budget Officers, *Fiscal Year 2005 State Expenditure Report* (Washington, November 2006).

4. Austan Goolsbee, "The Implications of Electronic Commerce for Fiscal Policy (and Vice Versa)," *Journal of Economic Perspectives* 25 (Winter 2001): 13–23.

5. Frederick M. Abbott, "NAFTA and the Legalization of World Politics: A Case Study," *International Organization* 54 (Summer 2000): 519–47.

6. "Aid to State and Local Governments," in *Analytical Perspectives: Budget of the United States Government, Fiscal Year 2005* (Government Printing Office, 2004).

7. Ibid.

8. Congressional Research Service, "Federal Spending by Agency and Budget Function, Fiscal Years 2001–2005," RL33228 (January 9, 2006).

9. Kent Weaver, *Automatic Government: The Politics of Indexation* (Brookings, 1988).

10. Sandra K. Schneider, "Medicaid Section 1115 Waivers: Shifting Health Care Reform to the States," *Publius: The Journal of Federalism* 27 (Spring 1997): 89–109.

11. See Office of Management and Budget, *Budget of the United States, 2007,* "Health and Human Services" (www.whitehouse.gov/omb/budget/fy2007/hhs.html).

12. "Aid to State and Local Governments."

13. National Association of State Budget Officers, *Fiscal Year 2005 State Expenditure Report.*

14. Lester M. Salamon, "The New Governance and the Tools of Public Action," in *The Tools of Government: A Guide to the New Governance,* edited by Lester M. Salamon (Oxford University Press, 2002), pp. 1–47.

15. Pietro Nivola, Jennifer Noyes, and Isabel Sawhill, "Waive of the Future? Federalism and the Next Phase of Welfare Reform," Welfare Reform and Beyond Policy Brief 29 (Brookings, March 2004).

16. Alice M. Rivlin, *Reviving the American Dream: The Economy, the States, and the Federal Government* (Brookings, 1992).

17. Joshua M. Wiener, Laurel Hixon Illston, and Raymond J. Harnley, *Sharing the Burden: Strategies for Public and Private Long-Term Care Insurance* (Brookings, 1994).

18. Timothy Conlan, *New Federalism: Intergovernmental Reform from Nixon to Reagan* (Brookings, 1988).

19. Tax Policy Center, "Tax Facts: Historical Amount of Revenue by Source" (Washington, March 12, 2007).

20. Michael Mazerov, "Making the Internet Tax Freedom Act Permanent Could Lead to a Substantial Revenue Loss for States and Localities," Center on Budget and Policy Priorities (Washington, August 30, 2007).

21. The Energy Independence and Security Act (P.L. 110-140), enacted in December 2007, is an omnibus energy policy law that consists mainly of provisions designed to increase energy efficiency and the availability of renewable energy, including a higher corporate average fuel economy. The law sets a target of thirty-five miles a gallon for the combined fleet of cars and light trucks by model year 2020.

22. See Gabriel Galati and Alex Health, "Triennial Central Bank Survey," Bank for International Settlements, April 2007 (www.bis.org/publ/rpfx07.pdf).

23. Tax Policy Center, "Tax Topics: Payroll Taxes, Fiscal Year 2006" (www.taxpolicycenter.org/taxtopics/Payroll-Taxes.cfm).

24. Alexander Hamilton, *Federalist* No. 32, in *The Federalist Papers,* by Alexander Hamilton, James Madison, and John Jay (New York: Mentor, 1961), pp. 197–201.

25. Charles E. McLure Jr. and Walter Hellerstein, "Congressional Intervention in State Taxation: A Normative Analysis of Three Proposals," National Governors Association, Washington, D.C., 2003.

26. "Budgetary Pressures Will Force Tax Reform, Panelists Conclude," *Tax Analysts,* December 9, 2005; Weinberger's comments were delivered at a Tax Analysts conference, "Tax Reform: Where Do We Go from Here?" Washington, December 9, 2005.

27. This question originally came to the author from the former Denver mayor Quigg Newton, from the New Year's Eve address he delivered as president of the National League of Cities, broadcast from Denver on December 31, 1949, by CBS.

28. "Percentage Change in Quarterly State Tax Revenue by Major Tax, National Data: 1991 to 2007," Rockefeller Institute of Government (www.rockinst.org/research/sl_finance/2column.aspx?id=828).

29. See Frank Shafroth, "An Interview with FTA Executive Director Harley Duncan," *State Tax Notes* 38 (November 14, 2005): 635–41.

30. The U.S. House of Representatives in July 2006 passed its version of preemptive business activity tax legislation, H.R. 1956, which the Congressional Budget Office has estimated as costing states $3 billion annually, calling it the largest unfunded mandate it has every calculated.

31. "Treasury Conference on Business Taxation and Global Competitiveness," background paper, U.S. Department of the Treasury, July 23, 2007, p. 11.

32. Ibid., p. 29.

33. Ibid., p. 23.

34. In 2004 states and local governments derived 22 percent (or $364 billion) of their total tax receipts from sales taxes.

35. *The Budget of the United States Government, Fiscal Year 2007* (GPO, 2007).

36. Shafroth, "Interview," p. 639.

II

TESTING THE INTERGOVERNMENTAL SYSTEM

Issues and Challenges

5

Developing a National Homeland Security System

An Urgent and Complex Task in Intergovernmental Relations

CHARLES R. WISE AND RANIA NADER

As the events of September 11 and Hurricane Katrina revealed, when a homeland security incident occurs, whether it is caused by terrorism or natural disaster, the government response at all levels must be coordinated and timely or thousands of people suffer. In both incidents, the lack of coordination and effective planning by the U.S. intergovernmental system was all too apparent. The nation's governments are now attempting to remediate those deficiencies.

As articulated by President George W. Bush in his Homeland Security Directive to all federal agencies, "The objective of the United States Government is to ensure that all levels of government across the Nation have the capability to work efficiently and effectively together, using a national approach to domestic incident management."[1] This is just one of many presidential and congressional pronouncements defining the homeland security policy of the United States as a national policy, including the state and local governments as partners, rather than an exclusively federal government policy. This constitutes a recognition that the federal government by itself does not have the resources to ensure the security of the homeland. A homeland security system for the United States is inherently intergovernmental, and the development of such a system requires participation of federal, state, and local officials and agencies. Such a national system also requires a degree of intergovernmental integration of homeland security management that is perhaps unprecedented in the nation's past experience.

The Organization of Intergovernmental Homeland Security Relations

As we have pointed out in an earlier article, the difficulty in organizing the intergovernmental dimension of homeland security is exacerbated by the difficulty in organizing at each level of government to accomplish the homeland security mission.[2] Soon after 9/11, it was observed that at the federal government level, lack of coordination and overlapping jurisdictions have resulted in fragmentation and often redundancies within the system.[3] Although some steps have been taken to sort out the jurisdictions and relationships to provide for an integrated federal effort, agencies with homeland security responsibilities in the federal government have been in a phase of continuing reorganization that is likely to continue. Moreover, the task of clarifying federal department and agency roles in homeland security became both more urgent and more complex following the widespread confusion among federal agencies regarding their roles in emergency response to Hurricane Katrina.

One of the reasons given for the creation of the Department of Homeland Security (DHS) was the need for a single point of contact in the federal government from which state and local homeland security partners could obtain information, provide assistance, and coordinate their efforts. The priority of a single point of contact has waxed and waned since the creation of the department.

In 2004 the secretary of homeland security, Tom Ridge, consolidated various DHS elements in an attempt to establish "a single point of entry, interaction, and information for assisting State and local governments, non-governmental organizations, and other Federal agencies and departments to prevent, deter, respond to, and recover from acts of terrorism." This consolidation came in response to numerous complaints by state and local officials about the fragmentation of federal programs and was meant to fulfill "Secretary Ridge's commitment to the Nation's first responder community to create a 'one-stop-shop' to better serve their needs."[4]

Nonetheless, the office's actual operation fell somewhat short of this goal, in part because so many homeland security programs are lodged within major departments and agencies outside the control of the department's secretary. The office was dismantled in 2005 under the second secretary,

Michael Chertoff, and its functions were reassigned based on the purposes they had served. Grant management and training were assigned to an assistant secretary for grants and training within a newly created Preparedness Directorate, and the office's role as liaison between state and local governments was merged with legislative relations under an assistant secretary for congressional and intergovernmental affairs. The Office of State and Local Government Coordination and Preparedness was in existence for such a limited time that it is probably not possible to determine how successful it could have been as a primary point of access at least for DHS.

Following a two-stage review process conducted to a large extent by DHS employees, in July 2005 Secretary Chertoff announced a set of structural realignments that were intended to "better integrate the Department, giving DHS employees better tools to help them accomplish their mission."[5] The secretary separated the preparedness function from the Federal Emergency Management Agency (FEMA) and assigned it to the new Preparedness Directorate. State and local officials expressed concerns that this move would result in a de-emphasis on preparedness for natural disasters and an overemphasis on terrorism preparedness, as well as increased difficulties in capturing the lessons from response and recovery and incorporating them into preparedness plans and activities. However, Congress reversed this decision and transferred most of the directorate into FEMA in the Post-Katrina Emergency Management Reform Act, enacted in September 2006. This continuous reshuffling within DHS reflects the tension between an internal departmental need for a clear chain of authority and accountability and the need of the department's clients for a single and permanent point of contact. The idea of a central point of contact for state and local governments has been displaced. "One-stop shopping" has been replaced with "several-stop shopping."

The first major legislative changes arising from the management failures during the response to Katrina were enacted by Congress in the Post-Katrina Emergency Management Reform Act of 2006 (P.L. 109-295). In the act, Congress made several structural changes in FEMA and the DHS with the apparent purpose of specifying how they were to integrate their activities with those of state, local, and tribal governments. The act places greater responsibility on FEMA regional offices to integrate the activities of federal agencies in a region with the state, local, and tribal governments in that region. It specifies that FEMA regional administrators will work in partnership with state, local, and tribal governments and emergency managers to establish one or more strike teams within each region to serve as the focal point of the federal government's initial response efforts for natural disasters or acts of terrorism and to coordinate the training and exercises of those strike teams with the state, local, and tribal governments and with private and nongovernmental entities. It also mandates regional advisory councils to advise on preparedness in the region and calls for nomination to these councils from state, local, and tribal governments in the region. The act further stipulates that membership in the National Advisory Council must represent a cross-section of state, local, and tribal officials, emergency managers, and emergency response providers.

In addition, the act authorizes the president, acting through the director of FEMA, to establish a minimum of three national response teams, each of which will work in coordination with state and local officials and on-site personnel associated with a particular incident. It establishes within FEMA a National Integration Center with specific responsibilities to periodically review and revise the National Incident Management System and the National Response Plan, including improving the use of federal, state, local, and tribal resources and ensuring effective use of emergency response providers at emergency scenes. Finally, it directs the FEMA administrator to enter into a memorandum of understanding with the administrators of the Emergency Management Assistance Compact, state, local, and tribal governments, and organizations that represent emergency response providers to collaborate on developing standards for deployment capabilities including typing of resources likely to be needed to respond to natural disasters and acts of terrorism.[6]

Congress's multiple mandates on the DHS and FEMA emphasizing integration with state and local governments have set an agenda for intergovernmental relations regarding homeland security. It remains to be determined whether this legislated approach will be effective in actually improving the operational integration of state, local, and tribal homeland security activities.

While Congress focused on establishing several legal mandates for the DHS and FEMA to, among other things, integrate their activities with those of state, local, and tribal governments, the White House was focusing on multiple federal departments other than the DHS. In its report on the response to Hurricane Katrina, the White House suggested stripping its lead-agency status from the DHS and giving it to the Department of Defense for catastrophic incidents.[7] The report also proposed that various emergency support functions (ESFs) be assigned to different departments, for example, putting the Department of Housing and Urban Development in charge of providing temporary housing and the Department of Justice in charge of the public safety and security function.[8] It was unclear whether, should these changes ever take place, the coordinating function would remain with the DHS or be split among these various departments. In the latter case, state and local governments, under dire circumstances, would have to coordinate with multiple federal agencies, yet another addition to "several-stop shopping." This is in no way a novel idea; various states already assign lead-agency status to different agencies in their emergency response plans. The state of Arizona, for example, gives primary agency status to the Department of Transportation for transportation infrastructure (ESF 1) and public works and engineering (ESF 3) and to the Department of Health Services for various subfunctions under public health and medical services (ESF 8). Coordination is achieved by having a representative from each primary agency in the State Emergency Operations Center, which is the nerve center of response operations, led by the Division of Emergency Management.[9] The three plans are clearly very different from one another, and the only thing we can be certain of at this point is that they represent only the latest stage of the ongoing process of reorganizing for homeland security that will continue for some time.

Planning of Intergovernmental Homeland Security Operations

The planning framework put forth by the Department of Homeland Security to combine federal, state, and local capabilities is still evolving. The lack of a planning framework for such capabilities has hindered the department's and the states' ability to identify first-responder needs and priorities. Never has this been clearer than in the response to Hurricane Katrina, when confusion over procedures and roles accentuated the gaps in coordination among participating organizations.[10] According to William Carwile, the federal coordinating officer responsible for the Katrina response in Mississippi, "There has been no operational planning developed by FEMA in over four years. In my view there is no clear understanding of the responsibilities of each level (Washington, the regions, deployed emergency response teams) and how they are to interact."[11]

Reports by the DHS's Office of Inspector General and the Government Accountability Office (GAO) indicate that efforts by state and local jurisdictions to prioritize expenditures for preparedness have been hindered by the lack of clear guidance in defining the appropriate level of preparedness and setting priorities to achieve it.[12] The GAO also reports that the lack of national preparedness standards, baseline information on preparedness and threat and risk scenarios, plans based on those tools, and reliable data to report on the status of initiatives are fundamental obstacles in achieving

desired levels of preparedness.[13] The difficulties of fulfilling these requirements for the planning processes should not be underestimated. Evaluating
the likelihood of any given terrorist attack, for example, is very difficult,
especially since there are so many potential targets in the United States.

There are four major initiatives to provide the planning framework for a
coordinated and comprehensive national response for homeland security.
The first is a National Response Framework that forms the basis of how the
federal government coordinates with state, local, and tribal governments and
the private sector during incidents. It is an all-discipline, all-hazards plan that
provides the structure and mechanisms for coordinating federal support to
state and local jurisdictions. The final framework became effective on March
22, 2008. The framework commits the federal government, in partnership
with local, tribal, and state governments and the private sector, to complete
strategic and operational plans for the incident scenarios specified in the
National Preparedness Guidelines. The second is the National Incident Management System, which was developed to help emergency managers and
responders from different jurisdictions and disciplines work together more
effectively to handle emergencies and disasters. It is intended to be adopted
and used nationwide, creating a standardized, unified framework for incident
management within which government and private entities at all levels can
work together effectively. The plan provides a set of standardized organizational structures such as the incident command system and standardized
processes, procedures, and systems.

The third plan is the National Infrastructure Protection Plan (NIPP), a
revised draft of which was issued in January 2006 to bring together all levels
of government and the private sector to identify and protect critical infrastructure throughout the nation. Beginning with fiscal year 2006, state and
local grant applicants' strategic plans for protecting critical infrastructure
based on the NIPP have been one criterion for evaluating the strategies of
grant applicants. The fourth plan is the National Preparedness Goal, which is
now mandated in legislation by the Post-Katrina Emergency Management
Reform Act of 2006. Its purpose is to provide national performance standards for assessing domestic preparedness capabilities and to identify gaps in
those capabilities that reflect national homeland security priorities for prevention, response, and recovery from major events, with an emphasis on terrorism. The Post-Katrina Emergency Management Reform Act orders that
within 180 days of enactment, the administrator will complete guidelines to
define risk-based target capabilities for federal, state, local, and tribal government preparedness and directs the administrator to ensure that the guidelines

are specific, flexible, and measurable. The act also mandates a comprehensive system to assess the nation's prevention capabilities and overall preparedness, including operational readiness. Specifically, it directs the administrator to ensure that each component of the national preparedness system, including the National Incident Management System and the National Response Plan, is developed, revised, and updated with clear and quantifiable performance metrics, measures, and outcomes.

The promulgation of performance measures has important implications for the operation and sustainability of a workable national intergovernmental system for homeland security. Federal homeland security programs that can systematically demonstrate their impact on preparedness have a greater chance of being sustained in competition with other programs through the congressional appropriations process, and if accountability can be established on the basis of measured results, there is a greater impetus for flexibility in how funds are used by state and local recipients of federal funds.[14] Effective response to highly unpredictable and localized situations requires highly adaptive behavior that cannot be achieved by a hierarchical ordering of responsibilities and resources but also needs flexibility for jurisdictions to reallocate resources among agencies and staff within and across jurisdictions.[15] At the same time, local officials have said that federal standards and guidance are needed and have acknowledged that sufficient incentives and technical expertise to fulfill homeland security expertise may be missing at the local level.[16] National standards can also serve to put a floor under competition with other jurisdictions, provide political cover to address internal political opposition, and answer the question of how much preparedness is enough.[17] A survey study of state and local officials in Florida has found that federal and state mandates and efforts at standardization have served to encourage—not discourage—intergovernmental cooperation and networking.[18] Thus national standards and measures of capabilities can potentially assist the implementation of a national intergovernmental homeland security system.

The planning framework will confront several challenges. Although standards carry with them the promise of increased accountability, they can also portend further centralizing of the federal government role in defining appropriate and acceptable policies for preparedness and response.[19] Several groups of state and local officials with responsibility for homeland security have charged that inappropriate centralization has characterized federal planning up to this point. A 2005 meeting of the National Emergency Management Association that focused on Homeland Security Presidential Directive 8, which calls for strengthening national preparedness and requires the preparation of a National Preparedness Goal, reported a consensus about what constitutes the "central challenge in our relationship with DHS (and, for that matter, at all levels of government)."[20] The report notes "a deep division between principles and actions. Specifically, while there appears to be almost universal acceptance of the doctrine that local and regional public safety, health, and emergency management professionals should be in the leadership role of identifying and implementing Homeland Security plans and strategies, the reality is that most strategic planning has been conceived and promulgated from a centralized, Federal system. . . . This creates a credibility gap that must be addressed as a matter of the highest priority."[21] Similarly, a report by the International Association of Chiefs of Police reports a consensus among chiefs of police around the premise that federally led efforts, while well intentioned, have not led to the development of a cohesive strategy that will allow state, tribal, and local public safety officials to protect their communities successfully. "Our current homeland security strategy," the report states, "is handicapped by a fundamental flaw: It was developed without sufficiently seeking or incorporating the advice, expertise, or consent of public safety organizations at the state, tribal, or local level."[22] Although the DHS has tried to consult with state and local government officials in many of its efforts, such as the development of the National Preparedness Goal and the target capabilities list, the perception remains that these are federal standards that fail to take into account local or even regional priorities and needs. The target capabilities list, for example, has been criticized for overemphasizing terrorist threats and neglecting natural hazards like floods that remain a major concern for many regions.

Planning for homeland security remains a shared responsibility, however, and states and local governments seem to be struggling as well. In its Nationwide Plan Review of emergency operations plans in states and urban areas, issued in 2006, the Department of Homeland Security concludes that "the current status of plans and planning gives grounds for significant concern. Current catastrophic planning is unsystematic and not linked with a national planning system."[23] Among the deficiencies, the report mentions inadequate planning for catastrophic events, the absence of a clearly defined command structure, improper procedures for communications among operational components, significant weakness in evacuation planning, and inadequate definition of resource requirements.[24]

All of these problems were clearly an issue during Hurricane Katrina. Hurricane Katrina was the first large-scale test of the Nationwide Plan Review and the National Incident Management System,[25] and it is now widely accepted that experience fell short of the plans in terms of coordination and the unified command structure they were supposed to achieve. The House committee investigating the response to Katrina has found that critical elements of the National Response Plan (the predecessor to the National Response Framework) were executed late, ineffectively, or not at all.[26] In its analysis of the federal response to the event, the White House has concluded that "key decision-makers at all levels simply were not familiar with the plans."[27]

However, in addition to the problems of execution and understanding, there were deficiencies in the plans themselves. Exercises conducted by the DHS before Katrina indicated a lack of clear guidance on how functions are supposed to interrelate within the Nationwide Plan Review.[28] The GAO seems to agree: "Although the Nationwide Plan Review framework envisions a proactive national response in the event of a catastrophe, the nation does not yet have the types of detailed plans needed to better delineate capabilities that might be required and how such assistance will be provided and coordinated."[29]

Another criticism of the NRP is that "there is no specific discussion of multi-state disaster-management options," a rather important omission when one considers that very few threats, whether natural or terror-related, would not involve more than one state.[30] The Post-Katrina Emergency Management Reform Act mandates that not later than fifteen months after the act's enactment, a state receiving federal preparedness assistance must submit a report on the state's level of preparedness. The report must include an assessment of state compliance with the National Response Plan, the National Incident Management System, and other related plans and strategies; an assessment of current capability levels and a description of target capability levels; and an assessment of resource needs to meet preparedness priorities.

The challenge for the federal planning framework, therefore, is to set standards that incorporate the analysis state and local officials have done and their experience and knowledge of their areas and to use a process that gives these officials confidence in the standards so that they use them as a basis for their own planning and programming. It is no easy task to strike a balance between the uniformity required to set minimum capabilities and foster integration among jurisdictions, on the one hand, and the flexibility required to adapt homeland security programs to local contexts, on the other. Nonetheless, achieving that balance will be crucial in determining whether there will be a national planning framework for homeland security.

Intergovernmental Financial Relations in Homeland Security

Increased demands for homeland security have placed additional fiscal demands on the federal government but also on state and local governments, and as security needs have increased, homeland security expenses have absorbed funds from other functions of government.[31] Both federal and state mandates for homeland security have placed additional financial and administrative burdens on city and county officials.[32] State and local governments have turned to the federal government for increased financial assistance, arguing that homeland defense is largely a federal responsibility and thus the federal government should provide assistance to overextended state and local governments.

The Fragmentation of Federal Grant Programs

Federal funding assistance for state and local agencies did not start with the events of 9/11. Numerous programs in various federal departments to assist first responders such as police, fire, and emergency workers predated those attacks and the creation of the Department of Homeland Security. Funding has been added to several of these existing programs as well as those that have come under the jurisdiction of the new department. Homeland security grant money is currently distributed through a multitude of programs both within the DHS and in other federal departments, such as the Department of Justice and the Department of Health and Human Services. Some of these programs are targeted to the states and others to local first responders, and there is considerable duplication among these grants, with several of them providing money for the same purposes, such as law enforcement equipment, firefighter training, and preparedness planning.[33] No public officials wanted to slow the flow of money to the first responders in order to rationalize the existing programs and to ensure they were adapted to the new purposes and context, and much of the money has gone out under the old structures.[34]

The fragmentation of federal assistance makes it difficult for local and state governments to develop integrated homeland security plans and coordinate activities like training, exercises, and spending on equipment. Additionally, the multiplicity of funding sources and the absence of a central coordinating authority at the federal level obscures the lines of accountability and makes it impossible to track where the money is going or to reach a conclusion about an actual link between spending and the level of preparedness. The GAO's review of federal funds allocated from multiple grant programs to the National Capitol Region concludes that "there is no established process or means for regularly and reliably collecting and reporting data on the amount of federal funds available to first responders in each of [the region's] eight jurisdictions, the planned and actual use of those funds, and the criteria used to determine how the funds would be spent. Reliable data are needed to establish accountability, analyze gaps, and assess progress toward meeting established performance goals."[35] The lack of benchmarks and performance goals also may contribute to difficulties in developing a regionwide plan for determining how to spend federal funds received and assess the benefits of that spending.[36]

Consolidation and rationalization of the grant programs is one option to make the grants easier to administer for state and local agencies as well as their federal partners. Some of this has been done. In fiscal year 2004, several state and local domestic preparedness grants administered by the Office for Domestic Preparedness (moved from the Department of Justice to the Department of Homeland Security upon the latter's creation), which were targeted for separate purposes such as equipment, training, and exercises, were consolidated into a single funding source, the State Homeland Security Grant Program (SHSGP). In addition, four FEMA grants now have a joint application process. Nonetheless, according to the GAO's review, in 2004 the National Capitol Region jurisdictions used sixteen funding sources.

Oversight

A GAO analysis has found that on-site visits by the Office for Domestic Preparedness decreased after September 11, 2001, because of the increase in workload and reported staff shortages. In 2004 the agency established new monitoring goals, which required at least one office file review and one on-site visit for each state each fiscal year.[37] These visits, in addition to the progress reports that states are required to file regularly, represent a minimal level of federal oversight and do not involve systematic performance measurement. The criteria and measures developed in the context of the National Preparedness Goal are intended to provide a basis of gauging preparedness, and procedures will need to be developed to link these to federal financial assistance programs in order to assess such programs' effectiveness.

According to the GAO, the management of homeland security grants should focus on the achievement of two equally important goals: distributing the grant funds to state and local first responders in the shortest time possible and ensuring accountability for the appropriate use of these funds.[38] The task has become increasingly more difficult as the amount of grant funds managed by the DHS's Office of Domestic Preparedness has grown from $91 million in fiscal year 2001 to almost $4 billion ($2.58 billion through the SHSGP and $1.02 billion in Urban Area Security Initiative grants) in fiscal year 2003.[39] Ensuring that these funds reach first responders in a timely manner and that they are used in a way that enhances the preparedness of state and local law enforcement agencies and their ability to respond to terrorist events, should they occur, offers several challenges on all three governmental levels.

Fund Allocation: Risk versus Spread

Before October 2005, USA PATRIOT Act funds had been allocated in accordance with a guarantee for each state of 0.75 percent of the total amount appropriated to the DHS for state terrorism preparedness grants. The need for an approach based on likely threat and vulnerability instead of population soon became apparent in both legislative and executive circles. However, although all parties seemed to agree on the necessity to allocate the largest share of homeland security funds to high-risk areas, they disagreed on the size of that share. The disagreement crossed partisan lines, with legislators from urban states favoring a model that concentrated the resources on areas most likely to be targeted by a terrorist attack opposing legislators from rural states, who favored a spread model that saw the potential for every state to become a target for terrorists. The House of Representatives passed a bill calling for a relatively concentrated allocation of funds, reducing the minimum guarantee to 0.25 percent of the funds for each state and 0.45 percent for states with international borders or a shoreline.[40] This bill was in line with the president's fiscal year 2006 budget proposal[41] and had the support of the 9/11 Commission. The Senate, on the other hand, over the objections of senators from urban states, which constitute a minority in that body, passed a bill that reflected a spread model of fund allocation, guaranteeing each state 0.55 percent of the funds and up to 3 percent for nineteen heavily populated states.[42] The matter was not resolved in conference, however, and the law that was finally signed by the president still provided for a minimum of 0.75 percent for each state. When the new Congress convened in 2007, the House approved a minimum of 0.25 percent for each state but also specified that any state with an approved state homeland security plan that also met specified high-risk criteria would receive no less than 0.45 percent of the available funds. Senate consideration was just beginning at that time. The most recent compromise gives every state 0.375 percent of total available funds as a minimum allocation. The rest is allocated based on an assessment of risk and effectiveness. The balance between risk and geographic distribution in fund allocation will continue to be subjected to high congressional politics for some time.

In accordance with the 2005 law, the Department of Homeland Security formed peer-review panels composed of representatives from forty-seven states and conducted an analysis combining both risk and the perceived effectiveness of measures proposed by states and urban areas in their applications. Risk was defined by threat (the likelihood of an attack), vulnerability (the potential success of an attack), and consequence (the potential impact of an attack). The analysis included geographic and asset-based components.[43] The process resulted in a 32 percent cut in state and local grants compared with fiscal year 2005. The bulk of the cuts were in the SHSGP, which was reduced 49 percent from the previous year. Funding of the Urban Area Security Initiative was cut for New York City (by 40 percent), Boston, and Washington. Funds were increased slightly for other cities, including Chicago and Louisville. Overall, twenty-eight states saw their funds reduced by at least 11 percent.[44] The grant awards generated heated and public arguments, especially with representatives and senators from New York City, who felt that the funding cuts would undermine the city's ability to protect itself from potential terrorism-related incidents. What these events show is that regardless of established procedures, the definition of risk and therefore the allocation of funds remains a political process, and acknowledging that fact may have allowed the DHS to foresee and perhaps prevent the confrontation that ensued.

Whatever the underlying reasons for these disagreements, there are serious accountability concerns. In fact, the larger the share given to states unconditionally, and without any requirement to demonstrate a link between these funds and actual preparedness, the greater the risk that the entire federal assistance program will lose support in Congress as the program progresses. While it was in existence, the Law Enforcement Assistance Act program, which distributed assistance to state and local law enforcement agencies largely on a spread model, was repeatedly criticized in Congress on grounds that no meaningful performance data regarding the impact of funds on crime were provided. This lack of demonstrated impact played a significant role in the abolition of the program.

Fund Allocation and Disbursement at State and Local Levels

To expedite the transfer of funds to local jurisdictions, program guidelines of the Office for Domestic Preparedness require states to transfer grant funds to localities within forty-five days of the grant award date. To ensure compliance, states are required to submit a certification form indicating that all grant funds had been transferred within the forty-five-day period or to explain why they had not been transferred and indicate when they would be transferred.[45] Many states still allocate their homeland security grant funds based on population, although some (for example, Wisconsin) have incorporated need and threat factors into their formulas. Different states use widely different risk-based formulas, however, because of the absence of federal guidance and insufficient sharing of threat and vulnerability information.[46]

Expenditure Planning at State and Local Levels

A major reason for the delays in drawing down grant funds is that planning how to spend the funds often occurs after the grants are received. As of March 2004, 43 percent of the counties in Ohio had not submitted the required spending plans for their share of the 2003 homeland security grants. Illinois and New York, on the other hand, are two examples of how advance planning can speed up the process. In cooperation with its local governments, Illinois developed spending proposals based on funding estimates before receiving the Office for Domestic Preparedness obligation. As a result, not only were state administrators able to obligate funds before the mandated forty-five-day deadline, but they also knew how the funds would be spent. New York required its localities to submit funding plans within the forty-five-day period, and as a result, as of February 2004, New York localities had spent around 65 percent of the 2003 SHSGP funds, the most efficient drawdown rate of any state in the country.[47] The elevated perception of risk in these two states is no doubt related to their eagerness to draw down the funds as quickly as possible.

Procurement and Reimbursement at State and Local Levels

Most states have a 100 percent reimbursement system, under which no funds are advanced to localities before the purchases are actually made. This can be a real problem for towns with small budgets. The state of Utah has addressed this problem by providing local governments with an advance payment option. Maine and Kentucky have done the same thing, requiring their localities only to submit an invoice or proof of purchase to qualify for reimbursement.[48] Burdensome procurement rules at the local level have also caused delays in the pipeline. Some states have addressed the problem by centralizing their purchasing systems and allowing equipment and services to be purchased by the state on behalf of local jurisdictions, freeing them from some local legal and procurement requirements. Other states have developed "statewide procurement contracts that allow local jurisdictions to buy equipment and services using a prenegotiated state contract." The DHS has also entered into agreements with the Department of Defense's Defense Logistics Agency and the Marine Corps Systems Command to allow state and local jurisdictions to purchase equipment directly from their prime vendors.[49]

In sum, intergovernmental financial assistance programs to aid state and local governments still display considerable fragmentation. In addition, some initiatives have been set in place to provide more focus on national homeland security goals and to begin to measure the impact of state and local programs, but they are still in the start-up stage. Furthermore, the issue of risk versus spread as a basis for fund allocation continues as a source of conflict and complicates the process of developing a national effort.

Intelligence and Information Sharing

The "National Strategy for Homeland Security" categorizes homeland security activities into six critical mission areas, the first of which is intelligence and warning: "Homeland security intelligence and information must be fed instantaneously into the Nation's domestic anti-terrorism efforts. . . . This effort must be structured to provide all pertinent homeland security and intelligence and law enforcement information—from all relevant sectors including state and local law enforcement, as well as federal agencies—to those able to take preventive or protective action."[50] Within the federal government, intelligence activities are undertaken by multiple units and agencies, including the Information Analysis and Infrastructure Protection Directorate, the Department of Homeland Security, and the Terrorist Threat Information Center, with reports to the Director of Central Intelligence, the Counterterrorism Center in the Central Intelligence Agency, and the Office of Intelligence and the Counterterrorism Division of the Federal Bureau of Investigation. The DHS and the FBI share the task of cooperating with state and local agencies to collect and share information.

The 9/11 Commission, in its report on needed improvements in the nation's system of intelligence, points out that "the FBI is just a small fraction of the law enforcement community in the United States, a community comprised mainly of state and local agencies." "The network designed for sharing information," the commission concludes, "and the work of FBI through local Joint Terrorism Task Forces, should build a reciprocal relationship, in which state and local agents understand what information they are looking for and, in return, receive some of the information being developed about what is happening, or may happen, in their communities. In this relationship, the Department of Homeland Security also will play an important part."[51]

The current intergovernmental arrangements for intelligence sharing appear to be some distance from the network the 9/11 Commission envisioned. A GAO survey of federal, state, and city homeland security officials notes that only 13 percent of federal officials, 35 percent of state officials, 37 percent of large-city officials, and 29 percent of small-city officials found sharing between federal, state, and local agencies to be effective or very effective. Of the states and big cities surveyed, 98 percent of both groups reported they needed specific and actionable threat information, but only 33 percent of states and 28 percent of big cities reported they received it. Ninety-eight percent of both states and large cities stated they needed information on the movement of known terrorists, but only 15 percent of both reported they received it.[52] The GAO has noted several initiatives by individual federal agencies (the FBI's Joint Terrorism Task Forces, the Defense Intelligence Agency's information-sharing partnership with the state of California and the City of New York, and the Massachusetts antiterrorism network of state, local, and federal agencies). However, the report concludes that these initiatives, though beneficial to the partners, presented challenges because they were not well coordinated, risked limiting participants' access to information, and potentially duplicated efforts of some key agencies at each level of government.[53]

A report of a meeting of the National Emergency Management Association that focused on Homeland Security Presidential Directive 8 issues reports the following problems:

—There is a general lack of confidence that intelligence information will be promptly, completely, and accurately transmitted. Emergency Management System directors, in particular, did not believe that they would be included in the loop to receive important intelligence information.

—Intelligence is still not a routine part of day-to-day operations. Information is shared only in the event of an alarming crisis-level need, and that is sometimes too little too late.

—The people who need the information the most—the officer on the street, the "end user"—seldom if ever receives it. Pushing information down the chain of command is a rare occurrence.

—Doctrinal and jurisdictional conflicts between the Department of Justice and the DHS (and even within the DHS) continue, creating inconsistencies, inefficiencies, and confusion. One example is in the area of security clearances and information sharing, where the FBI, under the Department of Justice, often operates at cross-purposes with the Office of Domestic Preparedness.

—The cost of putting operations into action (for example, health) based upon general, nonspecific intelligence is often prohibitive.[54]

Most of the respondents to a National Governors Association survey of state homeland security advisers were only somewhat satisfied with the timeliness, specificity, and actionable nature of the information received from the FBI and the DHS. Seventy-eight percent responded that more unity among key federal agencies, such as the Departments of Justice, Homeland Security, and Health and Human Services, would have a highly positive impact on their state homeland security efforts.[55]

In December 2005, President Bush issued an order that information be shared with heads of federal departments and agencies. The order designated specific officials within government departments to handle information-sharing activities. It also included guidelines and requirements to implement commonalities in technical standards and architectures to expedite the process of intragovernmental information sharing.[56]

The *Final Report on the 9/11 Commission Recommendations,* issued in December 2005 by the 9/11 Public Discourse Project (previously the 9/11 Commission), gave the government a D for information sharing. The report concludes, "Changes in incentives, in favor of information sharing, have been minimal. The office of the program manager for information sharing is still a start-up, and is not getting the support it needs from the highest levels of government. There remain many complaints about lack of information sharing between federal authorities and state and local level officials." It adds, "Designating individuals to be in charge of information sharing is not enough. They need resources, active presidential backing, policies and procedures in place that compel sharing, and systems of performance evaluation that appraise personnel on how they carry out information sharing."[57]

The overhaul of the federal government's intelligence agencies and their joint relationships has been a major preoccupation of the leadership of the agencies as well as the president and Congress. The relationships with state and local governments have tended to receive a lower priority[58] and have been affected by the volatility in the organization and structure of intelligence activities within the Department of Homeland Security, which has a major responsibility for the federal, state, and local interface in intelligence. As Gregory Treverton has pointed out, the department's Intelligence Directorate got off to a rocky start: "Apart from the infrastructure warnings, the information analysis arm of the DHS's Information Analysis and Infrastructure Protection Directorate has yet to carve out a clear mission and base of 'customers,' in part because it has not had clear or consistent leadership. . . .

The DHS's broader threat assessment mandate has effectively been ceded to the TTIC [Terrorism Threat Integration Center], and it remains uncertain how tightly the DHS's intelligence will be coupled to its infrastructure-protection mission."[59]

A task force of the Markle Foundation examined intelligence and information sharing and has concluded that the "DHS has yet to articulate a vision of how it will link federal, state, and local agencies in a communications and sharing network, or what its role will be with respect to the TTIC and other federal agencies. . . . Moreover, neither the TTIC nor the DHS has gotten very far in putting in place the necessary staff or framework for analyzing information and sharing it broadly among the relevant federal, state, and local agencies. Government at the federal level thus remains very much in need of an overarching decentralized framework for building an information sharing and analysis network."[60]

The task is further complicated by the addition of another bureaucratic layer to the intelligence infrastructure, namely, the new Office of the Director of National Intelligence. The final report issued by the former 9/11 Commission seems quite optimistic, giving the new position, which was part of the commission's recommendations, a grade of B. The report warns, however, that the director's challenge "is to exercise his authorities boldly to smash stovepipes, drive reform, and create a unity of effort—and act soon. He must avoid layering of the bureaucracy and focus on transformation of the Intelligence Community. The success of this office will require decisive leadership from the [director] and the president, and active oversight by Congress."[61]

Secretary of Homeland Security Michael Chertoff, in response to his internally appointed task force's review of DHS's operations, policies, and structures, announced that the department needed to combine the information and analysis it generated with information from other members of the intelligence community as well as information from its state, local, and international partners and that the department could do a better job of sharing intelligence with frontline first responders at the state and local level.[62] He decided to reorganize his department's Intelligence Directorate and designated an assistant secretary for information analysis as the chief intelligence officer, who would report to the secretary and head a strengthened information analysis division. The office is designated as the "primary source of information" for the department's state, local, and private sector partners. It will take some time to determine whether this "new start" for intelligence operations within the Department of Homeland Security will result in greater intelligence sharing with state and local government.

Just as Secretary Chertoff was directing changes designed to improve the sharing of intelligence related to terrorism with state and local first responders, Hurricane Katrina exposed large gaps in information gathering and sharing in intergovernmental emergency response operations. The inability to gain information about conditions on the ground in the various Gulf states and the inability to communicate about conditions that were known to a few scattered officials played a significant role in the inadequate and delayed response by agencies at all levels of government. The House committee investigating the Katrina response found that lack of communication and situational awareness paralyzed command and control.[63] The White House report on the federal response found that "federal, state, and local governments have not yet completed a comprehensive strategy to improve operability and interoperability to meet the needs of emergency responders. This inability to connect multiple communications plans and architectures clearly impeded coordination and communication at the Federal, state, and local levels."[64]

The Post-Katrina Emergency Management Reform Act orders the secretary of the DHS, in cooperation with state, local, and tribal governments and federal departments and agencies and the private sector, to develop a national emergency communications plan to support emergency response providers and government officials and to attain interoperable emergency communications nationwide not later than 180 days after enactment. Grant guidelines for states and localities have to be coordinated and consistent with the plan. Furthermore, the secretary of the DHS can prohibit any state, local, or tribal government from using homeland security assistance or emergency communications capabilities if they have not submitted a statewide interoperable communications plan or if the government has proposed to upgrade or purchase new equipment that does not meet or exceed any applicable national voluntary consensus standard for interoperability. Congress has clearly run short of patience with previous initiatives to achieve communications interoperability and is attempting to legislate it. It will be interesting to see whether the various interests that have resisted previous similar initiatives will continue their resistance in the face of this new legislative approach.

Although some new structures have been put in place to foster interchange, they do not form an integrated and coordinated system for intelligence collection and sharing. The effort to construct an intergovernmental intelligence network has been limited by the volatility in the structure and operations of the federal government's intelligence apparatus. Beyond this, however, numerous obstacles remain to integrating state and local operations with federal ones. The cultures of federal agencies long accustomed to segmenting and safeguarding information rather than sharing it, the limitations of information systems of federal, state, and local agencies, the lack of interoperability of communications systems, the different security clearance procedures, and the lack of processes to give state and local officials guidance about what to look for, or to collect and analyze what they discover, also present major challenges that have yet to be mastered. Added to these cultural and structural obstacles, however, are valid concerns about determining the proper threshold at which the benefits of disseminating intelligence outweigh the risks of divulging secret and often private information to thousands of law enforcement entities that may lack the safeguards that are in place in higher-level entities.

Conclusion

The integration of intergovernmental homeland security management and operations remains a work in progress. With respect to the organization of intergovernmental homeland security activities, integration has been and will continue to be impacted by volatility in the organization of homeland security in the federal government as well as the inherent difficulties and associated tensions involved in determining and securing agreement on the appropriate roles and responsibilities for tasks and activities that are largely local in nature but have national and international implications. The creation of the Department of Homeland Security did not result in a single point of interface between the federal government and state and local governments, and the experience of Hurricane Katrina revealed the still unsolved problems associated with coordination of multiple federal departments and agencies with state and local agencies. Reorganization within the Department of Homeland Security could provide further pluralization of necessary contacts among divisions of the department. Additional changes made by the administration and Congress during the post-Katrina period are likely to keep the organizational environment churning for some time. It will clearly be a challenge for state and local government agencies to establish working relationships with the various actors.

Although major planning frameworks have been initiated in the federal government, they have not been made fully operational with respect to state and local government agencies. Katrina exposed significant gaps in the federal planning initiatives, and these gaps have been exposed to intense scrutiny and significant revision, both of which are still under way. State and local governments are likely to react to these new planning frameworks, and further revisions may be in prospect.

Federal financial assistance to state and local governments has been characterized by some consolidation of grant programs, but considerable fragmentation remains. Up to this point, funds have been provided without specific performance goals or provision for their measurement. The National Performance Goal, which was issued in September 2006, is supposed to initiate the process of measuring state and local performance against national goals for homeland security. A source of significant conflict in the federal approach to financial assistance continues to be embedded in the basis for the allocation of funds—that is, the proportion of grant funds that should be allocated on the basis of risk versus the proportion spread across all jurisdictions. This divide is likely to continue in Congress.

Indications from state and local agencies demonstrate that systematic sharing of intelligence and information from federal government agencies with state and local agencies is still not a routine part of day-to-day operations. Although the federal government initiated some programs to designate officials responsible for information sharing in late 2005, it will be some time before these programs have a significant impact. Furthermore, Hurricane Katrina exposed significant shortcomings in the intergovernmental communications needed to respond to homeland security incidents.

Embedded in attempts to resolve these issues are three tensions that will condition policymakers' efforts at resolution. The first is the tension between the demand for leadership from the federal government in setting priorities for the changed homeland security threats facing the nation and the resultant efforts to set standards embodying these priorities, on one hand, and the need for the implementing agencies—federal, state, and local—to employ adaptive strategies that allow them to integrate their efforts according to changing threats and differing local conditions, on the other. The demand for federal standards implies certainty and national accountability through top-down decisionmaking, and adaptation implies requirements for flexibility and recognition of uncertainty through bottom-up decisionmaking.

The second tension is between the need to expedite spending on improving homeland security capacity nationwide and the need to demonstrate accountability for real change that is nationally meaningful. Failure to demonstrate nationally meaningful change in performance can undermine support for continued federal aid for state and local capacity building, but standards and measures that are ill suited to local threats and conditions can also undermine support from the local level for continued participation and funding. The third tension is that between the demonstrated need for increased information sharing among agencies at various levels of government and the need to maintain secrecy and safeguard individual privacy in highly sensitive areas. This involves the assessment of multiple risks of error possible among a large number of widely dispersed agencies.

The intergovernmental scene for homeland security has continued to be one of volatility and change. Major initiatives have been introduced, but it is too early to observe their implementation and impact on the integration of intergovernmental homeland security activities. At this point, integration efforts will have to navigate through a myriad of tensions between national accountability and local flexibility, between responsive and responsible funding, and between the sharing of information and the protection of privacy. There are no simple answers to any of these dilemmas; the only option is to continue to pursue an ever changing balance that will move in one direction or another depending on operational, financial, and political circumstances.

Notes

1. Office of the White House, *Homeland Security Presidential Directive 5,* February 28, 2003 (www.whitehouse.gov/news/releases/2003/02/20030228-9.html).

2. Charles Wise and Rania Nader, "Organizing the Federal System for Homeland Security: Problems, Issues, and Dilemmas," special issue, *Public Administration Review* 62 (September 2002): 44–57, p. 45.

3. Paul L. Posner, "Homeland Security and Intergovernmental Management: The Emergence of Protective Federalism," paper prepared for the annual meeting of the American Political Science Association, Philadelphia, August 2003.

4. Matt A. Mayer, *Statement before the U.S. House Committee on Homeland Security, Hearing on Enhancing Terrorism Preparedness for First Responders,* 109 Congress, 1 sess., February 10, 2005.

5. Michael Chertoff, *Testimony of Secretary of Homeland Security Michael Chertoff before the Senate Homeland Security and Governmental Affairs Committee,* 109 Congress, 1 sess., July 14, 2005 (www.dhs.gov/xnews/testimony/testimony_0037.shtm).

6. Resource typing is the categorization and description of resources by capacity and capability. It is designed to provide emergency responders with information they need to request resources during emergencies and to help make the response request and dispatch processes more efficient.

7. Office of the White House, *The Federal Response to Hurricane Katrina: Lessons Learned,* February 23, 2006 (www.whitehouse.gov/reports/Katrina-lessons-learned.pdf).

8. Ibid.

9. Arizona Division of Emergency Management, *State of Arizona Emergency Response and Recovery Plan* (www.dem.state.az.us/SERRP03%20-%20R1.0%20Indexed%20(Web).pdf).

10. Charles Wise, "Organizing for Homeland Security after Katrina: Is Adaptive Management What's Missing?" *Public Administration Review* 66 (May–June 2006): 302–18.

11. William L. Carwile, *Testimony before the House Select Committee to Investigate the Preparation for and Response to Hurricane Katrina,* 109 Congress, 1 sess., December 7, 2005 (www.katrina.house.gov/hearings/12_07_05/Carwile_120705.pdf).

12. J. Richard Berman, *Statement of J. Richard Berman, Assistant Inspector General for Audits, U.S. Department of Homeland Security, before the Subcommittee on Emergency Preparedness, Committee on Homeland Security, U.S. House of Representatives,* 109 Congress, 1 sess., April 12, 2005 (www.dhs.gov/xoig/assets/testimony/OIG_1st_Responder_Testimony_Berman_Apr05.pdf); U.S. Government Accountability Office (GAO), *Homeland Security: Management of First Responder Grant Programs Has Improved, but Challenges Remain,* GAO-05-121 (Government Printing Office, 2005).

13. U.S. Government Accountability Office, *Homeland Security: Management of First Responder Grants in the National Capital Region Reflects the Need for Coordinated Planning and Performance Goals,* GAO-04-433 (GPO, 2005).

14. Posner, "Homeland Security and Intergovernmental Management," p. 40.

15. Wise, "Organizing for Homeland Security after Katrina"; Louise Comfort, "Rethinking Security: Organizational Fragility in Extreme Events," special issue, *Public Administration Review* 62 (September 2002): 98–107.

16. Frank Fairbanks, "Intergovernmental Issues in Homeland Security," paper prepared for the American Society for Public Administration National Conference, Phoenix, Arizona, March 24, 2002.

17. Posner, "Homeland Security and Intergovernmental Management," p. 31.

18. Kiki Caruson and Susan A. MacManus, "Mandates and Management Challenges in the Trenches: An Intergovernmental Perspective on Homeland Security," *Public Administration Review* 66 (July–August 2006): 522–36, p. 533.

19. Posner, "Homeland Security and Intergovernmental Management," p. 42.

20. National Emergency Management Association, "Capturing the Issues: Homeland Security," paper prepared for the Executive Education Seminar for the National Homeland Security Consortium, Monterey, California, May 24–25, 2005, p. 1.

21. Ibid., p. 2.

22. International Association of Chiefs of Police, "From Hometown Security to Homeland Security: IACP's Principles for a Locally Designed and Nationally Coordinated Homeland Security Strategy," July 31, 2005 (www.theiacp.org/leg_policy/Homeland SecurityWP.pdf), p. 2.

23. U.S. Department of Homeland Security, *Homeland Security Grant Program: Risk Analysis,* 2006 (www.ojp.usdoj.gov/odp/newsreleases/HSGP_risk_analysis.pdf).

24. Ibid.

25. Wise, "Organizing for Homeland Security after Katrina."

26. U.S. House Select Bipartisan Committee to Investigate the Preparation for and

Response to Hurricane Katrina, *A Failure of Initiative: The Final Report of the Select Bipartisan Committee to Investigate the Preparation for and Response to Hurricane Katrina* (GPO, February 15, 2006), p. 132.

27. Office of the White House, *Federal Response to Hurricane Katrina.*

28. U.S. Senate Committee on Homeland Security and Governmental Affairs, Department of Homeland Security: *Second Stage Review,* 109 Congress, 1 sess., July 14, 2005, p. 15.

29. U.S. Government Accountability Office, *Statement by Comptroller General David M. Walker on GAO's Preliminary Observations Regarding Preparedness and Response to Hurricanes Katrina and Rita,* GAO-06-365R (GPO, February 1, 2006), p. 5.

30. Carwile, *Testimony before the House Select Committee to Investigate the Preparation for and Response to Hurricane Katrina,* p. 9.

31. Enid Beaumont and Bruce McDowell, "Will Homeland Security Transform Intergovernmental Management?" in *Meeting the Challenge of 9/11: Blueprints for More Effective Government,* edited by Tom Stanton (Armonk, N.Y.: M. E. Sharpe, 2006), pp. 293–331; Dale Krane, "The State of American Federalism, 2002–2003: Division Replaces Unity," *Publius: The Journal of Federalism* 33 (Summer 2003): 1–44, pp. 43–44.

32. Caruson and MacManus, "Mandates and Management Challenges in the Trenches," p. 528.

33. U.S. House Select Committee on Homeland Security, *An Analysis of First Responder Grant Funding,* 108 Congress, 2 sess., April 2004 (www.homelandsecurity.house. gov/files/FirstResponderReport.pdf); Posner, "Homeland Security and Intergovernmental Management."

34. Beaumont and McDowell, "Will Homeland Security Transform Intergovernmental Management?"

35. GAO, *Management of First Responder Grants,* p. 26.

36. Ibid.

37. GAO, *Management Has Improved.*

38. Ibid.

39. GAO, *Management Has Improved;* Mayer, *Statement before the U.S. House Committee on Homeland Security.*

40. U.S. House, *Budget Report: H.R. 1544: Faster and Smarter Funding for First Responders Act of 2005,* 109 Congress, 1 sess., April, 28 2005 (www.govtrack.us/congress/bill report.xpd?bill=h109-1544&type=cbo).

41. Mayer, *Statement before the U.S. House Committee on Homeland Security.*

42. U.S. Senate Committee on Homeland Security and Governmental Affairs, *Summary of Collins-Lieberman Amendment on Homeland Security First Responder Grants to H.R. 2360,* 109 Congress, 1 sess., August 2005 (www.hsgac.senate.gov/_files/homelandamend mentsummary.pdf).

43. U.S. Department of Homeland Security, *Homeland Security Grant Program.*

44. Jonathan Marino, "DHS Awards 32 Percent Less than Last Year in State, Local Grants," Government Executive, May 31, 2006 (www.govexec.com/dailyfed/0506/ 053106j1.htm).

45. GAO, *Management Has Improved.*

46. U.S. House Select Committee on Homeland Security, *An Analysis of First Responder Grant Funding.*

47. Ibid.

48. Ibid.

49. GAO, *Management Has Improved,* p. 427.

50. Office of Homeland Security, *National Strategy for Homeland Security* (July 2002), p. 17 (www.whitehouse.gov/homeland/book/nat_strat_hls.pdf).

51. 9/11 Commission, *Final Report of the National Commission on Terrorist Attacks upon the United States* (GPO, 2004), p. 427.

52. U.S. General Accountability Office, *Homeland Security: Efforts to Improve Information Sharing Need to Be Strengthened,* GAO-03-760 (GPO, 2003), pp. 18–21.

53. Ibid.

54. National Emergency Management Association, "Capturing the Issues: Homeland Security."

55. National Governors Association, Center for Best Practices, "Homeland Security in the States: Much Progress, More Work," January 24, 2005 (www.nga.org/Files/pdf/0502 HOMESEC.pdf).

56. Sarah Lai Stirland, "Bush Details Plan for More Effective Information Sharing," Government Executive, December 19, 2005 (www.govexec.com/dailyfed/1205/121905 tdpm1.htm).

57. 9/11 Public Discourse Project, *Final Report on 9/11 Commission Recommendations* (Washington, December 5, 2005 [www.9-11pdp.org/press/2005-12-05_report.pdf]).

58. Gregory F. Treverton, "Intelligence Gathering, Analysis, and Sharing," in *The Department of Homeland Security's First Year: A Report Card,* edited by Donald Kettl, pp. 55–75 (New York: The Century Foundation, 2004), p. 71.

59. Ibid., p. 58.

60. Markle Foundation, *Creating a Trusted Information Network for Homeland Security: Second Report of the Markle Foundation Task Force* (New York: Markle Foundation, May 3, 2003).

61. 9/11 Public Discourse Project, *Final Report.*

62. Chertoff, *Testimony of Secretary of Homeland Security Michael Chertoff,* p. 13.

63. *A Failure of Initiative: The Final Report of the Select Bipartisan Committee to Investigate the Preparation for and Response to Hurricane Katrina* (GPO, 2006), p. 191.

64. Office of the White House, *Federal Response to Hurricane Katrina.*

6

ACCOUNTABILITY AND INNOVATION

New Directions in Education Policy and Management

KENNETH K. WONG

O n the fourth anniversary of the passage of the No Child Left Behind Act (NCLB), President George W. Bush declared that the federally led reform was making measurable progress. In response to congressional efforts to amend the legislation, including those from his own party, the president stated, "I'll fight any attempt to do that. I'm just not going to let it happen. We're making too much progress."[1] Celebrating the occasion in a high-performing, predominantly minority school in suburban Baltimore, the president cited rising fourth-grade performance in reading and math as evidence that the law is working. This is in sharp contrast with another Republican administration a quarter of a century ago: in an interview with the *New York Times* during his first month as the U.S. secretary of education, Terrel Bell pledged his commitment to President Ronald Reagan's proposal to abolish the Department of Education and said that he was "not sure that we need department-level cabinet status."[2] Another failed attempt to abolish the agency was led by the Republican majority in the House of Representatives in 1995. Clearly, within a generation, elementary and secondary education has emerged as a priority in the Republican Party.

As education gains national attention, our system of intergovernmental governance and management faces the challenge of institutional redesign.

Two sets of policy developments tend to contribute to new ways of thinking about the organization of public education. One policy trend is related to the changing federal role, the other comes from state and local sources. There has been a gradual shift in the focus of federal education policy. Under the Great Society programs of the 1960s and the early 1970s, the federal government expanded its grants-in-aid system to promote equal educational opportunities in public schools. With the 1983 publication of the influential report *A Nation at Risk,* policymakers at all levels of the government began paying attention to school performance. By the time No Child Left Behind was signed into law by President Bush in January 2002, there was bipartisan support for holding schools and districts accountable for academic performance. Federal policy has evolved into a comprehensive framework of accountability that affects all states, districts, and schools.

To be sure, federal initiatives to strengthen accountability do not occur in a policy vacuum. State and local reforms proliferated before the federal No Child Left Behind program began, an important consideration that policy analysts have often overlooked. Since the early 1990s, an increasing number of states have adopted standards on core subject areas at certain grade levels. In 1997, for example, thirty-one states established standards in the core areas of English, mathematics, science, and social studies. By 2001 only three states had not adopted academic-content standards in those four subject areas. In twenty-nine states, mathematics and English assessments were closely aligned to the content standards at various grade levels.[3] Furthermore, state and local education policy systems have undertaken changes to accommodate alternative models of service delivery and management. A good example is charter schools, which are granted substantial autonomy from district and state regulations. The number of states with charter school legislation grew from twenty-five in 1996 to thirty-eight in 2001 and stayed at forty, in addition to the District of Columbia, from 2003 through 2007.[4] By the time Congress enacted NCLB, almost twenty-four hundred charter schools were in operation. In other words, state and local reformers have played an active role in experimenting with new governance arrangements and management practices.

The rise of accountability and the proliferation of management experimentation have redefined our intergovernmental system of education policy. In light of these developments, a new framework that specifies the new directions in education policy associated with federal initiatives and state and local reform efforts is needed. The interplay of accountability and experimentation has facilitated several types of management models and governance

Table 6-1. *A Framework on Intergovernmental Redesign in Education Policy*

	Intergovernmental initiatives in education innovation	
Expected institutional effects	*Federal led*	*State and city led*
Governmental boundaries redefined	Systemwide standards with consequences (NCLB)	Takeover of failing schools and districts
Public-private boundaries redefined	Federal start-up funds for charter schools; federally funded voucher program in Washington, D.C.; federally funded supplemental education services	State-funded vouchers; diverse service providers in charter and other public schools

arrangements and also has significant policy implications for intergovernmental relations.

Conceptualizing Policy Redesign in Education

Multiple strands of reforms at different levels of the federal system are likely to define the management of public education in the twenty-first century. For analytical purposes, two key aspects are important in understanding the evolving system of intergovernmental management. First, policy innovation occurs at different levels of government. These innovations are often implemented jointly at the federal, state, and local levels. While recognizing that the management of innovation involves intergovernmental collaboration, I see the need to differentiate the federal role from state- and city-led reforms because the political dynamics tend to vary at different levels of the system. Second, reforms are expected to change the terms of the institutional arrangements. Although some innovations aim at redefining existing boundaries among governmental entities, others tend to shift the dividing line between public and nonpublic sectors in the provision of education services. These major institutional aspects jointly generate four types of policy redesigns, illustrated in table 6-1.

First, federally led reform that redefines the authority among governmental entities is illustrated by the No Child Left Behind policy regime. Given the magnitude of NCLB reform, intergovernmental relations are likely to be complex and varied across different state and local political economies. Second, when state and city governments are involved in the reallocation of power in public schools, these initiatives are often characterized as takeover reforms of failing schools and districts. Third, several emerging federal initiatives are designed to change the long-established tradition of separating the public from the nonpublic sector in schooling services. These efforts generate federal start-up funds for charter schools, federally funded voucher program in the District of Columbia, and federally funded supplemental education services. Finally, states and districts are increasingly active in promoting alternative ways of management and governance arrangement, including state-funded vouchers and provision of diverse services in charter and other public schools.

Federal Role in Promoting Equity

The federal commitment to equal educational opportunities has been increasingly institutionalized in the past forty years. The pervasive impact of poverty and racial and ethnic inequality in public schools raises a fundamental tension in our federal system of government. Given our decentralized system of governance, the federal government is faced with a policy dilemma. On one hand, the U.S. Constitution, under the Tenth Amendment, recognizes the rights of the states to handle their own affairs, including public education.[5] Decentralization is clearly prevalent in public education, where power and decisions are dispersed among fifty states and fifteen thousand districts. On the other hand, there is a collective responsibility to address the needs of those who are less fortunate. In the nation's largest central-city school districts, for example, more than 60 percent of the students are eligible for the free and reduced-price school lunch program. States and districts, given the political reality of electoral disenfranchisement, often marginalize access and opportunities for segments of the at-risk populations.

An understanding of how the government manages this tension between local control and social responsibility lies in the changing distribution of power and functions between layers of government over the past several decades. The literature on federalism has looked for structural sources in explaining why antipoverty policy is more likely to receive attention at the national level. The federal government enjoys a broader revenue base, in which taxes are raised primarily on the principle of ability to pay, and it represents a constituency with diverse demands, including views that are not often supported by the majority.[6] In other words, the federal government has both the fiscal capacity and the political incentive (often facilitated by organized interest groups) to take a more active redistributive role. A good example is the evolving federal grants-in-aid system in public education.

The 1965 Elementary and Secondary Education Act, arguably the most important federal education program, signaled the end of dual federalism and strengthened the notion of what has been called "marble-cake" federalism, whereby the national and subnational governments share responsibilities in the domestic arena.[7] More important, the act marked the creation of a complex intergovernmental policy system. Federal engagement in education is evident in its spending priorities. According to an analysis of spending in public schools between 1970 and 2002, federal aid to redistributive programs showed persistent growth in real dollar terms.[8] During the thirty-two-year period, these programs increased from 36 percent to 63 percent of total federal spending in elementary and secondary schools. The school lunch program, for example, increased its funding from $299 million in 1970 to $10.3 billion in 2002. Spending for Head Start jumped from $326 million to more than $6.5 billion in real dollars over the same period.

With the passage of time, federal education grants have taken on several institutional characteristics. First, the grants-in-aid arrangement provides the federal dollars and sets the federal programmatic objectives. Categorical or single-purpose grants, for example, stipulate the use of supplementary services that aim at eligible at-risk students. The operational details, however, are handled by state and local agencies. Second, the grants-in-aid in education have received bipartisan support. Special-needs programs are often connected to deeply entrenched political interests—the child nutrition program (free and reduced-price lunch program), for example, was initiated by the agricultural business—and there are clearly tangible incentives for congressional representatives, since federal funds are widely distributed. In the 1990s, programs instituted under the 1994 education act provided supplemental resources to 64 percent of all the schools in the nation, covering virtually every congressional district. High-needs urban districts are not the only beneficiaries of compensatory education funds. Indeed, more than 20 percent of federal aid goes to districts with fewer than twenty-five hundred students. Districts with enrollments between twenty-five hundred and twenty-five thousand receive almost 45 percent of the funds. Because there are Title I programs in almost every congressional district, partisan conflict has generally been limited during the appropriations process.

Finally, the grants-in-aid system has evolved into a fairly stable administrative process. Although local and state noncompliance remains an issue in some programs and in some settings, state and local agencies seem more ready to meet programmatic standards as the federal government increasingly clarifies its antipoverty intent.[9] The lack of full federal funding to meet mandated standards is likely to be a continuing source of intergovernmental contention. The federal government, for example, promised to provide 40 percent of the funds for special education, but in reality, its funding level seldom went beyond 25 percent of the program cost. Nonetheless, funding debate on specific programs has not jeopardized bipartisan support for education equity at the federal level.

Emergence of Performance-Based Federalism

As education receives steady bipartisan support, its effectiveness is increasingly called into question in a climate of outcome-based accountability. The 1983 publication of *A Nation at Risk* marked the beginning of federal concern about academic performance. Drawing on political support from governors and businesses, the passage of the Improving America's Schools Act in 1994 signaled federal efforts to address accountability in its antipoverty programs. This legislation, sponsored by Bill Clinton, aimed at reducing program-induced isolation of at-risk students from their peers, creating incentives for whole school reform, and requiring districts and states to use their systemwide standards to assess the performance of at-risk students.[10]

As the U.S. Congress enacted the No Child Left Behind Act of 2001 with bipartisan support, the federal government broadened its involvement toward educational accountability for all children. In many ways, the act represents an unprecedented level of federal direction in core elements of public education, and it promises federally mandated restructuring of schools that fail to reach the performance goals. The federal law requires annual testing of students at selected elementary and high school grades in core subject areas, mandates the hiring of "highly qualified teachers" in classrooms by 2005–06, and grants state and local agencies substantial authority in taking "corrective actions" to turn around failing schools. Furthermore, the law provides school choice, allowing parents to take their children out of failing schools. Equally significant in terms of federal intervention is the legislative intent in closing the achievement gaps among racial-ethnic subgroups as well as income subgroups. To support these efforts, the federal government increased its allocation by $1.7 billion to a total of almost $11 billion in the Title I program, in addition to more than $900 million for early-reading initiatives during the first years of the legislation. Whether these performance-based initiatives will prove effective in reducing the academic gaps remains to be seen.

The emergence of federally led accountability policy has created new dynamics in the intergovernmental system. First, No Child Left Behind grants state and local agencies substantial authority in taking corrective actions to turn around failing schools. Consistent with the institutional practices in its decades-long grants-in-aid arrangement, the federal government relies primarily on state and local capacity to implement the policy. On one hand, NCLB expands federal influence. Building on the founding fathers' notion of a "compound republic," Paul Manna argues that "borrowing strength" from state governments can facilitate federal capacity in the education policy arena, where the social license is historically weak.[11] The emergence of performance-based accountability connects the concept of borrowing strength and the activities of policy reformers to license and capacity. On the other hand, tensions arise when many state and local systems have limited experience in analyzing large-scale data on student performance on an ongoing basis, in supporting alternative instructional services in failing schools, and in making information more transparent to parents in a timely manner.

Accountability policy also generates new political positioning in grantsmanship. In the current context of NCLB, Jennifer Hochschild suggests that accountability-based politics has been facilitated by "issue expansion" as a growing number of governors, mayors, and other institutional actors place education high on their programmatic agenda.[12] The literature on intergovernmental relations further suggests that governors and mayors are keen on using their lobbying capacity to negotiate for federal grants in various policy domains, such as community development and subsidized housing. In the context of NCLB, elected officials at the state and local levels stand ready to use their political stature and reputation to obtain additional intergovernmental resources. For example, Nashville's mayor, Bill Purcell, worked closely with his predecessor, the current governor Phil Bredesen, in obtaining state and federal funding for an early childhood education program. In Philadelphia, Mayor John Street, a Democrat, and U.S. senator Arlen Specter, a Republican, worked on a bipartisan platform to support the school chief, Paul Vallas, in bringing federal literacy funds to the city.

Performance-based accountability is likely to improve transparency in public education, thereby encouraging parental and community engagement. With NCLB, districts are now required to disseminate annual report cards on district and school performance in meeting or failing the adequate yearly progress goals. The challenge is to make sure that parents, particularly in disenfranchised neighborhoods, receive the necessary information on educational options in a timely manner. Advocacy groups and political leaders use their many communications channels to connect parents to their schools. Many cities work with employers to enable parents to take their children to classes on the first day of the new school year. Other cities, such as Nashville, have gained corporate support to donate supplies and backpacks the weekend before the start of the school year. City hall and the nonprofit sector often arrange transportation for inner-city parents to attend parent-teacher conferences and pick up their children's report cards.

Given the comprehensive and ambitious nature of NCLB, it is not surprising that implementation problems occur. A dramatic example is the first legal challenge against implementing the new education act, brought by districts in Michigan, Texas, and Vermont and the National Education Association, the nation's largest teachers union. The plaintiffs argued that NCLB imposed federal mandates without adequate financial support. In November 2004, a federal judge in the U.S. District Court for the Eastern District of Michigan rejected the challenge. The ruling stated that Congress had the authority to specify policy conditions on states.[13] In late 2007, however, the appellate court ruled in favor of the plaintiffs and allowed the suit to continue. Another suit has been filed by Connecticut against the U.S. Department of Education. The state not only seeks full financial support from the federal government to implement NCLB, it also claims that the department has acted in an "arbitrary and capricious manner" in deciding on state requests for waivers and exemption.[14] Connecticut cited as an example the department's rejection of the state's request to test students every other year instead of annually. Intergovernmental conflicts over specific NCLB provisions are likely to continue in specific settings.

Facing local and state reluctance, the Department of Education has relaxed certain requirements on a case-by-case basis. Chicago's success in gaining federal approval to provide tutoring programs for students in schools that failed the test of adequate yearly progress is one example of intergovernmental accommodation. Under NCLB, districts that do not meet these standards, including most large urban districts, are prohibited from providing supplemental instructional services after school to their students. The department required that Chicago replace its own services with outside vendors in January 2005. Mayor Richard Daley stepped in and put his political capital behind his education chief's decision to continue the district services. In a series of private meetings between the mayor and the U.S. secretary of education, Margaret Spellings, compromise was reached. In return for the district's continuation of its supplemental services, the city agreed to reduce barriers for private vendors to provide tutorial services. When the compromise was formally announced by Secretary Spellings in Chicago in early September 2005, Mayor Daley hailed the efforts as the "beginning of a new era of cooperation" across levels of government in education.[15] A similar waiver was subsequently granted in New York City. Clearly, intergovernmental negotiation can smooth the implementation of NCLB in complex urban systems.

In the long term, a critical challenge lies in the capacity of our intergovernmental system to effectively address achievement gaps among income and racial and ethnic groups. As federal policy evolves to give greater attention to outcome-based accountability, state and local agencies are likely to feel fiscal pressure to provide adequate schooling support to all students. As my colleague J. Y. Lee and I have reported elsewhere, states that were active in accountability during the 1990s did not focus their fiscal efforts on narrowing the resource gap between high-needs districts and their more affluent peers.[16] Clearly, a functional, federally funded policy system will continue to play an instrumental role in mediating the tension between decentralized governance and better student performance.

Takeover by State and City as a Restructuring Strategy

With the formal endorsement of takeover as a reform strategy in the No Child Left Behind Act, state and mayoral takeovers of failing districts have gained national attention. Because it involves extensive reallocation of power away from the locally elected school board, takeover is one of the most controversial strategies for raising the performance of local education agencies with significant fiscal, academic, or managerial deficiencies.

To be sure, takeover as a school reform strategy predates the federally led NCLB. In the late 1990s, twenty-four states allowed state officials to exert authority over a district in the case of academic crisis, or woefully low-performing schools, but only eleven states exercised this authority. Although state takeover laws permit extensive intervention, state agencies often refrain from entirely dismantling the local school district administration, such as replacement of the school board and the superintendent. Most state takeover laws allow state administrators to influence decisions behind the scenes in a more limited fashion in academically troubled districts, giving schools or districts an opportunity to improve before more drastic measures are taken.[17]

There were forty-five cases of state (as distinct from mayoral) takeover between 1998 and 2004.[18] Although twenty-six cases involved primarily financial and management reform, nineteen were related to academic failure. During this six-year period, nineteen districts remained under state control, including five that continued in that status for more than ten years (Newark and Paterson, in New Jersey; Roosevelt Union Free, in New York; Chester-

Upland, in Pennsylvania; and Central Falls, in Rhode Island). In nine states, the state agencies phased out their takeover of twenty-six districts and restored district authority to the local school board. These included East St. Louis, Missouri, and Jersey City, New Jersey, two districts that had been under state control for more than ten years.

One often cited example is Logan County, West Virginia. In that case, Todd Ziebarth, Kevin Bushweller, and Richard C. Seder all quote local officials who "credit the success of the takeover to working collaboratively with the local school board during the takeover."[19] Indeed, one study of Alabama and Kentucky has found that the key lies in a functional state-local partnership.[20] The multifaceted process often begins with a state management team whose members integrate their expertise with the local administration in the areas of finance, instruction, and operations. Local resistance to state assistance is likely to hinder the development of a functional intergovernmental process. Consequently, a central task is to forge a working relationship between state managers and district leaders. In Kentucky, for example, district officials worked closely with the state assistance team to compete successfully for federal grants. Furthermore, state takeover directs districts to pay greater attention to performance-based accountability. In Alabama, for example, when districts failed to keep track of financial and academic records, state officials took swift action to intervene in local operations with the installation of a functional accounting system. Finally, local officials earn their local control by making sure that the district's operation and standards are aligned with state goals on accountability.

State takeover is often met with local opposition and skepticism. In Philadelphia, when Pennsylvania governor Tom Ridge backed a state takeover plan of the district in 2000, the mayor received strong public support to challenge the gubernatorial intervention. Consequently, the plan was revised to enable the governor and the mayor to jointly appoint the Philadelphia School Reform Commission. More recently, in March 2006, when Maryland's superintendent, Nancy Grasmick, announced that the state planned to take over eleven low-performing schools in Baltimore, the city's mayor, Martin O'Malley, successfully leveraged a strong majority in the state legislature to block the implementation of the plan until June 2007.[21] From a policy perspective, the state proposal addresses an important education problem, namely, the need to look for alternative management models to improve performance in middle and high schools. In this case, the timing and the political context of state politics played a critical role. Grasmick was often mentioned as a likely running mate with the incumbent Republican governor Robert Ehrlich Jr., who later faced off against his Democratic challenger, Baltimore's O'Malley (who won the election). This unusually heightened partisan context hinders a collaborative process between the state and the city to address the challenge of academic performance.

Another form of takeover that has often been enabled by state legislation, the accountability-driven notion of mayoral takeover, began in the early 1990s when Bostonians passed a citywide referendum that granted mayoral control over education. With the 2002 addition of New York to a list of cities, including Boston (1992), Chicago (1995), Cleveland (1998), Baltimore (1999), and Philadelphia (2001), nearly 2 million students now receive their education in a school district that has been taken over by the city's mayor or jointly by the mayor and the governor. It should be noted that in Detroit, where the mayor did not have complete control over the school board, the district subsequently reverted to an electoral system. Mayoral takeover of urban districts tends to be associated with several factors, including a mayor's willingness to address education problems, broad public dissatisfaction with the school system, accountability-oriented state legislative leadership, strong business support, and weakened legitimacy of traditionally powerful service provider and service demand groups.[22] Policy analysts are particularly interested in the coattail effects of mayoral popularity and school reform. For example, the reelection of Michael Bloomberg, in New York City, and Thomas Menino, in Boston, raises the likelihood that both mayors will use their political capital to address union and bureaucratic issues.

Like state takeover, mayoral takeover is politically controversial. In redefining the distribution of power between existing entities, takeover as a reform results in winners and losers. An opponent of the reform is likely to be the teachers union, which seems concerned about the uncertainty of negotiating with the mayor or state-appointed board members and managers. Supporters of the reform are often members of the business and civic community who are frustrated with the lack of progress in district management and student performance. On the key challenge of raising student performance, mayoral takeovers have produced positive results.[23] Takeover also tends to improve district management, diversify administrative expertise, and institute fiscal discipline.

Federal Efforts to Promote School Choice

The federal government has played a key role in promoting charter schools. During the Clinton administration, appropriations in support of charter school planning grew significantly. Federal funds are used to support charter preplanning, planning, and development, as well as start-up activities. Federal influence is also seen in Washington, D.C., where a separate board was established in 1996 to oversee the growth of charter schools, whose enrollment by 2005 was close to 20 percent of the public school population. Based on multiyear surveys of parents conducted between 2001 and 2004, Jack Buckley and Mark Schneider observe differences between charter and traditional public schools in the District of Columbia: compared with their traditional public school peers, charter school students tended to be poorer, to have about the same level of special education needs and fewer needs to address limited English learning, to have about the same degree of civic tolerance, and to be less likely to use bad language and more likely to perform community service and volunteer work. The same study also analyzed electronic user patterns, which showed that parents, when shopping for charter schools, devoted a lot of attention to the demographic (including racial) characteristics of the schools. This study found that only the most active choosers, referred to as the marginal consumers, made the greatest effort to go through multiple steps in launching their school search, leading to a better match with their schooling preferences. Equally important is the finding that active choosers were tougher graders on school quality.[24]

A somewhat more recent and perhaps politically more visible development is the federal demonstration program in school vouchers in Washington. In January 2004, Congress enacted the District of Columbia School Choice Incentive Act of 2003. The legislation provides as much as five years of federal funding to students in the District of Columbia to use for private school attendance. Eligibility is limited to students whose family income level falls within 185 percent of the poverty line, a criterion similar to eligibility for the free and reduced-price lunch program. During its first year of implementation, the District of Columbia Opportunity Scholarship Program received 1,848 eligible applications. Seven of ten eligible applicants came from public schools, while the rest were already attending private schools. In the fall of 2004 the federal scholarship, which could be as much as $7,500 for each student depending on family income, was used by 1,047 students (75 percent of those who received vouchers) to attend fifty-eight private schools within the District of Columbia.[25] In other words, 53 percent of all the private schools in the District participated in the program. In schools in which the number of applicants exceeded capacity, a randomized lottery was conducted. During the first year, only the high school grades were substantially oversubscribed and had to resort to a lottery. The first-year evaluation found that compared with nonapplicants in District of Columbia public schools, voucher applicants scored better in reading and mathematics and were more likely to be African American.[26]

Congressional approval of the scholarship program signaled federal intention to support the use of vouchers as a school reform strategy. The controversy over school choice would have hindered the passage of this bill. However, this particular initiative was facilitated by several factors. First, the legislation specifically stated that the District of Columbia public schools would be "held harmless" and that the departure of voucher-using students would not result in financial loss for the district.[27] Second, the experimental nature of the program tends to limit the allotment of vouchers. According to an estimate based on Census Bureau data, about forty thousand children in the district would be eligible for this program. Yet slightly more than a thousand applicants were using their vouchers during the first program year. Finally, the unsatisfactory academic performance of the district's public schools called for more drastic actions.

That charter enrollment accounted for 20 percent of the District of Columbia public school population suggests parental and public demands for alternative services. Given the limited scope of the pilot voucher program, it is interesting to note that an evaluation of the program's first year did not find program effects on public school performance, as framed in terms of competition theory.[28] The same study, however, did find the African American voucher users were selecting schools that were more racially diverse than the district public schools. Finally, according to the findings of a follow-up evaluation, the voucher programs did not generate systemic effects in raising academic performance in the District of Columbia public schools.[29] Future studies are needed to determine whether these patterns continue.

State and Local Initiatives on Choice and Diverse Management

Public education in most urban districts can no longer be characterized as a monopoly.[30] Since the early 1990s, when the nation's first charter school was opened in Minneapolis, the scope and availability of choice programs have substantially expanded. Dissatisfied with poor performance in traditional public schools, an increasing number of states are focusing on market-like competition as a driving force to raise student performance.[31] Concentrating on the four primary types of school choice programs, Jay Greene has developed an "education freedom index" for each of the fifty states. The four categories of choice are government-funded charter schools, privately funded vouchers, homeschooling, and public school choice. According to Greene, Arizona provides the highest degree of school choice to families, while Hawaii maintains the least choice. During 2000 and 2001, Florida showed the greatest gain in school choice, while Utah seemed to regress.[32]

Choice has redefined the traditional demarcation between the public and nonpublic sectors as well as rearranged the relative balance of control between district and schools. With more than forty states and the District of Columbia operating a total of more than thirty-four hundred charter schools, charter school reform has taken on a national character as an alternative to failing public schools. Although charter schools are labeled as public schools, they are distinctive in several major aspects. The school's charter or contract explicitly states the conditions and expectations for outcome-based performance consistent with the state framework.[33] The authorizing agency can be the local school board or another legal entity, such as a university. Once established, charter schools enjoy substantial autonomy in setting teachers' salaries and work conditions, although they are governed by state regulations regarding safety, health, dismissal, and civil rights. School funding follows students to the charter schools, which are operated on a multiyear renewable contract. Enrollment in charter schools accounts for about 2 percent of the nation's public school student population. In Arizona, California, and Michigan, charter enrollment constitutes a much higher percentage of the public school population. About one-fourth of the public school students in Dayton, Ohio, are enrolled in charter schools, the highest share of charter enrollment in a single city.

Parents in Milwaukee and Cleveland can use state-funded vouchers to choose both public and nonpublic service providers. In all states, homeschooling has become a viable parental option for more than a million school-age children. In some states, as many as 20 percent of privately schooled students are homeschooled.[34] In many other cities parents have access to a variety of interdistrict and intradistrict options and magnet programs.

Recent policy changes may create additional demand for school choice options. The No Child Left Behind Act requires districts with low-performing schools to initiate a series of corrective actions, which must include one or more choice options for parents. Depending on local administrative conditions, students may be given broader schooling options when their schools fail to meet the adequate yearly progress goals for a second year in a row. In reality, the district's central administration may delay or limit this enabling process. The Supreme Court's *Zelman* decision in 2002 ruled that the state-funded voucher program in Cleveland did not violate the establishment clause in the First Amendment, thereby signaling the Court's readiness to set standards under which choice programs can pass the constitutional test.[35] However, Florida's state-funded vouchers were ruled unconstitutional by the state's high court in 2006, on the ground that state aid must be used to deliver a uniform educational system. Nevertheless, parental demands remain high. In 2003 the Center for Education Reform found that four out of ten charter schools had waiting lists estimated to be as high as 20 percent of the total charter enrollment in the nation. Yet more than 60 percent of the charter school states institute some form of ceiling on the total number of charter schools or on the charter appropriations.[36]

Political Constraints and Supply of Choice

As the charter school movement spreads, states and districts have gradually opened up the public school sector to diverse service providers, including both for-profit and nonprofit organizations. In 2002, for example, seventeen for-profit companies managed schools in twenty-six states. The largest for-profit organization is the Edison Project. The company acquired several other school management companies during the 1990s and held its initial public offering in 1999. It managed both contracted and charter schools in more than twenty states, including more than twenty schools in the Philadelphia school district. Among the smaller for-profit companies is Victory Schools, a privately held company headquartered in New York that started its business primarily in charter school provision. Another small privately held company is the Ohio-based White Hat Management, which focuses on charter schools.

Mayors, too, are beginning to consider choice-oriented strategies to raise student performance. The mayor of Indianapolis, for example, is the only mayor in the country who has the authority to create charter schools. Big-city mayors are beginning to recruit education management organizations (EMOs) to provide instructional management using programs such as KIPP and Edison. The number of charter schools in New York City is expanding, and Chicago has launched its Renaissance 2010 to promote charter and small schools.

An ambitious effort to promote alternative management is being carried out in Philadelphia, where the district recruits an extensive group of diverse service providers to manage dozens of schools. In September 2005, there were 19,000 students enrolled in schools managed by contracted service providers, and an additional 16,700 students were attending charter schools in the district. The Philadelphia reform started shortly after the state and the city entered into a joint partnership to take over the district in late 2001. Edison was commissioned by Pennsylvania's governor, Tom Ridge, to conduct an assessment of the academic and financial position of the district in the fall of 2001. The report provided the basis for the legislation that granted the governor appointive power over the school board. Subsequently, the Edison Project was hired as the lead district adviser to manage central administration between March and July 2002. When Paul Vallas was hired as the chief executive officer of Philadelphia schools in July 2002, the Edison Project became one of the seven outside managers that received five-year contracts to manage forty-five low-performing schools beginning in August 2002.

In Philadelphia, education management organizations were paid the regular per student cost plus an extra financial incentive ranging from $450 to $881 for each student. This contractual arrangement enabled the district school board to hold the service providers accountable for management performance and student outcomes. In April 2003, for example, the school board terminated the contract with one of the EMOs, Chancellor Beacon Academies, for unsatisfactory performance. Among the EMOs, the Edison Project, given its role in the early phase of the district reform, continues to manage the largest number of schools. In 2004–05, the third year of contracting out, forty-three schools were managed by four private companies and two local universities. In addition, fifty-two charter schools were operating in Philadelphia in 2004–05.

Using a cross-sectional analysis, the Accountability Review Council, an independent oversight entity established under the Pennsylvania reform legislation, has observed that the 2005 Pennsylvania System of School Assessment (PSSA) reading scores for grades 5 and 8 combined vary among different types of management. For the EMOs, the percentages range from the University of Pennsylvania's 27.2 percent to Temple University's 16 percent of students scoring at the advanced and proficient levels. The degree of change among the EMOs from spring 2004 to spring 2005 also varies. Whereas Universal and Victory showed negative achievement trends (–5.8 and –0.1 percentage points, respectively), scores for the other EMOs showed gains, ranging from 4.9 percentage points for Penn to 0.3 percentage point for Temple. In their study on Edison schools nationwide, RAND researchers have found that Edison's performance did not exceed the gains of matched comparison schools.[37] A RAND follow-up evaluation also finds no significant differences in student achievement gains between EMO-managed schools and other district schools after five years of reform, despite the additional funds.[38] The RAND study findings, however, have been called into question by an evaluation report conducted by a team of Harvard researchers.[39] In other words, it remains to be seen whether the diverse provider model constitutes the most effective way to raise student performance in failing schools.

Clearly, the market for education services is substantially regulated by legislative and administrative authorities. After all, charter schools exist because of enabling state legislation. It has long been recognized that the market for education services is a "quasi-market," and quasi-markets are not always well-functioning markets.[40] Economists have engaged in much work on the empirical realities of these markets.[41]

Recent work in this area points toward the political aspects of the education market. Charter schools are not simply firms supplying education services. Jeffrey Henig and his colleagues have theorized (and provided some evidence) that charter schools act not only as economic agents but as political agents as well.[42] In another study, Henig and colleagues suggest that the locational pattern of charter schools is affected by political and practical considerations.[43] In short, charter schools are linked in many ways to the politics and bureaucracy of their surroundings. Exactly how that interaction takes place will depend upon the context of local and state politics, but it could very well play a significant role in the effectiveness of teaching and learning.

Competitive effects of charter schools are often constrained by legislative compromise. Based on interviews and on policy and legal analysis in four states, Bryan C. Hassel has found that laws that cap the number of charter schools, cushion the financial blow to traditional district schools, or reduce the autonomy of charter schools all contribute to reducing the impact a charter school can make.[44] In a study of five urban districts, Paul Teske and his colleagues attribute the modest effects of competition to several factors. The effects of charter school competition are lessened by financial cushioning and by a lack of school-level penalties for losing students to charter schools. Growing student populations may also reduce the competitive effects; even though traditional public schools are losing relative market share, the absolute number of their students remains constant. In districts where charter schools did have an impact, piecemeal rather than systemwide changes had been made, mostly concerned with expanding the school day by offering new add-on programs.[45]

Political effects have been recognized in other contexts as well. Frederick Hess and Patrick McGuinn analyze the state-funded voucher program in Cleveland and note that competitive effects can be "muffled" by existing bureaucratic and political structures.[46] Hassel and Meagan Batdorff have shown that the charter reauthorization process can also be influenced by politics and a lack of needed information. Both of these limitations can hamper the way the market works. Always operating in the background are the politics of school choice, which tend to break down along traditional partisan lines.[47] Omer Gokcekus, Joshua Phillips, and Edward Tower have shown that politicians with stronger links to teachers unions are more likely to vote against such proposals, whereas representatives of districts with larger African American or Republican populations are more likely to vote in favor.[48] Hess and McGuinn point out that the attitudes of public school teachers to school choice can limit the institutional impact of choice. Using survey data, they find that many public school teachers are highly skeptical of school choice reform.[49] Some teachers feel that this is just another passing reform. Others consider choice a potential threat to their jobs.

Conclusion

As we progress toward the end of the first decade of the twenty-first century, education policy promises an unprecedented level of innovation and accountability. At all three levels of our intergovernmental system, multiple initiatives are designed to improve accountability by shifting the authority boundaries between governmental layers. While the No Child Left Behind Act challenges states and districts to meet increasingly high academic standards, state and city governments are taking over school districts that have traditionally been insulated from the broader political system. Equally important are new initiatives that begin to broaden the supply and demand of schooling services. The federal government has expanded its support from charter school start-up and planning to a major demonstration voucher project. At the state and local levels, an increasing number of diverse service providers are offered contracts to manage schools that have persistently failed the academic standards. The field of education policy and management is in the midst of a process of governance transformation.

To be sure, institutional redesign creates new opportunities for intergovernmental cooperation. At the same time, reform poses many challenges for intergovernmental governance. The first policy tension lies at the core of our intergovernmental system in education policy. The No Child Left Behind Act has fundamentally changed the distribution of authority in setting priorities in public schools. Given the extensive federal mandates in the act, the challenge is to maintain intergovernmental collaboration in resolving problems of design, implementation, and funding. At issue is whether state and local agencies can institutionalize NCLB-mandated services without extensive federal regulatory and financial commitment.

The second policy tension concerns the multiple, even conflicting, expectations on accountability and choice. In an ideal market, with free flow of complete information, the parent-consumers would show their preference by their decision on where to enroll their children. As currently implemented, however, such client accountability is often constrained by regulatory accountability to a state charter-authorizing board. The question of expectations is central as policymakers try to manage the tension between accountability and choice—do we expect schools of choice to raise student achievement or simply to make students and parents more satisfied? Nonetheless, under pressure from the NCLB Act to measure student proficiency, an increasing number of states and districts are placing charter schools and other alternative programs within the same accountability framework that applies to traditional public schools.

Third, and very much related to the first, is the analytic capacity of state and local education authorities in evaluating the design, implementation, and effects of their innovative initiatives. Innovation is most effectively implemented within a broader system of research and development. Such R&D functions can be performed by independent third parties or by a partnership of governmental and nongovernmental actors. The key lies in the extent to which data can be made readily available to the public and policymakers so that decisions can be grounded in evidence of what works. Initiatives need to be phased out if they do not provide evidence of success.

A fourth policy challenge is sustainability in the field of practice, particularly given the high turnover of superintendents and principals in large urban districts. Although the first-generation innovators are likely to show measurable progress, the feasibility of bringing successful pilot projects to a larger scale is still an open question. Practitioners at all levels of the policy system need to be empowered with the tools and methods required for ongoing self-assessment to enable them to fine-tune their innovative practices. In the context of accountability and transparency, the scope of self-assessment must be systematic, including proactive analyses that would form the basis for renewing the innovative vision in the future. In considering strategies to improve school quality, for example, practitioners need to pay attention to both formal and informal constraints, such as an inadequate pipeline of innovative leaders, complacent governing boards, and the inertia of risk-averse decision-making behaviors. Clearly, research and development on these kinds of issues will be critical to our ongoing efforts toward systemwide redesign and improvement.

Notes

1. Quoted in Elizabeth Bumiller, "Bush Visits School to Speak on Education Law," *New York Times,* January 10, 2006, p. A19.

2. Quoted in "Education: Secretary Bell's View of a Department in Transition," *New York Times,* February 3, 1981, p. 13.

3. Melissa McCabe, "State of the States," *Education Week* 25 (January 2006): 72–89.

4. U.S. Charter Schools, "State Profiles" (www.uscharterschools.org/pub/uscs_docs/sp/index.htm).

5. Also see Alexander Hamilton, James Madison, and John Jay, *The Federalist Papers* (New York: Mentor, 1961).

6. Kenneth K. Wong, *Funding Public Schools: Politics and Policy* (University Press of Kansas, 1999); Wallace Oates, *Fiscal Federalism* (New York: Harcourt Brace Jovanovich, 1972); Paul E. Peterson, *The Price of Federalism* (Brookings, 1995).

7. Morton Grodzins, *The American System: A New View of Government in the United States,* edited by Daniel J. Elazar (Chicago: Rand McNally, 1972).

8. Wong, *Funding Public Schools.*

9. P. E. Peterson, B. G. Rabe, and K. K. Wong, *When Federalism Works* (Brookings, 1986).

10. K. K. Wong and Margaret Wang, *Efficiency, Accountability, and Equity Issues in Title I Schoolwide Program Implementation* (Greenwich, Conn.: Information Age Publishing, 2002).

11. Paul Manna, *School's In: Federalism and the National Education Agenda, 1965–2001* (Georgetown University Press, 2006).

12. Jennifer Hochschild, "Rethinking Accountability Politics," chap. 5 in *No Child Left Behind? The Politics and Practice of School Accountability,* edited by P. E. Peterson and M. R. West (Brookings, 2003), pp. 107–23.

13. Michael Janofsky, "Judge Rejects Challenge to Bush Education Law," *New York Times,* November 24, 2005, p. A14.

14. Ibid.

15. Quoted in Sam Dillon, "Education Law Is Loosened for Failing Chicago Schools," *New York Times,* September 2, 2005, p. A12.

16. J. Y. Lee and K. K. Wong, "The Impact of Accountability on Racial and Socioeconomic Equity: Considering Both School Resources and Achievement Outcomes," *American Educational Research Journal* 41 (Winter 2004): 797–832.

17. J. G. Cibulka, "Ideological Lenses for Interpreting Political and Economic Changes Affecting Schooling," in *The Handbook of Research on Educational Administration,* edited by Joseph Murphy and K. S. Louis (San Francisco: Jossey-Bass, 1999), pp. 163–82.

18. K. K. Wong, W. E. Langevin, and F. X. Shen, "When School Districts Regain Control: The Political Economy of State Takeover of Local School and Its Withdrawal,"

paper prepared for the annual meeting of the American Political Science Association, Chicago, October 5, 2006.

19. Todd Ziebarth, "State Takeovers and Reconstitution," policy brief (Denver: Education Commission of the States, 2002); Kevin Bushweller, "Under the Shadow of the State," *American School Board Journal* 185 (August 1998): 16–19; quotation from R. C. Seder, "Balancing Accountability and Local Control: State Intervention for Financial and Academic Stability," Policy Study 268 (Reason Public Policy Institution, March 2000), p. 9.

20. Wong, Langevin, and Shen, "When School Districts Regain Control."

21. D. J. Schemo, "Lawmakers Vote to Block Takeover of Schools in Baltimore," *New York Times*, April 1, 2006, p. A13.

22. Kenneth K. Wong and Francis X. Shen, "Big City Mayors and School Governance Reform: The Case of School District Takeover," *Peabody Journal of Education* 78, no. 1 (2003): 5–32.

23. Kenneth K. Wong and others, *The Education Mayor: Improving America's Schools* (Georgetown University Press, 2007).

24. Jack Buckley and Mark Schneider, *Charter Schools: Hope or Hype?* (Princeton University Press, 2006).

25. Patrick Wolf and others, *Evaluation of the D.C. Opportunity Scholarship Program: First Year Report on Participation* (Government Printing Office, 2005).

26. Ibid.

27. Jay Greene and Marcus Winters, "An Evaluation of the Effect of D.C.'s Voucher Program on Public School Achievement and Racial Integration after One Year," Education Working Paper 10 (New York: Manhattan Institute and Georgetown University Public Policy Institute, School Choice Demonstration Project, 2006).

28. Ibid.

29. Marcus Winters and Jay Greene, *Second Year Evaluation of the Systemic Effects of the D.C. Voucher Program* (Washington: Georgetown University Public Policy Institute, School Choice Demonstration Project, 2007).

30. Milton Friedman, *Capitalism and Freedom* (University of Chicago Press, 1962); J. E. Chubb and T. M. Moe, *Politics, Markets, and America's Schools* (Brookings, 1990); Kenneth K. Wong and Herbert Walberg, eds., "Contemporary School Choice Research," special issue, *Peabody Journal of Education* 81, no. 1 (2006).

31. Albert Hirschman, *Exit, Voice and Loyalty* (Harvard University Press, 1970).

32. Jay Greene, "2001 Education Freedom Index," Civic Report 24 (New York: Manhattan Institute, 2002).

33. Kenneth K. Wong and Francis X. Shen, "Charter Law and Charter Operation: Re-Examining the Charter School Marketplace," in *Charter School Outcomes*, edited by Mark Berends and others, chap. 6 (New York: Lawrence Erlbaum, 2007); L. A. Bierlein, "The Charter School Movement," in *New Schools for a New Century*, edited by Diane Ravitch and J. P. Viteritti (Yale University Press, 1997), pp. 37–60.

34. Patricia Lines, "Homeschooling Comes of Age," *Public Interest* 140 (Summer 2000): 74–85.

35. *Zelman* v. *Simmons-Harris* 536 U.S. 639 (2002).

36. Gregg Vanourek, "State of the Charter Movement: Trends, Issues, and Indicators" (Washington: Charter School Leadership Council, 2005).

37. Brian Gill and others, *Inspiration, Perspiration, and Time: Operations and Achievement in Edison Schools* (Santa Monica, Calif.: RAND, 2005).

38. Brian Gill and others, *State Takeover, School Restructuring, Private Management, and Student Achievement in Philadelphia* (Santa Monica, Calif.: RAND, 2007).

39. Paul E. Peterson and Matthew M. Chingos, "Impact of For-Profit and Non-Profit Management on Student Achievement: The Philadelphia Story," PEPG 07-07 (Cambridge, Mass.: Program on Education Policy and Governance, Kennedy School of Government, Harvard University, November, 2007).

40. Nick Adnett, Spiros Bougheas, and Peter Davies, "Market-Based Reforms of Public Schooling: Some Unpleasant Dynamics," *Economics of Education Review* 21 (August 2002): 323–30; Elizabeth M. Caucutt, "Educational Vouchers When There Are Peer Effects: Size Matters," *International Economic Review* 43 (February 2002): 195–222.

41. C. M. Hoxby, *The Economics of School Choice: A National Bureau of Economic Research Conference Report* (Cambridge, Mass.: National Bureau of Economic Research, 2003).

42. Jeffrey Henig and others, "Privatization, Politics, and Urban Services: The Political Behavior of Charter Schools," *Journal of Urban Affairs* 25 (February 2003): 37–54.

43. Jeffrey Henig and Jason MacDonald, "Locational Decisions of Charter Schools: Probing the Market Metaphor," *Social Science Quarterly* 83 (December 2002): 962–80.

44. Bryan C. Hassel, *The Charter School Challenge: Avoiding the Pitfalls, Fulfilling the Promise* (Brookings, 1999).

45. Paul Teske and Mark Schneider, "What Research Can Tell Policy Makers about School Choice," *Journal of Policy Analysis and Management* 20 (Autumn 2001): 609–31.

46. Frederick Hess and Patrick McGuinn, "Muffled by the Din: Competitive Non-effects of the Cleveland Voucher Program," *Teachers College Record* 104 (June 2002): 727–64.

47. Bryan C. Hassel and Meagan Batdorff, *High-Stakes: Findings from a National Study of Life-or-Death Decisions by Charter School Authorizers* (Chapel Hill, N.C.: Public Impact, 2004).

48. Omer Gokcekus, Joshua J. Phillips, and Edward Tower, "School Choice: Money, Race, and Congressional Voting on Vouchers," *Public Choice* 119, nos. 1–2 (2004): 241–54.

49. Hess and McGuinn, "Muffled by the Din."

7

WELFARE REFORM

A Devolutionary Success?

JOCELYN M. JOHNSTON

In 1982 Helen Ladd and Fred Doolittle asked a fundamental American federalism question: Which level of government should assist the poor?[1] That essential question remains unanswered, in part because poverty programs in the United States reflect the structure, evolution, and ambiguity of our federal system.

In the early years of the republic, providing relief to the poor was a local enterprise, based on the tradition of the Elizabethan poor laws. In tandem with other major intergovernmental events, poverty relief has moved through a long cycle of centralization spawned by the progressive movement of the early twentieth century and the policies of the New Deal and the Great Society in the midcentury years.[2] The 1996 Personal Responsibility and Work Opportunity Reconciliation Act (PRWORA) represents the most recent rearrangement of poverty-directed welfare programs. Under PRWORA, states have gained new flexibility in the design and funding of their welfare programs and are no longer bound to honor a federal entitlement to cash assistance for the economically disadvantaged. The act was heralded by some as a significant reversal in intergovernmental policy direction, away from federal

I am grateful to Lamar Bennett for research assistance.

power and control and toward the originally local (that is, nonfederal) roots of assistance to the poor.

The term *devolution,* in its political sense, refers to the partial transfer of power and responsibility for policy from the federal government to the states. Although President Bill Clinton, who signed PRWORA into law, hailed it as "the end of welfare as we know it," the uncertainties of our federal system are likely to leave unresolved, at least in the longer term, the large question of how best to assign responsibility for poverty programs. American poverty relief exemplifies the diversity of the federal system, with some programs fully supported by the federal government, some funded jointly by multiple levels of government, and others operated and financed solely by state or local governments.[3]

Temporary Assistance for Needy Families (TANF), created by PRWORA, succeeds Aid to Families with Dependent Children (AFDC) as the major source of cash assistance for low-income families with children. The reforms embedded in TANF include an end to individual entitlement for cash assistance, expectations of work activity in return for cash assistance, and a revamped financing system that alters the federal subsidy collected by states.[4] In keeping with the general view on decentralization, PRWORA allows states to tailor services to meet the unique needs of their low-income populations. This arrangement is also consistent with the performance movement in that the federal government sets broad performance standards (for example, work participation rates for TANF recipients) but leaves it to the states to design strategies to meet those goals.

Like many national policies, PRWORA and TANF adopted key ideas rooted in earlier state innovations under AFDC. Three states—Wisconsin, Mississippi, and Oregon—had enacted AFDC waiver programs that served as models for PRWORA. Led by Republican governors, with the highly visible and influential Tommy Thompson of Wisconsin serving as a key policy entrepreneur, these states had reoriented their welfare programs around the work-first philosophy and time limits for cash assistance. Impressive caseload reductions attracted the attention of other state leaders. The federal reform resulted in part because these governors, joined by others, lobbied the Clinton administration and Congress, pushing for increased state flexibility and relief from the regulations associated with AFDC.[5]

Once PRWORA was enacted, caseload reductions took off (though caseloads had been declining). Observers were stunned by the numbers. Within four years of passage, caseloads nationwide had dropped by more than half, with Idaho, Wisconsin, and Wyoming reporting caseload drops of more than

80 percent. The combination of the strong job demand in the boom economy of the late 1990s and tough-love work-first provisions quickly stripped state welfare rolls of their most employable recipients. The increased demand for labor from an expanding economy then began to absorb a second tier of less employable enrollees. By 2000 many of the remaining welfare recipients were defined as hard to employ and were seen as least prepared to hold permanent jobs. In four short years, welfare looked very different from what it had under AFDC, and the fiscal, policy, and administrative relationships between the federal government and the states had been significantly altered. Caseload reductions began to moderate in 2001, owing in part to a recession, and national reductions have been fairly flat since then.[6]

More recently, however, the new flexibility afforded to states has been constrained by the Deficit Reduction Act of 2006, which stiffened federal regulation with regard to state TANF work requirements. Although the Republican Congress that created PRWORA in 1996 believed that the law imposed strict work rules, states quickly found that the federal work participation mandates were reduced significantly by the combination of a technical element of the law and steep caseload declines. The act required 25 percent of nonexempt TANF adults to participate in work activities for at least twenty hours a week, with expectations of a 50 percent participation rate by 2002. But the so-called caseload reduction credit, which reduced the stipulated rate as the number of caseloads declined, meant that by 2004, only about one-third of TANF adults were participating in work or work activities. In nineteen states, the required work participation rate had fallen to zero, the average state faced an effective rate of 6 percent, and only eleven states had to meet rates in excess of 10 percent.[7] Under these conditions, nearly all states were meeting their federal work obligations.

The PRWORA reauthorization debate drew increased congressional attention to work participation rates. Consistent with the recategorization dynamics observed in other block grant programs,[8] Congress shifted its priority from state flexibility to accountability, in this case, for putting welfare recipients to work. As it did with the No Child Left Behind Act and other George W. Bush administration policies, the Republican-majority Congress, dominated by conservatives who had traditionally championed states' rights, pushed its conservative agenda on the states. Traditional Republican criticism of Democratic congressional mandates for the states was forgotten for the moment, as predicted by theories contending that federalism concerns are typically superseded by other political considerations and by the propensity of those in power to use their authority to achieve their ideological, political, and policy objectives, regardless of their impacts on states' autonomy.[9]

Fiscal Impacts

The devolutionary reputation of PRWORA stems partly from its use of a block grant to fund TANF cash assistance, set at an annual allocation level of $16.5 billion for the first five years (1997–2002).[10] Because state officials have typically expressed preference for the greater flexibility associated with federal block grants, this provision was viewed as especially important to state interests. Aid to Families with Dependent Children, the predecessor to TANF, had been financed through open-ended matching grants.[11]

New Grant Design

The matching-grant design used to fund AFDC had several potential advantages over block grants. First, from the grantor's perspective, matching grants are thought to be more stimulative than block grants, in part because they minimize substitution of federal dollars for state programs that the federal government does not intend to subsidize.[12] Matching grants therefore may result in more targeted leveraging of federal aid dollars. In addition, federal matching funds can be used to help states deal with recessions—and the attendant revenue losses and higher demand for income support and related services associated with unemployment and other recessionary pressures.

Block (or fixed-sum) grants, like the one used to distribute TANF funds, can have other disadvantages compared with matching grants. To begin with, they tend to be eroded by inflation over time. R. Kent Weaver estimates that the value of the TANF block grant declined by 12 percent between 1997 and 2002, and other projections put the 2011 value of the TANF block grant at 70 percent of its 1997 value.[13] Unless states replace the lost value of the grants—a questionable assumption at best[14]—the capped block grant generates, in effect, a federal cut to state programs and beneficiaries. In addition, each TANF dollar spent beyond the block grant allocation must be fully funded through state revenues. The high marginal cost of spending beyond the federal block grant allocation imposes the greatest burden during recessions, when state revenues are strained, just as demand for poverty-related services increases.[15]

Yet despite the theoretically superior stimulative strength of open-ended matching grants, they have not always generated expected results. Two potential reasons include flaws in the matching rates, which are set through political bargaining, and the incentives for states to game the system by drawing down federal dollars without a state match.[16] In a review of research on AFDC matching grants, Howard Chernick concluded that the stimulative effects were small, despite the large matches given to some states. He attributes this anomaly to states' use of federally funded food stamps as a substitute for cash assistance. He also contended that the fiscal effects of converting from a matching grant to block grant mechanism for welfare might not be fully understood until after the reform has been in place for at least ten years, partly because of the boom economy of the late 1990s that sent caseloads plummeting.[17]

Thus far, the evidence suggests that state spending on TANF and related services has increased since the reform, including the period during and after the 2001 recession. The Government Accountability Office (GAO) reports that in a nine-state sample, a 17 percent median real increase in combined federal-state spending occurred between 1995 and 2004.[18] In all states but one, real spending from state sources also rose during the same time period, with a median increase of 17 percent. The extent to which this spending growth reflected state preferences is unclear, but state spending decisions were affected by federal pressure to spend TANF balances and by state concerns that Congress might reclaim those balances.[19]

Traditionally, states reduced AFDC cash benefit levels only through the real cuts imposed by inflation. This trend has continued under the TANF block grant. Between 1996 and 2004, the real value of state TANF cash grants to individual households (family of three) declined by as much as 32 percent (Montana) and by 15 percent in most states. Only eight states— Alabama, California, Louisiana, Maryland, Mississippi, New York, West Virginia, and Wisconsin—instituted real increases in the values of their cash grants during this period.[20]

One critique of the PRWORA block grant design is that it essentially froze preexisting interstate spending disparities.[21] The TANF federal block grant allocations to each state were based on that state's spending level in the final years of AFDC. But under AFDC, poorer states tended to offer lower benefits to fewer beneficiaries and spent less on each recipient, despite relatively high matching rates. Thus one important effect of TANF has been to award more funding for each TANF individual to wealthier states than to poor states.

Regardless of state fiscal responses, block grants reduce the federal spending uncertainty associated with entitlement programs. The fixed federal block grant allocation contrasts to the budgetary uncertainty associated with a matching-grant system. Under the AFDC open-ended matching-grant design, federal spending responded directly to state spending dollar for dollar, so federal aid levels were determined largely by state spending decisions.

Block Grants and Substitution

Although block grants theoretically facilitate states' use of funds for fiscal relief and other nontargeted priorities, federal maintenance-of-effort requirements constrain such substitution effects. The present welfare act gives states increased policy and administrative flexibility, but the law also includes maintenance-of-effort provisions that require states to spend 75 percent of their 1994 AFDC spending level on services designed to meet the objectives of the new law. For any state that does not meet federal work participation thresholds, the maintenance-of-effort level rises to 80 percent.

New spending priorities emerged as states sought ways to meet their maintenance-of-effort obligations. Allowable maintenance-of-effort activities include state earned income tax credit (EITC) programs, social service block grant programs, and others. Just as states have "Medicaided" formerly state-only health care programs for low-income individuals, some have "welfarized" preexisting cash and noncash assistance programs with PRWORA, using federal dollars to replace state-only dollars. In a ten-state study, the GAO found that all states replaced some state-only program funding with TANF dollars, and five states used up to 25 percent of their TANF block grants for this purpose. The dollars contributed by TANF were directed to fund a variety of state programs, including Medicaid, child welfare, early childhood development and prekindergarten programs, pregnancy prevention, homestead tax credits (Michigan), general fiscal relief (New York), K–12 education (Oregon and New Jersey), and property tax cuts (Wisconsin).[22]

For the most part, these purposes have been viewed as consistent with PRWORA's emphasis on support for low-income working families.[23] But because of the wide variety of spending priorities, and owing to the failure of federal government monitoring to keep pace with the new spending patterns as they have emerged, significant retooling is necessary in order for current systems to assess state accountability.[24]

New Spending Patterns

The big story of welfare reform in terms of state TANF spending patterns is the decline in spending on cash assistance and the increased spending on work supports. In addition to programs designed to enhance employability and help with job search, the most important work supports include child care, along with transportation and other work necessities. The states' new emphasis on work supports, an important result of PRWORA's devolutionary design, was both unanticipated and surprising to most observers of the reform.

This pronounced shift in spending patterns is explained not only by the financial windfall stemming from the strong economy and the spectacular drop in caseloads during the late 1990s but also by federal work participation expectations, strong federal maintenance-of-effort requirements, and large TANF surpluses that states saw as vulnerable to congressional reclamation.[25] Regardless of the impetus, the important development is that states used their new flexibility to increase spending per TANF case with generous work supports and to reduce the notorious welfare work disincentives.

Between 1996 and 2000, the percentage of combined state and federal TANF funds spent on cash assistance fell from 76 percent to 41 percent. During the same period, the portion allocated to child care rose from 4 percent to 19 percent, while the portion spent on work-related programs rose from 5 percent to 9 percent.[26] The GAO reported that in a nine-state sample, median increases in welfare spending priorities between 1995 and 2004 were lowest for employment and training services (21 percent), compared with 71 percent on work supports such as child care, transportation, wage subsidies, state EITCs, and others. The largest shift in work supports was in the area of child care, with a median spending increase among the nine states of 133 percent.[27]

What is not new under PRWORA is spending variations across the states. The broad shift in spending patterns—away from cash assistance and toward work support—took different forms in different states. One study of seventeen states has found that between 1995 and 1999, noncash TANF spending increased by only 4 percent in New York, compared with 115 percent in Colorado, and that between 1996 and 2000, spending on child care increased by 219 percent in Wisconsin but by only 34 percent in Oregon.[28] At the same time, in a study of sixteen states with high child-poverty rates, TANF spending per low-income child ranged from less than $400 to more than $1,600, and spending levels correlated inversely with child-poverty rates.[29] Consistent with cross-state disparities under AFDC, states with fewer resources tend to spend less on each case and less on each child and also devote fewer state-only dollars to welfare.

The First Post-PRWORA Recession

The stunning early success in TANF employment gains raised questions about how states would react to an economic downturn. Evidence indicates that state welfare spending reductions during and immediately after the 2001 recession were more modest than might have been expected and that most states did not cut cash benefit levels. Although cuts to work supports began to emerge early in the recession period, by 2003 only fifteen states had reduced or planned to reduce funding for TANF recipient skill improvement and employment preparation. Child care expenditures were more hard hit by recessionary spending adjustments.[30]

For many states, recessionary cuts resulted from the depletion of surplus TANF funds that had been available for several years in the late 1990s. The trends of heightened spending on each case and support for employed households began to slow late in the recession. By then, states had committed to a new focus on support services such as child care and transportation, and they began to use unexpended funds and to exhaust their block grant allocations.

In addition to the TANF carryover funds, states had the option to take advantage of two PRWORA provisions designed to blunt the impact of recession. Under the law, states were given authority to borrow from the federal government, and a special federal contingency fund was created for states to draw on during recessions. But because states were reluctant to borrow for welfare purposes, and owing to the difficulty of meeting the standards required to draw from the contingency fund, these provisions provided limited actual recessionary relief. In fact, according to the Congressional Research Service, no states drew from the contingency fund during the 2001 recession.[31] However, federal aid provided through other avenues, including general purpose and Medicaid assistance, offset some state revenue losses.

Policy Choices

State policy innovation is considered to be a key strength of a decentralized federal structure, wherein subfederal units serve as laboratories of democracy. Under PRWORA, state welfare policies have been crafted to reflect the unique political, economic, and demographic needs of the states. Interstate welfare policy differences existed under the comparatively restricted framework of the AFDC cash assistance program as well, in part because states had authority with regard to program eligibility, benefit levels, and other features. More recently, waivers granted by the George H. W. Bush and

Clinton administrations generated additional welfare policy variations across the states.

Although PRWORA stimulated policy innovation, state experimentation began to slow and level off two to three years into the reform, and policies began to converge around a small number of broad PRWORA themes.[32] As expected (and required) under PRWORA, states reoriented their programs to emphasize work for TANF cash assistance applicants and recipients. The emergence of policies that intensified work supports and extended cash assistance to employed TANF individuals was more surprising.

The Range of Choices

State PRWORA and TANF policy choices have been categorized in several ways. Thomas Gais and R. Kent Weaver, among others, differentiate between policies that enhance access to TANF services (with positive incentives, or "carrots") and those that restrict support (with negative incentives, or "sticks").[33] Nearly half of the states instituted "stick" policies by implementing family caps, electing stiff sanction policies for failure to participate in work activity,[34] or requiring work activities for TANF women with children under the age of twelve months. By 2003 more than half of the states had adopted "diversion" policies, whereby some potential applicants were paid lump sums after they agreed that they would not apply for TANF cash assistance for a specified time period. But only eight states restricted TANF lifetime limits to levels below the federal ceiling of sixty months. Roughly half of the states adopted the federal time limit, seven adopted no time limit at all, and the remainder fashioned unique time limit policies.[35]

In terms of "carrots," only twelve states provided transitional Medicaid for those leaving TANF beyond the federal requirement of twelve months. Some states also extended TANF benefits to qualified noncitizens, other immigrants, individuals in higher-education programs, the disabled, and victims of domestic violence in "separate state programs," using state-only funds.[36]

As noted earlier, one of PRWORA's greatest surprises was the substantial and widespread increase in state support for working TANF households, including continued cash assistance. By raising asset and income disregards, most states expanded the pool of eligible TANF recipients to include working households. In effect, states opted to reduce the implicit tax rate on new household earnings and to supplement earnings; the percentage of TANF households with wage income that also received cash assistance rose from 11 percent in 1996 to 26 percent in 2002. The Congressional Research Service has described the new focus on work support as one of the "most profound changes states made to their cash assistance programs, once freed from federal rules." Gais and Weaver note that this policy development "was in no way mandated by TANF. It emerged out of the new flexibility accorded to the states."[37]

By 2002 two-thirds of all TANF adults required to work were in unsubsidized employment, and state supports for working families were providing important supplements to family income. Research indicates that in California and some other states, the use of such earnings supplements actually encouraged employment and, together with other work supports such as child care assistance, led to higher household income and lower poverty rates among low-income families.[38]

There has also been substantial growth in the number and coverage of state policies designed to subsidize work through state income tax systems. By 2007 twenty-three states had state EITC programs in force, up from only thirteen states in 2000. (An important regional effect is revealed by the fact that most EITC states are located in the Northeast and Midwest. North Carolina and Louisiana are the only southeastern EITC states).[39] States also use their income tax systems to distribute other types of aid to working poor and low-income households, including property tax relief for homeowners, food tax rebates, and property tax credits for renters.

Thus most states adopted a set of common policies, and relatively few "pushed the envelope" with especially generous or harsh policies. The policies selected by the largest number of states include asset and income disregards (carrots) and work activity requirements before twenty-four months of TANF cash receipt has elapsed (sticks), with nearly two-thirds requiring immediate work activity. Nearly all states require participation in work-related activities for the twenty to thirty hours a week stipulated in the law, and nine states require more than thirty hours.[40]

Conclusions about the impact of reformed welfare policies on national poverty rates remain tentative and mixed, in part because of state policy variations. Scholars offer evidence of both reduced poverty rates, especially in the early years of the reform, and higher poverty rates, more recently. It is likely that poverty rates are more responsive to the overall economy than to changes in welfare policies and that some of the early poverty rate reductions were driven more by employment growth than by policy changes.[41] It does seem clear, however, that welfare reform has not led to widespread, significant, or sustained reductions in poverty rates for families and children and that the extent to which the reforms have alleviated poverty varies from state to state, determined in part by state policy choices. Although national caseloads have been declining recently, child poverty rates have risen, suggesting that TANF is helping fewer poor families in at least some states.[42]

How and Why Policy Choices Are Made

The wide variation in AFDC eligibility and benefit policies has been studied extensively. Scholars are now working to identify the determinants of state policy decisions under PRWORA and TANF, and the prevailing view is that in the area of welfare policy, executive branch actors, primarily governors, drove the policy changes.[43] Carol Weissert has found that in the Midwest, state policies were shaped by strong, entrepreneurial governors such as John Engler in Michigan and Thompson in Wisconsin and also by strong executive branch agency leaders in Ohio, Michigan, Wisconsin, and Kansas.[44] In states where governors were more involved in crafting policy, legislative bodies tended to be primarily reactive, responding to gubernatorial and bureaucratic policy initiatives. Advocacy groups, which might be expected to protect the interests of welfare families, often had relatively little voice in shaping welfare policy.[45]

Bureaucratic actors also had significant influence over the design of TANF policies, particularly when it came down to details, both because elected officials often lack interest in policy details and because of the expertise and institutional history of bureaucratic actors and their capacity to span intergovernmental and network boundaries through "picket-fence" connections with other social welfare professionals. Consequently, many of the variations in policy across states originated with bureaucratic decisions. This dynamic is consistent with research on the input of administrative officials in other social welfare arenas, such as Medicaid.[46]

One widely cited factor used to explain states' choice of welfare policy was articulated in 1949 by V. O. Key, a student of southern politics, who argued that state spending on "have-nots" tends to be higher in states with two or more competitive political parties. When Key formulated his theory, many southern states were effectively one-party states, with Democratic interests entrenched because of resistance to Republican policy before, during, and after the Civil War. Robert Plotnick and Richard Winters provide a more contemporary and comprehensive theoretical explanation of state welfare generosity, incorporating both political (ideology, interparty competition, interest group strength) and economic (state resident income, tax price for welfare programs) variables.[47] Many recent studies have found that states with more conservative ideologies and weaker interparty competition tend to choose less generous welfare policies. Most states, on the other hand, display a long-standing tendency to be more generous with those they consider the "deserving poor" through programs such as Medicaid and state supplements to federal Supplemental Security Income for the disabled.[48]

Joe Soss and his colleagues explain that analyzing interstate TANF spending variations has become complicated, in part because spending is now diffused across so may services. Under AFDC, analysts focused on comparing eligibility thresholds, benefit levels, and spending on cash assistance. Because of the wide range of programs and supports offered through TANF, however, these comparisons are not as clear. As a result, Soss and his colleagues have focused instead on variations in the common types of policies adopted and specifically on the extent to which choices on family caps, sanctions, work requirements, and time limits are more or less punitive (that is, the degree of "toughness"). They conclude that states' "old" AFDC policies are good predictors of TANF choices. They also find that political ideology matters and that more conservative states selected tougher policies and implemented them more quickly.[49]

One of the more consistent and most troubling conclusions in studies of current state welfare decisions is the continuing association between race and policy choices. More punitive welfare policies are the norm in states with TANF caseloads that have higher concentrations of African Americans and Latinos. Relative to whites, African Americans are more likely to live in states with stricter income and administrative barriers to welfare assistance, lower benefit levels, and fewer postemployment supports. Soss and his colleagues conclude that the "devolution revolution" has created openings for new forms of racial inequality that disadvantage African Americans in the United States.[50]

States' Race to the Bottom?

Scholars of federalism and public policy have also speculated on whether PRWORA set the stage for the states to "race to the bottom" in terms of welfare policies. The concept of "welfare magnets" suggests the possibility that state officials, loathe to attract poor residents from other states by offering generous welfare policies, will opt to reduce welfare generosity (or to avoid increasing benefits).[51] The underlying idea is that businesses and wealthier citizens have incentives to avoid jurisdictions that are more generous with social welfare programs because of perceptions of higher tax rates and less desirable populations.

The race-to-the-bottom theory has been disputed by several studies of TANF implementation,[52] and some studies refuted its validity during the

AFDC years as well.[53] Robert Lieberman and Greg Shaw conclude that national factors and trends (specifically, national caseload trends) are more important determinants of welfare policy choice than are interstate competitive pressures. William Berry, Richard Fording, and Russell Hanson, correcting for model specification problems in earlier studies, argue that state economic conditions are far more important determinants of welfare benefits than are neighboring state policies.[54] In a direct challenge to the welfare magnet thesis, Sanford Schram, Lawrence Nitz, and Gary Krueger conclude that "the migration routes of poor single mothers with children are not associated with higher welfare benefits" but rather are driven by considerations such as safety, better housing, schools, and economic opportunities. Although other scholars offer evidence that welfare benefits do influence interstate migration, the effect is small relative to motivations such as returning to one's home state to be near family members.[55]

At best, empirical evidence for the existence of welfare magnets and a race to the bottom is mixed. More time will have to pass before these dynamics can be clearly assessed with regard to TANF and PRWORA, although state behavior during the 2001 recession is not generally consistent with the two theories. Like the race-to-the-bottom theory, the welfare magnet idea is one that perseveres, and "its symbolic value in reinforcing prejudices against welfare recipients" may help explain its resilience.[56]

Managing Devolution

State welfare administrators faced the dual challenge of managing new authority and discretion under PRWORA while implementing a major policy reform. Although many states achieved the crucial institutional changes seen as necessary by many reformers, others have been less successful.

Institutional Change

State welfare officials were well aware that without substantial alteration of the culture of their welfare organizations, the new policy could be compromised. That culture—shaped by a mission of minimizing eligibility determination errors—worked against the new emphasis on employment and independence from public assistance. Realizing PRWORA's goals would therefore require a major retooling of state welfare agencies—a modification of such proportions that many state welfare agency leaders opted to bypass their organizations and outsource significant portions of their new TANF program to other public, nonprofit, and private entities.

Several states did successfully reorient their welfare offices around the new employment goals—and to a greater extent than expected. The implementation of PRWORA required states to develop new program services, direct client flow through a complex web of new services, and maintain accountability within both their own organizations and those with which they contracted for client services.[57] In essence, according to one report, "No longer are local [welfare] offices simply check-writing operations; now they are also programs that help people prepare for and find jobs. The typical welfare office has been transformed, personnel have been retrained, and the activities inside the welfare office—which most states have renamed 'Work Centers' or some similar term—have expanded to include job-related pursuits." In 2001 Gais and his colleagues remarked that "the rapidity and breadth of change [in welfare institutions] have been stunning. State and local human service systems may now be one of the most quickly changing components of American governmental institutions."[58] These administrative reconfigurations were possible in part because of the economic growth that occurred simultaneously with the reform and the resulting success in placing recipients into employment.

Yet the degree to which these cultural changes have taken hold remains a somewhat open question. Both PRWORA and TANF suffered to some extent from the classic "street-level bureaucracy" problem of resistance to change, wherein frontline workers use discretion to thwart the reform. For public managers, the key challenge was to mitigate the negative impacts of that discretion while using workers' expertise and experience to foster program success.[59]

In many states, TANF frontline caseworkers received new job titles, along with new job responsibilities that were often added to their previous eligibility determination and intake tasks. In other words, administrative change "occurred by augmenting, not transforming, the culture" of welfare agencies. Several of these new tasks involved directing client behavior toward desired goals, which required more intense interpersonal relationships between caseworker and client. This represented a critical—and difficult—shift for many former eligibility workers. As Irene Lurie notes, "Frontline [welfare] workers typically do not have an educational background in social work, and they often feel unprepared and reluctant to get involved with their clients' personal problems."[60]

The implementation of PRWORA also exposed new goal inconsistencies. The culture of eligibility determination remained entrenched in many states, in part because many managers in the system continued to focus on flawed performance measures such as intake accuracy and timeliness, thereby compromising efforts to refocus workers toward employment goals.[61] Although error rates and timeliness are legitimate concerns, they do not address the fundamental goal of TANF, which is to generate sustained employment and economic independence for applicants and recipients.

Managing "Delinked" Programs

The rapidity of institutional change helps explain the drop-offs in Medicaid and food stamp participation in the early PRWORA reform years. Cash assistance had been explicitly "delinked" from Medicaid and food stamps, but new administrative systems exacerbated the disconnect.[62] New, more rigorous policies at the "front door" of welfare offices meant that efforts to divert applicants often also discouraged participation in other critical entitlement programs such as Medicaid and food stamps—programs that were essential to supporting low-wage working households.[63] During the first year of the reform, national Medicaid enrollments decreased by 7 percent; Wisconsin had the highest enrollment decline at 19 percent. States later found that although Medicaid benefits were not subject to TANF's mandatory job search requirements, eligible applicants often received no Medicaid, food stamps, or other non-TANF assistance of any kind simply because cash assistance was not granted at the time of application. Diversion programs generated similar problems.[64]

Finding the right balance was a key policy and management challenge: too little administrative delinkage could mire programs in the preexisting welfare culture, while too much, especially if responsibility was spread across several organizations, could overwhelm existing capacity to coordinate.[65] Despite PRWORA's deregulatory flavor, federal officials were soon calling on states to revisit their intake and outreach processes to ensure that those eligible for Medicaid, food stamps, and other support services received those benefits, regardless of their TANF status.

Managing Second-Order Devolution

Second-order devolution—devolution from state to local governments or to local offices of state welfare agencies—has been widespread under PRWORA.[66] Most states constructed administrative systems that were centralized in state government, but fifteen ceded administrative responsibility to local governments, often counties,[67] and many centralized states extended more policy and management authority to their regional offices.

Another significant component of second-order devolution—"contractual devolution"—is also under way in many states.[68] Although not new, welfare agency reliance on other state, local, nonprofit, and for-profit organizations, especially to deliver employment-related services through formal agreements and contracts, is widespread and much more extensive under TANF and PRWORA than it was under AFDC. Richard Nathan and Gais suggest that this "downward push" may have been necessary to implement a reform designed around significant individual behavioral change. Similarly, Karin Martinson and Pamela Holcomb have observed that "the most striking institutional change" under PRWORA "is the development and expansion of organizational linkages" to pursue specific program goals.[69]

Welfare agencies contracted not only with other organizations for employment services—typically, state and local agencies funded by the U.S. Department of Labor—but also with nonprofits and for-profit entities for case management services, client tracking, compliance monitoring, and other specialized services. As of 2002, Texas, Florida, and Arizona were also contracting out eligibility determination. These "connections" with other organizations probably helped the states implement the reform sooner and diversify their client services more effectively.[70]

In essence, many welfare agencies have become more networked and therefore more heavily involved in contract and network management. Problems of communication, coordination, and maintaining accountability have generated new challenges for welfare administrators.[71] The intense management required in networks consumes substantial resources because roles and responsibilities must be defined and renegotiated, often through a system of trial and error.[72] Risk arrangements for these contracts also create difficulties, especially because incentives exist to treat relatively easy clients or because the promised enrollment levels that generate revenue never materialized.[73]

The performance systems borrowed from the private sector do not readily fit social welfare programs, and the transaction costs for these contracts are comparatively steep. The goal congruence sought by administrators in an intergovernmental system becomes even more elusive in a heavily networked system.[74] Flawed contract performance measures can give rise to goal displacement, and performance information is often difficult to obtain. Under these conditions, holding third parties accountable for specified performance is not a simple task.[75]

Clearly, institutional changes have materialized under PRWORA, and welfare administrators have faced enormous pressures to implement a very different program, to redesign welfare organizations resistant to change, and to manage extensive interagency provider networks. As Lawrence Mead indicates, this is not a cheap proposition. Mead documents administrative costs that grew continually during Wisconsin's waiver and postwaiver reform while federal grant values actually declined. Donald Boyd and his colleagues report state welfare administration cuts ranging from 5 percent to 22 percent during the early years of the 2001 recession.[76] Given the high expectations for welfare agencies under PRWORA, these cuts are problematic at best.

A Devolutionary Success?

Despite the rhetoric surrounding the new law, there are clear doubts about the extent of devolution and decentralization embodied in welfare reform.[77] Analysts note that states always had plenty of autonomy under AFDC, and they do not have "unprecedented liberty" now.[78] Constraints on state discretion are clearly demonstrated in the Deficit Reduction Act of 2006, which reauthorized the reform and imposes stringent new requirements on the states.

In view of the pervasive waiver activity before passage of PRWORA, one can legitimately question the marginal value of the law's devolutionary impact. More than forty states were using welfare waivers in the decade preceding the reform, and during the Clinton administration virtually all state waiver applications were approved.[79] The extent to which policy experimentation can be attributed to PRWORA must be measured in light of the fact that many of the individual state innovations adopted before the reform were grandfathered in by federal officials reviewing state TANF plans.

Instead, PRWORA may be better described as a "dubious devolution," in part because new flexibility for states is undercut by expectations with regard to work participation rates, by the termination of federal assistance when cases time out, and by the requirements of the 2006 Deficit Reduction Act.[80] Like most block grant programs, PRWORA has been and will continue to be increasingly curbed over time by the federal "recategorization" dynamic associated with demands for grantee accountability from the lawmakers who dispense the funds and from executive branch officials who oversee program and policy. The welfare block grants could also reinforce the distributive (place-based) tendencies of Congress, further eroding the redistributive (people-based) flavor of AFDC.[81] A related key issue surrounding the reform debate concerned whether a race to the bottom among states would materialize. Many analysts have concluded that any such race thus far has been modest. Whether the eroding value of the block grant and future economic pressures on states will prompt states to avoid becoming welfare magnets is an open question.

The federal government essentially used PRWORA to set a broad program objective—independence from reliance on welfare—and left it to the states to achieve that objective. This outcome-based approach is consistent with the devolutionary philosophy of New Public Management and other market-based government reforms, but it is also subject to many of their limitations, including reliance on output measures (such as job placements and work participation rates) in lieu of true outcome measures (such as sustained economic independence and family well-being), the difficulty of establishing performance standards and goals agreeable to all levels of government, and the use of a one-size-fits-all approach.[82]

The variations in policy choices across states implementing PRWORA represent the classic trade-off in American federalism. The new flexibility granted to states allowed them to tailor policies to their unique conditions. The states responded by adopting policies that had not been anticipated—especially with regard to the extensive work support system, including child care and cash assistance to working TANF households—but also by following the pattern set by AFDC. The wide range in welfare generosity under AFDC was preserved but took a new form. Preexisting state AFDC benefit and eligibility levels tended to remain the same, but states now had the opportunity to craft policies that created incentives for work. They could also remove families from cash assistance earlier and permanently, divert them from receiving cash assistance in the first place, require substantial individual effort in job seeking and other work-related activities, and sanction households for failure to comply with those requirements. The most generous and the most punitive policies tended to be adopted by a handful of states, with the majority adopting policies toward the middle of the generosity continuum. Evidence indicates that states' decisions have been generally consistent with their prereform policies in terms of relative generosity, reflecting the fact that in our federal system, state policy preferences are resilient and not easily altered. [83]

The troubling relationship between race and tough state welfare policies merits ongoing scrutiny. Soss and his colleagues are "struck by the extent to which welfare policy in the United States continues to be rooted in politics driven by race and ethnicity, gender and family relations, class and labor market conditions." States that have caseloads with high proportions of African Americans and other minorities have traditionally been among the least generous with regard to their social welfare policies, and PRWORA appears to have done little to alter that pattern. As Paul Peterson observes, the price of federalism—inequity across states—is paid with recognition that a centralized solution could make society worse off.[84] For individual recipients living in states with tough policies or less generous eligibility and benefit levels, however, that price can be very high.

The Future of Welfare Devolution

The Personal Responsibility and Work Opportunity Reconciliation Act was originally set to expire in 2002, but Congress and the Bush administration extended temporary program authority several times. On February 8, 2005, President Bush signed the Deficit Reduction Act, which finally reauthorized TANF through 2010. The law left the basic block grant at the same level but added $2 billion for recession contingency funds, up to $100 million for "healthy marriage" initiatives, and $200 million more for child care (with a state match required) for TANF recipients who are either working or involved in work-related activities.[85] The child care funding was especially contentious, and much higher levels had been recommended by some advocacy groups.

In keeping with block grant recategorization theory, PRWORA requirements were tightened through more stringent work participation rates, new and more restrictive definitions of what counts as work activity and how that work must be reported, reductions in the value of the caseload reduction credit, and new penalties for states that fail to meet the new rates. At the time of the reauthorization, most states were not meeting the new work participation standards. Advocacy groups and interest groups representing the states have criticized the new rules, expressing dismay that "there is so much micromanagement coming from the federal government on a block grant that was designed to be a flexible source of funds."[86] At the same time, the Deficit Reduction Act adds $319 million in supplemental grants for states with high poverty rates or high population growth rates, which could help mitigate policy and spending disparities that work against TANF beneficiaries in some states. In addition, new implementation directives provide some work participation relief for states with high unemployment and poverty rates.[87]

In essence, the Deficit Reduction Act constrains the opportunity for states to evade the original TANF work requirements. State reactions to the act have been driven in part by the reality that TANF cases have changed since the reform was enacted—with many of the "easy" to employ individuals no longer enrolled. Consequently, states are shifting their services to deal more effectively with hard-to-employ recipients, adopting mixed-services strategies for those with mental and physical disabilities, substance abuse problems, limited English proficiency, and other complex barriers to employment. Some states have also reconsidered their elimination of education and training programs (including higher education). Before PRWORA, more than one-third of beneficiaries in employment-related activities were actually in education programs. Because many of the jobs obtained by TANF individuals have not kept families out of poverty, there is increasing recognition that training for higher-skilled jobs may yield more-stable employment outcomes.[88]

Thus though PRWORA offered the states relief from some regulatory constraints, new fiscal flexibility, and the opportunity to get creative (or continue their creativity) with welfare policy, the law also pushed states to demand more of recipients and to limit their receipt of cash assistance. The federal government used the block grant tool to take advantage of states as policy innovators and distributive engines.[89] The states, led by key Republican governors who had crafted welfare reforms that drove the federal law, responded with broad changes to their welfare programs. Yet state policy choices essentially converged around a common set of policies and tended to reflect pre-PRWORA patterns with regard to generosity and demands on individual recipients.

Conclusion

If PRWORA was at all revolutionary, that revolution was short lived. There is no doubt that the welfare program has shifted from one of relatively unencumbered income assistance to one focused on employment and economic independence. But that trend was already under way in the states. As the reform was implemented, it became clear that conservatives in Congress are just as prone to block grant "recategorization" as liberals were during the Reagan administration. The accountability weaknesses of the block grant mechanism in terms of grantee performance and the achievement of grantor objectives persist,[90] and states, true to form, are complaining vigorously about new federal welfare requirements. Although the federal government has ceded some policy control to the states, it retains the fiscal upper hand.

Despite the changes in the American welfare system under PRWORA, federalism and the struggle to balance federal and state authority and responsibility are hardly settled issues. The Ladd and Doolittle question posed at the beginning of this chapter remains relevant and will endure as we continue to confront and address poverty and need among our fellow citizens. The 2006 welfare reform reauthorization, although crafted in an era of conservative executive and legislative branch politics, nonetheless reflects the classic tendency of those in power to push their policy agenda on the states.

Appendix 7A. Selected Welfare-Related Policies, by State, Various Years

State	Maximum monthly benefit for family of three, January 2004	Percent real change in maximum monthly benefit from July 1996 to January 2004	TANF exit point (gross earnings), January 2004	Percent change in AFDC or TANF families from August 1996 to September 2001	Mandatory job search required at application, July 2003	Lifetime time limit shorter than federal limit of sixty months, July 2003	State EITC[a]	Transitional Medicaid longer than twelve months
Alabama	215	11	$256 after three months; no limit first three months	−56	Yes	No	No	No
Alaska	923	−15	$1,961 in year 1, dropping to $1,363 by year 5	−54	No	No	No	No
Arizona	347	−15	$571	−46	No	No	No	Yes
Arkansas	204	−15	$696	−51	Yes	Yes	No	No
California	704	0.14	$1,613	−55	No	No	No	Yes
Colorado	356	−15	$1,227, dropping to $499 after two years	−71	No	No	Yes	No
Connecticut	636	−15	$1,272	−63	No	No	Yes	No
Delaware	338	−15	$1,520 months 1–4; $1,054 months 5–12	−47	No	Yes	No	Yes
District of Columbia	379	−22	$1,267	−38	No	Yes	Yes	Yes
Florida	303	−15	$768	−77	Yes	No	Yes	No
Georgia	280	−15	$740 months 1–4; $534 months 5–12	−63	No	Yes	No	No
Hawaii	570	−32	$1,343	−49	Yes	Yes	No	Yes
Idaho	309	−17	$631	−90	No	Yes	No	No
Illinois	396	−11	$1,185	−75	Yes	No	Yes	No
Indiana	288	−15	$1,148	−11	No	Yes	Yes	No
Iowa	426	−15	$1,040	−35	No	No	Yes	No
Kansas	429	−15	$788	−46	Yes	No	Yes	No

State								
Kentucky	289	−6	No limit months 1–2; $881 months 3–6; $628 months 7–14	−54	No	No	No	No
Louisiana	240	7	$1,250 for six months in lifetime; $350 thereafter	−73	No	No	No	No
Maine	485	−2	$1,023	−53	No	No	Yes	No
Maryland	477	8	$778	−66	Yes	No	Yes	No
Massachusetts	618	−7	$1,143	−56	No	No	Yes	No
Michigan	459	−15	$761	−60	No	No	No	No
Minnesota	532	−15	$914	−32	No	No	Yes	No
Mississippi	170	20	$441	−69	No	No	No	No
Missouri	292	−15	$1,116	−46	Yes	No	No	Yes
Montana	375	−27	$700	−49	No	No	No	No
Nebraska	364	−15	$751	−38	No	No	Yes	Yes
Nevada	348	−15	No limit months 1–3; $845 months 4–12	−32	Yes	No	No	No
New Hampshire	625	−4	$1,230	−40	No	No	No	No
New Jersey	424	−15	No limit month 1; $848 thereafter	−61	Yes	No	Yes	Yes
New Mexico	389	−15	$901	−50	No	No	No	No
New York	691	2	$1,272 (100 percent of poverty limit, all months)	−52	No	No	Yes	No
North Carolina	272	−15	No limit months 1–3; $681 after three months	−66	Yes	No	No	Yes
North Dakota	477	−6	$1,279 months 1–6; $984 months 7–9; $852 months 10–13	−29	No	No	No	No
Ohio	373	−7	$976	−65	Yes	No	No	No
Oklahoma	292	−19	$684	−64	No	No	Yes	No
Oregon	460	−15	$616	−42	No	No	Yes	No
Pennsylvania	421	−15	$822	−60	No		No	No

(Table continues)

Appendix 7A *(continued)*

State	Maximum monthly benefit for family of three, January 2004	Percent real change in maximum monthly benefit from July 1996 to January 2004	TANF exit point (gross earnings), January 2004	Percent change in AFDC or TANF families from August 1996 to September 2001	Mandatory job search required at application, July 2003	Lifetime time limit shorter than federal limit of sixty months, July 2003	State EITC[a]	Transitional Medicaid longer than twelve months
Rhode Island	554	−15	$1,258	−29	No	No	Yes	Yes
South Carolina	205	−13	$1,174 months 1–4; $704 after four months	−61	Yes	No	No	Yes
South Dakota	493	−2	$694	−60	No	No	No	No
Tennessee	185	−15	$1,020	−37	No	No	No	Yes
Texas	217	−2	$1,727 months 1–4; $327 thereafter	−46	No	No	No	No
Utah	474	−3	$1,050	−44	No	No	No	Yes
Vermont	709	−5	$1,082	−37	Yes	No	Yes	Yes
Virginia	389	−6	$1,252	−57	No	No	Yes	No
Washington	546	−15	$1,072	−49	No	No	No	No
West Virginia	453	52	$755	−53	No	No	No	No
Wisconsin	673	10	$1,462 (or 115 percent of federal poverty level)	−71	Yes	No	Yes	No
Wyoming	340	−20	$530	−92	No	No	No	No

Source: Data from Congressional Research Service, "TANF Cash Benefits as of January 1, 2004," RL32598 (September 12, 2005); U.S. Department of Health and Human Services, Administration for Children and Families, "Change in Number of AFDC/TANF Families, Fiscal Years 1996–2002" (www.acf.hhs.gov/programs/ofa/annualreport5/0203.htm); Gretchen Rowe and Jeffrey Versteeg, *Welfare Rules Databook: State TANF Policies as of July 2003* (Urban Institute, April 2005); State EITC Online Resource Center, "50 State Resource Map" (www.stateeitc.com/map/index/asp); Center on Budget and Policy Priorities, *Expanding Family Coverage: States' Medicaid Eligibility Policies for Working Families in the Year 2000* (Washington, February 2002).

a. These benefit amounts vary substantially, in terms of value and design. Several "piggyback" on the federal EITC, allowing a percentage of the federal credit. Some are refundable (available to those with no income tax liability), others are not.

Notes

1. Helen F. Ladd and Fred C. Doolittle, "Which Level of Government Should Assist the Poor?" *National Tax Journal* 25 (September 1982): 323–36.

2. Sarah F. Liebschutz, *Managing Welfare Reform in Five States: The Challenge of Devolution* (Albany, N.Y.: Rockefeller Institute Press, 2000). Despite the conservative, states' rights rhetoric of President Ronald Reagan, policy decentralization was actually quite limited during his tenure (Timothy J. Conlan, *From New Federalism to Devolution: Twenty-five Years of Intergovernmental Reform* [Brookings, 1998]).

3. For instance, the national government fully funds two critical programs: food stamps (through the Department of Agriculture) and Supplemental Security Income for the disabled. Since the 1960s, cash assistance for the poor has been financed and administered jointly by the federal and state governments but delivered through individual state PRWORA (formerly AFDC) programs. Medicaid health programs for low-income individuals are also operated through a shared federal-state arrangement. States have traditionally offered a variety of other poverty relief programs, including cash assistance for low-income individuals without children. Local governments also play a role, in some cases sharing funding and administrative responsibility for welfare and Medicaid. Other local contributions include city or county hospitals with substantial charity caseloads, programs for the homeless and indigent, and others.

4. In addition, PRWORA includes family policy provisions that establish funds for states to prevent and reduce out-of-wedlock pregnancies and to encourage the formation and maintenance of two-parent families. In general, state responses to these federal priorities have been far more limited and variable relative to responses to the employment emphases in the law (see Deborah A. Orth and Malcolm L. Goggin, *How States and Counties Have Responded to the Family Policy Goals of Welfare Reform,* report to the U.S. Department of Health and Human Services, Administration for Children and Families [Albany, N.Y.: Rockefeller Institute of Government, December 2003]).

5. David A. Breaux and others, "Welfare Reform, Mississippi Style: Temporary Assistance for Needy Families and the Search for Accountability," *Public Administration Review* 62 (January–February 2002): 92–104, p. 92; Troy E. Smith, "When States Lobby: Welfare Reform, 1993–1997," paper prepared for the annual meeting of the American Political Science Association, Boston, September 3–6, 1998.

6. National Conference of State Legislatures, "Welfare Caseload Watch," March 9, 2005.

7. Robert Pear, "New Rules Force States to Curb Welfare Rolls," *New York Times,* June 28, 2006, p. 14; LaDonna Pavetti, "The Challenge of Achieving High Work Participation Rates in Welfare Programs," Welfare Reform and Beyond Policy Brief 31 (Brookings, October 2004).

8. Margaret Wrightson and Timothy Conlan, "Targeting Aid to the Poor: What Have We Learned about Allocating Intergovernmental Grants?" *Policy Studies Journal* 18 (Fall 1989), pp. 21–46.

9. Richard P. Nathan, "There Will Always Be a New Federalism," *Journal of Public Administration Research and Theory* 16 (October 2006): 499–510; Conlan, *From New Federalism to Devolution*; Paul L. Posner, *The Politics of Unfunded Mandates: Whither Federalism?* (Georgetown University Press, 1998); John Kincaid, "The Devolution Tortoise and the Centralization Hare," *New England Economic Review* (May–June 1998): 13–40.

10. Federal spending on cash assistance for the poor comprises about 1 percent of federal expenditures (2 percent of discretionary spending) and only 2 percent of state expenditures (total or general fund), on average.

11. Under AFDC, the federal government established state matching rates annually, with each state's matching rate applied to both AFDC and Medicaid. The federal government then matched each state dollar spent on AFDC, based on the established rate. States were free to spend as much as they chose. The grants were open ended because the federal government imposed no spending caps on AFDC or Medicaid services.

12. In economic terms, open-ended matching grants invoke both an income and a price effect among recipients. The match subsidy meant that under AFDC, states received both more income and a reduced "price" for each state dollar of welfare spending. Block grants, on the other hand, generate only an income effect, putting more income into the hands of states but offering no price reduction or subsidy for any state dollar spent beyond the grant allocation.

13. R. Kent Weaver, " The Structure of the TANF Block Grant," Welfare and Beyond Policy Brief 22 (April 2002); Center on Budget and Policy Priorities and Center for Law and Social Policy, "Implementing the TANF Changes in the Deficit Reduction Act: 'Win-Win' Solutions for Families and States," May 9, 2006.

14. See Shama Gamkhar and Wallace Oates, "Asymmetries in the Response to Increases and Decreases in Intergovernmental Grants: Some Empirical Findings," *National Tax Journal* 49 (December 1996): 501–12.

15. Howard Chernick and Andrew Reschovsky, "State Fiscal Responses to Welfare Reform during Recessions: Lessons for the Future," *Public Budgeting and Finance* 23 (Fall 2003): 3–21.

16. Matching rates are designed to provide higher matches, or subsidies, to lower-income states. Because the AFDC matching rates took account of state resident income but not of state variations in other relevant factors such as poverty rates and the costs of provided services, the rates were flawed (U.S. Government Accountability Office [GAO], *Welfare Reform: Better Information Needed to Understand Trends in States' Uses of the TANF Block Grant,* GAO-06-414 [Government Printing Office, March 2006]). Those flaws, together with the political forces that overcompensated wealthier states by setting a minimum matching rate of 50 percent, reduced the capacity to offset AFDC spending differences. And there is no inherent reason why block grants cannot also be designed to offset fiscal disparities.

17. Howard Chernick, "Federal Grants and Social Welfare Spending: Do State Responses Matter?" *National Tax Journal* 53 (March 2000): 143–52.

18. GAO, *Welfare Reform: Better Information Needed.*

19. U.S. General Accounting Office (GAO), *Welfare Reform: Challenges in Maintaining a Federal-State Fiscal Partnership,* GAO-01-828 (GPO, August 2001).

20. Congressional Research Service, "TANF Cash Benefits as of January 1, 2004," RL32598 (September 12, 2005).

21. Weaver, "Structure of the TANF Block Grant."

22. GAO, *Welfare Reform: Challenges;* Chernick and Reschovsky, "State Fiscal Responses to Welfare Reform during Recessions"; Chernick, "Federal Grants and Social Welfare Spending."

23. GAO, *Welfare Reform: Challenges.*

24. GAO, *Welfare Reform: Better Information Needed.*

25. GAO, *Welfare Reform: Challenges;* Chernick and Reschovsky, "State Fiscal Responses to Welfare Reform during Recessions."

26. Most of the rest of combined federal and state spending went to, from largest to smallest, social service block grant programs, separate state programs, transportation, tax credits, out-of-wedlock pregnancy prevention, and family formation programs (Washington: Urban Institute, "Distribution of Federal and State Welfare Spending, 1996 and 2000," Fast Facts on Welfare Policy Series [May 2002]).

27. GAO, *Welfare Reform: Better Information Needed,* pp. 22–23, 25.

28. Donald J. Boyd and others, "Assessing State Social Service Spending under Welfare Reform," paper prepared for the annual meeting of the American Political Science Association, Boston, August 28–September 1, 2002.

29. Cathy Marie Johnson, Thomas Lewis Gais, and Catherine Lawrence, "Child and Welfare Reform: What Policy Theories Are Being Implemented in States Where Most Poor Children Live?" paper prepared for the annual meeting of the American Political Science Association, Boston, August 28–September 1, 2002.

30. Seven states actually increased cash benefits during fiscal year 2003, despite recessionary revenue constraints (see Chernick and Reschovsky, "State Fiscal Responses to Welfare Reform during Recessions"). See also Sharon Parrott and Nina Wu, "States Are Cutting TANF and Childcare Programs: Supports for Low-Income Working Families and Welfare-to-Work Programs Are Particularly Hard Hit" (Center on Budget and Policy Priorities, June 3, 2003); U.S. General Accounting Office, *Childcare: Recent State Policy Changes Affecting the Availability of Assistance for Low-Income Families,* GAO-03-588 (GPO, May 2003).

31. Congressional Research Service, "Temporary Assistance for Needy Families (TANF) Block Grant: FY 2007 Budget Proposals," RS22385 (February 21, 2006).

32. Thomas Gais and R. Kent Weaver, "State Policy Choices under Welfare Reform," Welfare Reform and Beyond Policy Brief 21 (Brookings, April 2002).

33. Ibid. Other typologies were devised by Rebecca M. Blank, "Evaluating Welfare Reform in the United States," *Journal of Economic Literature* 40 (December 2002): 1105–166; Joe Soss and others, "Setting the Terms of Relief: Explaining State Policy

Choices in the Devolution Revolution," *American Journal of Political Science* 45 (April 2001): 378–95; and Signe-Mary McKernan, Jen Bernstein, and Lynne Fender, "Taming the Beast: Categorizing State Welfare Policies: A Typology of Welfare Policies Affecting Recipient Job Entry," *Journal of Policy Analysis and Management* 24 (Spring 2005): 443–60.

34. Irene Lurie ("Changing Welfare Offices," Welfare Reform and Beyond Policy Brief 9 [Brookings, October 2001]) reports that in an average month in 1998, less than 1 percent of TANF families lost all cash benefits.

35. Gretchen Rowe and Linda Giannarelli, "Getting On, Staying On, and Getting Off Welfare: The Complexity of State-by-State Choices," A-70 (Washington: Urban Institute, July 2006).

36. Alan Weil, "Ten Things Everyone Should Know about Welfare Reform," policy brief (Washington: Urban Institute, May 9, 2002) (www.urban.org/url.cfm?ID=310484); National Conference of State Legislatures, "Welfare Caseload Watch," March 9, 2005.

37. Congressional Research Service, "TANF Cash Benefits as of January 1, 2004," p. 25; Gais and Weaver, "State Policy Choices under Welfare Reform," p. 6.

38. Pavetti, "Challenge of Achieving High Work Participation Rates"; Blank, "Evaluating Welfare Reform in the United States"; Center on Budget and Policy Priorities, "Recent Welfare Reform Research Findings: Implications for TANF Reauthorization and State TANF Policies," January 30, 2004.

39. Virginia, sometimes considered a mid-Atlantic state, has an EITC, and Florida has no income taxes. All other southeastern states have income taxes but no EITC. Louisiana and North Carolina only recently joined the EITC states, enacting their programs in late 2006 and early 2007, respectively.

40. Rowe and Giannarelli, "Getting On, Staying On, and Getting Off Welfare."

41. Howard Chernick and Cordelia Reimers, "Welfare Reform and Economic Well-being in New York City: The Jury Is Still Out," paper prepared for the annual meeting of the Association for Public Policy Analysis and Management, Washington, November 8–10, 2007; Signe-Mary McKernan and Caroline Ratcliffe, "The Effect of Specific Welfare Policies on Poverty" (Washington: Urban Institute, April 2006).

42. Sharon Parrott and Arloc Sherman, "TANF at 10: Program Results Are More Mixed Than Often Understood" (Center on Budget and Policy Priorities, August 17, 2006).

43. Smith, "When States Lobby."

44. Carol S. Weissert, "Learning from Midwestern Leaders," in *Learning from Leaders: Welfare Reform Politics and Policy in Five Midwestern States,* edited by Carol S. Weissert (Albany, N.Y.: Rockefeller Institute Press, 2000), pp. 6–9.

45. Interest groups are seen as more powerful in shaping policies for Medicaid and other health-related programs for low-income populations and less so for income support programs (James W. Fossett and Thomas L. Gais, "A New Puzzle for Federalism: Different State Responses to Medicaid and Food Stamps," paper prepared for the annual conference of the American Political Science Association, Boston, September 3–6, 2002).

46. Weissert, *Learning from Leaders;* Richard P. Nathan and Thomas L. Gais, "Early Findings about the Newest New Federalism for Welfare," *Publius: The Journal of Federalism* 28 (Summer 1998): 95–103; Jocelyn M. Johnston and Kara Lindaman, "Implementing Welfare Reform in Kansas: Moving, but Not Racing," *Publius: The Journal of Federalism* 28 (Summer 1998): 123–42; Deil Wright, "Federalism, Intergovernmental Relations, and Intergovernmental Management: Historical Reflections and Conceptual Comparisons," *Public Administration Review* 50 (March–April 1990): 168–78; Saundra K. Schneider, William G. Jacoby, and Jerrell D. Coggburn, "The Structure of Bureaucratic Decisions in the American States," *Public Administration Review* 57 (May–June 1997): 240–49.

47. Robert D. Plotnick and Richard F. Winters, "A Politico-Economic Theory of Income Redistribution," *American Political Science Review* 79 (June 1985): 458–73. Economists often use tax price as an explanatory economic demand variable in their interstate variation models, whereas political scientists focus more on such factors as state resident income and unemployment rates.

48. Charles Barrilleaux and Ethan Bernick, "Deservingness, Discretion, and the State Politics of Welfare Spending," *State Politics and Policy Quarterly* 3 (Spring 2003): 1–22; Charles Barrilleaux, Thomas Holbrook, and Laura Langer, "Electoral Competition, Legislative Balance, and American State Welfare Policy," *American Journal of Political Science* 46 (April 2002): 415–27. In a related vein, Soss and others and Richard Fording suggest that welfare generosity is negatively correlated with incarceration rates, suggesting that states are more punitive with both the "undeserving" poor and individuals—often poor—in their criminal justice systems (Soss and others, "Setting the Terms of Relief"; Richard Fording, "The Political Response to Black Insurgency: A Critical Test of Competing Theories of the Role of the State," *American Political Science Review* 95 [April 2001]: 115–30). Similarly, Donald Boyd and others note that welfare spending disparities are higher than disparities on Medicaid programs, which not only serve "more deserving" clients but also benefit state health care industries (Boyd and others, *Spending on Social Welfare Programs in Rich and Poor States,* final report prepared for the Department of Health and Human Services, Assistant Secretary for Planning and Evaluation [Albany, N.Y.: Rockefeller Institute of Government, July 2004]); also see Fossett and Gais, "New Puzzle for Federalism"; Charles Barrilleaux and Mark E. Miller, "The Political Economy of State Medicaid Policy," *American Political Science Review* 84 (December 2004): 1089–107.

49. Soss and others, "Setting the Terms of Relief." The authors note, however, that only five states selected the four toughest policy choices. It should also be mentioned that their model contains no economic variables, with the exception of the state unemployment rate. Also see GAO, *Welfare Reform: Better Information Needed.*

50. Soss and others, "Setting the Terms of Relief," p. 390; Gais and Weaver, "State Policy Choices under Welfare Reform"; Boyd and others, *Spending on Social Welfare Programs;* Weil, "Ten Things Everyone Should Know about Welfare Reform."

51. Paul E. Peterson and Mark C. Rom, *Welfare Magnets: A New Case for a National Standard* (Brookings, 1990).

52. Sanford Schram, Lawrence Nitz, and Gary Krueger, "Without Cause or Effect:

Reconsidering Welfare Migration as a Policy Problem," *American Journal of Political Science* 42 (January 1998): 210–30; William D. Berry, Richard C. Fording, and Russell L. Hanson, "Reassessing the 'Race to the Bottom' in State Welfare Policy," *Journal of Politics* 65 (May 2003): 327–49; Olivia A. Golden, *Assessing the New Federalism: Eight Years Later* (Washington: Urban Institute, 2005); Congressional Research Service, "Welfare Reform: An Issue Overview," IB93034 (October 28, 2004); Boyd and others, "Assessing State Social Service Spending under Welfare Reform"; Gais and Weaver, "State Policy Choices under Welfare Reform."

53. Robert C. Lieberman and Greg M. Shaw, "Looking Inward, Looking Outward: The Politics of State Welfare Innovation under Devolution," *Political Research Quarterly* 53 (June 2000): 215–40; Sanford F. Schram and Gary Krueger, "'Welfare Magnets' and Benefit Decline: Symbolic Problems and Substantive Consequences," *Publius: The Journal of Federalism* 24 (Fall 1994): 61–82; Schram, Nitz, and Krueger, "Without Cause or Effect."

54. Lieberman and Shaw, "Looking Inward, Looking Outward"; Berry, Fording, and Hanson, "Reassessing the 'Race to the Bottom' in State Welfare Policy."

55. Schram, Nitz, and Krueger, "Without Cause or Effect," p. 228; Michael A. Bailey, "Welfare and the Multifaceted Decision to Move," *American Political Science Review* 99 (February 2005): 125–35.

56. Schram and Krueger, "'Welfare Magnets' and Benefit Decline," p. 82.

57. Lawrence M. Mead, *Government Matters: Welfare Reform in Wisconsin* (Princeton University Press, 2004); Thomas L. Gais and others, "Implementation of the Personal Responsibility Act of 1996," in *The New World of Welfare,* edited by Rebecca Blank and Ron Haskins (Brookings, 2001), pp. 35–69; Karin Martinson and Pamela A. Holcomb, "Reforming Welfare: Institutional Change and Challenges," Assessing the New Federalism Paper 60 (Washington: Urban Institute, August 2002).

58. Ron Haskins, Isabel V. Sawhill, and R. Kent Weaver, "Welfare Reform: An Overview of Effects to Date," Policy Brief 1 (Brookings, January 2001); Gais and others, "Implementation of the Personal Responsibility Act of 1996," p. 37.

59. Michael Lipsky, *Street-Level Bureaucracy: Dilemmas of the Individual in Public Service* (New York: Russell Sage Foundation, 1980); Marcia K. Meyers and Nara Dillon, "Institutional Paradoxes: Why Welfare Workers Cannot Reform Welfare," in *Public Management Reform and Innovation: Research, Theory, and Application,* edited by H. George Frederickson and Jocelyn M. Johnston (University of Alabama Press, 1999), pp. 230–58; Marcia K. Meyers, Bonnie Glaser, and Karin MacDonald, "On the Front Lines of Welfare Delivery: Are Workers Implementing Policy Reforms?" *Journal of Policy Analysis and Management* 17 (Winter 1998): 1–22. This challenge of managing discretion arises in part because street-level workers often operate with norms and collective understanding that are not fully understood by their managers (Jody R. Sandfort, "Moving beyond Discretion and Outcomes: Examining Public Management from the Front Lines of the Welfare System," *Journal of Public Administration Research and Theory* 10 [October 2000]: 729–56).

60. Gais and others, "Implementation of the Personal Responsibility Act of 1996," p. 48; Lurie, "Changing Welfare Offices," p. 5.

61. Marcia K. Meyers, Norma M. Riccucci, and Irene Lurie, "Achieving Goal Congruence in Complex Environments: The Case of Welfare Reform," *Journal of Public Administration Research and Theory* 11 (April 2001): 165–201; Norma M. Riccucci, *How Management Matters: Street-Level Bureaucrats and Welfare Reform* (Georgetown University Press, 2005); Norma M. Riccucci and others, "The Implementation of Welfare Reform Policy: The Role of Public Managers in Front-Line Practices," *Public Administration Review* 64 (July–August 2004): 438–48.

62. Frank J. Thompson and Thomas L. Gais, "Federalism and the Safety Net: Delinkage and Participation Rates," *Publius: The Journal of Federalism* 30 (Winter 2000): 119–42.

63. Lurie, "Changing Welfare Offices."

64. U.S. General Accounting Office, *Medicaid Enrollment: Amid Declines, State Efforts to Ensure Coverage after Welfare Reform Vary,* GAO/HEHS-99-163 (GPO, September 1999); to illustrate, transitional Medicaid assistance, guaranteed in PRWORA for a period of twelve months for all TANF entrants into employment, was used by only 4 percent of eligible households leaving cash assistance in Utah. Other states did better—the comparable statistic in Connecticut was 94 percent (ibid., p. 24); diversion programs, together with the extraordinary success among applicants who never actually received cash assistance because they obtained jobs, meant also that welfare agencies collected little data on applicants who never made it through the entire application process, let alone on "leavers" who received cash assistance before finding employment. State administrators were simply unprepared for the results of their early work-first efforts.

65. Thompson and Gais, "Federalism and the Safety Net."

66. Nathan and Gais, "Early Findings about the Newest New Federalism for Welfare."

67. Chung-Lae Cho and others, "Translating National Policy Objectives into Local Achievements across Planes of Governance and among Multiple Actors: Second-Order Devolution and Welfare Reform Implementation," *Journal of Public Administration Research and Theory* 15 (January 2005): 31–54; Liebschutz, *Managing Welfare Reform in Five States.*

68. Nathan and Gais, "Early Findings about the Newest New Federalism for Welfare."

69. Ibid., p. 99; Martinson and Holcomb, "Reforming Welfare," p. vii.

70. U.S. General Accounting Office, *Federal Reform: Federal Oversight of State and Local Contracting Can Be Strengthened,* GAO-02-661 (GPO, June 2002); Martinson and Holcomb, "Reforming Welfare."

71. Edward T. Jennings and Dale Krane, "Coordination and Welfare Reform: The Quest for the Philosopher's Stone," *Public Administration Review* 54 (July–August 1994): 341–48.

72. Robert Agranoff and Michael McGuire, *Collaborative Public Management: New Strategies for Local Governments* (Georgetown University Press, 2004).

73. Gais and others, "Implementation of the Personal Responsibility Act of 1996"; Barbara S. Romzek and Jocelyn M. Johnston, "State Social Services Contracting: Exploring Determinants of Effective Contract Accountability," *Public Administration Review* 65 (July–August 2005): 436–49; Jocelyn M. Johnston, Barbara S. Romzek, and Curtis H.

Wood, "The Challenges of Contracting and Accountability across the Federal System: From Ambulances to Space Shuttles," *Journal of Federalism* 34 (Summer 2004): 155–82; Jocelyn M. Johnston and Barbara S. Romzek, "Contracting and Accountability in State Medicaid Reform: Rhetoric, Theories, and Reality," *Public Administration Review* 59 (September–October 1999): 383–99.

74. Jocelyn M. Johnston and Barbara S. Romzek, "Social Welfare Contracts as Networks: The Impact of Network Stability on Management and Performance," *Administration and Society* 40, no. 2 (April 2008: 115–46); Meyers, Riccucci, and Lurie, "Achieving Goal Congruence in Complex Environments."

75. Richard Fording, Sanford F. Schram, and Joe Soss, "Sanctioning Outcomes in the Florida TANF Program: Devolution, Privatization, and Performance Measurement," paper prepared for the annual meeting of the Midwest Political Science Association, Chicago, August 31–September 4, 2005; Paul Posner, "Accountability Challenges of Third-Party Government," in *The Tools of Government: A Guide to the New Governance,* edited by Lester M. Salamon (Oxford University Press, 2002), pp. 523–51. These dynamics help explain why the extensive welfare contracting system set up in Mississippi ultimately failed (see David A. Breaux and others, "To Privatization and Back: Welfare Reform Implementation in Mississippi," in *Managing Welfare Reform in Five States: The Challenge of Devolution,* edited by Sarah F. Liebschutz [Albany, N.Y.: Rockefeller Institute Press, 2000], pp. 43–56; Breaux and others, "Welfare Reform, Mississippi Style," p. 92). The state's ambitious model, which outsourced almost all welfare-related services, fell victim to many of the typical contract and network management pitfalls (see Robert D. Behn and Peter A. Kant, "Strategies for Avoiding the Pitfalls of Performance Contracting," *Public Productivity and Management Review* 22 (June 1999): 470–89). An additional challenge observed in many states involves the coordination of welfare information systems with the systems of other organizations serving clients, whether public or not (see Gais and others, "Implementation of the Personal Responsibility Act of 1996"; U.S. General Accounting Office, *Human Services Integration: Results of a GAO-Cosponsored Conference on Modernizing Information Systems,* GAO-02-121 [GPO, January 2002]). One analyst has investigated the challenges of integrating these information systems under PRWORA, noting that "information federalism" requires a major revamping of existing structures (see Terence Maxwell, "Working Paper on Informational Federalism: History of Welfare Information Systems" [Rockefeller Institute of Government, 1999]).

76. Mead suggests that this gap was filled in part by Wisconsin's moralistic, "good government" culture (as articulated by Daniel J. Elazar, *American Federalism: A View from the States,* 3rd ed. [New York: Thomas Y. Crowell, 1984]); Boyd and others, *Spending on Social Welfare Programs,* p. 67.

77. Cho and others, "Translating National Policy Objectives into Local Achievements"; Kincaid, "The Devolution Tortoise and the Centralization Hare"; Pamela Winston and Rosa Maria Castaneda, "Assessing Federalism: ANF and the Recent Evolution of American Social Policy Federalism," 07-01 (Washington: Urban Institute, May 2007).

Martha Derthick argues that the PRWORA reform is less a devolutionary act and more a compromise between a liberal president and a conservative Congress in the absence of a national consensus. In such situations, she contends, federalism provides a safety valve by ceding discretion to the states. She further suggests that one of the most important results of the law was to alter relations between Congress and the courts—by eliminating the entitlement to AFDC cash benefits that had been protected by federal judicial decisions. The Supreme Court had decided, in the 1970 *Goldberg v. Kelly* case, that welfare benefits were state "entitlements" rather than "privileges" and were protected under the Fourteenth Amendment's due process clause. By removing the entitlement to support, PRWORA has weakened this protection (Martha Derthick, "American Federalism: Half-Full or Half-Empty?" *Brookings Review* 13 [Winter 2000]: 24–27).

78. Soss and others, "Setting the Terms of Relief," p. 379.

79. Lieberman and Shaw, "Looking Inward, Looking Outward."

80. Sanford F. Schram and Joe Soss, "Making Something Out of Nothing: Welfare Reform and a New Race to the Bottom," *Publius: The Journal of Federalism* 28 (Summer 1998): 67–89, p. 69.

81. Paul L. Posner and Margaret T. Wrightson, "Block Grants: A Perennial, but Unstable, Tool of Government," *Publius: The Journal of Federalism* 26 (Summer 1996): 87–99; Wrightson and Conlan, "Targeting Aid to the Poor."

82. Beryl A. Radin, *Challenging the Performance Movement: Accountability, Complexity, and Democratic Values* (Georgetown University Press, 2006); Beryl A. Radin, "Intergovernmental Relationships and the Federal Performance Movement," *Publius: The Journal of Federalism* 30 (Winter 2000): 143–59; Robert D. Behn, "Why Measure Performance? Different Purposes Require Different Measures," *Public Administration Review* 63 (September–October 2003): 586–606; Meyers, Riccucci, and Lurie, "Achieving Goal Congruence in Complex Environments." As an example of the one-size-fits-all approach, PRWORA's federally required work participation rates were uniform, failing to account for economic and job opportunity differences across and within states.

83. Marcia K. Meyers, Janet C. Gornick, and Laura R. Peck, "Packaging Support for Low-Income Families: Policy Variation across the United States," *Journal of Policy Analysis and Management* 20 (Summer 2001): 457–83; Soss and others, "Setting the Terms of Relief"; Gais and Weaver, "State Policy Choices under Welfare Reform."

84. Soss and others, "Setting the Terms of Relief," p. 391; Boyd and others, *Spending on Social Welfare Programs;* Paul E. Peterson, *The Price of Federalism* (Brookings, 1995).

85. Congressional Research Service, "Temporary Assistance for Needy Families (TANF) Block Grant"; Scott W. Allard, "The Changing Face of Welfare during the Bush Administration," *Publius: The Journal of Federalism* 37 (Summer 2007): 304–31.

86. Michael A. Fletcher, "U.S. Moves to Get States to Put More Welfare Recipients in Work or in Training," *Washington Post,* June 29, 2006, p. A02.

87. Center for Law and Social Policy, "Two-Thirds of States Qualify for Extended Counting of TANF Job Search and Job Readiness Assistance," October 5, 2006.

88. Lurie, "Changing Welfare Offices"; Martinson and Holcomb, "Reforming Welfare." Essential questions are being raised about the "pendulum" of welfare reform—with suggestions that the emphasis on work-first may have become too strong. There is some evidence that a mix of services—focused, short-term education for some applicants and immediate job search and placement for others—generates better payoff in terms of income and the well-being of children in the welfare household (see Judith M. Gueron and Gayle Hamilton, "The Role of Education and Training in Welfare Reform," Welfare Reform and Beyond Policy Brief 20 [Brookings, April 2002]). Challenges related to cases that have "timed out" will increasingly capture policymakers' attention. In addition, there are concerns that roughly half of TANF-eligible households do not currently receive any aid, and that "nonreceipt" is growing (Center on Budget and Policy Priorities, "Recent Welfare Reform Research Findings").

89. Alice M. Rivlin, *Reviving the American Dream: The Economy, the States, and the Federal Government* (Brookings, 1992).

90. Timothy Conlan, "From Cooperative to Opportunistic Federalism: Reflections on the Half-Century Anniversary of the Commission on Intergovernmental Relations," *Public Administration Review* 66 (September–October 2006): 663–77.

8

MEDICAID WAIVERS

License to Shape the Future of Fiscal Federalism

CAROL S. WEISSERT AND WILLIAM G. WEISSERT

Although the United States is not unique in having its health care paid for from a variety of sources, it stands alone among industrialized nations in having no systematic plan for coverage and no effective way to get control of costs. The United States also relies more heavily on private payment than other countries: public sources account for 44 percent of total spending here compared with an average of 72 percent for member countries of the Organization for Economic Cooperation and Development.[1] If all public employees whose insurance is paid by public funds are included, as well as costs of tax forgiveness for health care expenses of corporations, the public share of health care spending in the United States rises to more than 50 percent—still well below that of other countries.

What the United States has in lieu of a unified policy is something more complex and perhaps less sensible—a product of combining our federal system of governance, our capitalistic economic system, and our pluralistic system of policymaking. The federal government tries periodically to get reform organized and enacted, but each time it fails, usually for roughly the same reasons: no one has figured out how to pay for it; many lack confidence that the national government will do a good job of managing it (though it has done a reasonably good, and reasonably efficient, job with Medicare); and a wide variety of interest groups benefit from the chaos of the status quo and resist key features of any plan suggested.

If there is a ray of hope for reform, it probably lies with the states. The states live within annual budgets, which makes them from the outset more realistic than federal would-be reformers, who have typically first designed reforms and later estimated costs and still later tried to figure out who will pay them. The states tend to start their reform efforts with the realistic assumption that their responsibility is going to be limited to those who are poor and do not have insurance. The states tend to use small-scale, targeted, trial-and-error approaches, start early to figure out how to control costs, and try to come up with schemes in which the national government will pay most of the costs.

Under a special provision of the Medicaid law (waiver authority), the states also have the option of limiting the size, scope, and geography of, as well as total enrollment in, any new pilot plan they try, so that they can predict and control costs. This alone makes state health care reformers more likely to win support in their state legislatures than federal bureaucrats and other reformers, who invariably must face the strong probability that any new national initiative will grow uncontrollably, owing to eligibility expansions, interest group pressures for adding services, regional demands for special exceptions, intense utilization rates per person, and a variety of other pressures.

The Medicaid program is unusual in that it encourages innovation—through waiver authority—in the delivery of long-term care services, in particular, the home and community-based care provision of the Medicaid statute, contained in and known as Section 1915(c). Waivers have special political milieus and have largely escaped classification in academic literature. Here, we offer a new approach to viewing waivers as intergovernmental licenses that allow states to suspend some legal requirements but increase the popularity of the activity; they involve negotiation or bargaining but, once established, have a fairly secure existence. Waivers seem to work and can be viewed as a political success story in modern fiscal federalism because they have survived, thrived, been widely adopted, and sometimes made permanent.

The Politics of Waivers

A waiver grants permission for states to fail to meet (that is, waive) certain federal requirements to operate a specific kind of program for a specific group. Under waivers, states seek permission to deviate from national standards to improve services, expand eligibility, or save money. The politics of waivers involve largely backroom bargaining, with the president—not Congress—as the primary agenda setter and force for policy change. Day-to-day activities fall to federal and state bureaucrats. Some have cautioned that the waiver process may involve risks to democratic values, bypassing, as it often does, state legislatures and Congress in favor of bureaucratic bargaining. This concern may be especially important when what gets waived are provisions in the law originally designed to protect poor minorities and other powerless groups. Examples are waiver of the Medicaid statutory requirements for "statewideness," so cities are not favored or shunned compared with rural areas, and the requirement for comparability of services provided to groups of eligibles such as white elderly women and black mothers. Medicaid patients may be locked into a set of providers or managed care plans, and expensive providers may be locked out of providing some Medicaid-covered services.

Although there may be little formal involvement by legislative bodies acting as a whole, individual committee and subcommittee members may intervene one-on-one with bureaucrats. They may make demands on behalf of constituents, their own personal preferences, or lobbyists' special pleadings. Loathe to offend powerful committee chairs, bureaucrats may move policy in directions it would not have gone if a fully deliberative legislative process had operated, involving rules committees, floor votes, conference committees, and the other mechanisms designed to protect the commons from moral hazard by committee action.

Waivers were first authorized in 1962 under Section 1115 of the Social Security Act, which gives states the ability to seek waivers of federal requirements for all programs authorized under the Social Security Act. Section 1115 waivers were intended to be used for experimental, pilot, or demonstration projects that in the view of the secretary of health, education, and welfare (now health and human services) would promote the purposes of the Social Security Act. Section 1115 waivers initially covered the major intergovernmental welfare program—Aid for Families with Dependent Children (AFDC)—and were later applied to Medicaid and the State Children's Health Insurance Program (SCHIP).

More-targeted waivers, called program waivers, authorize states to ignore specific program requirements in the law. In Medicaid, program waivers allow alternative delivery systems (such as home and community-based care) or alternative reimbursement systems (such as managed care). The freedom-of-choice exemption, in Section 1915(b) of the Social Security Act, permits states to send Medicaid recipients to specific providers; the home and community-based care exemption, authorized in Section 1915(c) of the same law, permits coverage of nonmedical services that would not normally be covered by Medicaid.[2] Program waivers are also available in education and job training programs. For example, in 1994 new legislation allowed the U.S. Department of Education to waive provisions of federal education law; more than 500 such waivers were granted in only four years, from 1995 to 1999.[3] The more recent No Child Left Behind Act (P.L. 107-110) allows the education secretary to grant waivers to state and local agencies to consolidate and redirect funds and suspend a wide range of requirements .

The experience with waivers is primarily from Medicaid and AFDC—the latter now part of the Temporary Assistance for Needy Families block grant. In both areas, the initial progress of waivers was slow, in part because of the reluctance of federal agencies to allow states to make changes in federal policy.[4] Presidents played a pivotal role in the use of waivers, beginning with Ronald Reagan, who brought to the White House the frustrations of having worked with federal agencies to achieve a welfare reform waiver in California while he was the state's governor. In the 1990s, some forty states received AFDC waivers to employ such provisions as time limits on welfare receipt, school attendance requirements, and substitution of school attendance for work requirements, many of which were put into the 1996 federal welfare reform law. Medicaid program waivers (1915[b] and 1915[c]) were similarly popular. In the 1990s, roughly forty waivers were granted each year.[5]

Presidents Bill Clinton and George W. Bush pushed to make waivers easier to obtain and thus a more attractive option for states. Bush promoted several new waivers in health care, including one to encourage states to use Medicaid and SCHIP dollars to cover uninsured parents. Indeed, the quest for more flexibility to states through waivers, especially during trying state economic conditions and changes, led to a new round of Section 1115 Medicaid waivers that allowed states to provide coverage or deliver services to low-income populations outside federal standards and rules.[6] Between January 2001 and March 2005, comprehensive Medicaid waivers (Section 1115 waivers) were approved for seventeen states.

It was not chance that led former governors turned president to support waivers. Like Reagan, Presidents Clinton and Bush remembered their own desires for freedom from sometimes onerous federal requirements and the ability to tailor programs to their own preferences. They also felt that waivers could be used to improve program efficiency and control expenditures. This is especially important in entitlement programs, such as Medicaid, that can grow substantially in the very times when state revenues are negatively affected by economic downturn. Waivers allow governors to take credit for major reforms from constituents and get special recognition from Washington.[7] Certainly the 1990s welfare reform waivers elevated Wisconsin governor Tommy Thompson and Michigan governor John Engler to national policy figures while also allowing them to take credit for actions to solve their own state's problems.[8]

But presidential support may derive from more than gubernatorial memory. Waivers allow presidents to pursue controversial policy goals without seeking approval from the often politically divisive and slow legislative process. Presidents can also curry favor with supportive governors, even gaining their support for other presidential priorities.[9] Finally, presidents can use their influence to prod a reluctant bureaucracy.

Congress sometimes chafes under the idea of waivers—recognizing that waivers can very much change the nature of the program devised by Congress. For example, in 1997 Florida representative Clay Shaw complained that welfare waivers were undermining the reform's primary mission of hurrying welfare recipients into the workforce.[10] In 2006 long-time Michigan representative John Dingell called for a Government Accountability Office investigation into the expeditious federal approval of sweeping state Medicaid waiver applications, specifically naming the Vermont and Florida Section 1115 Medicaid waivers.[11] In fact, in some sense the current congressional role with respect to waivers is less one of defining policy than of supporting state waiver requests from their state delegations, becoming advocates of state interest—in this case, getting a waiver approved.[12]

The question then becomes, Why does Congress allow extensive and growing use of waivers? There are several reasons. First, Congress likes to avoid complex and detailed issues, preferring to delegate them to the bureaucracy. Waivers are often extremely complicated and deal with issues that many of its members would prefer to ignore (long-term care populations, people with mental retardation or developmental disabilities, people with mental illness or major brain injuries or syndromes). Second, waiver-granting policies have been in place a long time, and change would require positive action by Congress. States do not have to first come to Congress or get the request onto the crowded congressional agenda to obtain a waiver. Thus waiver authority is the status quo position, and there has been little concerted call from ideological or political leaders to change the waiver mechanism. Third, Congress may recognize that the waivers are a way for experimentation and learning to occur. Certainly, the 1996 welfare reform law was built largely on state experiences made possible only through states' use of waivers of AFDC program provisions. Fourth, Congress can use waivers as a mechanism to avoid blame.

When states make cuts in the Medicaid program through waivers or transfer clients to managed care, members of Congress can heartily blame the states (and the bureaucracy) for such actions. Finally, from an individual member's perspective, waiver applications are a manifestation of Congress's commons problem. Even if the institution of Congress is ill served (if it is) by delegating its authority over program modification and budget expansion to administrative deals between the federal bureaucracy and the states, an individual member has an incentive to support such requests emanating from his or her own state. Since this is the extent of involvement in waivers by most members of Congress, there may be little enthusiasm for reining in their availability.

The increasing use of waivers is a component of what two scholars call executive federalism, the strategic exercise of executive powers to promote major changes in state policies or administrative practices without new legislation. Thomas Gais and James Fossett argue that major policy shifts in recent years have been driven by the federal executive branch and state leaders, not Congress.[13]

Waivers and Federalism

Waivers provide a mechanism for individual states to apply solutions to their own policy problems, and they do so. A quick look at recent waivers provides a case in point. Massachusetts and Florida launched major health care reforms with Section 1115 waivers in 2006, but the two plans provide near-opposite approaches to providing care, approaches that directly reflect their own states' political cultures and preferences.

Florida's plan specifically targets the Medicaid program, seeking to control costs and maximize market forces. It features payments to plans that are risk adjusted by the health status, age, and medical history of the recipient. Plans compete for recipients and their premiums by offering differing packages of care (apart from some required services). Plans include health maintenance organizations and other entities such as executive provider organizations, licensed health insurers, and provider service networks. The idea is that turning over the program to the private sector will save the state money and improve access (and quality) through competition.[14] The waiver—requested by the state whose governor was the president's brother—was approved by the federal government in a record sixteen days and began initially in two large counties, encompassing more than 200,000 recipients. An early internal review by the state Medicaid agency's Office of Inspector General noted many important problems, including service and information gaps, lower enrollment than expected, and no evidence as yet of cost savings. A too hasty rollout of the program proved problematic.[15]

The Massachusetts plan includes most of the state's citizens and relies much more on state oversight and control. The 2006 state law builds upon a Section 1115 Medicaid waiver first implemented in 1997 (called MassHealth). That waiver created an insurance partnership program to provide premium subsidies to smaller employers and their low-income employees. The 2006 law requires citizens of Massachusetts to obtain and maintain a minimum level of health insurance coverage (called an individual mandate), requires employers with eleven or more employees to provide health insurance, creates a subsidized insurance program for those not eligible for public or employer programs, and expands eligibility for children. The law sets up a major presence for the state—unlike the Florida program, which is highly privatized. The plan calls for a MassHealth Payment Policy Advisory Board to review and evaluate Medicaid rates and payment systems; an independent public authority, called the Connector, to administer the new safety-net fund; a new office, called the Health Safety Net Office, to administer the health safety-net trust fund; and a new Health Care Quality and Cost Council, to set quality improvement and cost containment goals.[16]

Other recent Section 1115 waivers further illustrate the variety of approaches states have undertaken using the additional flexibility of the waiver. Utah's 2002 Section 1115 waiver set up a primary care network in which the state reduced coverage for some recipients in order to expand primary care coverage to low-income adults who were not formerly eligible for the program. The program is made possible because of an informal agreement with the state's hospitals to provide a set amount of charity care for hospital, specialty, or mental health care.[17]

Another small state, Vermont, used a Section 1115 waiver to launch a new block grant–type Medicaid program. The state agreed to an overall ceiling of nearly $5 billion in Medicaid expenditures over five years. Any outlays above the cap must be covered entirely by the state. In return, the state will establish its own managed care organization and will have flexibility in how it provides care, selects benefits, manages enrollment, and requires cost sharing. The state can make changes in benefits and cost sharing of up to 5 percent without federal review.[18] Kentucky, Colorado, and South Carolina have also obtained Section 1115 waivers to reform their Medicaid programs to their own states' liking and needs.

Given their importance and increased use, it seems especially necessary for scholars to recognize waivers and include them in theoretical models. The two most likely areas of inclusion, however—fiscal federalism and policy tools—ignore this major intergovernmental mechanism. A brief look at those literatures follows.

Fiscal Federalism and Policy Tools

Research on fiscal federalism has focused on the stimulative or substitutive effects of various types of federal grants on recipient states and localities.[19] The impact of grants on state and local spending depends on the type of grant—matching or nonmatching—with the former more likely to stimulate spending than the latter. However, research has consistently found that even nonmatching grants stimulate spending in a manner that has been likened to dollars sticking like flypaper at the governmental level where they hit. Related research has also highlighted the role of mandates as a stimulant, showing that they are more effective than grants but lead to cutbacks in spending in other parts of the program or in related programs.[20]

Recent years have seen a movement away from research on federal grants and toward exploration of institutional relationship problems, including information asymmetry, agency failures, impacts of hard and soft budget constraints, determinants of stability, and risk-sharing arrangements.[21] Without completely abandoning the impact of federal grants, this newer literature has shifted the focus toward other issues and constraints.

Literature in the area of policy tools comes closer to encompassing waivers but only tangentially. Anne Schneider and Helen Ingram define policy tools as techniques the government uses to achieve policy goals.[22] Although this definition would seemingly include waivers, their policy tools are more focused on policy content, especially the wording of the law or regulation. They categorize policy tools into authority tools, incentive tools, capacity tools, symbolic and hortatory tools, and learning tools. Of these choices, waivers are most likely to fit into learning tools, in that they allow lower-level agents to experiment with different policy approaches; but they do not fit the authors' notion that agents and targets do not know what needs to be done or what is possible to do.

The literature on policy tools, unlike that on fiscal federalism, shows no agreement on how such tools should be classified. In addition to the Schneider and Ingram classifications, there have been a number of other efforts at creating a taxonomy, including those by Christopher Hood, Richard Elmore, and William Gormley.[23] The policy tools literature is wide and varied, dealing with behavior impact on recipients, policy implementation, its management and political implications, and democratic governance.[24] Given the scope of this literature, it is interesting that it has ignored waivers as a possible policy tool. In fact, the subfield seems to have moved away from the traditional governmental focus to encompass the new governance of complex networks of public and private engagement. In Lester Salamon's mammoth text on tools of government, fifteen policy tools are examined, with grants as one policy tool and no mention of waivers.[25]

Thus like the fiscal federalism literature, the literature on policy tools leaves a large theoretical hole in which the rather important policy mechanism of waivers resides. Waivers might be then a neglected child in both fiscal federalism and policy tools, or they could be something else. Perhaps a new term needs to be devised. Interestingly, more is known about the impact of waivers and their place in policy dynamics than about their institutional classification. Waivers are a means to enact incremental policies that are made possible by federalism and can lead to state innovation. Waivers also delegate initial review procedures to bureaucratic agents restrained by few criteria, demand little oversight and feedback, empower the states to design and implement policies in broad furtherance of national goals, involve substantial give-and-take between state and federal bureaucrats, and persist for years. These features share many of the qualities of a license, defined as "a right or permission granted by a competent authority (a government or a business, for example) to engage in some business or occupation, do some act, or engage in some transaction which would be unlawful without such right or permission."[26] Since they deal expressly with federal and state governments, perhaps waivers should be called "intergovernmental licenses."

Thinking of waivers as licenses highlights several important characteristics. First, while licensure can be thought of as curbing a practice by requiring certain standards for entry, in fact it often increases the popularity of the activity being licensed. Whether it be for massage therapists or new businesses, licensure can legitimate the function and spawn a number of adherents. Second, licensure takes place in the bureaucracy with few points at which vetoes are possible. Third, negotiation or bargaining can be important—particularly in the licensure of new areas or approaches. Finally, once approved, the life cycle of a license is fairly assured.

Intergovernmental Licensing Process

The process of initial licensure can be fraught with questions and concerns on the part of the license grantor, often resulting in negotiation or bargaining.

Once the license is granted, however, the bargaining ends and the parties assume that renewal will be near automatic—threats of denial being associated largely with gross failure. Both the initial bargaining component and the near-automatic continuation of the license apply to intergovernmental waivers. Helen Ingram was among the first to highlight the notion of bargaining in understanding federal-state relationships generally. Eugene Bardach has talked of implementation games in a similar manner. In more recent years, some initial efforts have been made to model federal-state relations as a game, but there is clearly more to be done there.[27]

Practitioners have long understood the role of bargaining in waivers, which involves an initial state application followed by a series of questions and responses and meetings in person and by telephone. In many cases, the initial state application follows a series of informal meetings with federal agency staff to iron out certain difficulties and avoid misunderstandings. The process can be laborious (as in California's early and unsuccessful efforts to enroll most of their mentally retarded and developmentally disabled population in 1915[c] waiver programs) or easy (as in Florida's Medicaid reform program).

Perhaps more important is that whatever bargaining occurs takes place in a venue with few veto points—in the bureaucracy and generally outside of Congress. With few actors involved in the bargaining and few veto points in the way, successful bargaining can lead to greater likelihood of waiver approval but also to a likelihood that risks will be ignored. When the president signals his support of waivers and encourages their use, the bargaining is made easier and a positive conclusion more likely. Secretary of Health and Human Services Tommy Thompson used his experience as Wisconsin governor to support expansion of waivers in a way that contributed to substantial growth in waiver use during his tenure. He paid little attention to evidence demonstrating that most proposals would not actually accomplish their usual goal of cost savings.[28]

Once approved, waivers tend to have a life of their own—that is, they continue indefinitely. Unlike grant programs, which must be reauthorized and reappropriated, waivers must be renewed—but renewal is expected. Although renewals must be sought on a regular basis, the renewal process is expedited; and it is typically only when states decide to cancel the program that the waiver is ended. Even the Section 1115 waiver for research and demonstration grants in Medicaid can continue for decades. Arizona's Medicaid program has operated under such a waiver since 1982.

There is one additional impact of waivers as intergovernmental licenses. Waiving federal requirements to accomplish state goals is a popular notion for state and local officials and interest groups. Individual legislators may press the bureaucracy to seek waivers, even though they may have limited support. Similarly, these advocates often encourage retention of certain waivers far beyond their apparent usefulness or value.

The Medicaid Home and Community-Based Care Services Waiver

One popular intergovernmental waiver, the Medicaid home and community-based care services (HCBS) waiver, provides a good illustration of the intergovernmental licensure notion and its effect on initial bargaining, near autonomic continuation, and political salience. In 1981, in the same bill that enacted President Reagan's unpopular proposal to turn Medicaid into a block grant, the Omnibus Budget Reconciliation Act added Section 1915(c) to the Social Security Act authorizing the Health Care Financing Administration (now the Centers for Medicare and Medicaid Services) to waive Medicaid requirements to allow states the option of including home and community-based services in their Medicaid programs.

The waivers were promoted as money savers in the Democrat-controlled House version of the bill, even though the House language permitted higher total expenditures under waivers so long as per capita payments were lower than the payment rates of daily nursing home care. The Republican-controlled Senate was more skeptical and tried to limit the scope of the waivers with restrictive language designed to limit total expenditures. Both sets of language were included in the law, despite their inherent conflict. Following the Senate language, the Reagan bureaucracy limited the initial waivers to those who might otherwise require nursing home care and to small numbers of clients whose spending would not raise total outlays. Under Reagan administration rules, the original waiver coverage was limited to those who, without the waiver, would require the level of care provided in a nursing home for the elderly or mentally retarded. Initially, states had to document that a bed was available in a nursing home or other institutional setting for each person in the waiver program. The intent of the provision, called the "cold bed policy," was to ensure that the services provided were substituting for, not supplementing, nursing home care.

In 1994 the Clinton administration—at the behest of governors—removed most limits on the program by directing the bureaucracy to follow the more generous House language in the law, ignoring the restrictive Senate language. Bureaucratic reviewers were also reined in, required to accept state documentation as valid without much checking. The "cold bed" stipulation was modified, so that states were no longer required to document specific substitution, making it more likely that waiver programs would be used to increase total federal matching dollars, as a broader group of clients was served than would be likely to actually use nursing homes or intermediate care facilities and mental retardation facilities.[29] Later changes were made to cover targeted groups such as adults and children with AIDS, children with disabling conditions, adults with physical disabilities, and those with serious mental illness.[30]

A critical feature of waivers is that states can control the number of persons served and limit overall expenditures in a way impossible under the Medicaid law. States can choose to apply the waiver to a small group of individuals or may limit the services they wish to provide. They may offer services such as transportation, respite care, nursing services, personal services, chore services, caregiver training, and home modification. Eligibility for these ambulatory services may also be extended to individuals who would not be poor enough to meet income and asset standards for institutional care. Clients must be disabled enough to meet institutional care admission standards (although few who meet such standards would actually go to a nursing home in the absence of home care alternatives).

The Increasing Popularity of HCBS Waivers

Interest groups and individual legislators (not to mention governors) understand the idea of waivers and push their usage if it advantages their position. In Florida, for example, it is common for legislation calling for some change in the Medicaid program to include a provision that authorizes the state health administration agency to apply for a waiver to cover the population, supply the services, or authorize a new delivery mechanism. State officials note that these occurrences are not tied to the need for a waiver: many times the desired change in coverage can be attained under existing law or a slight modification of the state plan. But the legislator who has taken action will be able to take credit. Moreover, it is an action—waiving of federal law—that constituents and lobbyists can understand, whether they understand the process or not.

The aging of the population and a 1999 U.S. Supreme Court decision requiring states to stop warehousing mentally impaired people have helped expand the scope of waivers. In the *Olmstead* v. *L.C.* case, the U.S. Supreme Court found that, under Title II of the Americans with Disabilities Act, states have a duty to provide care in a community setting when medically appropriate and that isolating people with disabilities in institutions when there is no medical reason for placement there is unlawfully discriminatory. Availability of waivered community care services was a crucial concern in the case.[31]

The growth of the waiver program in terms of the number obtained by states, the number of recipients, and the dollars spent is impressive. In its first year, 1982, six states were operating one program each.[32] Ten years later, there were 155 waivers. In 2001 every state was using waivers, and the number had grown to 231.[33] A year later, there were 252 waivers across all states.

Expenditures increased from $2.2 billion in 1992 to $14 billion in 2001.[34] The number of persons served increased from fewer than 50,000 throughout much of the 1980s to 236,000 in 1992 and 843,000 in 2001.[35] By 2004 the total number of participants in home and community-based waiver programs had reached 1,015,418, while expenditures that year were $31.2 million.[36] Between the years 1999 and 2004, growth averaged 44 percent annually.[37] In 2006 there were 280,176 people on waiting lists.[38]

The enormous growth of the program is most likely attributable to demographics as much as politics—specifically, the aging of the population and its extended life expectancy. During the twentieth century, while U.S. population growth for the those under the age of sixty-five increased threefold, the number of Americans aged sixty-five and older increased by a factor of eleven.[39] Both falling fertility rates and increased longevity are contributing factors. Americans now live, on average, more than twice as long as they did when the nation was founded.[40] But these aged growth rates pale by comparison with the projections through 2050 as the baby boomers retire.[41]

Few Veto Points

The waivers are initially approved for three years by Department of Health and Human Services staff in Washington. They can easily be renewed for another five years (eight years for some types of waivers); the renewal is substantially the domain of the regional offices of the Centers for Medicare and Medicaid Services. The enabling legislation greatly facilitates the renewal of the waivers, authorizing the secretary of the department to approve and extend waivers, unless certain assurances have not been met.

Among those assurances are that states have taken necessary safeguards to protect the health and welfare of waiver participants and that they have submitted annual reports on the impact of the waiver and the health and welfare of the recipients. Empirical support for such assurances varies. Congress typically is not involved in Section 1915(c) waivers except to encourage their adoption for home jurisdictions.

Intergovernmental Bargaining

In Section 1915(c) waivers the bargaining takes place between state bureaucrats and officials in Department of Health and Human Services regional offices. Washington staff often get involved as well. The interactions are both formal and informal and are generally collegial. Both sides can learn from the exchange—and neither fully trumps the other. Federal and state bureaucrats negotiate over specific program provisions and build into the programs failsafe mechanisms that would be difficult to negotiate in a partisan legislative context and might be unwise to write into statute. The Centers for Medicare and Medicaid Services routinely sets caps on how many clients can be served annually, sometimes even monthly, during a period of waiver approval.

Here is an opportunity not only for federal bureaucrats to participate in the states' laboratories of democracy but also for negotiators on both sides of the table to use mild political threats to enhance the likelihood of reaching compromise. That is, Centers for Medicare and Medicaid Services staffers can threaten to turn the matter over to higher authorities in the federal government, while states can hint that their political leadership is prepared to go over the federal agency's head to its congressional delegation and the White House. The result has been a give-and-take in waiver negotiation that typically satisfies both sides.

Near-Assured Existence

Like all waivers, home and community-based care services waivers tend to persist over time. Their persistence derives, in part, from the lack of oversight by Health and Human Services over the waivers, especially concerning quality assurance.[42] If it feels the state has not ensured the health and safety of beneficiaries, the Centers for Medicare and Medicaid Services can either terminate the waiver or bar the state from enrolling any new waiver beneficiaries unless corrective actions are taken. In fact, the agency provides little oversight and tends to extend waivers. As the General Accounting Office (now the Government Accountability Office) has noted, as of June 2002 about one-fifth of the waivers that had been in place for three years or more had either never been reviewed or were renewed without review.[43]

The Deficit Reduction Act of 2005 signed by President George W. Bush on February 8, 2006, made major changes in Medicaid and the home and community-based care waiver. The law contains six chapters and thirty-nine sections devoted to Medicaid. It allows states to offer home and community-based care and self-directed personal care services without a waiver and to include these as optional services in state plans. However, unlike other optional services, the home and community-based services can be provided only to a predetermined number of recipients. This provision essentially caps the program and ensures states more fiscal control than if the services were guaranteed to all those eligible. States can now also tighten the standard for admission to institutions and refine eligibility for home and community-based waiver services without a waiver.

Conclusion

Waivers have become an integral part of our intergovernmental system. They are familiar tools for solving policy problems, enjoying broad support in the White House, federal agencies, and the states. Yet they have been largely ignored by the academic literature on fiscal federalism and policy tools—perhaps because waivers do not fit into definitional parameters. Waivers may be viewed as an intergovernmental licensing arrangement that imposes some constraints on the states but tends to increase the popularity of the waiver, ensure its continuation, enjoy few veto points, and provide a politically salient option for politicians and interest groups. At its core is bargaining—not coercion or even cooperation—an area sorely understudied as well.

We have developed the notion of waivers as intergovernmental licenses and applied the implications of such a design to one case: Medicaid home and community-based care services waivers. The case makes clear the importance of the waiver as an intergovernmental mechanism—a program license that suspends laws and removes federal strictures on states. Viewing waivers through this lens helps highlight their persistence and importance in our modern intergovernmental system. We have not explicitly fit the notion of intergovernmental licenses to the broader Section 1115 waiver but believe that many of the elements in the licensure notion apply there as well.

Given the recent popularity of waivers in other areas, it might be appropriate to compare the experiences with home and community-based care and AFDC—another area in which federal law built on state waiver experimentation. In doing so, some caveats emerge. In AFDC, subsequent federal action limited state options rather than continuing or expanding them. This might serve as a caution for states in implementing the new Deficit Reduction Act: what is provided at one point can be taken away at another. Certainly, this is more likely in congressional follow-up to this legislation. However, unlike Temporary Assistance for Needy Families, which replaced AFDC, the Deficit Reduction Act did not establish a block grant that needs to be reauthorized. Rather, the act retains considerable authority in the executive branch as well as spelling out state choices as choices, not mandates. Perhaps, then, here is a different model, one that builds on the strengths of waivers and delegation to both the federal bureaucracy and the states. If prior experience is our guide, Congress will revert to its subsidiary role, leaving to executive federalism the maximization of incremental behavior in a federal system, using waivers—however classified in the literature—as an intergovernmental license.

Notes

1. Organization for Economic Cooperation and Development, "Health at a Glance: OECD Health Data, 2005," June 2005 (www.oecd.org/dataoecd/44/38/34957431.pdf).

2. There is also a 1915(b)(c) waiver, which allows states to provide nontraditional and community-based services in a managed care environment or with a limited pool of providers.

3. William Gormley, "Money and Mandates: The Politics of Intergovernmental Conflict," *Publius: The Journal of Federalism* 36 (Fall 2006): 523–40.

4. Steven M. Teles, *Whose Welfare? AFDC and Elite Politics* (University of Kansas Press, 1996).

5. Nancy Miller, Sarah Ramsland, and Charlene Harrington, "Trends and Issues in the Medicaid 1915(c) Waiver Program," *Health Care Financing Review* 20 (Summer 1999): 139–60.

6. Samantha Artiga and Cindy Mann, "New Directions for Medicaid Section 1115 Waivers: Policy Implications of Recent Waiver Activity," policy brief, Kaiser Commission on Medicaid and the Uninsured, March 31, 2005 (www.kff.org/medicaid/7286.cfm). The authors note that in 2001 the Bush administration launched the Health Insurance Flexibility and Accountability waiver initiative, which encouraged states to use Section 1115 waivers to increase the number of individuals covered with health insurance within Medicaid and SCHIP resources. To encourage more self-direction, the Bush administration in 2002 unveiled the Independence Plus initiative, which encouraged states to use both Section 1115 and 1915(c) waivers to allow beneficiaries to self-direct their own budgets for services to keep them from being institutionalized. The Bush administration's Department of Health and Human Services also expanded the scope of the program by determining that the waiver initiatives need only further the objectives of the Social Security Act, not Medicaid or SCHIP—for the first time in the history of the initiative.

7. Thomas Gais and James Fossett, "Federalism and the Executive Branch," in *The Executive Branch in Institutions of American Democracy,* edited by Joel D. Aberbach and Mark A. Peterson (Oxford University Press, 2005), pp. 486–522.

8. Carol S. Weissert, "Learning from Midwestern Leaders," in *Learning from Leaders: Welfare Reform Politics and Policy in Five Midwestern States,* edited by Carol S. Weissert (Albany, N.Y.: Rockefeller Institute Press, 2000), pp. 1–23.

9. Gais and Fossett, "Federalism and the Executive Branch," pp. 486–522; Teles (*Whose Welfare?* p. 127) recounts the experiences of Richard Nixon who as president tried to exchange support for a California AFDC waiver for Governor Ronald Reagan's backing of Nixon's pet Family Assistance Program (an early welfare reform effort). Reagan refused, even testifying against the proposal in congressional hearings, but was granted his waivers in a process that took a year and a half.

10. Marilyn Werber Serafini, "Welfare—Waivering," *National Journal,* January 11, 1997, pp. 66–69.

11. "Rep. Dingell Writes to Comptroller General Walker Asking GAO to Examine Use of Section 1115 Medicaid Waivers by HHS Secretary," *U.S. Fed News Service, Including U.S. State News,* May 4, 2006 (www.allbusiness.com/government/3663032-1.html).

12. Teles, *Whose Welfare?* pp. 142–43.

13. Gais and Fossett, "Federalism and the Executive Branch," p. 487.

14. Carol S. Weissert and William G. Weissert, *Governing Health: The Politics of Health Policy* (Johns Hopkins University Press, 2006).

15. Office of the Inspector General, "Program Review of the Medicaid Reform Pilot Project," Florida Agency for Health Care Administration (September 2007).

16. Commonwealth of Massachusetts, Executive Office of Health and Human Services, Office of Medicaid, "Section 1115 Waiver Amendment," submitted May 1, 2006 (www.mass.gov/Eeohhs2/docs/eohhs/cms_waiver_2006/amendment.doc).

17. Samantha Artiga and others, "Can States Stretch the Medicaid Dollar without Passing the Buck? Lessons from Utah," *Health Affairs* 25 (March–April 2006): 532–40.

18. Jocelyn Guyer, "Vermont's Global Commitment Waiver: Implications for the Medicaid Program," Kaiser Commission on Medicaid and the Uninsured, April 2006 (www.kff.org/medicaid/upload/7493.pdf).

19. See D. F. Bradford and Wallace E. Oates, "Towards a Predictive Theory of Intergovernmental Grants," *American Economic Review* 61, pt. 1 (June 1971): 440–48; John E. Chubb, "The Political Economy of Federalism," *American Political Science Review* 79 (December 1985): 994–1015.

20. Karl Kronebusch, "Matching Rates and Mandates: Federalism and Children's Medicaid Enrollment," *Policy Studies Journal* 32 (Summer 2004): 317–39; Colleen Grogan, "The Influence of Federal Mandates on State Medicaid and AFDC Decisionmaking," *Publius: The Journal of Federalism* 29 (Fall 1999): 1–30.

21. Wallace Oates, "Toward a Second-Generation Theory of Fiscal Federalism," *International Tax and Public Finance* 12 (August 2005): 349–73.

22. Anne Schneider and Helen Ingram, "Behavior Assumptions of Policy Tools," *Journal of Politics* 52 (May 1990): 510–29.

23. Christopher Hood, *The Tools of Government* (Chatham, N.J.: Chatham House, 1983), pp. 174–86; Richard Elmore, "Instruments and Strategy in Public Policy," *Policy Studies Review* 7 (Spring 1987): 174–86; William Gormley, *Taming the Bureaucracy: Muscles, Prayers, and Other Strategies* (Princeton University Press, 1989).

24. Anne Schneider and Helen Ingram, "Social Construction of Target Populations: Implications for Politics and Policy," *American Political Science Review* 87 (June 1993): 334–47; B. Guy Peters and F. K. M. Van Nispen, *Hammer and Tongs: The Study of Policy Instruments* (Cheltenham, U.K.: Edward Elgar, 1998); Donald Kettl, *Government by Proxy: (Mis?)Managing Federal Programs* (Washington: Congressional Quarterly Press, 1988); B. Guy Peters, "The Politics of Tool Choice," in *The Tools of Government: A Guide to the New Governance,* edited by Lester Salamon (Oxford University Press, 2002), pp. 552–64; Steven Rathgeb Smith and Helen Ingram, "Policy Tools and Democracy," in *Tools of Government,* edited by Salamon, pp. 565–84.

25. Salamon, *Tools of Government;* also see David Beam and Tim Conlan, "Grants," in *Tools of Government,* edited by Salamon, pp. 340–80.

26. *Merriam-Webster's Dictionary of Law,* s.v. "license" (www.dictionary. com).

27. Helen Ingram, "Policy Implementation through Bargaining," *Public Policy* 25 (Fall 1971): 449–501; Eugene Bardach, *The Implementation Game: What Happens after a Bill Becomes a Law* (MIT Press, 1977); Robert Stoker, *Reluctant Partners: Implementing Federal Policy* (University of Pittsburgh Press, 1991); Jeffrey Hill and Carol S. Weissert, "Implementation and the Irony of Delegation: The Politics of Low-Level Radioactive Waste Disposal," *Journal of Politics* 57 (May 1995): 344–69.

28. William Weissert, Cynthia Cready, and James Pawelak, "The Past and Future of Home and Community-Based Long-Term Care," *Milbank Quarterly* 83 (Fall 2005): 1–71.

29. William Weissert, Michael Chernew, Richard Hirth, "Titrating versus Targeting Home Care Services to Frail Elderly Clients: An Application of Agency Theory and Cost-Benefit Analysis to Home Care Policy," *Journal of Aging and Health* 15 (February 2003): 99–123.

30. Miller, Ramsland, and Harrington, "Trends and Issues in the Medicaid 1915(c) Waiver Program."

31. *Olmstead* v. *L.C.* (P.L. 98-536) is summarized in Sara Rosenbaum and Joel Teitelbaum, "Olmstead at Five: Assessing the Impact" (Kaiser Family Foundation, June 2004). The authors argue that the ruling left considerable ambiguity regarding what services must be provided and to whom. Subsequent lower-court cases have endeavored to apply what has come to be seen as crucial criteria included in the *Olmstead* decision relating to what is being sought by plaintiffs. If services or expansion of eligibility criteria are seen by the court as "reasonable" in light of the scope of the state's program, the court tends to side with the plaintiff. But if the services or expanded eligibility would require fundamental changes in the nature of the state's program, the courts have tended to side with the states.

32. William Weissert, "Hard Choices: Targeting Long-Term Care to the At Risk Aged," *Journal of Health Politics, Policy, and Law* 11 (Fall 1986): 463–81.

33. Martin Kitchener and others, "Medicaid Home and Community-Based Services: National Program Trends," *Health Affairs* 1 (January–February 2005): 206–12.

34. Ibid., exhibit 1, "National Medicaid Home and Community-Based Services Summary Program Trends, 1992–2001."

35. Ibid.

36. Kaiser Family Foundation, "Medicaid Home and Community-Based Service Programs: Data Update: Executive Summary," Kaiser Commission on Medicaid and the Uninsured (Washington, December 12), p. 3 and figure 1, "Medicaid Home and Community-Based Services Participants, by Program, 2004" (www.kff.org/medicaid/7720.cfm).

37. Ibid., figure 2, "Growth in Medicaid Home and Community-Based Services Participants, by Program, 1999–2004."

38. Ibid., table 11, "Waiting Lists for Medicaid 1915(c) HCBS Waivers, by State and by Enrollment Group, 2006."

39. U.S. Census Bureau, *Statistical Brief: Sixty-Five Plus in the United States* (U.S. Department of Commerce, Economics and Statistics Administration, May 1995 [www.census.gov/apsd/www/statbrief/sb95_8.pdf]).

40. Ibid.

41. Ibid.

42. U.S. Government Accountability Office, *Long-Term Care: Federal Oversight of Growing Medicaid Home and Community-Based Waivers Should Be Strengthened,* GAO-03-576 (Government Printing Office, June 20, 2003).

43. Ibid.

9

REGIONALISM AND GLOBAL CLIMATE CHANGE POLICY

Revisiting Multistate Collaboration as an Intergovernmental Management Tool

BARRY G. RABE

Regional strategies have periodically been embraced as a method of intergovernmental management in the United States and other federal systems, a halfway house of sorts between concentrating authority at federal and state levels. As early as the 1920s, Felix Frankfurter and James Landis envisioned a burgeoning set of regional institutions to address problems that were demonstrably multistate in nature. "Our regions are realities," they declared.[1] Analysts from other fields joined the regionalism chorus in subsequent periods, perhaps most notably sociologists in the 1930s and economists and planners in the 1960s.[2] More recently, the regional option continues to resurface, characterized in some quarters as "federalism at its maximum potential."[3]

The allure of regionalism is considerable, allowing multiple states to join forces to address common problems and seize joint opportunities. This allows for a scale beyond individual state boundaries, but one that can be tailored to regional realities rather than imposed across all states by a federal government. At the same time, the bulk of writing on regionalism presumes an active and constructive federal role, with regional governance seen as an

I am very grateful to Tim Conlan, Judi Greenwald, Kirsten Engel, Paul Posner, Stacy VanDeveer, and anonymous reviewers for helpful comments on this chapter.

outgrowth of cooperative federalism. In practice, regionalism has taken numerous forms, including more than 150 congressionally sanctioned interstate compacts that remain operational between two or more states.[4] But far more regional arrangements are of an ad hoc, almost improvisational nature. These are so diverse and numerous as to defy any reliable census, ranging from regional purchasing pools for prescription drugs to reciprocal agreements on emergency assistance and homeland security protection.

Perhaps no area of public policy has been such a target for regional strategies as environmental and natural resource protection. More than half of existing interstate compacts involve some form of cross-border environmental concern, and innumerable agreements have been struck between multiple states on environmental issues ranging from waste management to deterrence of exotic species. The continuing attraction of regional approaches is particularly understandable given the frequently poor fit between existing state jurisdictional boundaries and environmental problems, reflected in the penchant for cross-border spillovers. A growing body of scholarly work examines the prospects for so-called bioregionalism, which tailors organizational boundaries to ecosystem realities.[5] In turn, important contributions in "common pool resources" and subnational environmental governance suggest many models whereby units within a federal entity might devise effective policy strategies that fall somewhere between the familiar divide of state and nation.[6]

The exploration of regionalism in environmental policy has only accelerated in recent years. This reflects a simultaneous expansion of policymaking capacity in many states and an extended period in which the federal government has experienced considerable difficulty in reaching consensus on new initiatives or in revising much earlier legislation.[7] New regional activity has been evident on a number of policy fronts, from water quality management to common pursuit of new pollution reduction technologies. As the political scientist Ann Bowman has noted, "It is only a short leap, then, to begin to think of interstate accords as potential alternatives to federal legislation."[8]

The evolving role of regional institutions in environmental governance is well illustrated by greenhouse gas reduction efforts in response to the challenge of global climate change—perhaps the most robust example of state and, increasingly, regional policy leadership. Three distinct forms of climate policy development have arisen whereby individual state strategies have expanded into very different forms of multistate or regional engagement. All of these cases have emerged amid extended federal government inactivity and the possibility of eventual federal opposition that could take legal or administrative form. The case that has the most formal and complex framework for regional collaboration, the so-called Regional Greenhouse Gas Initiative (RGGI), is finalizing a carbon cap-and-trade program for ten states and may expand its geographic scope in coming years. The analysis that follows demonstrates the continuing promise of regional strategies but also underscores their political and legal fragility in the absence of a common mission with the federal government.

Global Climate Change as a State and Regional Issue

In many respects, an issue such as global climate change would appear tailor-made for domination by national governments working collectively through international agreements. This was clearly the intent behind the 1997 Kyoto Protocol, crafted through protracted negotiation among nations. The odyssey of Kyoto ratification, particularly U.S. withdrawal in the face of approval by most other developed nations, is a familiar tale. What is far less understood are the domestic politics of climate policy, namely, the highly variable ability of national governments, and in many instances subnational governments, to find ways to translate Kyoto pledges into real policy and emission reduction. That Kyoto ratification may not necessarily be a good predictor of actual climate policy development or emissions stabilization is perhaps the biggest surprise in climate policy formation to date. Among federal or federated systems of government, one finds highly uneven levels of policy development and emissions stabilization among states, provinces, and regions, whether the protocol was ratified, as in the European Union and Canada, or rejected, as in the United States.[9]

In the United States, the Senate never seriously entertained the possibility of ratification before the Bush administration formally disengaged in 2001. Coupled with extended congressional inaction on various legislative proposals relevant to greenhouse gas reduction, states received a clear indicator that the field of policy development had essentially devolved to them—if they chose to engage, either working individually or in partnership with other states.[10] One decade after Kyoto, well over one-half of the American states have designed at least one policy that promises significant reduction in greenhouse gas emissions, and more than one-third have established a cluster of integrative policies. States have pursued these policies for multiple reasons, often perceiving a simultaneous boost to economic development alongside environmental benefits such as reduced conventional air pollutants and greenhouse gas releases.[11] Consequently, the United States has continued to develop its own version of climate policy from the bottom up, raising the question of whether individual state policies ultimately converge and assume regional characteristics. Thus far, at least three types of regional initiatives on climate policy have emerged, including the Regional Greenhouse Gas Initiative.

De Facto Regionalism

Political scientists have long discerned patterns of regional clustering as policies diffuse across the American states.[12] This naturally produces questions over whether neighboring states with similar policies work independently or collaboratively with one another. Such a dynamic is evident among so-called renewable portfolio standards (RPSs), whereby states mandate that all electricity providers within a given jurisdiction steadily increase the amount of renewable energy. The number of state RPSs has grown consistently, jumping from fourteen in mid-2004 to twenty-five in early 2008, including a number of states with large populations and energy demand. Collectively, implementation of these programs will increase the share of the nation's energy that is provided by renewable sources from less than 2 percent in 2002 to more than 7 percent in 2020. This estimate excludes large hydroelectric sources, assumes continued growth in national electricity demand, and does not account for the interactive effect of other state renewable-energy programs or any future state policy adoption. Consequently, these policies could make a modest dent in national greenhouse gas emissions, although no common metric has been established to estimate the likely impact.

Although all twenty-five RPSs have been created through distinct intrastate political processes, issues of regional coordination and management are increasingly evident. These state policies can be trichotomized into distinct regions, whereby multiple state neighbors have enacted comparable policies. In the Southwest, a de facto regional RPS includes six states that stretch from California through Texas. In the Northeast, a regional RPS zone extends north through Maine, west through Pennsylvania, and south through Maryland. A similar clustering exists within the westernmost states of the Midwest. Electricity routinely moves across state boundaries, creating both interstate interdependence for energy and extreme difficulty in hermetically sealing state borders to capture any economic development benefits from cultivation of new renewable energy. This diffusion of policy in the absence of any federal support increasingly raises questions of regional governance of renewable electricity.

States with RPSs have increasingly come to confront the creation of mechanisms that allow for interstate cooperation. Virtually all have created some form of tradable renewable energy credits, which allow renewable electricity generated in one state to qualify for another state's RPS if used in the receiving state. In Massachusetts, for example, relatively slow development of within-state renewable sources has led to active use of tradable renewable energy credits from elsewhere in New England to meet its policy requirements. Some states have attempted to move toward uniform credit definition, oversight, and trading rules, including an eleven-state effort launched by the Western Governors' Association known as the Western Renewable Energy Generation Information System.

Development of such an open system has not been easy, however, as multiple states must negotiate collaborative arrangements after completing the design of their respective programs. There is considerable interstate variation between programs, ranging from the definition of renewable energy sources to the question of specialized provisions for preferred renewable sources.[13] These variations are compounded by state eagerness to maximize the likelihood that any new jobs or economic development stemming from RPS implementation occur within their state boundaries, complicating the development of regional governance. In turn, states continually modify earlier policies, and new states periodically enter the RPS fold, making any effort at regional collaboration a continually moving target. Adding to the complexity is growing congressional interest in developing a federal version of an RPS, with most legislative proposals devoting scant attention to the relationship between existing state programs and any new federal initiative.

Bicoastal Regionalism

A common theme in the state diffusion literature has been the tendency over many decades for policy innovation to begin in states along the East and West Coasts and then gradually migrate toward the central states. This pattern is not necessarily replicated in other areas of climate policy but is strikingly evident in the effort to legislate reduction of carbon dioxide emissions from vehicles. In this case, California has once again used the unique powers afforded to it under the Clean Air Act to attempt to set emission standards that are more rigorous than those of the federal government, based upon an exemption approved by Congress in the 1970s. This authority is contingent on approval of a waiver from the U.S. Environmental Protection Agency (EPA), although dozens of these have been granted in recent decades.[14] Enacted in 2002, the legislation calls upon the California Air Resources Board to establish vehicular emission limits that take effect in the 2009 model year. If fully implemented, the new standards are expected to reduce carbon emissions from vehicles sold in California by 18 percent by 2020 and by 27 percent by 2030 relative to emissions projected in the absence of the regula-tions.[15] This remains a central component of a more far-reaching climate pol-icy enacted in Sacramento in 2006, the Global Warming Solutions Act.

Only California has the authority to take such steps, but the possibilities of a regional effect stem from the fact that all remaining states may opt for either the California or the federal standard if EPA grants the waiver. Histori-cally, the remaining West Coast states of Oregon and Washington and many states of the Northeast have formally emulated California's policies, often resulting in noncontiguous clusters of states that maintain higher regulatory standards than the remainder of the nation. There is also precedent for the bicoastal region to then prompt federal embrace of what was initiated in Cal-ifornia, reflecting pressure from vehicle manufacturers who want to avoid contending with two distinct sets of standards within a national context.

History has thus far repeated itself in this latest case, with a set of sixteen states, many of which are lodged along the ocean coasts, having formally adopted the California standard. Both vehicle manufacturers and the Bush administration have registered opposition to this legislation, arguing that it is in essence a fuel economy provision and thereby the exclusive jurisdiction of the federal government. Litigation has ensued, and in 2007 the U.S. Supreme Court concluded by a 5-4 vote that EPA needed to revisit its refusal to classify carbon dioxide as an air pollutant under the 1990 Clean Air Act Amendments. Twelve states and several municipalities joined forces in bring-ing this suit, which has served to put considerable pressure on EPA to grant the California waiver request. The agency denied that request in December 2007, prompting a near-immediate return to the courts by California and allied states. This experience reinforces the pattern whereby formal agree-ments can produce a region that includes noncontiguous states. Other prece-dents for this exist, such as the compacts for low-level radioactive waste man-agement, whereby states from different parts of the continental United States have attempted to join forces to share responsibility for their own waste.

Ironically, greenhouse gases may present a particularly strong opportunity for this unique brand of regionalism. Unlike conventional air pollutants, which follow particular deposition patterns and raise enormous cross-border tensions, any reduction of greenhouse gases from any source affords a global benefit. As a result, as the legal scholar Kirsten Engel has noted, "States are thus not limited to their geographic neighbors when searching for climate partners and can enter alliances based upon economic or social advantages and compatibilities."[16] Indeed, states may not be confined to alliances with sub-national units within American boundaries, further stretching the potential geographical boundaries of regionalism. This is most evident in a series of evolving partnerships between clusters of American states and neighboring Canadian provinces on climate policy.[17] On the East Coast, the New England governors and eastern Canadian premiers have agreed to common but nonbinding greenhouse gas reduction targets for the region and for their individual jurisdictions, building on their long-standing history of collaboration on environmental protection, economic development, and energy matters. Somewhat similar relationships are emerging between the central plains states and Manitoba through an initiative called Powering the Plains and also among West Coast states and British Columbia. As with some forms of interstate collaboration, subnational policy engagement involving states and non-U.S. governments raises numerous questions, and yet there is abundant precedent for formal and semiformal entities that further expand the realm of what is possible under the umbrella of regionalism.[18]

Cap-and-Trade Regionalism

The idea of developing a system of carbon emissions trading as the primary vehicle for securing Kyoto compliance was generated in the United States and pushed aggressively by American negotiators on their reluctant counterparts. This proposal was based on earlier American experience in transitioning from traditional command-and-control regulation toward more flexible systems that were used effectively to phase out the use of lead in gasoline and reduce sulfur dioxide emissions from coal-burning power plants. In the run-up to Kyoto, the United States consistently argued that this method could deliver cost-effective reductions in greenhouse gases. Despite resistance from the European Union and some other Kyoto signatories, the American case prevailed, and the launch of Kyoto led to the exploration of a global mechanism for imposing a carbon emissions cap that would allow for substantial trading among various emission sources to reach reduction targets with maximal flexibility and efficiency.

Ironically, this very concept is now embraced enthusiastically in the European Union but resisted thus far in Washington. In January 2005, the original fifteen members of the EU launched their emissions-trading scheme (ETS). Heavily based on the American model for sulfur dioxide, the ETS is designed as a primary policy tool to enable Europe to reach its Kyoto target of reducing greenhouse gas emissions 8 percent below 1990 levels by the end of the current decade. The ETS has experienced a series of implementation problems, stemming from flawed understanding of actual emissions and excessive allocation of permits to EU member states. This has led to allegations of "windfall profits" for many European utilities and minimal evidence of demonstrable emission reductions thus far. Nonetheless, this system is being expanded to cover the newer members of the EU and will most likely be extended from its original coverage of large utilities and industries to other sectors such as aircraft emissions. Senators John McCain (R-Ariz.) and Joseph Lieberman (I-Conn.) have repeatedly introduced different versions of a cap-and-trade proposal in Congress, but these have never come close to passage. The 110th Congress has featured a flurry of new carbon cap-and-trade proposals, but all face an uncertain reception in both chambers as well as in the executive branch.

Federal inaction, however, is not the end of the American story for carbon emissions trading. Massachusetts established its version of a carbon cap-and-trade program for within-state utilities in 2001, and New Hampshire followed with its own legislation a year later. These early steps prompted a number of other states to consider the viability of enacting their own version of such a program, using their powers for regulating air emissions and governing the environmental performance of electricity-generating utilities. One of the most thorough review processes occurred in New York, in conjunction with a comprehensive analysis of various policy options for reducing greenhouse gases in the state. This review prompted New York governor George Pataki in 2003 to formally invite his six counterparts from New England as well as the governors of four other states to begin exploration of the viability of a northeastern regional strategy.

By 2006, after protracted interstate negotiations, eight states had agreed to establish and participate in the Regional Greenhouse Gas Initiative, and two more entered the fold in early 2007. At least two other states and the District of Columbia continue to monitor the process and will most likely consider membership in coming years. There is also ongoing discussion about linking the RGGI with somewhat similar initiatives emanating from Sacramento and neighboring western capitals and preliminary exploration of possible collaboration with states in the Great Lakes basin. The RGGI establishes a cap-and-trade system for carbon dioxide emissions on all power plants that generate more than half of their electricity from burning fossil fuels and produce more than twenty-five megawatts a year. The formal cap will go into operation in 2009, set at a level of 121.3 million short tons of carbon dioxide, which is "approximately equivalent to 1990 emissions."[19] That level will be maintained through 2014, when the emissions cap decreases by 2.5 percent a year, designed to reach a 2018 level that is 10 percent below 1990 emissions. Very much a work in progress, the RGGI offers numerous insights into the viability of regional governance and distinct challenges that emerge. Consequently, subsequent analysis focuses primarily on the RGGI experiment, although making periodic reference to the other forms of regionalism noted above.

Making Regionalism Work

The Regional Greenhouse Gas Initiative may rank among the most complex and ambitious regional undertakings in U.S. history, in environmental policy or in any other sphere. Its proponents make no small claims for its potential impact; the December 2005 memorandum of understanding that serves as RGGI's founding document declares that "the Signatory States wish to establish themselves and their industries as world leaders in the creation, development, and deployment of carbon emission control technologies, renewable energy supplies, and energy-efficient technologies, demand-side management practices, and increase the share of energy used within the Signatory States that is derived from secure and reliable sources of Energy."[20] Indeed, central figures within this regional process have laid claim to national, continental, and even international leadership in establishing the RGGI as a viable model for carbon emissions trading that could warrant emulation nationally or abroad.

Meeting such lofty objectives will not be easy. But the RGGI does retain a substantial base of political support and a number of design elements that give it considerable promise as a regional entity. Thus far, this has enabled most of the original RGGI coalition of states to sustain prolonged negotiations over many complex and contentious provisions involved in setting up a regionally based program to cap-and-trade carbon dioxide emissions. This resulted in the 2005 memorandum of understanding that set forth the basic operating framework and was signed immediately by the governors of Connecticut, Delaware, Maine, New Hampshire, New Jersey, New York, and Vermont. Maryland formally joined this group in April 2006, followed by Massachusetts and Rhode Island in the early months of 2007. This led to construction of a model rule, a detailed blueprint of all RGGI operations, which was released in draft form in early 2006 and continues to undergo extensive stakeholder review. Once a model rule is endorsed by participating states, each individual state will then formalize its role either through legislation, executive order, or administrative interpretation. Other states can formally enter the process at any point, including those that are officially designated as nonsignatory states. Several key elements have served both to facilitate the complex effort to assemble a regional cap-and-trade program and to sustain political support and momentum for a structure that relies exclusively on multistate collaboration in the absence of authorization from either the federal government or a central regional authority.

Path Dependence

The construction of the RGGI has been eased greatly by the substantial experience among participating states with previous forms of emissions trading. All states were involved in the national trading programs for lead in gasoline and sulfur dioxide. But the RGGI states also gained unique experience in operating the first regional cap-and-trade system for emissions of air pollutants, when the federal government delegated responsibility for reducing nitrogen oxide emissions to the northeastern states in the 1990s. Working under the auspices of the Ozone Transport Commission, nine participating states ultimately pursued a path with some similarities to the RGGI. This included a series of interstate agreements that outlined a regionally based emissions-trading system and resulted in significant emissions reductions with high compliance levels and no discernible signs of adverse economic impact.

This experience was embedded in long-standing collaboration on environmental and related matters among a set of states that the political scientist Daniel Elazar once described as a "sectional confederation."[21] This historic tendency to work on a regional basis was further reflected in institutional development that established a policy network that made the Northeast an ideal place to experiment with a multistate cap-and-trade program for nitrogen oxides. This network includes NESCAUM, the Northeast States for Coordinated Air Use Management, an unusually strong regional entity established in 1967 to develop common air quality strategies for eight states within the region (beginning with six but expanding to include New York in 1970 and New Jersey in 1979). The organization is empowered to address "the entire spectrum of air quality issues," ranging from conventional emissions from fixed and mobile sources to greenhouse gas emissions.[22] It maintains a thirty-member professional staff that advises states individually and collectively on air quality science and policy concerns.

Alongside this regional expertise, each state within the RGGI orbit had already demonstrated its own significant interest in greenhouse gas reduction and assembled professional staff in both environmental protection and energy agencies to pursue various policy initiatives. All RGGI states also have RPS policies and so possess in-house expertise on renewable energy issues and related environmental impacts. Like Noah's ark, interstate negotiations leading to the RGGI extended invitations to a lead official from each environmental and energy entity involved. These officials frame policy recommendations and report directly to their respective agency heads, who meet periodically to take key decisions and, where appropriate, seek support from their governors. Every state in the region, regardless of scope, had at least some staff with expertise on all relevant issues. "All of the staff involved in this process were very familiar with [nitrogen oxide] and the acid rain budget and many had worked together before," noted one senior state staffer in a June 2006 interview. "These are all pretty sharp people and they are fun to work with. It means we have a nice atmosphere to be collaborative and everyone believes in what they are doing."[23]

The RGGI case expands on a pattern discerned in numerous other states that have made some initial foray into climate policy. In most instances, a network of intrastate policy professionals, most of whom are embedded in state environmental protection agencies, has proved influential in early stages of policy development and coalition building. As a result, many state climate policies have been designed to maximize political support that crosses partisan divides.[24] This is clearly reflected in many state RPS experiences but was also a significant factor in the progress of the RGGI. Virtually every state entered into this process with an experienced set of policy entrepreneurs on climate change on staff, all of whom knew climate science and policy options and most of whom had actually played some role in state climate policy development. Given the clustering of so many experienced policy professionals within a region that had a history of cooperative collective action, a regional greenhouse gas cap-and-trade program was in many respects a natural extension.

Maximizing Flexibility

The absence of any federal marching orders concerning the design of the carbon emissions–trading system and the broad language in much of the memorandum of understanding left substantial room for state officials to weigh the pursuit of the intellectually optimal trading system against political realities and ways in which various provisions might be modified to sustain broad political support. Indeed, the various subcommittees of the RGGI staff working group have continually tinkered with key design features. They have attempted to remain consistent with the overall goal of the RGGI but take advantage of the latitude they had to try to keep every state—and participating state agency—on board. Contrary to much of the literature on emissions trading, which is dominated by economic analyses that have largely ignored political factors and imply that market-based emissions-trading systems largely implement themselves, the RGGI experience demonstrates the necessity of deft political maneuvering to sustain multistate and stakeholder coalitions. Bars of soap have been jokingly awarded to state officials who have insisted on "pure" decisions rather than temper them to reflect political pressures.

Even a provision as seemingly straightforward as allocating the annual carbon dioxide emission budgets among states, which would establish a baseline for the subsequent cap and reductions, served as a mechanism for political bargaining. Under a pure distribution system, a budget would be allocated in strict accord with actual carbon emissions in the baseline year. However, the final allocations approved in the memorandum of understanding give somewhat more generous treatment to states with the lowest overall emissions, such as Delaware, Maine, New Hampshire, and Vermont. Under the official formula, these states will actually be able to increase their carbon dioxide emissions somewhat from baseline levels during the first phase of operation. In contrast, the states with the largest overall emissions generally accepted initial allocations somewhat below baseline levels. This emerged as a political compromise, whereby larger states agreed to assume a somewhat disproportionate share of the overall responsibility for emissions reduction, keeping smaller states with fewer sources and potentially less latitude in securing reductions on board.

Developers of the RGGI also attempted to navigate among a range of diverse stakeholders, each of whom potentially stood to lose or gain financially depending upon the definition of the cap-and-trade arrangements. This resulted in a dizzying set of provisions known as early reduction credits, triggers, safety valves, and offsets, each of which was designed to maintain flexibility in cap-and-trade implementation and sustain support from various constituents. In the case of early reduction credits, carbon dioxide generators who would be covered under the RGGI cap were adamant that they receive flexible terms for any early action between the signing of the memorandum of understanding in 2005 and the launch of the cap in 2009. This would entail formal recognition of early reduction actions, leading to allowances that would be issued in addition to the state budget. The issuance of early credits has long been contentious in the phase-in of new regulatory programs, including those that have an emissions-trading provision, but this willingness to add flexibility boosted support among states and firms with plans for pre-2009 reductions.

Triggers and safety valves are parts of a complex set of formulas whereby any future increases above anticipated costs for emission allowances allow greater flexibility in compliance. This added flexibility might entail formal extension of deadlines for compliance or more liberal use of offsets to compensate for emission levels that remain within allowed levels. The list of activities eligible for consideration as an offset includes methane capture from landfill gas, afforestation strategies to sequester carbon, and end-use energy efficiency, among others. Offsets generated within the RGGI zone of states are to be approved on a ton-for-ton basis, whereas those generated outside the region "shall be awarded one allowance for every two CO2 equivalent tons of certified reduction."[25] Generators can use offsets to cover up to 3.3 percent of their reported emissions for any compliance period. "This number had nothing to do with climate science or economics," explained a senior state official. "One group wanted a high number, another wanted no number. This basically split the difference."

All of these provisions further complicate the trading process. For example, safety valves set an initial threshold equivalent to $7 a ton, set in 2005 dollars and adjusted for inflation. In the event that prices exceed the threshold, the RGGI allows for both expanded use of offsets and more favorable terms for those that are generated outside the region. In turn, the safety valve mechanism also allows for expansion of the geographic area for eligible offsets to include projects located outside the United States. Every dimension of this process is contentious, guided by a blend of science and policy analysis but tempered by political calculations. Utilities generally favor maximal flexibility in all areas, whereas many environmental groups fundamentally opposed the entire idea of offsets as antithetical to the mission of a cap-and-trade program. Policy development evolves within a multistate staff working group, with subcommittees assigned to each particular category. Once some degree of internal consensus is reached, public hearings are held that allow for input from any interested stakeholder within or outside the region. At that point, the staff working group revisits the issue and makes further modifications, with the intent of assembling a package in the final model rule that can sustain regional support and win formal endorsement within each participating state.

Navigating each of these provisions is not unique to this particular emissions-trading system but presents a particular challenge and opportunity for state staff working in a regional context. Individual staff must contemplate what is best for overall greenhouse gas reduction in the region, weighed against the interests of their particular state's pressures from various stakeholders. Thus far, the staff-driven policy process has successfully struck a nuanced set of agreements that have sustained a fairly broad and diverse coalition of support, using negotiations over each provision as a bargaining chip to sustain a large body of constituents. This political skill clearly draws on many years of prior experience for most of these state policy professionals, both in the design of previous emissions-trading programs and regulatory programs intended to operate on a regional basis.

The Case for Economic Development

All of the provisions designed to maximize compliance flexibility have been blended with an overarching argument that the RGGI represents a classic instance in which environmental protection can advance in harmony with economic development. Proponents of the RGGI routinely highlight projected environmental benefits, including greenhouse gas reduction as well as anticipated reduction of conventional air emissions as the various stages of the cap are implemented. But they are equally adept at making the economic case, indicating that it is in the economic self-interest of individual states and the RGGI region writ large to pursue this initiative. "We are looking at climate change not only as an environmental obligation but an economic opportunity for the state," said a senior adviser in 2006.

The staff of the RGGI and commissioned consultants from various think tanks and universities have invested heavily in developing and publicizing economic impact scenarios, all of which point to minimal or nonexistent projected increases in regional electricity costs as various stages of the program are implemented. Under one moderate and well-publicized scenario, full implementation of the RGGI would produce average retail rate price increases for all rate classes of well under 1 percent through 2015. This would result in a weighted average household increase by 2015 of $3–16 annually for each household. Some analysts suggest that these increases may, in fact, be exaggerated. For example, RGGI-sponsored analysis has concluded that improvements over time in end-use energy efficiency, attributable to both the cap-and-trade program and a set of other state energy policies, may produce average household savings that exceed the price impact of the RGGI itself.

At the same time that analyses have played down likely implementation costs, other RGGI-supported studies have emphasized anticipated economic benefits from the RGGI that could be derived over the longer haul. These note that the states that make up the RGGI already hold "a particularly strong position in research and innovation related to energy and the environment," measured in related venture capital investments, patents, and federal research funding.[26] As a result, the region could indeed be positioned for further advancement in regional as well as national and international markets, through pursuit of the RGGI and the attendant impact on seeking carbon emission reductions. Current leadership is evident across a range of technologies that might, at least in theory, be further stimulated through a first-mover advantage linked to pursuit of the regional cap-and-trade program. According to the political scientist David Levy, "There are, in fact, strong grounds for projecting that the proposed greenhouse gas–trading system could substantially enhance the competitiveness" of the region in a number of economic sectors.[27] Individual states within the RGGI have undertaken similar kinds of economic development impact analyses, both in weighing participation in the regional agreement and in exploring supplemental climate policy initiatives.[28] These analyses have served to mitigate concerns about projected costs from unilateral development of a cap-and-trade zone for only one portion of North America, instead allowing proponents to contend that the RGGI is a tool for economic development as well as electricity reliability and environmental protection.

The Challenge of Sustaining Regional Collaboration

The evolution of the RGGI from George Pataki's 2003 letter of invitation to his gubernatorial colleagues into something approximating a full-blown regional system for cap-and-trade regulation of carbon emissions a half decade later underscores the political feasibility of large-scale development of regional policy. In many respects, it goes well beyond the other forms of climate policy regionalism discussed above, in terms of institutional complexity, cross-state network development, and collective scope of intent. Indeed, the RGGI appears well on its way to joining the European Union's emissions-trading scheme as the world's second multijurisdictional entity to oversee implementation of a sophisticated emissions-trading program to achieve reduction of greenhouse gas emissions.

At the same time, the RGGI remains a work in progress rather than a finished product. Interstate negotiations have continued over several years, with numerous issues remaining to be resolved before any regional agreement can be individually approved through appropriate political channels in each state. Before arriving at that final stage, however, a number of fault lines emerged. These do not necessarily undermine the long-term viability of the RGGI. But collectively they serve to underscore the political fragility of a regional venture that is so complex and operates exclusively through sustained multistate cooperation rather than any central coordinating mechanism provided by the federal government or any other external source. Some of the most significant challenges to sustaining the RGGI over its planned period of operation are outlined below.

The Secession Threat

Many federal systems, including Canada, continue to cope with the challenge of maintaining participation of all system members amid periodic threats to leave the union.[29] This has long since seemed resolved in U.S. federalism but reemerges frequently on issues of regional governance. In the case of the RGGI, participation by each state is purely voluntary, even after the point at which governors have signed formal agreements that commit them to long-term participation. The RGGI bylaws include provision for "withdrawal of a signatory state," which merely entails a thirty-day written intent to abandon the regional entity. In such circumstances, "the remaining Signatory States would execute measures to appropriately adjust allowance usage to account for the corresponding subtraction of units from the Program."[30]

None of the original signatories has given any indication of taking such a step, including New Jersey, despite a gubernatorial transition shortly after the memorandum of understanding was approved. However, the RGGI has already confronted decisions by two states that participated actively throughout the policy development process and then decided at the point of approval to reject the agreement, at least at that juncture. Both Massachusetts and Rhode Island remained nonsignatory states for extended periods, during which they generally continued to send representatives to RGGI meetings and held out the possibility of rejoining at some future point. But their decisions complicated the ongoing deliberations, reducing the overall scope of the region by approximately one-fifth (measured in terms of projected carbon emissions removed from the zone), necessitating recalculation of governance duties, and adding some degree of uncertainty to the viability of the regional pact.

The Massachusetts decision was particularly surprising given its earlier development of its own state-based cap-and-trade program and very active and enthusiastic support for the RGGI throughout its formative stages. The commonwealth was widely perceived as second only to New York in terms of its support and level of engagement in all aspects of RGGI development. Governor Mitt Romney and commonwealth development secretary Douglas Foy repeatedly cited the RGGI as one of many Massachusetts climate protection provisions that made it a national leader on the issue.[31] Moreover, Romney and Foy designated a senior staff person, Sonia Hamel, as the state's point person on the initiative. Hamel forged a strong partnership with her New York counterpart, Franz Litz, and was widely seen as a driving force in all areas of the initiative. "Sonia and Franz literally went everywhere, like a pair of Energizer bunnies, on behalf of RGGI," noted a senior official from another state. "They had a common passion for this issue, above and beyond their governors on this issue, and, in many ways, Sonia was the spiritual leader of RGGI."

But Hamel and Foy endorsed positions that Romney initially seemed to support but ultimately rejected. In particular, Romney insisted upon a firm price cap on electricity rates, whereby additional allocations would be made available if these caps were exceeded. By this point, Hamel and Foy had already agreed to exclude such a cap but instead insert various triggers and safety valves. Romney then decided to pull the plug, and Rhode Island, which closely adhered to the Massachusetts position throughout the deliberations, took a similar step.[32] The Massachusetts legislature subsequently considered enactment of a state agreement on the RGGI, and Romney introduced an expanded version of the state-based cap-and-trade system that did feature a firm price cap. But neither made much progress leading up to the November 2006 elections. Many observers contend that Romney's actions were designed to bolster his 2008 presidential prospects by showing concern for climate change but assuming a more fiscally responsible position than his potential rival, Pataki.

Both Massachusetts and Rhode Island returned to the RGGI fold in February 2007, as Deval Patrick shifted gears upon replacing Romney as governor in January, followed shortly thereafter by Rhode Island. But their earlier withdrawal illustrates the fragile context in which multistate regional partnerships operate, particularly given the flexible arrangements for withdrawal even after formal engagement. Unlike the European ETS or the U.S. federal cap-and-trade program for sulfur dioxide emissions, the RGGI allows any member to jump ship at any point in the process, without formal sanction or financial penalty. With considerable turnover of political leaders expected in coming elections in those states that have endorsed the RGGI, it remains unclear whether the initiative in future years will expand, contract, or retain its present shape. It is also uncertain how destabilizing this unpredictability might be for developing longer-term networks and levels of trust necessary to sustain institutions in the long term.[33]

Institutional Uncertainty

The RGGI has, in many respects, been a model of multistate collaboration and cooperative networking between lead state officials. But translating this initial cooperation into a more permanent governance structure remains an ongoing process. During its first four years of operation, the RGGI had little organizational form other than a staff working group, a website, and an ongoing set of stakeholder meetings that rotated from place to place. These years of deliberations focused primarily on many technical provisions, from offsets to safety valves, with far less attention devoted to the question of longer-term institutionalization of this regional partnership.

The RGGI memorandum of understanding did call for the establishment of a "regional organization with a primary office in New York City." Such an organization would operate on a nonprofit basis and be guided by an executive board comprising two representatives from each state. According to the memorandum, this body would serve as "the forum for collective deliberation and action among the Signatory States in implementing the Program," with responsibility for managing emissions trading, allowance tracking, offsets development and implementation, and numerous other responsibilities inherent in the operation of an emissions-trading program.[34] In July 2007 RGGI, Inc. was unveiled, a nonprofit entity that followed the basic lines set out in the memorandum of understanding. The organization has recruited for an executive director and projects a five-person staff with an estimated operating budget of about $1 million a year. But there is little detail beyond that in terms of funding support, organizational leadership and design, or staffing arrangements. "Clearly, there is a need for a secretariat of some sort, but it is not at all sure how this would work for RGGI," acknowledged one state official. "This is all to be determined, all on the path of negotiations," noted a colleague from another state. "New York wanted it in New York City, but that's about all that's been decided," confirmed an official from another state.

Conspicuous by its absence is any significant role for NESCAUM, the northeastern regional body for air quality, which has nearly four decades of experience, a strong track record on sustaining multistate collaboration, and a charge that includes climate change. Independent of the RGGI, NESCAUM has been working for a number of years on development of a regional registry for greenhouse gas emissions and a demonstration program for greenhouse gas credit trading. It maintains a large and permanent staff with considerable expertise in all of the technical and policy areas relevant to a regional cap-and-trade program for greenhouse gases. But to date it has largely been relegated to the role of observer, attending public meetings and occasionally playing an advisory role and thereby serving in a capacity similar to that of such other organizations as the Pew Center on Global Climate Change, Resources for the Future, and the World Resources Institute. It does not currently represent two of the RGGI signatories, Delaware and Rhode Island, although it has considerable experience working collaboratively with neighboring partners outside of its formal boundaries on other issues.

Any role that NESCAUM might play, both in policy development and as a long-term institutional home for key elements of the RGGI, has been actively opposed by some of the larger states in the collective, whereas smaller states have generally tended to favor its assumption of a more central role. At the same time, there has also been limited discussion about the coordination between the RGGI and a complementary but potential rival tool, the renewable portfolio standard, which exists in every state in the region. There is no regional institution that approaches NESCAUM in promoting coordination among individual state RPSs or renewable energy policy in general, reflected in significant and expanding state-by-state variation in these policies. Ideally, an RPS and a carbon cap-and-trade program like the RGGI would harmoniously coexist, but these appear to be evolving along separate policy tracks. There has been little discussion of common policy infrastructure, such as metrics for translating new renewable energy supply into a cap-and-trade program, how best to avoid double counting of credits in multiple programs, or how the allocation and pricing of cap-and-trade credits may influence prospects for successful RPS implementation.

Power Asymmetries

The progress of the RGGI to date has hinged on a high level of cooperation achieved through multiple rounds of interstate bargaining. Indeed, the network of state policy professionals who constitute the core of the RGGI have built on established relationships and facilitated this extended collaboration in an atmosphere of considerable trust, displaying many of the qualities of a robust epistemic community in domestic policymaking.[35] At the same time, tensions have surfaced within the RGGI that reflect the relative imbalance of influence among member states and call into question whether New York has attained disproportionate influence and thereby dominates most key decisions.

This dynamic suggests a potential power asymmetry that has been mitigated in part by giving all states full participation in all regional deliberations and the right to decide unilaterally whether they will remain engaged in the RGGI. It has been further eased by New York's willingness to offer generous terms of engagement, such as on carbon emission allowances, to relatively smaller states. Nonetheless, concerns have arisen among both moderate and small states about disproportionate New York influence. These concerns intensified during the hiatus from the RGGI of the "second-banana" state, Massachusetts, although the commonwealth's subsequent return to the fold may foster greater balance.

New York's influence is evident in many instances, from the decision to locate headquarters in New York City to the fact that the state formally chairs the staff working group. It is also one of only two states with staff representation on each of the five subgroups of the staff working group, which range from model rule development to energy modeling and analysis. Moreover, New York has covered a disproportionate share of overall RGGI costs to date and has offered to do so, at least in the early years of launching a regional office, as long as it is housed in-state. "It is no secret that New York considered this their show, that RGGI was New York's game," explained a senior state official. "In a good way, someone had to take this on their shoulders. But there has been a pernicious part to this. In a lot of cases, if an idea for RGGI was floated that was not New York's, it was seen as not being a good idea. Often, a very strong point of view has been expressed by New York staff and it is often hard for smaller states to counter that."

The viability of sustaining such an imbalanced set of interstate relationships is further compounded by the longer-term uncertainty of RGGI membership. Just as states like Massachusetts and Rhode Island can leave the fold and become official nonsignatory states, they can indeed leap back into the regional collective at any point, thereby altering interstate dynamics. Signatory states can disengage with only a month's advance notice, potentially destabilizing interstate comity. Perhaps more complicating, however, other states outside the current orbit may choose to seek formal membership. In fact, the RGGI remains amenable to the idea of expanding its zone to include other contiguous—and noncontiguous—states. Pennsylvania, for example, has remained a formal observer in RGGI deliberations and, as it has become an increasingly active player in many dimensions of climate policy, could indeed seek to join the initiative at some future point.[36] Governor Edward Rendell and senior advisers expressed growing interest in RGGI membership in a number of public pronouncements in 2007. The commonwealth, however, has nearly double the total carbon emissions from power plants as New York and exports more than one-third of the electricity that it generates into RGGI states; it would presumably expect a large role in future RGGI governance.

Another big-coal state, Illinois, also indicated increasing interest in joining the RGGI, as the state's Climate Change Task Force began discussions with RGGI leaders in fall 2006 about possible membership. In turn, the Canadian province of New Brunswick has remained a formal observer, although it rarely attends RGGI meetings. Its emissions are modest in comparison with those of Pennsylvania and New York, but its possible engagement raises still further governance questions, not only because it is a subnational unit of a foreign government but also because it is part of a nation pledged to ratify the Kyoto Protocol.

The RGGI could also expand to include far more distant noncontiguous states, as has been the case in the bicoastal form of regionalism evolving for regulating carbon emissions from vehicles discussed above. Most notably, California's 2006 Global Warming Solutions Act has started in motion a range of greenhouse gas reduction mechanisms that may be emulated by neighboring western states. Governor Arnold Schwarzenegger has formally emphasized the role of a cap-and-trade program under this new legislation, albeit one that would most likely include a wider range of emission sources than are covered under the RGGI. The details of any California program of this sort have been delegated to state agencies such as the California Air Resources Board and would require careful stitching together to allow "interoperability" for carbon credit trading with western neighbors or northeastern states. Cross-continental conversations about this possibility are only at early stages of development but demonstrate the potential fragility of the current RGGI power structure and the need to realign respective roles if states with larger populations and emissions were to enter the RGGI framework.

Circling the Wagons and Deterring Leakage

However the final boundaries of the RGGI are defined, any regionally based cap-and-trade zone will have to confront the challenge of leakage, whereby electricity produced outside the regulated area could prove less expensive because of the absence of carbon regulation. This is an inevitable problem for many kinds of potential climate programs that lack a fully global scope, reflected in the European Union's concerns about importation of electricity produced outside the zone of its member states, which are bound by the ETS. It may be particularly salient in a region such as the northeastern United States, where there is substantial movement of electricity across American state and Canadian provincial jurisdictions and no easy mechanism to encapsulate power generated exclusively within RGGI territory.

The current set of states that make up the RGGI already spans three interconnected power markets, each of which is operated by a separate transmission region.[37] A considerable portion of New Jersey sits within the so-called PJM Interconnection, which means that at least twelve states may feed electricity to its providers, only one of which (Maryland) is a RGGI signatory. There is also a large pool of states that provide some portion of electricity to New York and many New England states, as do Quebec and the Maritime provinces. Many of these jurisdictions already generate electricity below the average price for power produced within the RGGI region; any potential cost increase in RGGI states owing to carbon emissions trading could create a further incentive to import electricity and thereby bypass the carbon caps. Ultimately, the impact of significant leakage could be to neutralize any potential carbon reduction of the RGGI and even create substantial sinks that could accentuate the attractiveness of electricity produced in nonregulated states and provinces.

The leadership of the RGGI, cognizant of this possibility, commissioned an emissions leakage multistate working group to prepare a report outlining possible responses. An initial report released in March 2007 delineates a diverse and complex set of policy options but does not endorse any particular approach and readily acknowledges potential points of litigious vulnerability.[38] States that are members of the RGGI cannot impose a formal restriction or ban on electricity imported from states that are not RGGI signatories, as any such strategy will almost surely draw constitutional challenge and "clearly run afoul" of the commerce clause restraints against impeding the interstate movement of goods and services.[39] Another option is to expand the RGGI zone, and this is indeed part of the attraction of bringing states such as Pennsylvania into the fold. Even such annexation of sorts would not resolve the problem, however; it would instead simply push outward the zone of potential cross-state pressures. Pennsylvania, for example, is divided into three separate regional transmission organizations, making it an importer of electricity from far more states than other current RGGI members. At present, RGGI states are continuing to explore methods to impose greenhouse gas emission restrictions on imported electricity without triggering constitutional concerns. One emerging option involves some emulation of California's plan to create so-called performance standards, which would establish emission caps on all electricity used in the state regardless of its origin, but this has already provoked controversy and constitutional questions on both coasts.

Leaders of the RGGI lack any short-term remedies for this issue but take heart from the economic projections that suggest little if any impact on electricity costs for power generated within RGGI states. Thus far, the RGGI's primary response to the leakage threat has been development of allowance set-asides for each state that can be used to purchase offsets. The RGGI memorandum of understanding also calls upon signatory states "to pursue technically sound measures to prevent leakage from undermining the integrity of the Program."[40] But it is highly uncertain how much impact the allowance and offset provisions would have in deterring leakage, as well as what other measures that might pass constitutional muster would entail, resulting in enduring concern about the potential impact of leakage on long-term RGGI viability.

This sensitivity was further inflamed in 2007, when some RGGI states began to discuss the possibility of auctioning all allowances rather than adhering to the long-standing plan to distribute most of them free of charge. This triggered vehement opposition from many electricity generators and large consumers, who contend that this shift constitutes a late-stage "bait and switch" that deviates markedly from earlier agreements over how the process would unfold. "It is clear that the balance promised in the multistate process has been lost," lamented one set of utility and industry leaders in response. On the heels of the European controversy stemming from the initial ETS decision to allocate allowances without cost, the RGGI allowance allocation issue underscores the enormous political sensitivity of this aspect of cap-and-trade policy development, particularly for as complex and ubiquitous an emissions source as carbon dioxide.[41]

Federalism without the Federal Government?

Perhaps the single most surprising dimension of the RGGI is that such a complex, multistate endeavor is being undertaken without any significant state government conversation with, much less engagement by, the federal government. There is, of course, ample precedent for multistate ventures to operate without federal involvement, including the experience of neighboring states' RPSs to attempt to work out common terms of definition and trade. But the RGGI represents, in many respects, an extension of existing federal clean air legislation and experience in emissions trading to carbon dioxide. It involves a conscious decision by a collection of states to act in the absence of current or imminent federal action, as well as a decision by those states to bypass any formal interaction or negotiation with Washington.

Under other circumstances, one indeed might anticipate that the RGGI would be a candidate for an interstate compact. This would allow for formalization of its provisions and provide a formal endorsement by the federal government. One can envision many scenarios, perhaps building on the nitrogen oxide Ozone Transport Commission process or involving regional entities such as NESCAUM or EPA regional offices in constructive ways. Indeed, many scholars have deemed formal and constructive federal engagement as highly valuable in making regional strategies viable, serving as a catalyst for interstate cooperation, an honest broker of information, and a safeguard against noncompliance by individual members.[42] However, RGGI proponents have been skeptical that they could secure formal support from Congress or federal agencies and have instead decided that the initiative can be handled through a memorandum of understanding between state participants that is then ratified by actions of individual state governments and monitored by a nonprofit regional oversight body, to be known as RGGI, Inc.

An enduring concern of state officials engaged in the RGGI is that not only are federal institutions unlikely to be supportive but they might actually attempt to undermine the initiative. State officials repeatedly invoke the fear that the federal government will pursue some variation of a preemption strategy that attempts to strip state governments of any ability to develop a cap-and-trade system for carbon, either unilaterally or on a multilateral basis.[43] Most proposed federal cap-and-trade bills introduced in the 110th Congress call for some form of protection for state policies that were put into operation before any federal steps were taken. However, such divergent figures as Senator Dianne Feinstein (D-Calif.) and the National Association of Manufacturers president (and former Michigan governor) John Engler began in 2007 to suggest that total preemption of prior state legislation could become part of a grand bargain leading to federal legislation.

Beyond the legislative branch, many contend that the Bush administration and senior levels of EPA have worked to undermine the RGGI. "At one level, the feds are kind of a nonplayer in all of this," explained one state official involved in RGGI deliberations. "But they have actually spent more than two years trying to sabotage it, whether by trying to rally corporations and [think tanks known for their opposition to early action on greenhouse gas reduction] to oppose it or bombarding RGGI with information requests." Ironically, state participants note a different relationship at lower levels of EPA and with select congressional staff eager to advance some version of a national cap-and-trade program. "There are many folks at EPA who are privately cheering us on and helping us where they can," noted one senior staff official. "And there are a few congressional staff who have talked with us about how to reward early state action in any future federal program."

Nonetheless, while its member states generally view federal institutions and policy processes with considerable skepticism, the RGGI continues to evolve. Regardless of partisan affiliation, leaders of each of the RGGI states have not seen the federal government as a constructive ally and have as a result constructed a process designed to minimize federal involvement and possible intervention. Ironically, RGGI officials may have had considerably greater contact with officials from the European Union ETS and states outside their current membership roster than with their own federal government. These interactions have primarily entailed technical discussions about early lessons in carbon emissions–trading system development. But they have led to some initial conversations about the possibility of linkages between the RGGI and not only noncontiguous American states but also members of the European Union's ETS and what that would entail,[44] which has largely been missing in the state-to-federal relationship.

Looking Ahead: Prospects for Expanded Regionalism

The RGGI experience, along with other forms of regionalism for developing climate policy among multiple states, underscores the continuing dynamic of bottom-up policy development in U.S. environmental and energy policy of recent decades. Collectively, these policies do not add up to a comprehensive U.S. climate plan. But as they expand and take some semblance of a regional form, they become increasingly significant, both in terms of potential reductions of greenhouse gases and in constructing an extensive laboratory for testing what does and does not work effectively in climate policy. As of early 2008, more than 60 percent of Americans live in states with operational RPSs, more than 35 percent reside in states that have embraced the California carbon vehicle emissions standards, and more than 30 percent live in states covered by some form of a cap-and-trade program for utility sector emissions. Not only do these programs include states with considerable populations, but they literally represent regions that generate large amounts of greenhouse gases. Moreover, the kinds of policies reflected in these various regional formulations are far more than modest, voluntary experiments. They call for significant changes, whether increasing renewable energy to supplant thermal sources or steady reductions in carbon emissions from vehicles or power plants. Although all of this functions amid a classic patchwork quilt, some regional zones of the United States now operate climate protection policies that clearly rival those of other federal or federated systems of government that have ratified Kyoto, such as the European Union, Japan, Australia, and Canada.[45]

At the same time, all of this U.S. subnational experimentation goes forward in the awkward never-never land that is the current state of American federalism. States are keen to capture any economic and environmental benefits from taking early action and yet step cautiously so as not to trigger potential federal political challenges in the form of preemption or legal challenges in the form of litigation over constitutional powers granted to states. Almost eerily, there has been stunningly little constructive conversation between increasingly active states and continually disengaged federal entities such as regulatory agencies and Congress. All of these state efforts, perhaps most notably the cap-and-trade provisions of the RGGI, could indeed benefit from constructive dialogue with the federal government. Instead, U.S. climate policy has lumbered forward in two parallel but essentially isolated intergovernmental worlds, potentially fused at some future juncture through some form of collision.

Proponents of the RGGI have already begun to prepare for that potential confrontation, though many remain hopeful that their efforts will ultimately serve as a model for federal legislation. "All of the states involved in RGGI would love to see a national model," explained Franz Litz of New York, who left his post after the state gubernatorial transition in 2007 from Republican Pataki to Democrat Eliot Spitzer. "We would love to see an international program. You have to start somewhere."[46] In signing the RGGI memorandum of understanding in 2005, virtually each participating governor made similar statements. "I also see the potential for this program serving as a national model," noted Delaware governor Ruth Ann Minner, in a representative comment.[47] In anticipation of such a step down the road, RGGI leaders have already begun to position themselves for maximal advantage in negotiation over the terms of transition from a regional to a federal program. Indeed, the RGGI memorandum of understanding lays out the terms under which RGGI states would envision such a transition taking place: "When a federal program is proposed, the Signatory States will advocate for a federal program that rewards states that are first movers. If such a federal program is adopted, and it is determined to be comparable to this program, the Signatory States will transition into the federal program."[48]

There is, of course, no guarantee that any future federal program would be so accommodating of early state movers and significant precedent from other examples of preemption to suggest that first-movers are not always rewarded in later rounds of federal policy. For now, considerable uncertainty remains about next steps, owing in part to the paucity of serious intergovernmental conversation between state and federal officials during the current decade.[49] "What if, under RGGI, our states get 10 percent below a baseline and have plans to cut even more?" asked one senior state official. "And then the feds come in and say 5 percent is enough or what we did doesn't count. What happens then, and how do we work that out? Right now, no one knows."

In the absence of intergovernmental dialogue, the various state climate regions continue on the path of implementation. Each of the twenty-five RPS states continues to work out details on tradable renewable energy credits and other provisions essential for implementation, just as California and its bicoastal allies continue to press for federal approval of the regulations designed to achieve their carbon emission reduction goals from vehicles. At the same time, RGGI states must contend with countless challenges, from stemming the threat of emissions leakage to devising a sustainable regional governance structure where only memorandums and handshakes exist at present. Much like the European ETS, the RGGI has assembled considerable policy architecture in a short period of time, building on substantial precedent and a strong network of devoted policy professionals. But it demonstrates that emissions-trading arrangements are inherently political and technically complex entities, particularly when the federal government in which the regional effort is embedded is indifferent at best and hostile at worst.

Notes

1. Felix Frankfurter and James Landis, "The Compact Clause of the Constitution: A Study in Interstate Adjustments," *Yale Law Review* 34, no. 7 (May 1925): 685–758, p. 729.

2. Martha A. Derthick, *Between State and Nation: Regional Organizations of the United States* (Brookings, 1974), p. 3.

3. Henry N. Butler and Jonathan R. Macey, *Using Federalism to Improve Environmental Policy* (Washington: American Enterprise Institute, 1996), p. 58.

4. G. Ross Stephens and Nelson Wikstrom, *American Intergovernmental Relations: A Fragmented Federal Polity* (Oxford University Press, 2007).

5. Jonathan R. Strand, "The Case for Regional Environmental Organizations," in *Emerging Forces in Environmental Governance,* edited by Norichika Kanie and Peter M. Haas (New York: United Nations Press, 2004), pp. 71–85.

6. Elinor Ostrom, *Governing the Commons: The Evolution of Institutions for Collective Action* (Cambridge University Press, 1990).

7. Barry G. Rabe, "Environmental Policy and the Bush Era: The Collision between the Administrative Presidency and State Experimentation," *Publius: The Journal of Federalism* 37 (Summer 2007): 413–31.

8. Ann O'M. Bowman, "Horizontal Federalism: Exploring Interstate Interactions," *Journal of Public Administration Theory and Research* 14 (October 2004): 535–46, p. 545.

9. Barry G. Rabe, "Beyond Kyoto: Climate Policy Development in Multi-Level Governance Systems," *Governance: An International Journal of Policy, Administration, and Institutions* 20 (July 2007): 423–44.

10. Henrik Selin and Stacy D. VanDeveer, "Political Science and Prediction: What's Next for U.S. Climate Change Policy?" *Review of Policy Research* 24 (January 2007): 1–28.

11. Barry G. Rabe, *Statehouse and Greenhouse: The Emerging Politics of American Climate Change Policy* (Brookings, 2004).

12. Jack L. Walker, "The Diffusion of Innovation among the American States," *American Political Science Review* 63 (September 1969): 880–99; William D. Berry and Brady Baybeck, "Using Geographic Information Systems to Study Interstate Competition," *American Political Science Review* 99 (November 2005): 505–20.

13. Coral Davenport, "A Clean Break in Energy Policy," *CQ Weekly,* October 8, 2007, pp. 2920–27.

14. James E. McCarthy, *California's Waiver Request to Control Greenhouse Gases under the Clean Air Act,* RL34099 (Congressional Research Service, August 20, 2007).

15. Susan Brown, *Global Climate Change and California* (Sacramento: California Energy Commission, 2005).

16. Kirsten H. Engel, "Regional Coordination in Mitigating Climate Change," *New York University Environmental Law Journal* 14, no. 1 (2005): 54–85, p. 83.

17. Henrik Selin and Stacy D. VanDeveer, "Canadian-U.S. Environmental Cooperation: Climate Change Networks and Regional Action," *American Review of Canadian Studies* 35 (Summer 2005): 353–78.

18. Joseph F. Zimmerman, *Interstate Economic Relations* (State University of New York Press, 2004).

19. Regional Greenhouse Gas Initiative (RGGI), "Memorandum of Understanding," December 20, 2005.

20. Ibid., pp. 1–2.

21. Daniel J. Elazar, *American Federalism: A View from the States* (New York: Harper and Row, 1984).

22. Zimmerman, *Interstate Economic Relations,* p. 192.

23. A number of quotations appear in this chapter without direct attribution. These are drawn from interviews with more than twenty-five state, regional, federal, environmental advocacy group, and private sector officials with direct involvement in the regional policy process. Owing to the political sensitivity of these discussions, all interview participants were assured that there would be no direct attribution of their comments in any subsequent publication.

24. Rabe, *Statehouse and Greenhouse.*

25. RGGI, "Memorandum of Understanding," p. 4.

26. David L. Levy, "Sectoral Economic Benefits from the Regional Greenhouse Gas Initiative," draft report prepared for the Northeast States for Coordinated Air Use Management (September 5, 2006), p. 9.

27. Ibid., pp. 7–8.

28. Massachusetts Climate Action Network, "Mass. DOER Study Shows RGGI Could Cut Electric Bills for Most Businesses and Residential Customers," May 2, 2006, pp. 1–2; Center for Integrative Environmental Research, *Economic and Energy Impacts from Maryland's Potential Participation in the Regional Greenhouse Gas Initiative* (College Park: University of Maryland, Center for Environmental Research, January 2007).

29. Ugo M. Amoretti and Nancy Bermeo, eds., *Federalism and Territorial Cleavages* (Johns Hopkins University Press, 2004); Mikhail Filippov, Peter C. Ordeshook, and Olga Shvetsova, *Designing Federalism: A Theory of Self-sustainable Federal Institutions* (Cambridge University Press, 2004).

30. RGGI, "Memorandum of Understanding," p. 9.

31. Commonwealth of Massachusetts, Office of Commonwealth Development, "Massachusetts Climate Protection Plan," Boston, May 6, 2004.

32. John Pendergrass, "Seven States Forge Power Plant Pact," *Environmental Forum* 22 (November–December 2005): 8.

33. Eric Montpetit, *Misplaced Distrust: Policy Networks and the Environment in France, the United States, and Canada* (University of British Columbia Press, 2003).

34. RGGI, "Memorandum of Understanding," pp. 7–8.

35. Montpetit, *Misplaced Distrust.*

36. Stephen R. Dujack, "Welcome Back, Katie," *Environmental Forum* 22 (July–August 2005): 34–37.

37. William R. Prindle, Anna Monis Shipley, and R. Neal Elliott, *Energy Efficiency's Role in a Carbon Cap-and-Trade System: Modeling Results from the Regional Greenhouse Gas Initiative* (Washington: American Council for an Energy-Efficient Economy, 2006).

38. Regional Greenhouse Gas Initiative, "Potential Emissions Leakage and the Regional Greenhouse Gas Initiative (RGGI): Evaluating Market Dynamics, Monitoring Options, and Possible Mitigation Mechanisms," March 14, 2007.

39. Engel, "Regional Coordination in Mitigating Climate Change," p. 23.

40. RGGI, "Memorandum of Understanding," p. 10.

41. Leigh Raymond, *Private Rights in Public Resources: Equity and Property Allocation in Market-Based Environmental Policy* (Washington: Resources for the Future, 2003).

42. Butler and Macey, *Using Federalism to Improve Environmental Policy,* pp. 44–45; Derthick, *Between State and Nation,* p. 214.

43. Paul L. Posner, "The Politics of Preemption: Prospects for the States," *PS: Political Science and Politics* 38 (July 2005): 371–74; Paul Teske, "Checks, Balances, and Thresholds: State Regulatory Re-enforcement and Federal Preemption," *PS: Political Science and Politics* 38 (July 2005): 367–70.

44. Engel, "Regional Coordination in Mitigating Climate Change."

45. Rabe, "Beyond Kyoto."

46. Jon Goodman, "Greenhouse Gumption," *Governing* 19 (May 2006): 60–62, p. 62.

47. State of Delaware, "Governor Minner and Six Other Governors Announce Agreement on Regional Greenhouse Gas Initiative," December 20, 2005.

48. RGGI, "Memorandum of Understanding," p. 10.

49. Rabe, "Environmental Policy and the Bush Era."

III

ISSUES OF GOVERNANCE IN THE INTERGOVERNMENTAL SYSTEM

10

FROM OVERSIGHT TO INSIGHT

Federal Agencies as Learning Leaders
in the Information Age

SHELLEY H. METZENBAUM

J ustice Louis Brandeis's observation that "states are the laboratories of
democracy" is frequently quoted.[1] Unfortunately, these ostensible laboratories too often lack scientists. Few study state and local experiments taking
place across the country. Little attention is directed to documenting key
details and distinguishing studies with positive from those with negative or
no results. Few resources are devoted to writing up experimental findings,
weeding out unsubstantiated conclusions, and distributing lessons to interested parties.

Federal agencies that depend on other levels of government to accomplish
their objectives need to play a much stronger role studying experiments in state
and local laboratories of democracy or causing such study to occur and then
sharing the findings. Especially in the information age, federal agencies that
depend on states and localities to accomplish their objectives need to assume
both a learning role and a leadership role. They need to be learning leaders.

Federal agencies can promote learning by building the capacity to learn
which state and local actions improve outcomes, stimulate experiments that
complement those already occurring, disseminate findings, and encourage
uptake of effective and discard of ineffective approaches. This implies a much
stronger federal role in the creation, management, and transfer of knowledge.

The federal government can exhibit leadership by providing inspiration, a direction for action, motivation, expert coaching, and insights that enable genuine achievement.[2] To function as learning leaders, many in federal agencies need an attitude adjustment. They need to shift their emphasis from conducting oversight to generating outcome-focused, evidence-based insights. They need to pay less attention to ensuring that specific activities take place or specific amounts of money get spent and more to helping states and localities understand problems, then find and adopt effective solutions. Federal agencies need to identify what works, motivate uptake of effective interventions, and encourage the ongoing search for ever more productive ways to prevent, mitigate, and treat problems. That is not to suggest that federal agencies compromise their accountability to Congress and the public nor relax intergovernmental accountability expectations. States and localities will always need to ensure that taxpayer dollars are spent legally, efficiently, and honestly. Federal domestic policy agencies can no longer concentrate on procedural and fiscal matters, such as requiring the establishment of a single fund-receiving agency and maintenance of prior spending levels at the state and local level, to the neglect of performance accountability that "motivate[s] better performance than would otherwise occur" and democratic accountability that promotes government responsiveness to the choices and preferences of its citizens.[3] Instead, federal agencies need to act as intergovernmental learning leaders. They need to enhance performance accountability by helping states and localities learn how to improve outcomes and by motivating adoption of promising practices, avoiding the temptation to push specific means for achieving goals without compelling evidence of their effectiveness. They need to boost democratic accountability by clearly articulating priorities and supporting debate about the appropriateness of targets given available resources.

Incentives are also an important tool in the intergovernmental accountability toolkit. They should not, however, be used primarily to reward governments that meet their targets and punish those that do not, as is so often assumed. Incentives work best as a companion to goals and measurement to motivate the collection of standardized data, win attention to goals, enlist goal allies, and compel the attention of reluctant goal adopters. Incentives must be employed with great care, though, lest they stimulate dysfunctional responses owing to fear, frustration, or goal opposition.

Interestingly, the intergovernmental literature focuses most of its attention on incentives, especially grants, as the primary mechanism of federal influence on other levels of government. It rarely pays attention to goals and measurement as discrete intergovernmental tools. When it does, it is primarily in the context of a principal-agent relationship, in which goals reflect the principal's objective (assumed to differ significantly from the agent's) and measurement provides the means for monitoring agent fulfillment of obligations to the principal. The power of goals and measurement as tools for inspiration, communication, and knowledge management has only recently begun to garner attention.[4]

More attention is warranted because federal agencies can use goals and measurement to inspire, motivate, and illuminate performance-improving opportunities and pair them with incentives to enlist goal allies, generate measurement, and stimulate analysis. Mastering use of these three intergovernmental tools will improve both performance and accountability while at the same time reducing the rancor that so often arises when federal agencies place primary emphasis on state and local compliance with grant conditions. Of course, federal-state relations will not always be smooth even when federal agencies act as learning leaders. Political perspectives on which problems need attention inevitably vary across people and parties and therefore, not surprisingly, across levels of government. Intergovernmental battles about goals, especially specific targets, will be common. But battles about outcome priorities rather than administrative matters constitute healthy democratic debate rather than wasteful wrangling.

Federal agencies cannot function solely as learning leaders. When Congress sets national standards to protect basic rights or minimum standards of well-being, federal agencies must also serve as basement border guards, ensuring that states (and their residents) not trespass nationally set boundaries. Furthermore, when state and local delivery capacity is inadequate, as was the case with Hurricane Katrina in 2005, the federal government may need to provide direct service or catalyze creation of intergovernmental service delivery networks.

Strengths and Stresses of the Intergovernmental Governance Structure

In the United States, multiple levels of government serve the American people for both practical and political reasons. A multiparty governance arrangement is well established in domestic policy areas such as education, the environment, poverty reduction, and transportation.[5]

Well-functioning multilevel operations, if not too rule bound and controlling, have great practical advantage both in government and the private sector. Thus practicality argues for intergovernmental delivery of government services. Centralized units of well-functioning multilevel organizations or networks open possibilities for economies of scale, expertise specialization, and risk-spreading, while local units afford agility and adaptability. Intergovernmental arrangements also afford a practical means for handling cross-jurisdictional costs such as environmental pollution, cross-jurisdictional benefits such as highways, and cross-jurisdictional free-rider problems that arise when local governments offer redistribution programs. Poorly executed multilevel arrangements can, however, be cumbersome, inefficient, and infuriating.

In the United States, the political argument for multilevel governance dominates the practical one. The country's founders feared that an overly powerful government, acting on behalf of the majority and influenced by the wealthy and well organized, might trample the rights of the minority. They adopted a federalist system to counter this, with separately sovereign national and state governments. Together with the checks and balances of three branches of government, the federalist arrangement is designed to protect civil rights and deliver more responsive government.[6] When citizens do not like policies advanced at one level of government, they can organize politically to bring about changes at another. Although effective in protecting the minority, the ongoing quest for political responsiveness inevitably creates intergovernmental policy inconsistencies and recurring contention.[7]

The federal government seldom exercises force to assert hierarchical authority. Instead, it has long used grants to persuade states and localities to pursue federally selected goals.[8] When states and localities accept federal dollars to advance a specific objective, they agree to a set of conditions defined by law, regulation, guidance, or grant agreement. The legitimacy of this intergovernmental control mechanism has been challenged, but the courts have consistently "conceded to Congress the right to attach any regulations to any aid Congress provides."[9] Federal agencies dependent on states and localities to accomplish their objectives are not limited to using conditioned grants to motivate intergovernmental action. They can also use goals and measures. When federal agencies use grants to support the leadership potential of goals and the learning potential of measures rather than to control, multilevel governance thrives.

Government Performance and Results Act

In 1993, convinced of the logic of using outcome-focused goals and measurement to improve both performance and accountability, the U.S. Congress passed the Government Performance and Results Act (GPRA). The law requires every federal agency to set strategic (five-year) and annual goals, measure performance, and report performance annually to the public.[10] Perhaps surprisingly, the law "[pays] scant attention to federalism—a fundamental feature of the American political system that profoundly shapes program implementation."[11] It leaves it to each federal agency to sort out how to use goals and measurement in its intergovernmental arrangements.

In chapter 11 in this volume, Beryl Radin asserts that the GPRA and the Performance Assessment Rating Tool (PART), an executive branch review process introduced by the U.S. Office of Management and Budget to increase agency use of outcome-focused goals and measures as mandated by the GPRA, exacerbate intergovernmental difficulties.[12] Cantankerous conflicts can indeed erupt when the federal government tries to impose goals on states and localities. States and localities do not like another level of government telling them what their priorities should be, even when they agree with the goal itself, and often see measurement requirements associated with federal grants as a drain on resources needed to get the job done. Yet intergovernmental use of goals and measurement can defuse contention and speed program effectiveness when goal debates pertain to program priorities rather than power and when federal agencies use collected measurements to generate performance-improving insights rather than to control.

The GPRA requires every federal agency to set outcome-focused goals and measure progress. Federal agencies dependent on other levels of government to accomplish their objectives therefore must figure out how to use goals and measurement in an intergovernmental context within the bounds of their existing laws. These bounds vary greatly. Some laws set state and local goals; others instruct federal agencies to set them. Some restrict federal agency authority to set goals; and others charge states with goal-setting. Many also explicitly link goals and measurement to incentives.

Core Tools of Intergovernmental Performance Management

The core tools of intergovernmental management for performance are goals, measurement, and incentives. Goals and measurement can operate as intergovernmental tools independent of incentives. The most common incentives are the promise of grants and the threat of penalties.

Goals

John F. Kennedy intuitively appreciated the inspirational value of goal setting in government when he announced his plan to land a man on the moon within a decade. Goals, especially those that are specific and challenging, fulfill a remarkably powerful performance-driving function for both individuals and organizations.[13] Goals affect performance through four mechanisms: a directive function, an energizing function, persistence, and a stimulating function that encourages discovery and the use of task-relevant knowledge and strategies.[14] Goals can also frustrate, though, when targets are unrealistic relative to available knowledge, skills, or resources. To inspire effectively, goals need to be challenging, but they also need to be realistic. Otherwise, they simply enrage or discourage.[15]

Goal setting has received limited attention as a tool of government influence. One exception, a study of school mission statements, tentatively concludes that the framing of a mission statement can affect performance. Statements phrased in an active voice, with a few outcome-oriented goals, improve school performance more than those stated passively with either multiple goals or goals focused on processes or behaviors.[16] Goals have received even less attention in the intergovernmental literature, except when combined with incentives.

Experience in the health area suggests the potential power of well-set federal goals. The federal government issued the first Healthy People report in 1979, providing a health vision for the country by setting five specific national outcome targets, one each for five distinct age groups, to be achieved within ten years. This goal-setting report was followed one year later by a report setting specific targets for fifteen priority program areas, such as immunization and accident prevention, to reach the five national goals. The federal government has updated the health goals and objectives for the American people each successive decade, setting targets for the decade to follow.[17]

Healthy People goals and objectives are set based on a review of the evidence about deaths and illness, their causes, and the effectiveness of prevention efforts. The reports select high-level goals, such as the current Healthy People goals of increasing quality and years of healthy life and reducing health disparities, and specific objectives for specific focus areas. Data on risks associated with illness and death guide the selection of objectives and focus areas. Health care system problems, behavioral factors, environmental hazards, and human biological factors are also considered in the selection of objectives. The reports classify preventable risks and tally them to find the best opportunities for risk reduction.

Healthy People goals do not have the force of law, only the power of persuasion. Nonetheless, they have proved contagious, guiding priorities, informing decisions, and influencing government spending. Other federal agencies, states, localities, and the private sector have embraced these goals. The New York City Department of Health and Hygiene uses Healthy People goals to guide and gauge its own performance. Forty-four states, the District of Columbia, and Guam have replicated the Healthy People model and adopted their own health promotion and disease prevention objectives to guide local health initiatives.[18]

Congress incorporated Healthy People objectives into several laws and programs, including the Indian Health Care Improvement Act, the Maternal and Child Health Block Grant, and the Preventive Health and Health Services Block Grant. Indeed, the positive congressional response to Healthy People goals suggests that federal agencies can use goal setting as a way to start (or continue) a conversation with Congress about appropriate priorities.

The federal government did not assume other levels of government would embrace Healthy People targets; it worked hard to build support. It offered technical assistance to encourage states and localities to undertake their own tailored Healthy People efforts and created the Healthy People Consortium, made up of 350 national membership organizations in addition to state and territorial health agencies.[19]

The Healthy People initiative also stimulated nongovernmental financial support to advance its goals. The Robert Wood Johnson Foundation, for example, awarded a grant in 1997 to direct the attention of American businesses to Healthy People goals.[20] A Healthy People Business Advisory Council was created to encourage attention to Healthy People goals in the workplace.

The intergovernmental trajectory of one Healthy People objective suggests how federal goal setting can influence others. The 1979 Healthy People report identified cigarette smoking as the single most preventable cause of death and adopted a smoking cessation target.[21] Since that time and without central coordination, other federal agencies, states, and local governments have adopted a wide variety of actions to prevent smoking. These include taxes, lawsuits, warning labels, and bans on smoking in public places. Uncoordinated goal-focused intergovernmental action, led at different times by different levels of government, has driven U.S. smoking levels down dramatically since the mid-1960s, when the surgeon general first issued a report warning of the dangers of smoking.[22]

Well-selected federal goals, these vignettes suggest, have a powerful persuasive effect when they deal with issues that concern people and are backed by evidence showing the relative importance of a problem and the existence of effective prevention practices. They inspire effort and investment by others. Experience with the Healthy People initiative suggests that federal agencies can use the federal bully pulpit to set goals that persuade, even without incentives.

Is Healthy People an exception or does it offer a model for other policy areas? Arguably, four replicable attributes of the initiative caused states and localities to align voluntarily with federally nominated objectives. First, its goals focused on issues that concern the public. Second, goal selection was informed by accumulation, analysis, and publication of data about the relative seriousness of problems needing attention. Third, Healthy People reports tally not only problems but also their preventable causes, suggesting a path for problem reduction. Fourth, the federal government used the goals to reach out broadly to recruit experts and implementers whose independent actions and decisions could improve health outcomes.[23]

It has been suggested that Healthy People is unique because the health field is rich with data and is an area with high goal congruence across government levels. However, Healthy People lacked data for about one-third of the objectives it set when it started. A decade later, it had reduced that gap to 20 percent because agencies started to generate the data they needed. In addition, data shortages in federal agencies are not always as desperate as claimed. Many agencies collect reams of data they never analyze, forgoing opportunities to understand the relative import of problems, their causes, and prevention possibilities.[24]

With regard to concern about goal congruence, intergovernmental goal dissonance undoubtedly exists. Differing values and the cost of goal pursuit make debates about government's goal selection and the appropriate portfolio of goals common. Those conflicts intensify across levels of government, especially when goals set by one level impose costs on another. Goal dissonance is less an issue with hortatory federal goals. Contention rises when Congress makes state or local goal adoption mandatory and threatens penalties. It can also rise when goal adoption is required as a new condition added to existing intergovernmental grants routinely awarded every year.

Even with agreement about specific goals, states and localities can get testy about federal goal setting. When the U.S. Department of Transportation first adopted GPRA goals and selected safety as its number-one priority, states protested. They urged the department to select a customer service target instead. The department declined. Despite their protest, state officials eventually adopted the same shared priority goal the federal government had selected: safety. In this situation, the problem was not goal dissonance but resistance to federal goal selection without state input and fear that the goal would eventually be used in ways that embarrassed states, such as report cards.

Because the federal agency chose a priority goal that concerned the public and promised not to generate report cards, the goal conflict subsided.[25]

The Healthy People and Department of Transportation examples suggest that many federal agencies may miss opportunities to tap the performance-driving power of specific, challenging goals, especially those chosen based on data about problems and their preventable causes. Moreover, when agencies share data about the relative import, characteristics, and causes of the problems they are trying to reduce, they can influence state and local goal selection. Even within constraints of laws they implement and limited data availability, federal managers can turn to specific, challenging goals to activate and orchestrate other levels of government. These are two of the three key skills Lester Salamon identifies as key to managerial success in third-party arrangements.[26] And, as with Healthy People, federal agencies can use evidence-informed goals to converse with Congress about priorities.

Measurement

Without measurement, goals are merely words. Measurement brings a goal alive. Measurement serves multiple functions that contribute to performance improvement. It motivates, illuminates, and communicates.[27] Measurement also informs the selection of goals, strategies, and tactics. The rich, outcome-focused measurement of Healthy People supported goal setting, goal reinforcement, and goal attainment.

Measurement motivates because people (and organizations) take pride in their accomplishments and like to do well. Measurement illuminates problems, programs, or places needing attention. It reveals which problems have a higher incidence and greater consequences, causal factors linked to the problems, and their frequency. It also reveals malfunctioning processes that need fixing. Measurement also illuminates promising prevention and treatment practices. Comparable measurement of similar performance units identifies top performers worth studying to determine whether their actions merit replication. Tracking changes before and after the introduction of a new government practice suggests possible effects of the practice. Investigating anomalies to understand why they occur can lead to the discovery of unexpected solutions as well as unknown problems.

In addition, measurement communicates. Measuring progress toward priority goals reinforces their importance. The failure to measure progress toward a priority goal signals that the espoused priority is, in fact, not a priority. Measurement also supports cooperation among multiple parties. It shifts attention from turf battles about assumed solutions to an examination of the evidence, strategy formulation, and assignment of responsibilities.[28] In addition, well-communicated measurement informs electoral and consumer choice, serving as a sort of market mechanism leading to improved societal outcomes.[29]

Measurement also helps organizations better calibrate the ambitiousness of a goal and their strategies. Without measurement, researchers find, people tend to judge their past practices as more effective than they in fact were, resulting in adoption of overly ambitious goals and subsequent investment in wasteful strategies.[30]

Although goals need measurement to be effective, measurement does not always need a goal to be useful. Comparison with the past, peers, or other problems naturally sets de facto goals, although caution must be exercised when using peer comparison to avoid discouraging those who do not like to compete and encouraging others to game the system.[31]

Experience suggests that the kind of information federal agencies collect from states and localities and the way they use it affects both outcomes and intergovernmental contentiousness. When federal agencies gather information primarily for knowledge management, to help states and localities learn from their own and others' experience, measurement is a powerful intergovernmental tool that improves performance and enhances accountability without dampening state and local flexibility. When they use it primarily to determine grant eligibility, document compliance with grant conditions, or motivate improvement by embarrassing low performers, measurement rankles.

The experience of the federal road (now highway) program illustrates the potential of measurement as a tool of influence.[32] When the first federal road office was established in 1904, it made information the center of its strategy for working with states. It gathered information about road conditions, mileage, and program characteristics in every county and conducted experiments to find effective road- and bridge-building practices and then frequently disseminated its findings to other levels of government. Information collection, analysis, and dissemination was and is a core federal highway function.[33] In 2000 the Federal Highway Administration modernized its knowledge management role by launching online versions of its publications and databases to reach more interested users.[34]

Congress requires the secretary of transportation to report annually on the condition and performance of the nation's roads but does not mandate inclusion of state-specific data in the annual report. The Federal Highway Administration opted to establish state reporting requirements through regulation.

Despite the absence of federal law mandating state reporting, states have willingly delivered data to the federal government for more than fifty years. Why? According to one agency official, "We have been doing highway statistical information for 50 to 60 years, and have turned it back [to the states] from the beginning. We have always done some value-added work when we turned it back to the states. It lets them see what other states were doing, and they see the data as a really valuable resource."[35] By functioning as a knowledge manager serving states and localities, the federal road agency built a performance-improving partnership with states that has flourished more than 100 years.

As automobile use increased, so did accidents. In 1966 Congress responded by adopting a new federal goal: highway traffic safety. It required every state to establish a highway safety program in accordance with uniform federal standards.[36] The National Highway Traffic Safety Administration (NHTSA) funds state employees in every state to review and code incident reports, such as police crash and coroner reports, collected for local purposes. State staff record data about traffic-related fatalities before, during, and after each accident, noting key characteristics of physical, social, and environmental conditions associated with the accident such as the state of the operator, type of equipment, and accident costs. They submit the information to a national highway fatality database. A dozen states voluntarily supplement the NHTSA's fatality database with their own data about nonfatal crashes.

The NHTSA not only supports and collects measurement, it also functions as the scientist in Brandeis's laboratories of democracy. It studies the data it collects to look for patterns of problems, such as accident levels correlated with driver age and alcohol use. It determines the most prevalent problems needing attention. It also looks for anomalies and tries to understand their causes. For example, the NHTSA helped one state understand why it had a higher right-angle crash rate than other states: as it turned out, more driveways in the state feed directly onto major thoroughfares than in other states. When states change their laws, the NHTSA compares changes in fatality rates in changed and unchanged states. Studying the effects of changes in state laws enabled the NHTSA to discover that when states allow police to pull people over to check safety belt use (instead of checking only when police stop drivers for other reasons), it increases belt use and lowers fatality rates.[37]

The NHTSA also uses measurement to help states find and replicate effective practices.[38] North Carolina identified an interesting program in Canada that combined a media campaign with a "stop-and-check" blitz to increase seat belt use. North Carolina replicated the program, with good results. South Carolina wanted to try it but lacked primary enforcement ("stop-and-check") authority, so the state sought help from the NHTSA to adapt the North Carolina program. The NHTSA developed audience-focused outreach materials to increase public awareness of the importance of wearing safety belts, including sample materials packaged for key target audiences such as schools (for example, morning announcements), law enforcement officials, parents, and others.[39] The adaptation worked; after adoption, belt usage increased 9 percent in South Carolina and other southeastern states.[40] The NHTSA then rolled the approach out nationally, simultaneously promoting state adoption of primary enforcement laws. It used grants to recruit volunteer states to participate in a controlled, measured experiment. Ten states tested the NHTSA Click It or Ticket campaign, four states served as a control group that did nothing, and four states tested programs of their own design. The NHTSA funded observers to measure belt use before and after the campaign, using a common measurement methodology. Belt use increased 8.2 percent in full implementation states, 2.7 percent in states using programs of their own design, and 0.5 percent in the control group of states.[41]

The NHTSA's data-rich, audience-focused work with states and localities dramatically improves outcomes. Automobile fatality rates have fallen in all but two of the past twenty-five years, and safety belt use climbed from 58 percent in 1994 to 81 percent in 2006.[42]

Intergovernmental measurement efforts are not always so successful. Data collection for early urban grant programs was more troubled because program offices used the data "as a means of control rather than a means of knowing."[43] Programs used data to determine grant eligibility or calculate grant size, or they required planning and needs assessments for grant applications. Unfortunately, programs did not analyze the plans or the data they collected to understand the nature of urban problems, nor did they search for state and local programs that might be worthy of replication. They measured simply to monitor compliance or justify spending, forfeiting a valuable opportunity to make measurement useful to data suppliers, key decisionmakers, and the public.

The evolution of intergovernmental measurement in the education field is also revealing. States began voluntarily supplying education data to the federal government in 1869, which the federal government organized and published in data tables. Several problems limited the performance-improving value of state education data. It was not standardized across states or even within a single state. Few states gathered outcome information, so the federal government could not determine whether any had improved outcomes over time. And although looking at local variations in educational outcome is essential to finding effective approaches because education is delivered locally, the federal government did not collect local data.[44]

Changes in education data measurement have evolved to fix these problems. Data standardization began in the 1950s, and the federal government began gathering data from local governments in the mid-1970s. Collection of educational outcome information did not begin until the 1990s, however. As with federal managers of urban grants, managers of federal education programs resisted efforts to collect educational outcome data along with the data they already collected about students and spending because outcomes are hard to control and might show problems that put program funding at risk.[45]

Congress finally decided it needed outcome data to inform its decision-making and created the National Center for Education Statistics in 1965. State education officials initially supported the creation of the office but changed their position as data-supplying proposals emerged. They feared an increased workload, being embarrassed by poor comparative performance, and meddling by Washington. Without strong state support, even with a congressional mandate, the newly formed educational statistics unit could not fight the resistance of powerful "program managers . . . [who] had no intention of relinquishing control over data they were collecting to establish eligibility for federal funding, to monitor state and local compliance with federal regulations, and to justify the program's existence to Congress."[46]

The first successful federal attempt to gather educational outcome data came in 1969 with the creation of the National Assessment of Educational Progress (NAEP). Again fearing embarrassment, state program officials sought to water it down. They made sure the NAEP measured educational outcomes only at the national level and could not detect state- and local-level performance differences. This, of course, prevented the National Center for Education Statistics from analyzing variations to find effective practices that would help states and localities improve.[47]

State attitudes about outcome data began to change in the 1980s when federal and state political leaders got exercised about educational quality. In 1981 the U.S. secretary of education convened the National Commission on Excellence in Education. The commission's 1983 report, *A Nation at Risk,* showed Americans scoring last on seven out of nineteen international academic tests and never scoring first or second.[48] Like the Healthy People reports, *A Nation at Risk* used measurement to nominate an issue for national attention.

State governors responded. Concerned about the economic consequences of inadequate education for students in their states, the nation's governors overrode the objections of their own state program officials and asked the federal government to administer state-level NAEP tests. Because not every governor wanted this information, the governors requested it on a voluntary basis. By 1996 forty-four states had voluntarily requested some form of NAEP testing.[49]

The 1984 cohort of governors, one of whom eventually became president and two of whom eventually became secretaries of education, pressed aggressively for a stronger federal role in educational outcome measurement throughout the 1980s and early 1990s.[50] In 1994 Congress responded by passing the first federal law mandating that every state measure educational outcomes. It took the governors, acting collectively, to lead the charge for federal action to produce measurement of educational outcomes. Even with the state-initiated push to require every state to measure outcomes, the 1994 law let each state set its own standards and explicitly prohibited federal agency action on national standards, even voluntary ones.[51]

A confluence of political events, including the presidential election of another governor who strongly supported mandated state measurement of educational outcomes, moved common outcome measurement one step further with the No Child Left Behind Act of 2001 (NCLB).[52] NCLB delicately balances intergovernmental measurement and federal mandates. It lets states set their own standards of educational performance but mandates that every state participate in NAEP testing. The law also strengthens sanctions on states that fail to measure progress toward state-set standards, since many states had not complied with that requirement in the 1994 law, and requires each state to ensure that every school makes adequate performance progress against its own standards.

NCLB quickly stirred up the perennial intergovernmental tug-of-war. The Connecticut attorney general, citing the high cost of measurement, sued the federal government.[53] Yet despite state pressure to change some provisions of NCLB, including great unhappiness with NCLB sanctions, the nation's governors urged federal adoption of a common method for measuring high school dropout rates and remain supportive of the federal government's collecting common outcome data. Much to the surprise of their own program officials, several years after the law's passage, governors continued to endorse the idea of the federal government's holding states accountable for student learning while calling for greater flexibility.[54]

NCLB's focus on outcomes has not changed the control orientation of federal Department of Education program offices. The law includes statutory deadlines and punishment-triggering accountability mechanisms that keep program offices consumed with control rather than the search for and promotion of replication-worthy practices.

NCLB has, however, resulted in a stronger research and statistics office that is beginning to play a learning leadership role. The Department of Education now funds an annual compilation of school-level performance measurement from every grade in every school in every state, normalizing school scores by comparison with state median scores for each grade and using the NAEP to put state scores in perspective. The Department of Education makes these normalized school data available to the public, inviting analysis by those outside government. A nongovernmental organization, Education Trust, has accepted this implied invitation every year, releasing an annual report identifying high-performing schools in high-poverty, high-minority areas. Education Trust encourages other researchers to look for distinguishing practices that are evident in these high-performing schools but not in low-performing ones, practices that others might want to adopt.[55] The Department of Education has also built a "what works" clearinghouse and provides online data-mining tools to facilitate comparisons along specific dimensions (for example, math performance trends in grade 8 in urban schools) to aid the search for models with useful lessons.[56]

Block grants that combine existing categorical grants advancing narrowly specified federal goals into a single more flexible grant can be particularly challenging for federal agencies that want to create an outcome-focused measurement system that helps grantees learn from one another's experience, especially when Congress constrains federal agency flexibility in promulgating regulations implementing the laws.[57] Yet even with block grants, federal agencies can work with states to acquire the needed outcome-focused information if they adopt a learning and leadership attitude. In implementing the maternal and child health block grant, the U.S. Health Resources and Services Administration negotiated with states a common set of outcome indicators every state would report. Each state can choose its own priorities, but all states must report the same outcome indicators. Indicator selection is an ongoing process and improves as everyone learns. Healthy People targets provide the context for, but do not dictate, indicator selection. The health resources agency also posts national and state priorities and performance on the web.[58]

The experience with measurement in urban grant programs, education, transportation, and maternal and child health suggests federal agencies that depend on states and localities to accomplish their objectives would speed performance improvements, reduce intergovernmental contention, and enhance democratic and performance accountability if they made the knowledge management function more central to their intergovernmental relationships, especially since passage of the GPRA. Laws such as the Paperwork Reduction Act, the Federal Education Rights and Privacy Act, and other federal legal restrictions can make this difficult, yet the experience with Healthy People, the NHTSA, the Health Resources and Services Administration, and the Department of Education suggest it is an effort worth making. Agencies should place greater emphasis on building measurement systems that advance understanding of problems, probable causes, and effective prevention, treatment, and mitigation practices rather than monitoring primarily for control.

Incentives

What happens when incentives, both negative and positive, are used with goals and measurement? Answering this question is critical for containing unconstructive intergovernmental tensions and improving societal outcomes.

Incentives can be remarkably effective. Even with knowledge that fewer fatalities occur at fifty-five miles an hour than at eighty, many more people would speed down the highway if they did not fear the threat of a traffic ticket and higher insurance rates. But incentives can also discourage people and organizations, triggering high levels of stress and dysfunctional responses.[59]

Structuring incentives appropriately is a tricky business. Managers need to master what Salamon calls "modulation" skills "to decide what combination of incentives and penalties to bring to bear to achieve the outcomes desired."[60] Experience suggests that federal managers should use grants primarily to identify, strengthen, and sometimes create goal allies and to stimulate common outcome measurement across states and localities. They should use penalty threats to compel adoption of goals dealing with serious but locally ignored problems and spur development and implementation of cogent strategies.

GRANTS. Both grants and penalties require prior congressional authorization. Federal grants account for about a quarter of state and local expenditures.[61] Grants are often seen as "the initial tool used to stimulate interest and adoption."[62] But grants have limited value as a performance driver unless paired with outcome-focused goals and measurement. Without them, grants risk generating "ineffectual" data and "useless forms of window dressing."[63] When paired with outcome-focused goals and used to stimulate standardized outcome-focused measurement, though, grants are remarkably effective.

The federal government uses grants "to influence the conduct of state and local governments in such a way as to promote the realization of its own goals." The simple act of offering a grant, especially a categorical grant for a specific purpose, nominates an item of federal interest for local political attention. Grants can stimulate healthy local debate about goals and the right balance among competing priorities. Federal grants essentially initiate an extended intergovernmental negotiation regarding both ends and means.[64]

One way grants influence the selection of state and local goals is by lowering the cost of pursuing a specific objective, but federal grants seem to work most powerfully in another way: they identify, strengthen, and sometimes even create local goal allies. By applying for a grant, states and localities indicate their shared interest in a problem that concerns the federal government.[65]

The availability of a grant strengthens a local ally's bargaining position in the battle for local resources, and grant deadlines give local goal allies a reason to move an issue up on the local action agenda.[66] Federal grants have successfully created a core of professional counterparts in the states, often a single state agency, who function as perennial goal allies. Their ability as allies to improve outcomes is limited, however, if grant conditions tend more to administrative matters than to outcomes.[67]

Even when grants are allocated by formula rather than competitive application, they can boost existing local goal allies. Block grants help local allies by providing them with resources to do what they already want to do without local strings attached. Categorical formula grants that routinely get distributed to the same program every year sustain local goal allies' ability to devote time to federally nominated problems.[68]

In addition to identifying and strengthening goal allies, federal grants can stimulate the generation of standardized data and state and local measurement capacity. When these data aid the public in understanding outcomes, data-stimulating grants enhance democratic accountability. When agencies require measurement simply to determine funding levels or document the completion of required activities, such grants have little democracy-enhancing value.

Federal agencies can also use grants and in-kind assistance to enrich the value of collected data. The Federal Highway Administration provided grants to states to develop software that transformed data collected for federal purposes to information useful for state budgeting and planning.[69] The Centers for Disease Control and Prevention purchased business intelligence software licenses to enable it to work more closely with states on epidemiology, disease detection, and response activities.[70]

Federal grants can also support experimentation and innovation to find more effective and cost-effective interventions. Federal agencies can use grants to attract participants to measured experiments, as the NHTSA has done. Nonrecurring grants are useful as seed capital to test new approaches or to pay one-time costs for equipment upgrades.[71] For these kinds of grants to be useful, however, their effect needs to be assessed. Otherwise, ineffective practices are likely to be repeated.

Perhaps the biggest challenge with intergovernmental grant management arises in setting and managing grant conditions.[72] Grant conditions are established to ensure that the federal government gets what it thinks it is buying for its money, rather than simply relieving the local tax burden or supporting local projects that do not advance federal objectives. Grant conditions can successfully catalyze constructive change in states and localities, but they can also result in wasteful activities.[73]

Federal agencies often stipulate administrative conditions. These are very effective when a clear link has been established between the administrative action required and the target outcome. Administrative conditions have been effective in creating in-state goal allies and measurement capacity and in motivating adoption of practices demonstrated to be effective. Administrative conditions also minimize unethical and illegal grant uses.

Problems arise from the number, nature, and way grant conditions are interpreted. Just staying in compliance with the sheer number of not-always-consistent grant conditions can consume so much grantee time that it precludes pursuit of more productive endeavors. Another problem arises when grant conditions fail "to cover the questions of major substantive importance" and focus instead on administrative, personnel, and fiscal practices.[74] Yet federal agencies opt for administrative rather than outcome-focused grant conditions for several sensible reasons: the need to recruit local allies who might not apply if they fear grant conditions will expect them to change societal conditions they cannot fully control; the relative ease of tracking administrative matters instead of outcomes; and the political difficulty of selecting specific outcome targets, especially values-based ones.[75]

The problem is that administrative grant conditions often become ends in and of themselves that interfere with outcome gains. Many federal laws, for example, require states and localities to write plans as a grant condition. Agencies confirm plan completion but fail to learn from plan content. They do not look for what the plans say about changes in local conditions that might be instructive for other communities nor for patterns of problems across communities that might respond to common solutions. Sometimes, they do not even expect grantees to use the plans they prepare.[76] As a consequence, many grantees simply complete minimal plans to meet grant conditions but never use them. Grantees submit copious quantities of data as required that are neither analyzed nor returned to data suppliers with enhanced value. When federal agencies use data for control rather than knowing, state and local grantees tend to treat their data-reporting obligation as a task to be completed rather than a contribution to a shared knowledge base from which they will benefit. A vicious cycle is thereby established wherein data suppliers stop worrying about data quality, making the data useless if federal agencies eventually try to analyze them for lessons worth sharing.

Overly rigid interpretation of grant conditions by either the grantee or grantor can also trigger silly decisions. For example, to deal with the worry that federal funds will simply substitute for state or local spending with no net benefit to the community, federal laws and agencies often establish maintenance-of-effort requirements and then try to follow the money trail.[77] This created an absurd situation in one program studied by researchers: a community pulled their educationally disadvantaged students out of the classroom for tutorial instruction. Although "pull-out" programs had been found educationally inferior to in-classroom training and stigmatized students, hiring tutors made it easier to track spending to satisfy federal reporting requirements.[78]

With so many oversight bodies in government looking for problems, grantees seeking to avoid problems must follow rules strictly rather than exercise commonsense discretion. Failure to do so can get them into trouble. One state environmental agency learned this the hard way. The inspector general of the federal Environmental Protection Agency (EPA) criticized the state agency when it let its water quality program borrow a video camera purchased for the air quality program, even though the air program was unable to use the camera full-time.[79]

Following the money also creates the impression that federal budget watchers can calculate return on federal spending. When federal money gets put in a pot with state and local money to advance a shared objective, determining what those federal dollars bought becomes a practical impossibility. To deal with this problem, federal agencies opt to track activities, people, and equipment bought rather than changes in societal outcomes because they are easier to measure. But measuring activities instead of outcomes makes it harder to find out what federal spending, or even federal spending combined with state and local funds, did or did not accomplish.

In sum, grants can be an effective tool of federal influence. They can lower the cost for localities of tackling specific objectives the federal government has judged as important. They can identify, strengthen, and sometimes create goal allies. They can also stimulate generation of standardized data, state and local measurement capacity, local use of collected data, innovation, and program modernization. But grants do not always have a positive effect. When grant conditions are too numerous and rigid, a problem common to mature grant programs, and when attention to administrative matters overwhelms attention to outcomes, grant conditions can cause wasteful activity and compromise program productivity.[80] To drive performance improvement, Congress and federal agencies should first and foremost use grants to persuade states and localities to collect and report credible and comparable outcome and program information. The federal government should also use grants to encourage adoption of specific, challenging outcome-focused targets by the federal government when there is a reason for national targets and by states and localities when there is not. With passage of the GPRA, Congress has, in most cases, given federal agencies implicit authority to make this happen.

Federal agencies must do more than use their grant authority to encourage states and localities to supply outcome information, though. They also need to organize, analyze, and disseminate the data they collect in ways that help state and local decisionmakers make wiser choices about priorities and program design, choices that are informed by evidence about problems and effective interventions. In addition, federal agencies need to encourage analysis by others as the Department of Education has begun to do by making its databases easily accessible on the Internet with online tools to support public analysis. Federal agencies should place a priority on returning knowledge to state and local data suppliers in a way that catches their attention and aids their decisionmaking. They should also regularly engage grantees in discussions of the data to enhance discovery and the learning process.[81] If agencies fail to do this on their own, the U.S. Office of Management and Budget should encourage them to do so during OMB program reviews. Congress, too, should adopt laws requiring agencies to assume a value-adding knowledge management function.

One final observation on grants: many experts describe the intergovernmental arrangement as a principal-agent relationship.[82] The evidence reviewed here suggests that this is not the appropriate conceptual framework. A principal-agent relationship assumes divergent interests of the federal government as the principal and state or local governments as the agent. The grant is seen as a mechanism for aligning the interests and objectives of the principal and agent, and measurement is seen as a monitoring device used to confirm that the agent is serving the needs of the principal. The examples and studies reviewed here, however, suggest that grants should instead be seen as a tool for recruiting, activating, and strengthening those whose interests are already aligned, for orchestrating cooperation and learning among them, and for securing the outcome-focused indicators every state must supply. Measurement, in turn, should be seen not so much as a monitoring mechanism but as a device for strengthening goal allies, supporting their ability to recruit and motivate others, illuminating problems and possibilities, and communicating lessons.

PENALTIES. Grants are a positive, preperformance incentive, whereas penalties are a negative, postperformance motivator. Perhaps the key difference between grants and penalties in the intergovernmental context is that grants invite state and local attention to a goal, whereas penalties compel it. Penalties can be a useful tool to force attention to externalities, the costs one party imposes on another. They are also useful when federal policymakers decide that all states or localities should protect specific rights or ensure a minimum level of well-being for their residents.

Because they are coercive, penalties are far more contentious than grants. Penalties can effectively drive performance gains and stimulate democratic debate, but they can also polarize political positions. In addition, they can galvanize organized opposition that successfully constrains federal program authority and contributes to performance declines. The federal government must therefore exercise great caution when using penalties to avoid positional stalemates, measurement manipulation, implosion of the measurement system, or elimination of its penalty power. It must master its modulation skills.

Penalties can effectively compel others to adopt a target and to take actions necessary to meet that target even when significant expenditure of local resources is needed to do so. With the Clean Air Act Amendments of 1990, for example, Congress succeeded in getting local attention to air quality problems by threatening the loss of lucrative federal highway funds (an exception was made for highway safety projects) and curbs on development. Under this law, sanctions are automatically triggered if a community does not meet various federally set air quality standards by specified dates. Over nearly two decades, the potential loss of this big pot of dollars has successfully convinced states and localities to adopt costly actions, such as vehicle air emission inspection programs. It has also improved air quality. States and

localities have seldom embraced these measures enthusiastically or immediately, but they have eventually adopted numerous practices resulting in
improved air quality.

Penalties are useful not only for forcing attention to a problem but also for
motivating states to measure outcomes. Little progress was made reducing
tobacco sales to minors until Congress adopted a penalty for states that did
not use a common and credible method to measure sales. Since then, all fifty
states have reported tobacco sales to minors annually, and tobacco sales have
steadily declined.[83] Smoking among minors has also declined significantly in
the same period, although not solely owing to reduced sales to minors.[84]

Penalties can also increase the use of data by local communities, contributing to better informed decisions. The 1968 Intermodal Surface Transportation and Efficiency Act required states to adopt six different information
management systems or lose up to 10 percent of transportation monies
awarded under the act. The mandate infuriated states, who successfully lobbied Congress to eliminate it. Ironically, even after the penalty was eliminated, most states ultimately adopted the mandated management systems
anyway because they found them useful.[85] Penalties proved an effective
short-term way to promote adoption of learning tools that persisted even
after the penalties were removed.

Federal penalties to encourage state adoption of universal motorcycle helmet laws have been similarly effective, albeit highly contentious. The Highway Safety Act of 1966 threatened states that did not adopt universal helmet
laws with the loss of 10 percent of federal-aid highway funds. Although no
states had universal helmet laws in 1966, all but California and Utah had
adopted them by 1975.[86] When the secretary of transportation moved to
penalize these two noncompliant states, his action galvanized intense opposition. Already furious about the loss of their freedom to ride without a helmet
which they valued more highly than the personal safety benefit of a helmet,
motorcycle riders convinced Congress to eliminate federal penalty power and
restore their freedom to ride as they choose. Soon thereafter, twenty-eight
states dropped their universal helmet laws.

Congress again authorized federal penalties in 1991. This time, the
National Highway Traffic Safety Administration moved quickly to penalize
more than half the states for failure to adopt universal helmet laws. It moved
too fast. In 1995 Congress repealed federal helmet penalty authority at the
insistence of newly elected Colorado senator Ben Nighthorse Campbell, a
motorcycle rider who liked neither helmets nor federal mandates.[87] As of

March 2008, only twenty states and the District of Columbia had universal helmet laws, twenty-seven required younger riders to wear helmets, and three states had no helmet law at all.[88] As the number of states with universal helmet laws has fallen, motorcycle fatalities have steadily climbed.[89]

When do penalties work, compelling local attention to a goal and local actions to attain it, and when do they backfire? Several factors may explain the success or failure of a penalty: the size of the penalty, its structure, the validity of mandated actions (dependent on the quality of the evidence about changed outcomes), the strength of organized opponents compared with that of organized proponents, and the presence of interstate externalities.

The size of the penalty matters. The 1991 motorcycle helmet penalty law allowed the federal government to shift a portion of federal highway construction funds for noncompliant states to state transportation safety programs, a far weaker threat than the 1975 penalty of a 10 percent holdback of federal aid for highways. All but two states eventually changed their practices in response to the 1975 penalty threat, but only two states adopted new universal helmet laws between the passage of the 1991 law and its 1995 repeal.[90]

Penalty structure also matters. A pyramid of escalating responses motivates compliance more effectively than a one-size-fits-all penalty.[91] Under the Clean Air Act as amended in 1990, a state's failure to meet a nationally set air quality target triggers the commencement of an escalating response process, not immediate curtailment of highway funding and development flexibility. A state that does not meet its target must develop a cogent strategy to do so, the state implementation plan. It must get the plan approved and then implement it. Each state develops its own strategy, using air quality data gathered with federal financial support in accordance with national standards and evidence about effective interventions. The federal EPA uses a model to project whether a state's proposed pollution control measures will meet the standards by the target date. When it deems proposed actions inadequate, it negotiates with the state other actions needed. The agency cuts funding and development flexibility only as a last resort, when a state refuses to develop and implement an acceptable implementation plan. The performance accountability approach used in the federal air quality law, exercising the extreme penalty of funding cuts and development restrictions not if a state fails to meet its target but only if it fails to measure air quality, develop cogent strategies, and implement them, has also been used successfully in other federal programs.[92] The approach also corresponds to the performance accountability principle attributed to former New York City police commissioner

William Bratton for precinct captains: "No one ever got in trouble if the crime rate went up. They got in trouble if they did not know why it had gone up and did not have a plan to deal with it."[93]

One mistake federal agencies sometimes make is to penalize states and localities for failure to adopt specific practices that are not backed by evidence of their effectiveness. Early versions of the EPA model used to review the adequacy of state plans to achieve air quality targets, for example, used assumptions about the effects of air pollution control actions that even EPA regional staff did not understand and could not explain to states. Not surprisingly, this enraged the states. The agency subsequently relieved this problem by updating the models it uses to assess state plans, making the underlying evidence and assumptions transparent, and engaging states in model development. Intergovernmental tensions on plan reviews have subsided significantly. They have not abated completely, of course, because few like having their discretion restricted and being required to obtain another's approval.

Despite state fury about the initial EPA black-box review and penalty threat under the Clean Air Act, states were unable to eliminate penalties as motorcycle helmet opponents had. The penalty threats of both laws catalyzed organized, powerful, and sustained opposition, but in the case of the federal air quality law, highly organized proponents including the American Lung Association successfully countered the opponents and preserved federal penalty authority.[94]

Another possible reason for the survival of the penalty threat is that states themselves have different views about federal penalties. Downwind states bear health care and compliance costs from upwind polluters. They want the EPA to have the power to reduce negative interstate externalities.

Penalties need not be financial to be effective; they can also be reputational. External advocates commonly use comparative data to try to embarrass government agencies into better performance. Federal agencies, however, are likely to encounter trouble if they try comparisons to embarrass or otherwise penalize low-performing states and localities.[95] Such actions can trigger resistance to outcome-focused measurement and prompt "cream skimming," whereby programs opt to serve clients that boost their own performance ratings rather than those with the greatest need or potential for gain. In addition, it can lead to submission of data so poor they are useless.[96] Federal agencies are likely to be more successful when they use comparison to find programs worth replicating, not to penalize.

Penalties, like grants, appear to be an effective federal tool for catalyzing local debate about a federally nominated problem. Unlike grants, which invite the debate, penalties force it. This makes them particularly useful for dealing with interjurisdictional externalities and national minimum standards that are costly for states and localities to address. More than just stimulating debate, federal penalties compel other levels of government to adopt and pursue federally nominated targets, as they did with air quality improvements around the country and, while they lasted, reduced motorcycle fatalities. They can also be effective in getting jurisdictions to use common measurement methods. They compelled measurement of tobacco sales to minors. Penalties also increased state and local use of infrastructure management software tools. But penalties are provocative, especially when they compel actions that seem unreasonable to those asked to take them or violate values held dear. They are especially provocative when a federal agency quickly exercises the most costly version of a penalty, rather than holding it in reserve as an available threat. A modulated, escalating response strategy that uses the harshest punishments only as a last resort is likely to be more effective. If no proponents are strong enough to counter opponents galvanized into action when penalties are used, federal penalty authority can be eliminated as a tool in ongoing intergovernmental negotiations about the right balance of government goals to pursue.

Conclusion

How can federal managers dependent on other levels of government to accomplish their objectives manage most effectively to improve performance and enhance accountability? Answering this question is especially important since passage of the GPRA, which requires every federal agency to set outcome-focused goals and report progress annually to Congress. Goals, measurement, and incentives are powerful tools federal agencies can use to navigate the practical and political aspects of intergovernmental program delivery.

Federal agencies can exercise effective leadership by engaging experts and stakeholders in reviewing the evidence and then nominating goals needing national, state, and local attention, as the Department of Health and Human Services does with its decennial Healthy People reports, inspiring, activating, and orchestrating goal allies and stimulating healthy democratic discussion about priorities among the levels and branches of government. They can do this even without an explicit link to positive and negative incentives.

Federal agencies can promote learning in states and localities by encouraging measurement, using grants and regulations to stimulate common outcome-focused measurement as needed. They can give the data they collect greater value by organizing, analyzing, disseminating, and using them to understand problems and identify solutions, as the NHTSA does routinely and as the Department of Education did when it normalized state and local perform- ance data, assembled them into a single database others could analyze, and supported analysis by providing online data analysis tools.

Federal agencies should use grants to recruit, strengthen, and sustain goal allies and to stimulate the generation and sharing of standardized outcome- focused measurement, negotiating the content, timing, and technical aspects of data submission. If a federal agency lacks the authority to require out- come-focused data submission, it should make the case to Congress to obtain that authority. Federal agencies can even make this work when using block grants, as the Health Resources and Services Administration did with the maternal and child health block grant, whereby each state chooses its own priorities but all states report on a common set of outcome indicators.

Federal agencies should use penalties with care to compel attention to fed- erally set goals and obtain useful measurements. The most extreme penalties are more powerful as a threat than when imposed, when they can so upset those threatened by penalties that they provoke formation of an opposition coalition. Before penalizing another level of government because it has failed to achieve a target or to take a specific action, federal agencies should focus first on getting grantees and those threatened by penalties to adopt outcome- focused targets set by Congress (or at congressional instruction, by the agency) or set their own outcome-focused goals, measure progress toward goals using common indicators, develop cogent strategies based on the best available evidence, and implement the strategies. If local political views make it difficult even to get the goal adopted, federal agencies should help local goal allies make the case for change, using penalty threats incrementally to help them win local attention and allies.

More research is clearly needed to understand under what circumstances goals, measurement, grants, and penalties are likely to work in an intergovern- mental context. It is hoped that this chapter inspires that research. It is also hoped that this discussion provides useful interim guidance to Congress in writing new laws and to federal agencies in managing programs that require them to depend on other levels of government to accomplish their objectives.

Notes

1. *New State Ice Co.* v. *Liebmann,* 285 U.S. 262, 52 S.Ct. 371, 76 L.Ed. 747 (1932).

2. For an introductory discussion of knowledge management, see Robert M. Grant, "Toward a Knowledge-Based Theory of the Firm," special issue, *Strategic Management*

Journal 17 (Winter 1996): 109–12. For a discussion of leadership, see David M. Messick and Roderick M. Kramer, eds., *The Psychology of Leadership: New Perspectives and Research* (Mahwah, N.J.: Lawrence Erlbaum, 2005).

3. Martha Derthick, *The Influence of Federal Grants: Public Assistance in Massachusetts* (Harvard University Press, 1970); Timothy Conlan, "Grants Management in the Twenty-First Century: Three Innovative Policy Responses," IBM Center for the Business of Government, 2005, pp. 10–12; quotation is from Eugene Bardach and Cara Lesser, "Accountability in Human Services Collaboratives: For What? And to Whom?" *Journal of Public Administration Research and Theory* 6 (April 1996): 197–224, p. 201.

4. Steven Kelman, "Improving Service Delivery in the United Kingdom: Organization Theory Perspectives on Central Intervention Strategies," *Journal of Comparative Policy Analysis* 8 (December 2006): 393–419; David G. Frederickson, "The Potential of the Government Performance and Results Act as a Tool to Manage Third-Party Government," PricewaterhouseCoopers Endowment for the Business of Government, August 2001; Shelley Metzenbaum, "Strategies for Using State Information: Measuring and Improving Program Performance," PricewaterhouseCoopers Endowment for the Business of Government, December 2003 (http://businessofgovernment.org/pdfs/Metzenbaum_Report.pdf).

5. Paul E. Peterson, *The Price of Federalism* (Brookings, 1995).

6. The powers of the states and people are laid out in the Tenth Amendment to the U.S. Constitution. The system of checks and balances is the subject of James Madison, *Federalist* No. 51, in *Federalist Papers,* by Alexander Hamilton, James Madison, and John Jay (London: Penguin Classics, 1987).

7. Daniel J. Elazar, *American Federalism: A View from the States,* 2nd ed. (New York: Thomas Y. Crowell, 1972); Thomas R. Dye, *American Federalism: Competition among Governments* (Lexington, Mass.: Lexington Books, 1990).

8. Conlan, "Grants Management in the Twenty-First Century," p. 13.

9. Peterson, *Price of Federalism,* p. 13.

10. An outcome-focused goal is one that focuses on the real-world conditions that a program seeks to change, such as water quality, percentage of people living in substandard housing, and commute times, rather than on agency activities, such as the number of permits issued, inspections conducted, or penalties collected.

11. James Fossett and others, "Federalism and Performance Management: Health Insurance, Food Stamps, and the Take-Up Challenge," in *Quicker, Better, Cheaper: Managing Performance in American Government,* edited by Dall W. Forsythe (Albany, N.Y.: Rockefeller Institute Press, 2001), pp. 207–44.

12. Radin and others see the GPRA and the Program Assessment Rating Tool as two distinct and incompatible entities. According to the Office of Management and Budget, PART was developed "to give true effect to the spirit as well as the letter of the law [GPRA]" (Office of Management and Budget, "Rating the Performance of Federal Programs," in *The Budget for Fiscal Year 2004* [2003] [www.gpoaccess.gov/usbudget/fy04/pdf/budget/performance.pdf]). Thus PART can be seen as the guidance developed by the federal budget office to advance GPRA adoption in federal agencies, not distinct from the GPRA. For a discussion of the specific weaknesses of PART, see Shelley Metzenbaum,

"Performance Accountability: The Five Building Blocks and Six Essential Practices," IBM Center for the Business of Government (2006).

13. Edwin A. Locke and Gary P. Latham, "Building a Practically Useful Theory of Goal Setting and Task Motivation: A 35-Year Odyssey," *American Psychologist* 57 (September 2002): 706–07; Alvin Zander, *Motives and Goals in Groups* (New Brunswick, N.J.: Transaction Books, 1996).

14. Locke and Latham, "Building a Practically Useful Theory."

15. Gary P. Latham, "Motivate Employee Performance through Goal-Setting," in *Handbook of Principles of Organizational Behavior,* edited by Edwin A. Locke (Malden, Mass.: Blackwell, 2004), pp. 107–19.

16. Janet A. Weiss and Sandy Kristin Piderit, "The Value of Mission Statements in Public Agencies," *Journal of Public Administration Research and Theory* 9 (April 1999): 193–223.

17. U.S. Department of Health and Human Services, Public Health Service, *Healthy People 2000: National Health Promotion and Disease Prevention Objectives,* GPO 017-001-00474-0 (Government Printing Office, 1991); U.S. Department of Health and Human Services, Public Health Service, "Promoting Health/Preventing Disease: Objectives for the Nation," Fall 1980 (www.eric.ed.gov/ERICDocs/data/ericdocs2sql/content_storage_01/0000019b/80/2e/23/e0.pdf); U.S. Department of Health and Human Services, Public Health Service, *Healthy People: The Surgeon General's Report on Health Promotion and Disease Prevention* (U.S. Department of Health, Education, and Welfare, Office of the Assistant Secretary for Health and Surgeon General, 1979 [http://profiles.nlm.nih.gov/NN/B/B/G/K/segments.html]); U.S. Department of Public Health, Public Health Service, *Promoting Health/Preventing Disease: Objectives for the Nation* (http://odphp.osophs.dhhs.gov/pubs/hp2000/pdf/midcours/appdx_b.pdf); U.S. Department of Health and Human Services, *Healthy People 2010: Understanding and Improving Health,* 2d ed. (GPO, November 2000 [www.healthypeople.gov/Document/pdf/uih/2010uih.pdf]).

18. Thomas R. Friedan, M.D., New York City Department of Health and Mental Hygiene, "Mayor's Management Report," September 2007 (www.nyc.gov/html/ops/downloads/pdf/2007_mmr/0907_mmr.pdf); Deborah R. Maiese and Claude Earl Fox, "Laying the Foundation for Healthy People 2010," *Public Health Reports* 113 (January–February 1998): 92–95 (www.phf.org/hp2010/ac1/dm_ef.htm). Also see "How Will the Objectives Be Used?" at the Healthy People website (www.healthypeople.gov/About/objused.htm).

19. *Healthy People 2000 Midcourse Review,* appendix B, "History of the Objectives Development and the Midcourse Review Process" (http://odphp.osophs.dhhs.gov/pubs/hp2000/pdf/midcours/appdx_b.pdf).

20. Maiese and Fox, "Laying the Foundation for Healthy People 2010."

21. Public Health Service, *Healthy People: The Surgeon General's Report on Health Promotion and Disease Prevention,* p. 1–7. This report builds on several earlier surgeon general's reports identifying smoking as a problem.

22. American Lung Association Epidemiology and Statistics Unit, "Trends in Tobacco

Use," November 2004 (www.lungusa.org/atf/cf/%7B7A8D42C2-FCCA-4604-8ADE-7F5D5E762256%7D/SMK1.PDF).

23. It is often suggested that those who set their own goals will have a stronger sense of goal "ownership" and therefore a stronger drive to achieve the goal. Research on goal setting, however, finds that goals set by third parties can be as powerful as self-set goals provided the externally set goals are plausible and the external goal setter possesses sufficient authority to be accepted as a goal setter. The five Healthy People 1979 goals targeting the major life stages were set by a small group in the office of the assistant secretary for health. A broader group of experts convened from around the country set the fifteen priority areas in the 1980 document. Subsequent Healthy People goals and objectives were informed by engagement of the broader public. This suggests that an iterative goal-setting process can work well, with the federal government proposing specific outcome-focused targets based on analysis of the evidence and states and others proposing adjusted targets based on more precise evidence about local conditions and expected effects on known treatments.

24. U.S. General Accounting Office, *Results-Oriented Government: GPRA Has Established a Solid Foundation for Achieving Greater Results,* GAO-04-38 (Government Printing Office, March 10, 2004).

25. Metzenbaum, "Strategies for Using State Information," p. 31.

26. Lester M. Salamon, "The New Governance and the Tools of Public Action," in *The Tools of Government: A Guide to the New Governance,* edited by Lester M. Salamon (Oxford University Press, 2002), pp. 1–47.

27. Metzenbaum, "Performance Accountability."

28. Robert B. Cialdini, *Influence: Science and Practice,* 4th ed. (Boston: Allyn and Bacon, 2001), pp. 157–58.

29. Charles M. Tiebout, "A Pure Theory of Local Expenditures," *Journal of Political Economy* 64 (October 1956): 416–24; Ginger Z. Jin and Phillip Leslie, "The Effects of Information on Product Quality: Evidence from Restaurant Hygiene Grade Cards," *Quarterly Journal of Economics* 118 (May 2003): 409–51.

30. Charles A. Keisler, *The Psychology of Commitment* (Orlando: Academic Press, 1971), cited in Zander, *Motives and Goals in Groups;* Locke and Latham, "Building a Practically Useful Theory."

31. See Metzenbaum, "Performance Accountability," pp. 22–25, for a discussion of the literature on peer comparison as a motivational tool.

32. Except where noted, the discussion of the federal roads and traffic safety office comes from Metzenbaum, "Strategies for Using State Information," pp. 22–33, 57–61.

33. The Federal Highway Administration's "Highway Statistics" for the year 2000 is described in its preface to the "56th of an annual series" (U.S. Department of Transportation, Federal Highway Administration [www.fhwa.dot.gov/ohim/hs00/preface.htm]).

34. "Editor's Notes," *Public Roads* 64 (November–December 2000) (www.tfhrc.gov/pubrds/nov00/ednotes.htm).

35. Quoted in Metzenbaum, "Strategies for Using State Information," p. 23.

36. *Highway Safety Act,* P.L. 89-564.

37. California was the first adopter of "stop-and-check" laws, with police having primary enforcement authority, and the NHTSA was quickly able to see how the changes affected outcomes in the state (U.S. Department of Transportation, *National Highway Traffic Safety Facts 2000: Occupant Protection,* DOT HS 809 327 [www-nrd.nhtsa.dot. gov/Pubs/2000occfacts.pdf]).

38. See, for example, U.S. Department of Transportation, *Strong Legislation: The Key to Saving Lives,* DOT 809 823 (www.nhtsa.dot.gov/people/injury/research/6thAnnual BUAReport/pages/StrongLegislation.htm).

39. See National Highway Traffic Safety Administration, "Click It or Ticket Planner 2006" (www.buckleupamerica.org/ciot-planner/planner/index.cfm). Even before the Internet, the NHTSA and the Federal Highway Administration made their data and research findings available to the public in annual compendiums and newsletters.

40. Metzenbaum, "Strategies for Using State Information," pp. 32–33.

41. Mark G. Solomon and others, *Evaluation of Click It or Ticket Model Programs,* Technical Report DOT HS 809 498, National Highway Traffic and Safety Administration, September 2002 (www.nhtsa.dot.gov/people/injury/airbags/clickit_ticket/clickit composite/clickit_composite.pdf).

42. Fatalities fell from more than 3.0 per 100 million vehicle miles traveled to less than 1.5 (National Highway Traffic Safety Administration, National Center for Statistics and Analysis, *Motor Vehicle Traffic Crash Fatality Counts and Estimates of People Injured,* August 2006, updated December 13, 2006, DOT HS 810 639 [www.nrd.nhtsa.dot.gov/pdf/nrd-30/ncsa/ppt/2006/810639.pdf]); on safety belt use, see National Highway Safety Administration, *Traffic Safety Facts 2006 Data: Occupant Protection,* DOT HS 810 807 (www. nhtsa.gov/portal/site/nhtsa/menuitem.6a6eaf83cf719ad24ec86e10dba046a0/).

43. Judith deNeufville, "Federal Statistics in Local Governments," in *The Politics of Numbers,* edited by William Alonso and Paul Starr (New York: Russell Sage Foundation, 1987), pp. 343–62, 349. The study looked at urban renewal, public housing, area redevelopment, and hospital construction categorical grants and community development block grants.

44. Janet A. Weiss and Judith E. Gruber, "The Managed Irrelevance of Federal Statistics," in Alonso and Starr, *Politics of Numbers,* pp. 363–91.

45. Ibid.

46. Ibid., p. 368.

47. Ibid.; Metzenbaum, "Strategies for Using State Information."

48. National Commission on Excellence in Education, *A Nation at Risk: The Imperative for Educational Reform* (GPO, 1983 [www.ed.gov/pubs/NatAtRisk]).

49. David Grissmer and others, *Improving Student Achievement: What State NAEP Test Scores Tell Us* (Santa Monica, Calif.: RAND, 2000), p. 21.

50. One of the governors leading the 1984 charge, Lamar Alexander, became Bush's secretary of education in 1991. Another, Bill Clinton, was elected president in 1992 and appointed a third governor who had been involved in the 1984 effort, Richard Riley, to be his education secretary. All three urged federal support to help states measure their performance, and all three urged the adoption of voluntary national standards. The

Improving America's Schools Act (P.L. 103-382), reauthorizing the 1965 Elementary and Secondary Education Act, linked Title I funding to the creation and content of state performance standards in the 1994 reauthorization of federal education law. For a more detailed discussion of the governors' role, see Maris A. Vinoskis, "The Road to Charlottesville: The 1989 Education Summit," National Educational Goals Panel, September 1999 (http://govinfo.library.unt.edu/negp/reports/negp30.pdf).

51. Andrew Rudalevige, "No Child Left Behind: Forging a Congressional Compromise," in *No Child Left Behind? The Politics and Practice of School Accountability,* edited by Paul E. Peterson and Martin R. West (Brookings, 2003), pp. 23–54.

52. As Rudalevige ("No Child Left Behind," pp. 34–42) explains, by the time the 1994 education law was up for reauthorization in 2000, educational performance had become a priority for yet another governor, George W. Bush of Texas. In Texas, Bush built on his predecessor's policies to test all students in reading and math in grades 3 to 8 and require that they pass state-issued tests to graduate. Educational accountability through measurement and other means became a campaign theme when Bush ran for president, one described in a campaign position paper that adopted as a goal the mission of the Children's Defense Fund, "to leave no child behind." The new president made action on the education campaign theme among his first postelection legislative moves.

53. In August 2005, the attorney general of the state of Connecticut sued the U.S. government for violating the Unfunded Mandates Reform Act, arguing that the No Child Left Behind law imposed large additional testing costs in violation of federal law (Sam Dillon, "Connecticut Sues the U.S. over School Testing," *New York Times,* August 23, 2005 [www.nytimes.com/2005/08/22/nyregion/22cnd-child.html?st=cse&sq=Blumenthal +education&scp=5]).

54. Regarding dropout rates, see "Governors Sign Compact on High School Graduation Rate at Annual Meeting," news release, National Governors Association, July 17, 2005. Regarding the governors' support for continuing strong federal accountability authority in NCLB, see Alyson Klein, "Governors Enter Fray over NCLB; State Chiefs, Boards Join Plan for Revisions to Law," *Education Week,* April 10, 2007. Klein quotes Mary Kusler, assistant director of government relations for the American Association of School Administrators representing district superintendents, as observing, "It seems strange to me that three state organizations did not harp on the whole federalism issue."

55. Metzenbaum, "Strategies for Using State Information," pp. 34–42. See also the Education Trust website (www2.edtrust.org/edtrust). As of 2006, the Department of Education's database of school-level performance scores was maintained under contract to the Department of Education by the American Institutes for Research.

56. See, for example, Institute of Educational Sciences, "What Works Clearinghouse" (http://ies.ed.gov/ncee/wwc/) and "State Comparisons" (http://nces.ed.gov/nationsreport card/nde/statecomp/).

57. See, for example, *Personal Responsibility and Work Opportunity Reconciliation Act,* P.L. 104-193, sec. 103, amending Part A of Title IV, with sec. 417, limiting federal authority to regulate the states except as expressly required in the new law.

58. See U.S. Department of Health and Human Services, Health Resources and Services Administration, Maternal and Child Health Bureau, *Child Health USA 2006,* 2006 (ftp://ftp.hrsa.gov/mchb/chusa_06/c06.pdf).

59. William T. Gormley and David L. Weimar, *Organizational Report Cards* (Harvard University Press, 1999).

60. Salamon, "New Governance and the Tools of Public Action," p. 17.

61. "Analytical Perspectives," in *Budget of the United States Government Fiscal Year 2007* (GPO, 2007), p. 108, table 8-3.

62. Paul L. Posner, "Federal Grant Design: What Washington Should Know and Why It Should Know It," paper prepared for the Ninety-Fourth Annual Meeting of the American Political Science Association, Boston, September 3–6, 1998, p. 4–5.

63. DeNeufville, "Federal Statistics in Local Governments," p. 344.

64. Derthick, *Influence of Federal Grants,* pp. 7, 201; Helen Ingram, "Policy Implementation through Bargaining: The Case of Federal Grants-in-Aid," *Public Policy* 25 (Fall 1977): 499–526; Paul E. Peterson, Barry G. Rabe, and Kenneth K. Wong, *When Federalism Works* (Brookings, 1986).

65. Derthick, *Influence of Federal Grants;* Peterson, Rabe, and Wong, *When Federalism Works,* p. 90; Richard P. Nathan, "State and Local Governments under Federal Grants: Toward a Predictive Theory," *Political Science Quarterly* 98 (Spring 1983): 47–57.

66. Derthick, *Influence of Federal Grants,* pp. 201–02; John W. Kingdon, *Agendas, Alternatives, and Public Policy,* 2nd ed. (New York: Longman, 1995).

67. See, for example, Peterson, Rabe, and Wong, *When Federalism Works;* Derthick, *Influence of Federal Grants.*

68. Peterson, Rabe, and Wong, *When Federalism Works;* see especially the discussion of Baltimore's use of community development block grant funds; also see Derthick, *Influence of Federal Grants.* If the block grant has a large matching requirement that increases the overview of local legislators or is in a state where the legislature must approve the receipt of a grant, it would garner considerably less local support.

69. Metzenbaum, "Strategies for Using State Information," p. 24.

70. Michael Hardy, "SAS Undergoes Identity Shift," *Federal Computer Week,* March 20, 2006.

71. Peterson, Rabe, and Wong, *When Federalism Works.*

72. Derthick (*Influence of Federal Grants,* p. 7) suggests that grants work in two ways: to "induce other levels of government to engage in [a specified] function or if they are already doing it, to do more of it" and by attaching "conditions that accompany the grants."

73. Congress often adds conditions, such as minimum small business purchasing expectations, to grants to advance wholly new objectives. Other conditions seek to prevent the recurrence of problems that previously occurred. Local goal allies often pursue numerous federal grants to fund single programs or projects and must meet the conditions, often incompatible, set for each of the grants. Block grants are created to address this problem. As organized advocates for the narrower objectives funded by categorical grants lose funds

locally and as problems gain attention on the political action agenda, conditions get added to popular block grants to compel state and local attention to their concerns.

74. Derthick, *Influence of Federal Grants,* p. 195. For a good discussion of the reasons for grant conditions and interpretations of them, see Conlan, "Grants Management in the Twenty-First Century," and Derthick, *Influence of Federal Grants,* pp. 193–218.

75. See discussion of vocational education in Peterson, Rabe, and Wong, *When Federalism Works.*

76. For example, in its early GPRA reports, the EPA reported the number of completed water plans but paid more attention to confirming data submission than using the data it gathered. It did not report water quality conditions, despite having collected biennial water quality–monitoring data from every state. Nor did it identify which water bodies were getting cleaner and which were getting dirtier, despite the fact that states collected the data and the law sets a clear goal of zero discharge to the navigable waters of the United States. That analysis might have illuminated unknown problems and possible solutions or shown trends in pollutants discharged. Following the GPRA and PART, and with development in information technology, the EPA has begun the transition to measuring water quality conditions and discharge trends.

77. Federal laws and the federal budget office like to make sure grantees do not use federal money as a substitute for existing local spending (Posner, "Federal Grant Design"; Conlan, "Grants Management in the Twenty-First Century").

78. Peterson, Rabe, and Wong, *When Federalism Works,* pp. 140–42.

79. Shelley H. Metzenbaum, "Making Measurement Matter: The Challenge and Promise of Building a Performance-Focused Environmental Protection System," CPM 98-2 (Brookings, October 1998), p. 29.

80. On problems in mature grant programs, see David R. Beam and Timothy J. Conlan, "Grant," in Salamon, *Tools of Government,* p. 351.

81. Harry P. Hatry and others, "How Federal Programs Use Outcome Information: Opportunities for Federal Managers," in *Managing for Results 2005,* edited by John M. Kamensky and Albert Morales (Lanham, Md.: Rowman and Littlefield, 2005), pp.197–274.

82. Posner, "Federal Grant Design," p. 6.

83. Before 1992, federal law required states receiving federal alcohol, mental health, and substance abuse funding to prohibit the sale of tobacco to anyone under the age of eighteen, but few states enforced the law. The 1992 Synar amendment to the Public Health Service Act requires states to conduct random unannounced inspections to measure vendor compliance with the law and report compliance rates annually to the federal government. A state that fails to measure according to federal requirements can lose up to 40 percent of its mental health and substance abuse grant; the Substance Abuse and Mental Health Services Administration keeps track of compliance rates by state (www.prevention.samhsa.gov/tobacco/01synartable.aspx). See also Jim Hood, Mississippi attorney general, "Cigarette Sales in the U.S. Reach Historic 55-Year Low," press release, March 20, 2006 (www.ago.state.ms.us/pressreleases/cigsalesdown.pdf).

84. See "Cancer Trends Progress Report," National Cancer Institute, January 7, 2008 (http://progressreport.cancer.gov/doc_detail.asp?pid=1&did=2007&chid=71&coid=702 &mid=#trends). Tobacco sales control is one of several intervention strategies the government has encouraged to slow smoking among minors.

85. Metzenbaum, "Strategies for Using State Information," p. 25.

86. Ibid., p. 29.

87. Ibid.

88. Insurance Institute for Highway Safety, "Helmet Use Laws: March 2008" (www.iihs.org/laws/state_laws/helmet_use.html).

89. National Highway Traffic Safety Administration, *Motor Vehicle Traffic Crash Fatality Counts.*

90. Metzenbaum, "Strategies for Using State Information," p. 29.

91. Ian Ayres and John Braithwaite, *Responsive Regulation: Transcending the Deregulation Debate* (Oxford University Press, 1992).

92. Hatry and others, "How Federal Programs Use Outcome Information."

93. This accountability principle is explored more fully in Metzenbaum, "Performance Accountability." The quotation was attributed to Bratton in a slide presentation made by a police chief during a performance management training session the author ran. Bratton has since been contacted about this phrase being attributed to him and had no objection to it.

94. James Q. Wilson discusses this political phenomenon in *Political Organization* (Basic Books, 1973), pp. 327–46. See also Mancur Olson, *The Logic of Collective Action: Public Goods and the Theory of Groups* (Harvard University Press, 1965).

95. Metzenbaum, "Performance Accountability."

96. On resistance to outcome-focused measurement, see Weiss and Gruber, "Managed Irrelevance of Federal Statistics," pp. 374–76. On "cream skimming," see Carolyn J. Heinrich, "Setting Performance Targets: Lessons from the Workforce Investment Act System," in Kamensky and Morales, *Managing for Results 2005,* pp. 351–74, 370.

11

PERFORMANCE MANAGEMENT AND INTERGOVERNMENTAL RELATIONS

BERYL A. RADIN

This chapter deals with two complex processes—performance management activities and intergovernmental relations management. Taken individually each of these processes demands attention to the trade-off between multiple values and goals. Combined, the two efforts create an overwhelmingly difficult and complex task. Because many federal programs involve intricate intergovernmental relationships, federal agencies have struggled with ways to structure these relationships. Federal agencies are balancing two competing imperatives. On one hand, they are attempting to hold third parties accountable for the use of the federal monies; on the other hand, they are constrained by political and legal realities that provide significant discretion and leeway to third parties for the use of these federal dollars.

One of the expectations of the performance movement has focused on the realities of the intergovernmental system, particularly the tension between those who devise programs as well as fund them (at least in part) and those who actually implement them. For some, performance measurement is viewed as the bridge between the accountability goals of the federal government and

This discussion is drawn from Beryl A. Radin, *Challenging the Performance Movement: Accountability, Complexity, and Democratic Values,* Georgetown University Press, 2006.

the demands of state or local government for discretion and flexibility. In this sense, the performance movement and performance measurement are seen as ways to avoid the traditional command-and-control perspective of the federal government and to substitute performance outcome requirements for input and process requirements.[1] According to some proponents of the performance movement, the traditional forms of accountability that are seen to evoke a compliance mentality will be replaced by performance measures that emphasize results.

Many third-party arrangements are crafted to minimize the federal role; despite the transfer of federal funds to these parties, there is often significant political conflict over the appropriate role of the federal government. Although the federal government may pay (at least partially) for programs, the extent of its role is disputed by both the third parties and their political supporters.

The federal efforts dealing with performance move against the devolution tide. The 1993 Government Performance and Results Act (GPRA) is the law passed by Congress in 1993 that requires all federal agencies to develop strategic plans, annual performance plans, and performance reports. The Program Assessment Rating Tool (PART) is the effort developed by the George W. Bush administration in which the Office of Management and Budget (OMB) requires federal agencies to report their performance. Both of these programs are linked to the federal budget process.

Efforts to hold federal government agencies accountable for the way programs are implemented actually assume that these agencies have legitimate authority to enforce the requirements that are included in performance measures. In some cases, the federal agencies have worked closely with other partners to devise a set of performance measures that are mutually agreed upon. These efforts thus become collaborative. More often, however, these other partners—especially states—have worked to protect their discretion in programs that are politically sensitive, such as Medicaid and Temporary Assistance for Needy Families (TANF). In addition, some states have taken action to ignore provisions of the No Child Left Behind Act, arguing that the federal requirements conflict with state goals, are intrusive, and require state expenditure of funds. For example, the Utah legislature passed a bill overriding some provisions of the No Child Left Behind law, the attorney general of Connecticut announced he would sue the Department of Education, and Texas openly defied an expansion of standardized testing for disabled children.[2]

In the performance context, third-party perspectives can create a significant problem in determining who defines the outcomes that are expected. States that already have performance measurement systems in place also do

Table 11-1. *A Comparison of the Government Performance and Results Act and the Program Assessment Rating Tool*

Issue	Government Performance and Results Act	Program Assessment Rating Tool
Focus	Offices and organizational units	Programs
Branch of government involved	Congress and the executive branch	Executive branch, centered in Office of Management and Budget
Organizational approach	Bottom up, beginning with program units	Top down, Office of Management and Budget must approve measures
Requirements	Multiple; strategic plan, performance plan, performance report	Performance measures
Approach to measures	Multiple types but highlights outcomes	Efficiency outcomes

not want to shift to a national system if their current activities provide them with the information they view as useful. In this sense, if performance measurement is taken seriously, it can lead to centralization—an increase in the federal role.

Intergovernmental Relations and Federal Performance Tools

Although both the GPRA and PART have an impact on intergovernmental relations, they differ in the way they approach this task. The GPRA has an outcome orientation and approaches the task in a one-size-fits-all manner. The Program Assessment Rating Tool also emphasizes outcomes but has attempted to differentiate between different program types. Table 11-1 notes some of the differences between the two.

Government Performance and Results Act

Although there was minimal attention to third-party grants in the design of the GPRA legislation, at least one arm of Congress did acknowledge the special problems involving the balance between flexibility and accountability in the performance activities. Two reports from the Advanced Studies and Evaluation Methodology General Government Division of the General Accounting Office (GAO—now the Government Accountability Office) did warn about these problems.[3] However, the warnings do not appear to have had much impact either on other GAO reports or comments from Republican congressional leaders. The GAO reports acknowledge the special problems experienced in the implementation of performance measurement in programs with limited federal authority. And they emphasize the special problems involved in block (or what they call flexible) grants, issues related to availability of performance data, and suggested strategies that could be of use in addressing these problems.

The two GAO reports highlight three design features of federal programs. First, they note that objectives of grant programs can be characterized as either primarily performance related or primarily fiscal. Performance-related objectives, according to the GAO study, focus on services, whereas fiscal or financial assistance objectives focus on providing dollars (such as support for goods or services) and targeting funding to needed jurisdictions. The second critical feature addresses the question whether national objectives are best achieved through a grant-specific operating program or by simply adding to the stream of funds supporting ongoing state or local programs. The report notes that "grants that operate as a *funding stream* are not federal 'programs' in this sense. Here, the federal agency provides funds that are merged with funds from state or local sources (and sometimes from other federal sources as well) to support state or local activities allowable under the flexible grant." The third feature deals with the activities supported by grant programs; some flexible grants focus on a single major activity or a limited set of activities, whereas others allow unrestricted choice among a wide variety of allowable activities.[4]

A GAO official, testifying on the program, pointed to limitations of performance data in the flexible grant context. She noted that "few grant programs are able to obtain these data program-wide," descriptive information is useful to convey the variety of conditions under which programs operate, and formal evaluation studies—if available—can be helpful. Whatever sources are used, she stated, are likely to be helpful "when backed by statutory authorization and budget resources than when it is not."[5]

In a report issued more than five years later, the GAO acknowledged that one of the persistent challenges in setting outcome-oriented goals, measuring performance, and collecting useful data is the difficulty encountered in meeting GPRA reporting requirements for intergovernmental grant programs. Unlike the general tone of the report, this commentary was hardly optimistic.

Programs that do not deliver a readily measurable product or service are likely to have difficulty meeting GPRA performance measurement and reporting requirements. Intergovernmental grant programs, particularly those with the flexibility inherent in classic block grant design, may be more likely to have difficulty producing performance measures at the national level and raise delicate issues of accountability. . . . Relatively few of [the programs reviewed] collected uniform data on the outcomes of state or local service activities. Collecting such data requires conditions (such as uniformity of activities, objectives, and measures) that do not exist under many flexible program designs, and even where overall performance of a state or local program can be measured, the amount attributable to federal funding often cannot be separated out.[6]

Program Assessment Rating Tool

When the Bush White House developed its own performance measurement system after assuming office, the initial design of the system acknowledged that different types of programs had special attributes. A range of program approaches was defined; among them were block-formula grant programs.[7] In the initial instructions for agencies, the OMB noted that

some block grant programs provide resources to non-Federal levels of government to focus on specific program areas, such as education, job training, or violence prevention. While the funds can often be used for a variety of activities, they are for a specific purpose. In these cases, national goals can be articulated that focus on outcomes to highlight for grantees the ultimate purpose of program funds. Targets for these measures may be set by surveying grantees to gauge the expected scale of their work or by looking at historical trend data. A system could be developed that uses performance measures and national standards to promote "joint" accountability for results. With this approach, after agreeing on an appropriate set of performance measures, program targets can be set at the local level and aggregated up to national targets. . . .

Some Federal programs are both large and diverse. They may be designed to address multiple objectives or support a broad range of activities or both. Block grant programs often have these characteristics, with the added feature of allowing grantees the flexibility to set priorities and make spending choices. Increased flexibility at the local

Table 11-2. *Block and Formula Grant Program Ratings, Fiscal Year 2005*
Percent

Rating	All programs	Block grant or formula programs	Block grant programs only
Effective	11	< 3	0
Moderately effective	26	27	14
Adequate	21	20	14
Ineffective	5	10	43
Results not demonstrated	37	40	28

Source: Data from President's Budget, Fiscal Year 2006.

level can limit efforts to set national goals and standards or create obstacles for ensuring accountability. In other cases, the program may focus on a limited set of activities which in turn are used for multiple purposes by many distinct stakeholders. Establishing performance measures for these types of programs can be challenging.[8]

Specific questions were devised to rate performance according to a set of criteria. Theoretically, the questions would be sensitive to the structure and demands of each type of program. Yet the questions developed for the intergovernmental programs did not reflect the challenges that had been raised both by the GAO and by the OMB itself. A program that had fiscal objectives, was designed to operate within a broader funding stream, and supported diverse activities, for example, would not fare well in the PART evaluation process because a number of these questions would be difficult to answer, given that the federal funds were not self-contained and separable from other sources.

In fact, this was the case for the block and formula grant programs that were included in the PART analysis for the fiscal year 2005 budget. During that year, PART analyzed 399 programs; 70 of which were designed as block-formula grant programs, and 7 were designated specifically as block grant programs. Table 11-2 compares the distribution of ratings for the block-formula grant programs with the broader pattern for the 399 programs.

Compared with all programs, the block-formula grants were rated least effective, and twice as many block-formula programs were rated by the OMB as "ineffective." Some block-formula grants have a history of more active federal presence, while others have a clear agenda of relative autonomy for the grantees. Looking only at the seven block grants, the pattern is even more divergent. No program was rated effective, and three (43 percent) were rated ineffective. The only block grant program that was rated as adequate was the community mental health services block grant. Yet its sister grant, the substance abuse block grant, was rated as ineffective. Both of the programs could be viewed as efforts designed with fiscal objectives that sought to operate within a broader funding stream and supported diverse activities. But the PART framework did not provide a way to acknowledge those realities, and observers believed that the differences in rating were attributable to differences between OMB budget examiners.[9]

It is important to remember that many of the grant programs involved policy areas that have been criticized by the Bush administration. These programs faced performance reviews highlighting the federal government's oversight role, even though the premise of block grants is that funds are sent to the states with various degrees of freedom from complex federal oversight requirements. Many states and local governments have their own performance and accountability review processes; overlaying federal PART reviews has the effect of overriding state and local government self-management, contrary to the intent of block grant projects. This set of problems is likely to continue unless the OMB acknowledges that the federal role is passive, not active, in some program areas.

Third-Party Government and Performance

Another way of describing the conflict between federal performance requirements and patterns of federalism is found in the literature on third-party government. Paul Posner has written about the accountability challenges posed by third-party government. Third-party government refers to collaborative actions of governments and private institutions at multiple levels. Posner notes that the major challenge stems from diffuse political authority embedded in third-party relationships. These players have independent bases of political power and often have conflicting goals and interests. Posner suggests that these third-party partners often have the upper hand in both policy formulation and implementation and thus require the federal role to be a partner involved in bargaining relationships.[10]

Posner argues that there are a number of features in third-party relationships that have implications for accountability. First, these providers (including states, nonprofits, universities, and defense contractors) influence both the setting of goals and implementation of these goals. Second, the participation of these parties is voluntary. Third, these providers often have monopolies over the means of program production. Fourth, these players often have inside knowledge that creates information asymmetries that tilt in their favor. Fifth, these providers are involved in efforts that Posner terms "complex implementation chains," in which the federal activity is only one of a number of actions.[11]

Many third-party arrangements are crafted to minimize the federal role; despite the transfer of federal funds to these parties, there is often significant political conflict over the appropriate role of the federal government. Although it may pay (at least partially) for programs, the extent of its role is disputed by both the third parties and their political supporters. The classic dichotomy between principals and agents becomes difficult to put in place when the principal (the federal government) has not been given authority to control the agent (the third party).

Thus third-party perspectives create a major problem in the performance context determining which party defines the outcomes that are expected. States that already have performance measurement systems in place also do not want to shift to a national system if their current activities provide them with information that is useful to them. In this sense, if performance measurement is taken seriously, it can lead to centralization—an increase in the federal role. This occurs despite the political decision by Congress to minimize the control role of the federal government.

David Frederickson and George Frederickson's book on third-party government provides an interesting comparison of two programs within the Centers for Medicare and Medicaid Services.[12] Although both programs involve third-party players, one (Medicare) involves contracts with health insurance and service carriers while the other (Medicaid) provides grants to states and territories. The authors note that though neither program is a direct service supplier, Medicare serves as an overseer or regulator around a single program; by contrast, the federal government's Medicaid role is more indirect and is diversified around fifty-six separate programs.

Medicare is thus able to define specific program goals both for its integrity program and its operations. In addition, the Centers for Medicare and Medicaid Services are able to establish performance goals that deal with customer service issues. By contrast, the Medicaid relationships are described in terms of fiscal intergovernmental relations. The Fredericksons find that "goal setting and performance measurement at Medicaid appear to be heavily influenced by changing relations regarding health care policy and implementation between the federal government and the states and territories."[13] This is reinforced by the reality that the states and territories contribute about half of Medicaid funding. Thus, according to the Fredericksons, Medicaid is very decentralized, has few and limited GPRA goals and performance measures, is the least accountable to federal goals of the agencies and programs studied, in large part because it is fiscal intergovernmental relations at work, and experiences continual tension regarding who should pay for the Medicaid safety net.

Proposals were made in 2005 to consolidate the Community Development Block Grant (CDBG) program and eighteen other grant programs into a single block grant called the Strengthening America's Communities Initiative. To justify this decision, the OMB's PART assessment for the program was rated as ineffective. Although the GPRA assessments had indicated that the CDBG program was meeting or exceeding its goals, the PART evaluation criticized the program for lack of purpose and an effective design or strategic planning process. The evaluation seemed to ignore the reality that the CDBG was a block grant and that federal officials had limited ability to determine how state and local governments would choose to spend the funds.

Major Issues Confronted

Since passage of the GPRA in 1993, a series of issues have arisen that have made it difficult to implement the federal performance management requirements within an intergovernmental environment. They include data availability, the level of federal fiscal contribution, questions related to program design and instruments used, legitimate differences between jurisdictions, and differences between a federal reality and state or local realities.

Two issues, however, stand out as of particular concern to those who face the federal performance assessment requirements. First, the process does not acknowledge that the federal agencies frequently do not have control over the outcomes that will flow from the federal funds. Second, the federal requirements (particularly those in PART) tend to ignore the reality that many programs contain multiple goals and outcomes, rather than focusing on a single goal or outcome. These multiple goals and outcomes are often contradictory to each other. Yet PART pushes agencies to focus on single goals.

Strategies to Address Tension between Levels of Government

Although the implementation of the GPRA and PART have provided the framework and a point of focus for federal performance efforts, other efforts have been undertaken within federal agencies to balance the two often conflicting imperatives: to provide states with flexibility and yet maintain a commitment to performance outcomes that acknowledges the expectations of those who fund and authorize programs.

The analysis that follows is an effort to explore some techniques that have been used by the federal government as it has attempted to bridge the goals of funders with the demands of those who carry out programs. It suggests that the initial expectations of those who believed that performance measures would be a relatively easy way to address intergovernmental tensions were naïve and quite unrealistic. Such research would also build on the extant literature that deals with the more technical questions focusing on development of performance outcomes, particularly the techniques that have been devised to deal with multiple stakeholders and situations in which competing values are at play.

The discussion highlights six approaches that have been taken recently within federal agencies to deal with issues of performance. Some of these efforts predate both the GPRA and PART initiatives, some are distinct from them, and others have been melded into the GPRA and PART framework. Some have been devised as a result of legislation and others through administrative action. All are struggling with the tension between federal agency accountability on the one hand and devolution and discretion provided to state and local agencies on the other. These include performance partnerships, incentives, negotiated measures, building performance goals into legislation, establishment of standards, and waivers.

Performance Partnerships

Over the past decade, a number of federal agencies have adopted or at least explored the possibility of moving categorical programs into performance partnerships. These partnerships have become increasingly popular as agencies realize the limitations of their ability to achieve desired changes in complex settings. Partnerships between various agencies and government have been around in some form for some years, but the performance orientation of the contemporary effort is new. However, these efforts do build on the concept of grantors and grantees as coequal, not as principals and their agents. The image of the relationship is one in which partners discuss how to combine resources from both players to achieve a prespecified end state. This end state is expected to be measurable in order for a partnership to be successful.

The design of a performance partnership addresses what some have viewed as one of the most troubling problems faced by federal managers: lack of control over outcomes. Although the managers may have control over inputs, processes, and outputs, they cannot specify end outcomes. Performance partnerships may involve agreements between federal officials and state or local agencies; they may be ad hoc or permanent.

The performance partnerships entered into by the Environmental Protection Agency (EPA) and the states during the 1990s have been among the most visible of these arrangements. However, there have been proposals for the development of performance partnerships involving health programs, programs for children, and the Office of National Drug Control Policy. According to the EPA, "Performance Partnerships establish a new working relationship whereby the States and EPA determine on an annual basis what and how work will be performed. Traditionally, the process for funding and addressing environmental and public health priorities has been conducted with a single media focus. States have submitted up to sixteen annual work plans and received multiple grants to support air, drinking water, hazardous waste, and other pollution control programs."[14]

The GAO also has noted that states and EPA disagreed over the degree to which states would be permitted to vary from the national core measures and the composition of the measures. Because each of the EPA regional offices enters into the arrangements with the states in their region, there is some variation between agreements across the country. This was of concern to the GAO analysts.[15]

The Environmental Protection Agency's experience with performance partnerships illustrates some of the problems that are intrinsic to this performance strategy and agreement form. The individual negotiation between the federal agency and (in this case) states is likely to result in variability of agreements across the country. In fact, to some the individual tailoring of agreements is the strength of the mechanism. However, others are concerned that this variation results from differential treatment of jurisdictions.

The problems with data identified by the GAO are also a predictable factor in any performance partnership agreement. The idea of performance partnerships can be attractive to federal agencies charged with the implementation of programs that involve policy sectors that lack well-established data systems or even data definitions. In such settings, it is difficult to establish and to garner data for more traditional approaches to performance measures.

Incentives

Over the past several decades, as the economics paradigm has increasingly influenced policy, some policy analysts have focused on the use of incentives as a way to change behavior. Incentives seek to induce behavior rather than command it.[16] According to David Weimer and Aidan Vining, bureaucrats and politicians have tended to be less enthusiastic about this approach than are those trained in economics.[17] This has occurred, they argue, because bureaucrats and politicians tend to be attracted to direct regulation because they believe that incentives also require governmental intervention and therefore involve regulation.

To some degree, however, incentives have been at play in the past in a number of federal programs through matching fund requirements. When the federal government offers funds as an incentive to induce states to provide their own funds, the matching requirements do serve an incentive function. In many cases, however, performance expectations are not made explicit, particularly in programs carried over from the past.

Probably the most dramatic example of performance incentives in the contemporary American scene was found in the High Performance Bonus program attached to the TANF welfare program. That 1996 legislation called on the secretary of health and human services, in consultation with the National Governors Association and the American Public Welfare Association, to develop a formula measuring state performance relative to block grant goals. Bonuses to an individual state could not exceed 5 percent of the family assistance grant. In addition, the law established a bonus for states that could demonstrate a reduction in the number of out-of-wedlock births and abortions in the most recent two-year period compared with the previous period. The top five states would receive a bonus of up to $20 million each, and if fewer than five states quality, the grant would be increased to $25 million each.

The first high-performance bonus awards were made in December 1999. The awards, totaling $200 million, were made to twenty-seven states; states were chosen on the basis of their ranking in each of the four categories. The states ranked the highest in each category were Indiana for job placement, Minnesota for job retention and earnings, Washington for the biggest improvement in job placement, and Florida for the biggest improvement in job retention and earnings. Eleven states received bonuses in two categories, and one state (Minnesota) was successful in three.

The bonus effort within TANF was a subject of some controversy both during the period when the criteria for awarding the funds were established and following the first awards. At one point, a proposal was made to simply divide the $200 million available annually for these awards equally among the fifty states and others eligible for the funds. Some critics of the bonus requirement argued that the categories that were established for the allocations were not directly related to the behavior of the state welfare agencies charged with implementing the TANF program. Economic conditions within the state were thought to be more responsible for the increases or decreases than the action of the state agency. Others have argued that the criteria that were established do not measure the real goal of TANF—the well-being of children. They called for the establishment of performance measures that highlight child welfare, child care, Head Start, and other noncash programs rather than focus only on the employment behavior of adults. The availability of data, however, were viewed as one of the reasons why other criteria had not been used.

The TANF experience illustrates the dilemma involved in using an incentive strategy. It is difficult to ascertain the direct relation between the behavior of the state or local government and specific outcomes. In addition, complex programs such as TANF have an array of program goals and expectations, and it is not easy to achieve agreement on performance standards. Some critics of the incentive strategy argue that state or local jurisdictions will attempt to game the system and develop policies that may meet the performance measures rather than achieve the basic expectations of the legislation. Others argue that this already occurs and so the situation is not much different from what it has been in the past. Similar problems were experienced in the Job Training and Partnership Act. Burt Barnow and Jeffrey Smith have noted how difficult it is to apply the principal-agent framework to that program because of the difficulty the federal government had in defining goals.[18]

Negotiated Performance Measures

One of the most common complaints by state and local governments is that the federal government attaches a set of requirements to its funding that do not meet the needs of the nonfederal jurisdiction. Indeed, this is one of the arguments that have been used to justify the transformation of categorical program grants into block grant efforts. Block grants have proved to be one of the most difficult grant forms on which to impose performance requirements. Balancing the flexibility of the block grant (allowing states and localities to meet their own particular needs) with a desire for greater accountability for the use of those funds has been problematic for federal officials.

The Maternal and Child Health Services Title V Block Grant has operated in some form as a federal-state partnership for most of its sixty-year history. Even after the program was converted from a categorical grant program to a block grant in 1981, the professional relationship between the federal agency charged with implementing the program and the state maternal and child health (MCH) agencies continued to be relatively close. The Omnibus Budget Reconciliation Act of 1989 did require states to report on progress on key maternal and child health indicators and other program information.

In 1996 the Maternal and Child Health Bureau, in the Health Resources and Services Administration of the Department of Health and Human Services, began a process with states that would establish a set of mutually agreed-upon measures with data sources to be used in the program. In the development phase of this process, the MCH Bureau created an external committee of thirty experts, representing various interests in the field of maternal and child health, that would help set overall direction for the process, provide technical expertise, and endorse the final results. Participants from associations and advocacy groups were expected to engage their own constituencies to ensure accurate representation. Review and comment from the state agency officials was solicited at various points during the process.

In March 1997, draft performance measures and guidance revision principles were presented at the annual meeting of the Association of Maternal and Child Health Programs; this meeting was attended by virtually all the relevant directors in the country. Eight representative states, chosen from seventeen volunteers, were selected to pilot test the measures for practicality and data collection issues. The consultation process that was used was approximately two years in duration; one year was spent on the development of the measures, and one for pilot testing the process.

By the end of 1997, the MCH Bureau had established eighteen national performance measures that were incorporated into the application and reporting guidance for the Title V block grant funds. These measures were drawn from goals related to Healthy People 2000 objectives over which grantees exercised substantial control. The performance measures were categorized as capacity measures (related to ability to affect the delivery of services), process measures (related to service delivery), and risk factors (involving health problems). Each individual state also was required to establish and report on between seven and ten of its own supplemental performance measures to provide a more complete picture of the program within that state. In addition, the MCH Bureau set six national outcome measures—ultimate goals toward which the performance measures are directed and for which ultimate achievement depends on external factors beyond the control of the state grantee.

As a result of this process, MCH block grant applications and annual reports contain a wealth of information concerning state initiatives, state-supported programs, and other state-based responses designed to address their MCH needs. The electronic information system that has been developed in this program, based on the applications and reports, collects both qualitative and quantitative data that are useful to a number of audiences.

The MCH experience indicates that when certain conditions are met it is possible to achieve agreement on performance measures. Programs that are not politically volatile or do not have a widely disparate set of expert opinions are appropriate for this process. In addition, prior work and data systems (in this case, involving Healthy People 2000) laid the foundation for consensus on many outcome and process objectives. The measures recognized and separated objectives over which grantees exercise influence and control from those that depend on external factors beyond their control. Even when these conditions are present, however, the negotiation process is time consuming and requires an investment of staff and resources by federal agencies.

Performance Goals in Legislation

Over the past few years various pieces of legislation have been crafted with attention to performance goals. Unlike the GPRA and PART approaches, which focus on the appropriations process, this approach emphasizes the authorizing role in Congress. Two pieces of legislation illustrate this strategy: the modifications to the vocational education program and the creation of the Workforce Investment Act as a replacement for the Job Training Partnership Act. In both cases, the legislation represented a move from an emphasis on input or process requirements to a focus on performance outcomes.

The Workforce Investment Act, signed into law in August 1998, reforms the federal job-training programs and creates a new comprehensive workforce investment system. It was constructed on top of the Job Training and Partnership Act experience. The reformed system is intended to be customer focused, to help Americans access the tools they need to manage their careers through information and high-quality services, and to help U.S. companies find skilled workers. Increased accountability is one of the principles embodied in the legislation. The act specifies core indicators of performance that become the structure for reporting by state and local governments. These core indicators include measures of entry into unsubsidized employment, earnings received, and attainment of a credential involving work skills. Indicators for eligible youth and customer satisfaction measures are also specified in the legislation. States are expected to submit expected levels of performance for these indicators in their state plans. Similar indicators of performance were also established in the Carl D. Perkins Vocational and Applied Technology Education Amendments of 1998. The modifications to the existing program emphasize the importance of establishing a state performance accountability system. The legislation requires states to identify core indicators in their state plans involving student skill achievement, attainment of educational credentials, and placement in education, employment, or military service.

Further refinement of these requirements was established by both federal departments through the regulations development process. In drafting these pieces of legislation, Congress assumed that the core indicators reflect common practices across the country and that data systems are available to report on achievement of the goals. This assumption has not been supported in practice.[19] Although this approach has the potential of establishing a framework in which performance measures might be used, the complexity of the employment system makes it extremely difficult to implement the intent of the effort.

Establishment of Standards

In some cases, the role of the federal government has been to establish performance standards that are meant to guide the behavior of state and local governments. At least theoretically, these standards are to be voluntary, and the ability of a state or locality to conform to them is not tied to eligibility for specific federal dollars. The federal role in this strategy may involve the development of the standards and provision of technical assistance and at times could include payment for meeting these norms and guidelines.

The Clinton administration's proposal for the development of voluntary national testing in reading and mathematics serves an example of this approach. In contrast to the No Child Left Behind legislation developed by the Bush administration, the Clinton standards were voluntary and did not have sanctions attached to them that could be imposed on states and localities. But the response to the limited Clinton proposal, particularly by some governors and education leaders, illustrates the types of problems that may emerge from this strategy.

Although several governors were supporters of this administration proposal in 1997, others expressed concern about the initiative.[20] A number of states already had test systems in place and did not want to replace their existing performance accountability systems with the national approach. Still others were uncomfortable with the content of the tests, particularly their accuracy and validity in measuring achievement and their substantive scope.

The proposal for voluntary tests in mathematics and English also uncovered another problem that is likely to be confronted whenever the standards strategy is employed: fear that the information gathered through these assessments has a life of its own and will be used inappropriately. This is particularly problematic because the information that is collected was meant to illustrate achievement at the individual level. Questions of privacy and information security have been raised and were not answered to the satisfaction of critics.

Waivers

Authority to grant waivers to state or local governments for specific programs has been in place for many years. Although the waiver authority has been viewed as a way to meet the unique needs of individual states, it has also been closely tied to a research and development strategy, providing latitude to nonfederal jurisdictions to experiment with new innovations and new ways to deliver services. For example, the secretary of health and human services had the authority under Section 115 of the Social Security Act to waive specified provisions of the act in the case of demonstration projects that were likely to promote the objectives of the act. These waivers were expected to be rigorously evaluated. The waiver authorization has usually been defined in the context of specific programs, and the criteria for granting the waivers are established within the authorizing legislation or implementing regulations. Certain requirements (such as civil rights requirements or filing performance information) cannot be waived.

This authority has been employed extensively in the past in several program areas, particularly involving welfare, Medicaid, and the Job Training Partnership Act. Waivers have been used to allow states to establish their own approach and to eliminate or modify input or process requirements. Many of the waivers require the proposed modification to be budget neutral—that is, it does not incur new costs for either the waiving jurisdiction or the federal government. For some, the waiver process is a mechanism that can be used to make a case for policy change. The experience with waivers in the earlier welfare program (Aid to Families with Dependent Children) and in the program implemented under the Job Training and Partnership Act became an important part of the justification for major changes in each of the programs, leading to the TANF program and the Workforce Investment Act.

At least one House member, Representative Major Owens (D-N.Y.), expressed concern about the waiver process. He asked, "In this process of rushing to grant waivers and place our faith in the State governments, do we have some safeguards? And can we have more safeguards and some stringent penalties for people who violate the law because the waivers give them a situation where nobody will be watching, monitoring, holding them accountable?"[21]

As Owens suggested, the proposed legislation did not focus on questions of performance. Although some of the existing waiver authorities did highlight performance issues when they required evaluation as a condition of the waiver, the proposed legislation accentuated the streamlining of the process, not the results that emerged from the changes.

Conclusion

The appropriate role of the federal government in the intergovernmental system has been debated for many years. Despite the rhetoric that is used to describe one perspective or another (for example, a strong federal government or a federal presence that defers to other levels of government), most of the shifts that have occurred over the years have taken place as specific legislation is crafted. The pendulum swings both in terms of the rhetoric used and specific policy design; the past few decades, however, have seen an emphasis on the devolution of responsibilities (at least rhetorically) to states and localities for the implementation of programs that are partially or mainly funded with federal dollars. Fewer and fewer federal domestic programs are entirely implemented by federal staff.

Efforts to hold federal government agencies accountable for the way that programs are implemented assume that these agencies have legitimate authority to enforce the requirements that are included in performance measures. Despite the ubiquitous nature of the performance rhetoric, the examples discussed here suggest that there are many pathways that can be taken to join the federal-level concern about performance with sensitivity to the needs of the governmental third parties involved in implementing the programs. In some cases, the two goals are not compatible; in others, it is possible to work out a mutually agreeable scenario. In this age of fiscal scarcity, both the federal government and states are extremely conscious of requirements that actually increase their costs for program implementation.

It is not easy to craft a strategy for performance measurement activity that addresses the tensions surrounding the intergovernmental system. The approach that is taken must be sensitive to differences among policies and programs, differences among the players involved, the complexity of the worlds of both the federal and nonfederal agencies involved, and the level of goal agreement or conflict. One of the most vexing problems in the performance area involves the availability of good data—data that have been verified and believed to be valid by all parties to the relationship. The data problem cuts across all of the strategies. Few policy sectors have the tradition or past investment in the creation of good data systems that would allow one to know whether performance has actually been achieved. In addition, the experience with all of these efforts indicates how difficult it is to achieve a performance measurement system that focuses on outcomes. Part of the problem relates to the lack of control many agencies have over the achievement of program goals and the difficulty of linking program activities to results, even when those results can be measured.

This repertoire of performance efforts also indicates that government-wide policies such as the GPRA and PART are not particularly effective because they do not respond flexibly to the differences in programs with third-party and intergovernmental dimensions. Without acknowledging these differences, the performance agenda leads to increased centralization and definition of outcomes by the federal government. It collides with strategies of devolution and a diminished federal role. The process of defining performance measures seems to work when it is devised in the context of specific programs, modest in its reach, and sensitive to the unique qualities surrounding those initiatives. If performance requirements are not sensitive to the differences in program and policy design, they are likely to fan increased conflict between levels of government. That is likely to lead to behaviors that diminish the possibility of emphasizing outcomes and performance because the actors in the system do not trust one another enough to develop appropriate measures.

Notes

1. See, for example, Deil S. Wright, *Understanding Intergovernmental Relations,* 3rd ed. (Pacific Grove, Calif.: Brooks/Cole, 1988), pp. 244–48.

2. See Sam Dillon, "Utah Vote Rejects Parts of Education Law," *New York Times,* April 20, 2005, p. A14.

3. Susan S. Westin, *Balancing Flexibility and Accountability: Grant Program Design in Education and Other Areas,* testimony before the Senate Committee on the Budget, Education Task Force, 105 Congress, 2 sess., February 11, 1998 (GAO/T-GGD/HEHS-98-94); see also U.S. General Accounting Office, *Managing for Results: Measuring Program Results That Are under Limited Federal Control,* Report to the Senate Committee on Labor and Human Resources, GAO/GGD-99-16 (Government Printing Office, December 1998).

4. Westin, *Balancing Flexibility and Accountability,* pp. 3–4.

5. Ibid., p. 13.

6. U.S. General Accounting Office, *Results-Oriented Government: GPRA Has Established a Solid Foundation for Achieving Greater Results,* GAO-04-38 (GPO, March 10, 2004), pp. 90–91.

7. The OMB chose to combine block and formula grants into one category. However, the two can be quite different from one another. Block grants establish general goals but give explicit discretion to the state or locality receiving the money. Formula grants may actually have more detailed requirements and thus provide less discretion to the state or locality.

8. Ibid., p. 11.

9. A similar argument is made in U.S. Government Accountability Office, *Performance Budgeting: Observations on the Use of OMB's Program Assessment Rating Tool for the Fiscal Year 2004 Budget*, GAO-04-174 (GPO, January 2004).

10. Paul L. Posner, "Accountability Challenges of Third-Party Government," in *The Tools of Government: A Guide to the New Governance*, edited by Lester M. Salamon (Oxford University Press, 2002), pp. 523–51, 525.

11. Ibid., pp. 525–28.

12. See David G. Frederickson and H. George Frederickson, *Measuring the Performance of the Hollow State* (Georgetown University Press, 2007).

13. Ibid., p. 93.

14. U.S. Environmental Protection Agency, *New Directions: A Report on Regulatory Reinvention*, EPA 100-R-98-002 (May 1998).

15. Ibid., pp. 3–4.

16. See discussion in David L. Weimer and Aidan R. Vining, *Policy Analysis: Concepts and Practice*, 2nd ed. (Englewood Cliffs, N.J.: Prentice Hall, 1992), p. 152.

17. Ibid., p. 153.

18. Burt S. Barnow and Jeffrey A. Smith, "Performance Management of U.S. Job Training Programs: Lessons from the Job Training Partnership Act," *Public Finance and Management* 4, no. 3 (2004): 247–87.

19. Burt S. Barnow, "The Effects of Performance Standards on State and Local Programs," in *Evaluating Welfare and Training Programs*, edited by Charles F. Manski and Irwin Garfinkel (Harvard University Press, 1992).

20. Rene Sanchez, "Education Initiatives Off to a Slow Start," *Washington Post*, July 11, 1998, p. 18.

21. Major Owens, statement before the House Subcommittee on Government Management, Information, and Technology, September 30, 1999.

12

BLOCK GRANTS AND DEVOLUTION
A Future Tool?

CARL W. STENBERG

Since the 1970s, American presidents have sought to reduce the size, increase the performance, and constrain the expenditures of federal domestic departments, agencies, and programs. Launched by both Republican and Democratic presidents, these efforts have had common themes: the national government was too large, and its elected and appointed officials were out of touch with grassroots needs and priorities; the federal bureaucracy was too powerful and prone to regulation; the United States Congress was too willing to preempt states and localities and to enact mandates without sufficient compensatory funding; the national government was too involved in domestic activities that were properly state or local affairs; there were too many narrow, overlapping federal grant-in-aid programs; and state governments were too often considered mere administrative subunits of the national government rather than the vital "laboratories of democracy" envisioned by Justice Louis Brandeis.[1]

Remedial proposals and actions to address these and related concerns about big government and nationally centered federalism have taken a variety of forms. These have included enactment of the General Revenue Sharing

The author wishes to express appreciation to David Leonetti for research assistance on this chapter.

program in 1972; establishment of standard federal administrative regions and federal regional councils in the early 1970s; passage of the Omnibus Budget and Reconciliation Act of 1981, the Government Performance and Results Act of 1993, and the Unfunded Mandates Reform Act of 1995; proposals to "sort out" and "trade off" national and state functional responsibilities; promulgation of federalism executive orders; and initiation of various federal regulatory relief measures.

Block grants have been considered instruments of federalism reform. They have been used as a tool for redistributing power and accountability through devolution and decentralization of authority.

Key Distinctions

During the 1990s, practitioners, academicians, and the media focused increased attention on what was called the "devolution revolution."[2] Former Michigan governor John Engler, in a statement to the Republican Governors Association meeting on November 23, 1996, said devolution consists in "pushing more power down to state and local governments." However, as it has turned out, devolution has been more rhetorical, or at best evolutionary, than revolutionary.[3] According to Joseph F. Zimmerman, there have been only a handful of successful efforts to shift functional responsibilities fully from the national to the state governments through legislative, executive, or administrative devolution. These include regulation of marine port pilots, insurance, interstate horse racing, shipping, and boundary waters.[4]

Instead of full devolution, featuring total removal and reassignment of federal policy, funding, regulatory, and administrative responsibilities, proposals have been made to restructure categorical grant programs to reduce federal requirements and oversight and give states opportunities for leadership and innovation in certain areas. These approaches are more accurately termed "partial devolution," in that while the states exercise significant authority and discretion, the national government continues to be involved in major policy, programmatic, and financial ways. Although it is unlikely that the partially devolved responsibilities will be rescinded, Congress and federal administrators may reassert authority, if performance fails to meet national standards and expectations by withholding funds, establishing set-asides of funds for particular purposes, demanding reimbursement for improper expenditures, or delaying application approvals.

A third approach that has been confused with devolution is intergovernmental decentralization. Here, although state and local officials may be accorded more responsibility and discretion, the national or regional offices of federal agencies continue to set policy and standards, enforce program and crosscutting regulations, and oversee fund allocations. Recentralization of authority occurs if performance is unsatisfactory. Decentralization also does not usually involve major restructuring of existing federal categorical grants.

Intergovernmental decentralization was a component of the Clinton administration's Reinventing Government agenda through the National Performance Review. Substantial decisionmaking authority was decentralized to regional offices of certain federal agencies, most prominently the Department of Housing and Urban Development. For example, owing to previous civil unrest, the city and county of Los Angeles received a temporary exemption from the department's community development block grant (CDBG) regulations, allowing the city and county to spend 25 percent of its CDBG funding on public service activities. Under normal circumstances, grantees can spend only 15 percent of their funding on this purpose.[5] Performance partnerships also were negotiated with state agencies, under which qualified state agencies were given greater authority over priority setting, reporting, and other administrative aspects of federal program delivery. The Department of Health and Human Services, for instance, waived federal regulations and other requirements to allow states to experiment with redesigned welfare delivery systems. President Bill Clinton's 1996 budget called for creation of twenty-seven performance partnerships involving 271 programs and amounting to $66 billion; state and local officials would negotiate with federal administrators to shift funds among the covered programs.[6]

The results of these three approaches to federalism reform are difficult to assess. Clearly, full devolution has not been popular. From a systemic perspective, the block grant record has not been impressive. David Beam and Timothy Conlan conclude that "the block grants device has proved hard to adopt, even more difficult to maintain, and has not at any rate reduced the number of separate grants overall."[7] Moreover, there is some indication that devolution has had at most a modest effect. Although administrative decentralization approaches have not been widely adopted by federal domestic agencies, state agency heads reported less intrusive national fiscal and regulatory influence in 1994 and 1998 surveys from the American State Administrators Project. Interestingly, this trend in reported declining national influence continued in the 2004 survey results. According to Chung-Lae Cho and Deil Wright, "This suggests that devolution as political strategy had an identifiable and noteworthy policy impact. Its effects, however, were modest and more evolutionary than revolutionary."[8]

Evolution of the Block Grant

The block grant is a tool for partial devolution of federal domestic responsibilities that has been used for more than four decades. A block grant is defined as a federal aid instrument that provides funding for a wide range of functionally related purposes and activities and gives recipients considerable flexibility in using these funds. States and local governments may use discretion in identifying problems, establishing outcomes, setting priorities, designing delivery systems, and monitoring performance. Block grants feature simplified planning, application, and administrative procedures and reduced financial reporting and auditing requirements. Most federal funds are allocated through a statutory formula, usually without recipient matching or maintenance-of-effort expectations. From a public management perspective, block grants potentially enhance efficiency and effectiveness values in the federal system.[9]

According to the U.S. Advisory Commission on Intergovernmental Relations (ACIR), the block grant is the "preferred instrument to provide federal financial assistance" when the following set of conditions is present: "A cluster of functionally related categorical programs has been in existence for some time; the broad functional area to be covered is a major component of the recipients' traditional range of services; heavy support for those recipient services that Congress determines to also have national significance is intended; no more than mild fiscal stimulation of recipient outlays is sought; a modest degree of innovative undertakings is anticipated; program needs are widely shared, both geographically and jurisdictionally; and a high degree of consensus as to general purpose exists among Congress, the federal administering agency, and recipients."[10]

The block grant concept can be traced to 1949, when the Commission on the Organization of the Executive Branch (known as the Hoover Commission) recommended that "a system of grants be established based upon broad categories—such as highways, education, public assistance, and public health—as contrasted with the present system of extensive fragmentation."[11] Not until 1966, however, was a block grant enacted, through the Partnership for Health Act (now the preventive health and health services block grant), followed two years later by the Omnibus Crime Control and Safe Streets Act of 1968. Under the Nixon administration, three other block grants were approved—through the Comprehensive Employment and Training Act of 1973, the 1973 amendments to Title XX of the Social Security Act, and the Housing and Community Development Act of 1974.

Interest in block grants languished until the Omnibus Budget and Reconciliation Act of 1981, in which nine new or restructured block grants were created by consolidating seventy-seven categorical programs amounting to $6.5 billion, about 7 percent of the $95 billion federal aid total. Most of these programs had been previously ignored or turned down by congressional authorizing committees, their restructuring buried in a lengthy bill. In a sense, these block grants could be considered more historical accidents than carefully conceived restructurings of categorical programs.[12]

Between that time and 1995, only five new block grants were added to the *Catalog of Federal Domestic Assistance:* for surface transportation, prevention and treatment of substance abuse, community mental health services, transition from homelessness, and child care and development. Three existing block grant programs—Community Youth Activity, Criminal Justice Assistance, and Alcohol, Drug Abuse, and Mental Health Services— were terminated. The U.S. General Accounting Office (GAO) and the ACIR both reported a total of sixteen operational block grants as of 1995.[13]

Over the thirty years from the mid-1960s until the mid-1990s, there was lukewarm interest in and mixed motivation for block grants. Twenty-three block grant programs were created during this time, four of which were converted into other block grants, and four block grants were eliminated.[14] Meanwhile, the number of categorical programs grew from 395 to 617.[15]

Although serving various needs and constituencies, these "old-style" block grant programs shared three key characteristics: none accounted for a majority of total federal aid in the functional area authorized, and in most cases the block grant existed alongside much larger categorical programs; collectively they represented a relatively small share of federal assistance to states and localities, about $36 billion—16 percent—of the $225 billion fiscal year 1995 aid total; and they were chiefly instruments of administrative decentralization, not devolution, owing to their relatively small financial magnitude, limited programmatic scope, and congressional recategorization over time.[16]

It is not surprising that block grants have been dwarfed by the categorical aid programs preferred by members of Congress. Congress has been unwilling or reluctant to turn over significant funds and discretion to state and local officials because of concerns about recipients' management capacity, recipients' ability to make the "right" allocation choices, and members' eagerness to take political credit. When unhappy with recipient decisions in using federal funds, congressional committees have recategorized programs through set-asides and cost ceilings. For example, as a result of concerns that states and localities were allocating too much of their Safe Streets funds to law enforcement, three years after creating the block grant Congress added a separate program to the act, setting aside 15 to 20 percent of the block grant award for financial assistance to correctional institutions and facilities.

The motives of block grant proponents changed between the 1960s and the 1980s. The block grants of the Lyndon Johnson and Richard Nixon administrations were instruments for administrative "cleanup" through consolidation, like the CDBG, and for making modest new or increased investments of federal funds in the program or activity areas authorized, such as the Omnibus Crime Control and Safe Streets Act.[17] Most block grants proposed by Ronald Reagan and George H. W. Bush, however, were accompanied by caps on or reductions in total appropriations available for consolidated programs, which were justified on the basis of projected cost savings of 10–15 percent resulting from a shift from federal to state administrative leadership. For example, although the amounts varied from program to program, the overall decrease of federal funding for the nine Omnibus Budget and Reconciliation Act block grants was 12 percent.[18] In contrast, CDBG program appropriations under the bill signed by President Nixon were 15 percent above the level of the merged categorical grants.[19]

In addition to cutbacks, the block grants of the Reagan and Bush administrations bolstered the governors' role. These block grants were federal-state ventures; local governments no longer received funds directly from the federal government except for the Nixon era comprehensive employment and training and community development block grants.

From Old-Style to New-Style Block Grants

Expectations and stakes have been raised considerably by the "new-style" post-1995 block grant proposals, of which the Temporary Assistance for Needy Families (TANF) program was the precursor. President Bill Clinton's signing of the Personal Responsibility and Work Opportunity Reconciliation Act on August 22, 1996, signaled bipartisan recognition that the time was opportune to turn greater responsibility over to the states and to rein in federal domestic spending and regulation. The act illustrates a successful attempt to convert a categorical program into a new-style block grant. The legislation broadly authorized states to use federal funds to accomplish the purposes of welfare reform. The architects of TANF gave states significant opportunities to exercise flexibility in setting priorities, determining eligibility, integrating state programs, streamlining and reengineering delivery systems, and transferring monies to related child care and social services block grant programs.

These breakthroughs were dampened by continuing concerns about accountability, managerial capacity, and fairness. The price tag for partial devolution was capping federal financial participation in meeting the needs of low-income persons by shifting individual entitlements to fixed grants (an indicator of future block grant design), continuing certain minimum national requirements, and imposing federal restrictions, such as those limiting aid to five years, requiring welfare recipients to find work within two years and to spend a certain number of hours each week working or seeking work, and curbing benefits for legal and illegal immigrants. As a result, though at $16.7 billion annually TANF became the largest block grant enacted to date, like others it was a hybrid program balancing stringent federal standards against significant state flexibility.[20] Also like its predecessors, more federal requirements were added to the program during TANF's reauthorization, calling on states to provide documentation that at least half of all families and 90 percent of two-parent families receiving welfare assistance met TANF work requirements and requiring states to include in these calculations anyone receiving benefits under separate state welfare programs. Failure to do so leads to a loss of from 1 to 5 percent of TANF funds in the first year of noncompliance and 2 percent thereafter.[21]

Whether other block grant proposals will follow the path of welfare reform remains to be seen. Historically, program overlap and duplication have provided a rationale for creating block grants through consolidation of categorical aids, and there are now more categorical programs than ever before. In 1995 the ACIR's "fragmentation index" found that these programs were becoming increasingly splintered.[22] This trend has continued in the ensuing years, raising concerns about efficiency and effectiveness.[23]

In the 104th Congress, for example, several bills were introduced that together would have consolidated 49 programs, with a combined annual appropriation of approximately $217 billion, into ten block grants. Only one of these proposals was approved in 1995—authorizing $503 million for local law enforcement. The two houses of Congress approved different versions of an employment and training block grant, which would have merged about 150 programs into one or three block grants amounting to about $25 billion, but no agreement was reached.[24]

The approval record of block grants remains modest, with only 23 programs existing as of 2006, depending on definitions.[25] Interestingly, according to the latest edition of the *Catalog of Federal Domestic Assistance,* 108 new programs have been added, only 1 of which is a block grant, enacted in 2004. The Specialty Crop Block Grant program awards $7 million in project grants to states for initiatives to increase fruit, vegetable, and nut consumption and to bolster the competitiveness of U.S. specialty crops producers. Annual performance reports are required of recipients.

As indicated in appendix 12A, at least twelve block grant proposals were introduced in Congress between 2001 and 2005. They covered a range of programs, chiefly health and social welfare related, in contrast to the transportation and community development emphasis of earlier block grants. These legislative proposals included Medicaid, community development, low-income housing, low-income employment transportation services, child welfare, job training, Head Start, and homeland security. Compared with their predecessors (excluding TANF, the CDBG, and social services grants, which rank among the twenty largest federal grant programs), these block grants represented potentially big dollars. According to the Urban Institute, if all of them were enacted (an unlikely prospect), the block grant portion of total federal assistance would jump from around 20 percent to 61 percent, mainly owing to Medicaid.[26]

The goals of contemporary block grant advocates have been wide-ranging and not necessarily complementary. They include reducing the federal budget deficit by cutting appropriations levels for discretionary programs; capping and constraining federal domestic spending by converting open-ended entitlements to close-ended fixed appropriations; realigning functionally related programs to reduce overlapping, simplify and streamline administration, and improve management efficiency; removing the national government from certain domestic areas; replacing one-size-fits-all approaches to program design and delivery; promoting innovation and competition through pilot programs; ensuring that recipients meet performance standards and demonstrate accomplishment of program outcomes; and targeting federal financial assistance on needy communities and individuals. Because of the potential extent of shifting authority to recipients, like TANF some of these new-style block grants could be vehicles for partially devolving federal domestic responsibilities as well as for decentralizing decisionmaking.

A controversial example of how some of these goals were advanced in President George W. Bush's fiscal year 2006 budget was the Strengthening America's Communities Initiative, which sought to combine eighteen existing grant programs into a single $3.75 billion block grant. The initiative called for relocation of the CDBG program from the Department of Housing and Urban Development to the Department of Commerce and its inclusion in the grant program merger. The funding level for the entire new block grant program was more than $400 million less than the amount allocated to the CDBG alone in fiscal year 2005. The Strengthening America's Communities

Initiative was intended to eliminate duplication of services provided by a number of different programs existing in different federal departments. Placing all community and economic development programs under the Department of Commerce was meant to reduce inefficiency, facilitate their administration, and cut costs. The proposal also authorized challenge grants, which allow municipalities to compete for additional funding as an incentive for enacting certain economic development programs. Congress rejected the transfer proposal and funded the CDBG program at $3.748 billion for fiscal year 2006, which was down from $4.15 billion in fiscal year 2005. The fiscal year 2007 budget maintained the Bush administration's commitment to the Strengthening America's Communities Initiative but did not include relocation of the CDBG.[27]

Concerns

After more than four decades of experience with block grants, many state and local officials remain uncertain about the fiscal impacts of contemporary block grant candidates. In part, this is a result of the message being sent— more devolution of authority, flexibility in administration, and freedom to innovate in exchange for a restrained federal financial role and increased performance expectations.

Some new-style block grants would cap spending and close previously open-ended entitlements. This shift was a key component of TANF, and spending caps and cost control measures are an important feature of the Bush block grant proposals for housing vouchers, food stamps, and Medicaid. With inflation factored in, state and local government leaders could face at least three unpopular choices: making cutbacks in funding or benefit levels for certain services, eliminating some recipients from eligibility, or shouldering new expenditures to cover the gaps.

Another cause for concern is the mixed federalism record of the Bush administration. Articulation and action on the administration's philosophy toward intergovernmental relations was put on the policy back burner by international events following September 11, 2001. However, despite the positive devolution thrust of new-style block grant proposals, state and local officials point to the centralizing effects of other Bush administration initiatives, such as the Department of Homeland Security, the USA PATRIOT Act of 2002, the Real ID Act, and the No Child Left Behind Act, together with the administration's support for a reduced funding ceiling for the social services block grant and for transfer of the community development block grant to the Department of Commerce.

Other skeptics and opponents are concerned that these shifts from categorical to block grants would diminish congressional oversight and control and also blur needs-based targeting. Yet the advantage of block grants in efficiency and effectiveness is diminished to the extent that recipients make allocation decisions that do not meet with the approval of congressional and federal agency program stewards, which could lead to recategorization. Given the fungibility associated with federal discretionary monies, additional concerns are raised about accountability for results in accordance with the Government Performance and Results Act of 1993 (GPRA), as block grants are passed through state agencies to a plethora of governmental and nongovernmental service providers. As a result of these tracking difficulties, federal oversight has often focused more on the proper fiscal use of the funds than on program outcomes. According to the GAO, for example, the Substance Abuse and Mental Health Services Administration monitors programs to ensure funds are being used properly, but it does little to assess program effectiveness on a national level.[28]

Finally, the desirability of turning over significant authority to states has been questioned by some, who point out that a primary reason for expansion of federal domestic programs was the states' inability or unwillingness to assume responsibility and that partial devolution could lead to a race to the bottom, owing to interstate competition for federal dollars. This argument is pressed by special interest groups who are skillful at lobbying Congress seeking federal preemption. Local officials also argue that channeling increasingly limited funds through state bureaucracies is inefficient and leads to diffusion rather than targeting of resources, and they complain about excessive state administrative and reporting requirements.[29]

These concerns are critical components of the block grant devolution debate. They are not easily addressed.

Lessons Learned

Research and evaluations provide a number of lessons from previous experience with implementing old-style block grants that may prove instructive. Generalizing about how fifty states and thousands of substate units have handled block grants, however, is risky business. The following eight observations are offered as points of departure for consideration.

First, block grants have a life cycle; and as they have matured, they have tended to become recategorized and less flexible. During the reauthorization process, congressional committees have often established categorical programs within the block grant, set cost ceilings on particular purposes, and required minimum set-asides for other purposes. For instance, according to the GAO, Congress imposed or changed cost ceilings or set-asides fifty-eight times between 1983 and 1991. Often these actions have been taken in response to complaints about state funding allocation decisions.[30]

Second, block grants have been recentralized. Although state reporting burdens were initially reduced, over time congressional authorizing committees have micromanaged block grant implementation, substituting the judgment of members of Congress and staff—usually after the fact—for that of recipients. Similarly, federal agencies have required more stringent reporting requirements and administrative conditions in response to concerns about state and local performance and competence and to ensure compliance with the GPRA. Recent experience with TANF's reauthorization suggests that "creeping categorization" continues.[31]

Third, although advocates of block grants, especially since the late 1980s, have touted administrative cost savings as a key advantage of this instrument, there has been no empirical evidence that total administrative costs borne by federal and state agencies have been significantly reduced. For example, according to Timothy Conlan, the Office of Management and Budget claimed that the nine 1981 Omnibus Budget and Reconciliation Act block grants would reduce state and local paperwork requirements by 5.9 million work hours and that for the seven merged health and human services programs, the states would save $52 million in paperwork costs.[32] On whether block grants are more efficient and effective than categorical grants, as has been claimed, the jury is still out. Overhead burdens may only have been shifted from the national to the state to the local levels through block grants.

Fourth, the designs of administrative systems or processes and accountability mechanisms in federal block grants have not adequately taken into account widely varying recipient managerial capacities and commitments. Recipients with demonstrated managerial competence have usually not been accorded more flexibility and discretion, nor those with questionable competence given more oversight of and control over less competent states. Exceptions to the one-size-fits-all practice included the performance partnership negotiations, in which the Clinton administration encouraged federal agencies to adopt differential treatment approaches to the states and grant waivers of regulatory and administrative requirements to those demonstrating compliance with managerial capacity criteria; the practice of Housing and Urban Development granting waivers of CDBG program funding ceilings to qualifying cities and counties; and Bush administration initiatives to grant states Medicaid waivers to allow them to control costs and coverage.

Fifth, the buying power of block grants has not kept pace with inflation. In addition, block grants have not effectively used state maintenance-of-effort or matching requirements to reduce the potential for substituting federal for state spending.[33]

Sixth, there is partial evidence from studies conducted by Richard Nathan, Fred Doolittle, and their research associates, as well as the GAO, that in response to the block grants of the Reagan era, some states—chiefly larger and urban ones—were willing to appropriate their own funds to fill gaps in service delivery created by federal funding reductions, particularly in program areas to which they were historically committed. The record of the remainder of states—a majority—in restoring cut funds was mixed.[34] There is evidence that states will use their flexibility to transfer federal funds from one block grant (TANF) to a related program (social services) or use carryover categorical monies to fill gaps created by federal funding caps and cutbacks.[35] However, there is no assurance that states will include compensation for reductions in federal aid programs now or soon to be covered by block grants in spending priorities for their own funds.

Seventh, block grants have not been well targeted, using programmatic needs, fiscal capacity, and service cost factors. Given the range of authorized activities, the number of recipients, and nonspecific statutory formulas, it has been difficult for state-administered block grants, as well as the CDBG, to adequately focus on communities and individuals with relatively greater needs and fewer resources. Yet with federal funding on the decline, targeting will most likely remain a sensitive intergovernmental friction point.[36]

Finally, local governments have not been major participants in negotiations on either old-style or new-style block grant design. Nor have they been beneficiaries in terms of greater program flexibility and reduced administrative burdens.[37] Two exceptions are TANF, under which states whose welfare administration had previously been decentralized continued to give localities significant discretion, and the CDBG, which was saved from transfer and elimination by pressure from mayors on members of Congress.

Implications

The lessons from prior experience provide a reality check for partial devolution attempts through the block grant tool. They suggest a number of political and managerial implications that may well accompany block grants and warrant consideration by elected officials and public administrators.

Channeling and Targeting

A reoccurring point of debate in the design of block grants has been whether all funds will be distributed initially to the states or whether some will be sent directly to certain local governments, usually large cities and counties in metropolitan areas, as in the CDBG program. The era of direct federalism ended with Ronald Reagan, and proponents of the nation's local governments have been unsuccessful in achieving rebirth. Although they recognize that block grants will be more effective to the extent they are targeted on communities having the greatest related needs and that risk will be diluted if the grants are sent through state bureaucracies, presidents since Reagan have favored channeling block grants through states and giving governors discretion over their reallocation among local units. But the philosophical and political debate over channeling versus bypassing persists and is unlikely to diminish.

At least two recent proposals signaled a possible shift in block grant funding strategy. The Homeland Security Block Grant Act, proposed by Senator Hillary Rodham Clinton in the aftermath of the September 11, 2001, terrorist attacks, would have distributed funding directly to localities, which were considered best equipped to address public safety issues, but the bill was not enacted by Congress.[38] The State and Local Housing Flexibility Act of 2005 sought to devolve substantial authority to local public housing authorities in the context of performance standards to be developed by the Department of Housing and Urban Development. These agencies would have been given wide latitude to waive statutory provisions that impeded local housing authorities from designing more-efficient programs, including determining family eligibility, targeting aid strategies, and altering rent rules. But it too failed to pass.[39]

Planning and Reporting

Consistent with the use of block grants as instruments for achieving partial devolution, congressional and administration architects, in particular, were initially reluctant to require states to prepare detailed comprehensive plans, submit quarterly financial reports, and conduct periodic evaluations of performance. As a result, there may be widely varying information systems or databases available to guide state planning and priority setting or to inform federal agencies and congressional committees as to how funds have been invested and what results have been achieved. Inadequate or inaccurate data may create problems as governors and federal agency heads are called upon during reauthorization proceedings to describe and defend their resource allocation decisions, and this could lead to recategorization. Therefore, it will be essential for states to put in place data collection, reporting, and tracking systems relative to block grant spending and service delivery. In doing so, care must be taken to avoid imposing costly and burdensome reporting requirements on local governments and agencies.

Performance Measurement

The GPRA committed the national government to strategic planning, benchmarking, and performance measurement on an agencywide basis, and grant-related conditions have caused recipients to make greater use of these tools. The Office of Management and Budget's Program Assessment Rating Tool (PART) reviews also have emphasized demonstrated accomplishment of program goals. The agency's assessment of the CDBG, for example, concludes that the program has been "ineffective," as, despite positive anecdotal evidence, there was no empirical proof that the program had been accomplishing its purposes. The PART review cited unclear program goals, inefficient fund targeting, and a lack of quantifiable performance measures as examples of the program's shortcomings.

The CDBG results are consistent with reviews of other block grants. According to Beryl Radin (chapter 11 of this volume), in fiscal year 2005 no block grants were rated effective by the Office of Budget and Management, compared with 11 percent of all grant programs, and 43 percent of the block grants were rated "ineffective," compared with 5 percent overall. In Radin's judgment, "overlaying federal PART reviews has the effect of overriding state and local government self-management, contrary to the intent of block grant projects."[40] By fiscal year 2007, some improvements had been made. A review of ratings for twelve block grants identified in the PART report indicated four programs (TANF, Child Care and Development, Maternal and Child Health, and Transition from Homelessness) that were rated moderately effective and two programs (Community Mental Health Services and Indian CDBG) rated adequate. The ratings for the remainder were "results not demonstrated" or "ineffective."

Because both the GPRA and the PART are likely to remain in force, specification of clear statements of purpose or objectives and measurable outcomes for block grants and establishment of processes for self-tracking and benchmarking progress toward their attainment will be the key to developing program records, which ultimately will need to be defended by recipients. But as the CDBG experience indicates, this will most likely prove difficult, given the basic purpose and design of block grants: to allow recipients to make their own choices from among a range of statutorily authorized purposes and programs and to target resources on their priorities consistent with federally authorized purposes. As has been done in the Family Investment Program, both state departments of human resources and local social services offices will need to identify and track outcomes, including compliance with federal work and other requirements. Federal agencies responsible for block grant oversight will also need to invest in sufficient monitoring staff if they intend, through periodic spot checks and routine visits to state grantees, to check on performance. Congress, as well as governors and state legislators, will want to know not only where the money went but also what it achieved and how it made a difference, if partial devolution is to be sustained.

Inclusion and Information Sharing

In a September 9, 1995, *National Journal* article, Douglas Seay, the director of the Heritage Foundation's Governors' Forum, observed, "I get calls all the time saying, 'O.K. this block grant is coming down, do you have any idea of what we're supposed to do?' I don't know of anybody who has sat down, in any consistent way, and said: 'Here's a model. Here's what the state should do.'"[41] Not much has changed since that time. To the extent that block grants are silent on intergovernmental process matters, concerns may be raised about the inclusiveness and representativeness of decisionmaking by state officials. Block grants will require new roles and relationships on the part of state and local governments, including working with nonprofit and for-profit third-party service providers. In addition to provisions for public involvement in planning and other aspects of program administration, procedures for obtaining the input of municipal and county officials will need to be developed. It will be critical to find ways to regularly share information, experiences, and perspectives and to make decisions transparent. During the 1990s, for example, the governors of Maryland and North Carolina issued executive orders setting up partnership councils to serve as forums for considering statewide issues and local concerns and developing principles and procedures for block grant implementation. Although neither body was successful, these initiatives exemplify actions states could take to remedy the problem Seay describes.[42]

Local Variation and Oversight

In managing federal block grants, state governments will need to take into account wide variances in city and county fiscal capacities, personnel competencies, and planning, management, and record-keeping systems, among other factors. States should consider developing differential oversight systems, based on criteria developed by state and local officials, for tailoring the amount of discretion and oversight accorded local governments in administering block grants to the capabilities and past performance of individual jurisdictions. A guiding principle here is that jurisdictions and other providers with strong capacities and performance records should require less supervision by state agencies.[43]

Conclusion

Experience demonstrates that the block grant as a tool for devolution offers mixed prospects. The good news for state officials is that devolution, albeit partial and evolutionary, will shift some of the intergovernmental spotlight from the nation's capital to the "laboratories of democracy." There are promising signs—such as those indicated in the American State Administrators Project survey data—that the trend toward national centralization of domestic affairs over the past fifty years may be restrained or weakened, at least in the grant system. Whether local governments benefit from this rebalancing remains to be seen.

On the other hand, the use of the block grant to close entitlements, cap and constrain the federal financial role in major domestic areas, target federal funds, and consolidate popular categorical programs will be a cause of concern to both state and local officials. In particular, they may be called on to fill significant gaps in program coverage with their own resources or to take politically unpopular steps to reduce covered services and recipient eligibility. And though their data collection and measurement systems may have improved since enactment of the GPRA, PART accountability and performance expectations for block grant recipients may be incompatible with the discretion and flexibility inherent in the block grant tool.

Finally, given the enactment track record since 1966, the fate of the pending block grant proposals is not promising. The categorical "beat goes on," and there is no assurance that Congress will be willing to relinquish the categorical reins on recipients, resist micromanagement, and put a halt to creeping categorization of existing block grants. Unless these financial, managerial, and political hurdles can be overcome, it is unlikely that the new-style block grant will be a major tool for devolution.

Appendix 12A. *Block Grant Proposals, 2001–05*

Proposal	Year proposed	Details of proposal	Is the proposal a consolidation of previous programs?	Total funding level	Performance requirements, maintenance-of-effort provisions, or set-asides
Job training	2005 (similar proposal in 2004)	Consolidates four major job training programs into a single block grant	Yes	Decreased	Performance standards and limits on overhead costs
Community development	2005	Consolidates eighteen existing grant programs into a $3.71 block grant	Yes	Decreased	Performance standards, including job creation and business growth. Challenge grants give incentives to adopt certain economic development measures.
Housing	2005 (similar proposal in 2004)	Calls for flexible vouchers that would give more latitude to local housing authorities to design programs that are more efficient	No	Remains the same	None
Food stamps	2005 (similar proposal in 2004)	Allows up to five states to receive their funding allotment as a block grant	No	Based upon the total amount state received for food stamps in either fiscal year 2005 or fiscal years 2003–05, whichever is higher	Yearly audit of program expenditures. No specific requirements with regard to program outcomes. State needs to ensure program is available statewide and that no one can receive benefits in two jurisdictions.

(Table continues)

Appendix 12A (*continued*)

Proposal	Year proposed	Details of proposal	Is the proposal a consolidation of previous programs?	Total funding level	Performance requirements, maintenance-of-effort provisions, or set-asides
Child welfare	2004	States allowed to receive funding allotment as a block grant	No	Based on previous expenditures	None
Head Start	2004	Up to nine states would receive their funding as a block grant.	No	Approximately the same	States required to fund preschools at current rate. State match of 5 percent. Administrative costs cannot exceed 15 percent of program funding.
Job access and reverse commute	2004	Enacts a block grant for developing employment transportation services for low-income people	No	Based on the number of low-income people in a state	Federal share cannot be more than 80 percent of capital costs for capital projects and 50 percent of operating expenses
Justice assistance grant	2004	Consolidates various judicial and law enforcement grant programs into a single block grant	Yes	Decreased	Funds cannot be used to replace state and local spending. Forty percent of funds must be passed to local governments

Program	Year	Description		Allocation	Requirements
New Freedom program	2004	Promotes access to alternative transportation for disabled persons	No	Based on number of disabled and elderly persons in state	Federal share cannot be more than 80 percent of capital costs for capital projects and 50 percent of operating expenses. No more than 15 percent of funds can be used for administration and planning.
Surface transportation	2004	Up to five states can use federal program funds as a block grant.	No	Remains the same	Spending must remain at or above levels for the past three years.
Medicaid	2003	Converts Medicaid from an entitlement program to a block grant issued to the states	No	Increases in first few years of the program, then decreases in later years	None
Homeland security	2001, 2002, 2003	Provides block grants to local governments to help fund first responders	No	$3.5 billion, with $3 billion going to local governments	Ten percent local match required

Source: Data from Kenneth Feingold and others, "Block Grants: Details of the Bush Proposals," A-64 (Urban Institute, April 2004); Joseph J. Schatz and Andrew Taylor, "Special Report: The Bush Budget," *CQ Weekly*, February 14, 2005; *Homeland Security Block Grant Act*, S. 1737, 107 Congress, 1 sess.; Ed Somers, "Homeland Security Block Grant Introduced in Senate," *Front Page*, December 3, 2001, United States Conference of Mayors (www.USmayors.org); Jeanne M. Lambrew, "Making Medicaid a Block Grant Program: An Analysis of Past Proposals," *Milbank Quarterly* 83 (March 2005): 6–7.

Notes

1. *New State Ice Co.* v. *Liebmann,* 285 U.S. 262, 52 S.Ct. 371, 76 L.Ed. 747 (1932).

2. Richard P. Nathan, "The 'Devolution Revolution': An Overview," *Rockefeller Institute Bulletin* (1996): 5–13.

3. David R. Beam and Timothy J. Conlan, "Grants," in *The Tools of Government: A Guide to the New Governance,* edited by Lester M. Salamon (Oxford University Press, 2002), pp. 340–80; John Kincaid, "The State of U.S. Federalism, 2000–2001: Continuity in Crisis," *Publius: The Journal of Federalism* 31 (Summer 2001): 1–69; Richard I. Cole, Rodney V. Hissong, and Enid Arvidson, "Devolution: Where's the Revolution?" *Publius: The Journal of Federalism* 29 (Fall 1999): 99–112.

4. Joseph F. Zimmerman, "The United States Federal System: A Kaleidoscopic View," paper prepared for a research seminar, The Federal Nations of North America, Rothermere American Institute, Oxford University, Oxford, England, November 23, 2004, p. 23.

5. U.S. General Accounting Office, *Los Angeles CDBG Public Service Funds,* GAO-02-726R (Government Printing Office, June 28, 2002).

6. U.S. Advisory Commission on Intergovernmental Relations, *Intergovernmental Accountability: The Potential for Outcome-Oriented Performance Management to Improve Intergovernmental Delivery of Public Works Programs* (GPO, May 1996); Beryl A. Radin, *The Accountable Juggler: The Art of Leadership in a Federal Agency* (Washington: CQ Press, 2002); Jonathan Walters, "The Black Hole of Block Grants," *Governing* 9 (February 1996): 11.

7. Beam and Conlan, "Grants," p. 365.

8. Chung-Lae Cho and Deil S. Wright, "The Devolution Revolution in Intergovernmental Relations in the 1990s: Changes in Cooperative and Coercive State-National Relations as Perceived by State Administrators," *Journal of Public Administration Theory and Practice* 14 (October 2004): 447–68.

9. Paul L. Posner and Margaret T. Wrightson, "Block Grants: A Perennial, but Unstable, Tool of Government," *Publius: The Journal of Federalism* 26, no. 3 (Summer 1996): 87–108, pp. 90–92.

10. U.S. Advisory Commission on Intergovernmental Relations, *The Intergovernmental Grant System: Summary and Concluding Observations: An Assessment and Proposed Policies,* A-62 (GPO, 1978), p. 24.

11. Ben Canada, *Federal Grants to State and Local Governments: A Brief History,* RL30705 (Congressional Research Service, February 19, 2003), p. 8.

12. Timothy Conlan, *From New Federalism to Devolution: Twenty-five Years of Intergovernmental Reform* (Brookings, 1998), pp. 110–21.

13. U.S. General Accounting Office (GAO), *Federal Grants: Design Improvements Could Help Federal Resources Go Further,* GAO/AIMD 97-7 (GPO, December 1996), p. 16; Posner and Wrightson, "Block Grants," pp. 88–89; U.S. Advisory Commission on Intergovernmental Relations, *Characteristics of Federal Grant-in-Aid Programs to State and Local Governments: Grants Funded FY 1995* (GPO, 1995), p. 8. According to the Advisory

Commission on Intergovernmental Relations, block grants were in existence as of 1995 for the following purposes: social services (1973); community development for entitlement communities (1974); community services (1981); community development (states' program) (1981); federal transit capital and operating assistance (1981); educational improvement (1981); job training partnerships (1981); preventive health and health services (1981); primary care (1981); maternal and child health services (1981); low-income home energy assistance (1981); transition from homelessness (1986); child care and development (1989); surface transportation (1991); community mental health services (1992); and prevention and treatment of substance abuse (1992).

14. Bruce D. McDowell, "Is There a Block Grant in Your Future?" *Assistance Management Journal* 8 (Summer 1996): 53–62.

15. GAO, *Federal Grants: Design Improvements*, p. 16; David B. Walker, *The Rebirth of Federalism: Slouching toward Washington* (Chatham, N.J.: Chatham House, 1995), pp. 16–17.

16. See U.S. General Accounting Office (GAO), *Block Grants: Characteristics, Experience, and Lessons Learned*, HEHS-95-74 (GPO, February 1995), p. 4; GAO, *Design Improvements*, 17; Beam and Conlan, "Grants," pp. 351–52.

17. See U.S. Advisory Commission on Intergovernmental Relations, *Community Development: The Workings of a Federal-Local Block Grant* (GPO, 1977); U.S. Advisory Commission on Intergovernmental Relations (ACIR), *Block Grants: A Comparative Analysis* (GPO, 1977), pp. 18–28, 31–36.

18. Conlan, *From New Federalism to Devolution*, pp. 278–92.

19. ACIR, *Block Grants*, p. 35.

20. Center on Budget and Policy Priorities, "A Brief Guide to TANF Reauthorization Issues in 2005," November 29, 2005 (www.cbpp.org/4-21-05tanf.htm).

21. John Dinan and Dale Krane, "The State of American Federalism, 2005: Federalism Resurfaces in the Political Debate," *Publius: The Journal of Federalism* 36 (Summer 2006): 327–74.

22. U.S. Advisory Commission on Intergovernmental Relations, *Federal Grant Profile 1995: A Report on ACIR's Federal Grant Fragmentation Index* (GPO, September 1995).

23. Paul L. Posner, *Federal Assistance: Grant System Continues to Be Highly Fragmented*, testimony before the House Subcommittee on Technology, Information Policy, Intergovernmental Relations, and the Census, Committee on Government Reform, GAO-03-718T, 108 Congress, 1 sess., April 29, 2003.

24. Posner and Wrightson, "Block Grants," p. 90; McDowell, "Is There a Block Grant in Your Future?" pp. 58, 62.

25. This total includes TANF and the child care block grant established within it, the local law enforcement block grant, the Indian housing block grant (2002), the Native Hawaiian housing block grant (2000), the juvenile accountability incentive block grant (2002), and the newest block grant, the specialty crop block grant. However, block grants are sometimes counted differently. For example, although there has been a CDBG entitlement program since 1974, other "block grants" have been added to CDBG for states,

small cities, Native Americans, and brownfields economic development. These may be counted as separate programs or included within the general CDBG program.

26. Kenneth Finegold, Laura Wherry, and Stephanie Schardin, "Block Grants: Historical Overview and Lessons Learned," New Federalism Issues and Options for States, A-63 (Washington: Urban Institute, April 2004), p. 4.

27. *An Act Making Appropriations for the Departments of Transportation, Treasury, and Housing and Urban Development, the Judiciary, the District of Columbia, and Independent Agencies for the Fiscal Year ending September 30, 2006,* P.L. 115, 109 Congress, 1 sess. (November 30, 2005); *An Act Making Appropriations for Foreign Purposes, Export Financing, and Related Programs for the Fiscal Year Ending September 30, 2005,* P.L. 447, 108 Congress, 2 sess. (December 8, 2004); Joseph J. Schatz and Andrew Taylor, "Special Report: The Bush Budget," *CQ Weekly,* February 14, 2005, p. 379; U.S. Department of Commerce, *Report of the Strengthening America's Communities Advisory Committee,* July 2005 (www.commerce.gov/SACI/SACAC_Report_Final_d.pdf), pp. 25–29.

28. U.S. General Accounting Office, *Drug Abuse Treatment: Efforts Under Way to Determine Effectiveness of State Programs,* GAO/HEHS-00-50 (GPO, February 2000), p. 25–26.

29. See Jonathan Walters, "Block That Grant," *Governing* 16 (September 2003): 12; Paul E. Peterson, "Devolution's Price," *Yale Journal on Regulation* 13 (1996): 101–11; Laurie Clewett, "New Kid on the Block," *State Government News* (August 2003): 5–8; Maureen Berner, "A Race to the Bottom? Exploring County Spending Shortfalls under Welfare Reform in North Carolina," *Journal of Public Budgeting and Finance* 25 (December 2005): 86–104.

30. GAO, *Block Grants,* p. 11.

31. See ACIR, *Block Grants,* pp. 37–47; Conlan, *From New Federalism to Devolution;* Finegold, Wherry, and Schardin, "Block Grants"; Cheryl D. Hayes, *Rethinking Block Grants: Toward Improved Intergovernmental Financing for Education and Other Children's Services* (Washington: Finance Project, April 1995).

32. Conlan, *From New Federalism to Devolution,* p. 200.

33. GAO, *Federal Grants: Design Improvements,* pp. 17–18; Beam and Conlan, "Grants," p. 363; U.S. Government Accountability Office, *Community Development Block Grant Formula: Targeting Assistance to High Need Communities Could Be Enhanced,* GAO-05-622T (GPO, April 2005).

34. Richard P. Nathan, Fred C. Doolittle, and others, *Reagan and the States* (Princeton University Press, 1987); Hayes, *Rethinking Block Grants,* pp. 7–9.

35. Kristina T. Lambright and Scott W. Allard, "Making Tradeoffs in Federal Block Grant Programs: Understanding the Interplay between SSBG and TANF," *Publius: The Journal of Federalism* 34 (Summer 2004): 153–54; Finegold, Wherry, and Schardin, "Block Grants," p. 4.

36. Finegold, Wherry, and Schardin, "Block Grants," p. 5; GAO, *Block Grants,* pp. 9, 15.

37. Anthony Downs, "The Devolution Revolution: Why Congress Is Shifting a Lot of Power to the Wrong Levels," Brookings Policy Brief 3 (July 1996).

38. *Homeland Security Block Grant Act,* S. 1737, 107th Congress, 1st sess., *Congressional Record* (November 28, 2001); Ed Somers, "Homeland Security Block Grant Introduced in Senate," paper prepared for the United States Conference of Mayors, Washington, D.C., December 3, 2001 (www.usmayors.org/uscm/us_mayor_newspaper/documents/12_03_01/security_block_grant1.asp).

39. *State and Local Housing Flexibility Act,* H.R. 1999, 109 Congress, 1 sess.

40. Beryl A. Radin, *Challenging the Performance Movement: Accountability, Complexity, and Democratic Values* (Georgetown University Press, 2006), p. 166.

41. Quoted in Council of Governors' Policy Advisors, *The States Forge Ahead despite the Federal Impasse: CGPA's January 1996 Survey of States on the "Devolution Revolution"* (Washington, February 1996), p. 40.

42. See State of Maryland, Office of Planning, Governor's Partnership Policy Council on Block Grants, *Report from the Governor's Partnership Policy Council on Block Grants* (October 1998); State of North Carolina, Office of the Governor, "Executive Order 21" (August 12, 1993); State of North Carolina, Office of the Governor, "Executive Order 65" (October 20, 1994); Governor James B. Hunt, "Administration of Federal Block Grants," memorandum to cabinet secretaries, November 16, 1995.

43. See Jonathan Walters, "Busting the Welfare Bureaucracy," *Governing* 10 (March 1997): 19–23.

13

MANDATES

The Politics of Coercive Federalism

PAUL L. POSNER

O ver the past forty years, mandates and preemptions have become two of the primary tools relied on by Congress and the president to project national priorities and objectives throughout the intergovernmental system.[1] The trend toward the use of coercive tools has been durable and lasting, albeit punctuated by episodes of reform. Although the enactment of unfunded mandates reform in 1995 most certainly has led to some restraint, the underlying forces prompting national leaders to use these tools have proved to be persistent and compelling. These trends have so far resisted partisan changes, as both parties engage in the extensions of federal roles through the instruments of coercive federalism, albeit for differing programs and purposes. Understanding the wellsprings of this secular shift in national strategies for federal programs is important in assessing the current and future status and prospects for our federal system.

Mandates: A Taxonomy

The concept of mandates covers a wide range of policy actions with centralizing and coercive effects on our system. Intergovernmental regulations can

Some material for this chapter was drawn from my article "The Politics of Coercive Federalism," *Publius: The Journal of Federalism* 37 (Summer 2007): 390–413.

range from direct orders imposed on state and local governments by federal statute to more indirect actions that force state and local policy change as a consequence of other independent federal policies, such as the implications of federal immigration policies for local health clinics. The U.S. Advisory Commission on Intergovernmental Relations has usefully defined a taxonomy of "federally induced costs," which suggests discrete policy actions the federal government can take to increase state and local costs. These include the following:

—statutory direct-order mandates

—grant conditions, both program specific and crosscutting

—total statutory preemption

—partial statutory preemption

—federal income tax provisions affecting state and local tax bases

—regulatory actions taken by federal courts and agencies

—regulatory delays and nonenforcement

—federal exposure of state and local governments to liability lawsuits[2]

Such policy actions could consist of either affirmative obligations for state and local governments to take action on a policy issue—what might be generically termed a mandate—or a constraint preventing or preempting certain actions. The intergovernmental impacts, though conceptually distinct, can be quite similar. For instance, the fiscal impacts of preemptions of state or local revenue sources can be every bit as costly as mandates ordering cleaner water. Many other distinctions can be drawn: some federal regulatory actions affect public and private sectors equally, such as fair labor standards, while others, such as voting or educational requirements, specifically focus on state and local governments.

The breadth of the instruments of coercive federalism goes well beyond the popular concept of unfunded mandates. This conceptualization was formalized when Congress passed the Unfunded Mandates Reform Act (UMRA) in 1995. Although passage of this act did, indeed, mark an attempt to reverse or at least arrest the growth of intergovernmental regulation or coercive federalism, in fact, UMRA primarily addresses only one of these instruments, statutory direct orders. Given the range of potential actions covered under the broad rubric of intergovernmental regulation, national actions can be best characterized along a continuum of centralization and fiscal impact. Rather than an on-off switch with bright lines of demarcation, coercive federal actions span a wide range of tools that also at times include classic elements of cooperative federalism, such as the presence of federal grant funding covering some of the costs. The relatively narrow definition embraced in UMRA has served to limit not only our understanding of the implications of national policy decisions for our federal system but also the potential effectiveness of this reform in influencing these policy decisions.

Centralizing Trends in Recent Decades

The secular trend toward a more coercive and centralized federalism has survived both Republican and Democratic administrations and Congresses. The Nixon administration, though it followed a principled federalism approach both in creating block grants and in revenue sharing, nonetheless presided over a major expansion of federal regulation with important implications for federalism.[3] The Reagan administration, notwithstanding major policy proposals to rebalance the federal role, nonetheless found itself endorsing new federal mandates in areas including environmental protection, highway safety, health care, and social welfare policy.[4] These trends continued through the 1990s and are reflected in the growth of federal mandates and preemptions over the decade.[5]

What political and social forces prompted this secular shift toward a more coercive federal system? As late as 1960, our federal system was undergirded by systemic political factors as well as social and economic forces that placed limits on the role of the federal government, reflected in a general forbearance and restraint that federal officials demonstrated in policy formulation. The position of state and local governments in the federal system was protected by the party system itself. As Morton Grodzins has noted, the party system was decentralized, with its power base concentrated at the state and local level. National officeholders, whether presidents or members of Congress, owed their nominations and political allegiances to state and local party leaders, embedding a sensitivity to the prerogatives of state and local officials in fundamental political incentives. Federalism was an important line of cleavage between the parties, with the Republican Party dedicated to preserving states' authority and constraining the growth of federal power. The interest group system served as a bulwark of federalism as well; business was the preeminent interest in our system, and such groups saw their interests as being better protected by states than by the federal government. In fact, national policymakers did observe forbearance and restraint on federalism issues before the 1960s. Daniel Elazar writes that before the 1960s, Congress generally protected states in federal legislation.[6] Even as the federal role expanded over the economy in such landmark statutes as the Fair Labor Standards Act, the Social Security Act, and Title VII of the Civil Rights Act of 1964, state and local governments were exempted. Indeed, federalism was accepted as one of the primary rules of the game.

Many of these forces have shifted dramatically, leading to the unraveling of the constraints that bolstered the position of states in the system. Since Grodzins's time, the party system has fundamentally changed as candidates for national office have been forced to assemble their own coalitions to compete for nominations and elections. Interest groups and media have eclipsed state and local parties as gatekeepers of candidate recruitment and legitimation; national elected officials have been converted from ambassadors of state and local party leaders to independent political entrepreneurs anxious to establish their own visible policy profiles to appeal to a diverse coalition of interest groups, media, and an increasingly independent base of voters. Far from being allies, congressional officials and state and local elected colleagues from their districts seem to be in a competition among independent political entrepreneurs for money, visibility, and votes.

These nationalizing trends were echoed and bolstered by other trends in our political system and the broader economy. The growth of national media institutions focused on Washington created a powerful resource for those groups wishing to nationalize problems and issues, and reporting increasingly sought to find national dimensions or applications for state and local problems or solutions. The advent of lobbies representing broad, diffuse interests, the so-called public interest groups, has fueled national policy advocacy as many of these groups have settled in Washington rather than the states. Perhaps the most important development in the interest group sector was the pronounced but little noticed shift of business groups from allies of the states to advocates of national regulation by federal agencies. This trend underscores the impact of the nationalization and globalization of the economy on our federal system. As corporations increasingly operate in a global environment, coping with fifty separate state regulatory regimes is seen as a hindrance to economic efficiency and competitiveness. This trend is reinforced by trade agreements that have been interpreted by the courts and international bodies as having preemptive effects on state and local laws.

Significant Mandate Actions in Recent Years

The beginning of the twenty-first century witnessed the marshalling of new political forces that might be expected to prompt national officials to shift away from the instruments of coercive federalism. The election of President George W. Bush presaged a period of unified government presided over by unprecedented conservative political leadership not seen since before the Great Depression. President Bush himself proved to be more committed to conservative ideological principles than many had expected, given his self-proclaimed profile as a consensus leader with democratic state legislators in Texas.[7] The president was able to work with Republican majorities in both House and Senate, albeit with a brief period of Democratic Senate control owing to Senator James Jeffords's conversion from a Republican to an Independent. The Republicans controlling Congress were far more conservative than previous Republican regimes in Congress. Moreover, the 1995 passage of the Unfunded Mandates Reform Act reflected a bipartisan commitment to curb the use of mandates in Congress.

Notwithstanding these forces, the period of the Bush presidency in fact witnessed the continuation of the centralization and nationalization of priorities and policies that had characterized previous administrations, Republican and Democrat alike. Although mandate reform served to provide a modest restraint, federal goals and priorities were extended to new intergovernmental service arenas heretofore primarily controlled by states and localities. Education testing, elections administration, fire protection and emergency response, and tax policy were important arenas that were once relatively off limits for federal officials but fell under the influence of major new national programs. The persistence of centralizing and coercive national policy decisions reflects the continued attenuation of federalism as a value commanding loyalty from elites and publics in the face of numerous other more politically compelling national values and interests.

Following is a profile of major new actions adopted from 2001 through 2006. Many of these actions, not surprisingly, are covered elsewhere in this volume, but I provide a brief discussion of how the actions taken fit within the pantheon of coercive federalism.

Education

Perhaps no area has been as sacred to our tradition of federalism and local governance as local control of our schools. Given this backdrop, passage of the No Child Left Behind Act with the leadership of President Bush and congressional Democrats marked a turning point in the centralization of our federal system. Skirting the Unfunded Mandates Reform Act, the program's requirements were couched as conditions of federal assistance, a category that exempted it from the mandates point of order. As Kenneth Wong notes in chapter 6 in this volume, the new mandates were broad reaching indeed, as the testing, teaching, and accountability requirements established a daunting new framework for local education policy and practice. Significant concessions were made to the state and local sector as well: states could define the standards used for tests, parents were consigned to find alternatives for failing schools only among other public schools within the school district, and federal funding rose significantly in the years following passage.[8] Ironically, the years of cooperative federalism characterizing the prior period of federal education had succeeded in both promoting greater state and local dependence on federal funding and gaining state and local buy-in for federal education policy goals, reflected in the endorsement of stronger national educational standards by the nation's governors in 1990.[9]

Welfare Reform

The passage of welfare reform in 1996 marked a signal shift in federal social welfare policy. Converting an open-ended federal grant program into a block grant to the states, the act devolved significant authority to the states to define eligibility and to use funds for a wide range of activities related to supporting lower-income persons. Although the new law was popularly celebrated as a triumph of state innovation, Republicans in the White House and Congress watched the states carefully—as Democratic committee chairs had during the Reagan block grants of the 1980s—lest the states undermine their ideological agenda by sidestepping the spirit of the program's work requirements. Some twenty states were able to entirely avoid placing additional welfare recipients in work, thanks to a Temporary Assistance for Needy Families provision that let them take credit for job placements that were in fact attributable to the expanding economy. As Jocelyn Johnston notes in chapter 7 of this volume, the 2006 reauthorization significantly increased the strength of the work mandates associated with the program. In addition to increased work participation requirements, the caseload reduction credit was no longer available to offset the states' compliance obligations. Moreover, the definition of work activities has narrowed, curtailing the time that education or training could be counted toward the work requirement. States in compliance under the old rules suddenly found themselves facing the burden of increasing their welfare clients' work participation by more than 100 percent. The new requirement for 90 percent of two-parent families to work a minimum of thirty-five hours a week is acknowledged to be "pretty much unattainable" by Wade Horn, the assistant secretary of the Department of Health and Human Services responsible for the program.[10] As it had with prior recategorizations of block grants, Congress also made significant changes in reporting requirements and oversight over the states, including extending new requirements to cases funded entirely from state dollars.

Election Administration

The Florida election crisis in 2000 prompted a veritable stampede toward federal action, as both parties realized that the failure to act on what was perceived to be a national crisis could constitute a liability for their party. Cross-partisan bargaining between Democratic and Republican leaders culminated in passage of the 2002 Help America Vote Act. The act instituted sweeping new federal standards requiring new voting systems, provisional ballots, statewide voter databases, and access to polling places for disabled persons. Federal error rate standards must be met, and voters must be allowed to correct errors. The law requires the centralization of the registration and elections process at the state level, specifying uniform processes for vote definitions across the state as well as new requirements for statewide voter databases.[11] Congress also has provided $3 billion in funding for state and local costs, primarily associated with modernization of election machines, though the amount fell well short of actual costs incurred.[12]

Tax Policy

Changes in tax policy over the Bush years have had significant, albeit often indirect, consequences on state tax policies and administration. Although not mandates in the classic sense and not covered under the Unfunded Mandates Reform Act, the tax cuts of 2001 and 2003—central to the Bush economic agenda—constituted unilateral federal policy changes to federal-state shared tax bases that threatened to unravel a system of cooperative tax policy and administration that had evolved over many years. Although cuts to individual and capital gains tax rates themselves do not threaten the tax bases of states, major changes in depreciation, dividends, and estate taxes presented states with a significant erosion of their income tax bases. Such changes force states to acquiesce and accept their consequences or decouple from the federal tax base. In some respects, unilateral changes to federal income tax bases were a continuation of trends from prior presidential eras. However, recent tax policy actions broke new ground in some areas. In the area of estate taxes, a shared federal-state regime begun in 1924 to encourage states to continue their own estate taxes through a federal credit was overturned. Under the 2001 legislation, the federal estate tax is phased out through 2010 by gradually raising the threshold that triggers the tax (the tax is then reinstated in 2011, but the state credit is not, unless Congress acts). With state revenue losses estimated at as much as $9 billion annually, twenty states have decided to decouple from the federal estate tax laws, complicating tax planning and tax administration.

Moreover, the pace of federal preemptions of state and local tax law has accelerated in recent years. As early as 1985, Congress acted to prohibit states from imposing business taxes on out-of-state companies with limited nexus.[13] This policy was reinforced by Supreme Court decisions that prevented states from collecting sales taxes on the sale of goods produced by remote sellers, although the Court left the door open for Congress to overturn this preemption by statute.[14] Congress has not acted on this invitation to enable states to extend their sales tax to mobile sales, despite the efforts by a majority of states to adopt a more uniform sales tax base through the Streamlined Sales Tax Project. Congressional preemptions of state taxation went further than the Court's ruling. Congress extended the preemption of state authority to tax Internet access, an action that was recently extended through 2014. The Congressional Budget Office (CBO) estimates that this recent action will reduce state and local revenues by $80 million annually.[15]

Homeland Security

The tragic events of September 11, 2001, forced federal officials to recognize that the intergovernmental system constituted the nation's first line of defense in dealing with the consequences of terrorist attacks. However, the presence of a strong national consensus, high externalities, extensive interdependencies, and high stakes ultimately led the Bush administration and Congress to adopt intergovernmental grants and mandates that together served to centralize emergency preparedness, infrastructure, and other state and local services (see chapter 5 in this volume).

The story of the adoption of the Real ID Act illustrates the centralizing pressures on the system, as federal and state leaders both were motivated to insulate themselves from blame for future incidents through the development of regulatory standards that can be argued to protect against future attacks and future political opponents alike.[16] Federal standards to promote a secure driver's license were recommended by the state motor vehicles administrators themselves as a way to force recalcitrant states to adopt uniform procedures that they had failed to do under voluntary compacts.[17]

In the "be careful what you ask for" category, Congress responded with passage of legislation ultimately going well beyond the suggestions made by the states. Initial legislation enacting federal standards was passed in 2004, partly in response to recommendations issued by the 9/11 Commission.[18] The 2004 legislation removed harsher mandates proposed by Representative James Sensenbrenner, the House Judiciary Committee chair, and contained significant concessions to the states, such as providing for negotiated rule making with states and applying the standards only to new licenses. A cagey conservative policy entrepreneur, Sensenbrenner persisted and, with support from the Bush administration, succeeded in passing a stronger measure—the Real ID Act—as part of a must-sign legislation funding U.S. troops in Iraq and Afghanistan.[19] Sensenbrenner and his coalition succeeded in including provisions prohibiting states from issuing federally approved identification cards to illegal aliens, the practice in ten states at the time.

The Real ID Act establishes federal standards for state driver's licenses that must be met by May 2008, although the administration has provided additional time for implementation. Although technically not a direct-order mandate, the effect is the same, as residents of states lacking this new secure ID will not be able to board airplanes. State associations originally estimated the costs to exceed $11 billion over five years, and so far little funding has come from the federal government.[20] The most burdensome provisions include reenrollment of all current license holders, new verification processes with original documentation, such as birth certificates, and new tamper-proof security features for the card itself.

This litany of enacted mandates should not obscure some of the notable concessions achieved by state and local governments over the same period. Of most fiscal importance, the states succeeded in derailing the Bush administration's proposals to shift funding for the Medicaid program from uncapped grants to states to a limited fixed grant. In various formulations, this took the guise of a block grant and an entitlement with fiscal limits, all of which inspired intense lobbying by the governors and other state officials, which succeeded in defeating these proposals in Congress. The state and local sector also achieved a significant victory in forestalling a House-passed provision in the energy bill of 2005 protecting producers of the gasoline additive methyl tertiary butyl ether from suits by local governments recovering damages for groundwater pollution.[21] The liability waiver was strongly promoted by Tom DeLay, majority leader of the House, but opposed by a wide range of environmental groups. The impact on local government cleanup costs was a significant part of the debate, which was fueled by a CBO estimate projecting state and local costs that would exceed the threshold needed to raise a point of order against the legislation.[22]

The Evolution of Mandates as a Tool of Government

How do these actions compare with the types of regulatory policy instruments used in earlier eras? As before, Congress and the president reached for a wide range of regulatory strategies to impose mandated requirements on the state and local sector: direct orders, grant conditions, preemptions, and crossover sanctions were all used to implement the regulatory policies of the past five years. However, newer policy instruments gained traction and have become more important influences on intergovernmental policy and management.

—Revenue nationalization: The Bush era witnessed a marked shift toward the erosion of cooperative federalism and federal forbearance in the area of tax policy. The unwinding of the framework for the estate tax and the preemption of state tax bases both portend a new front in coercive federalism that could erode the fiscal wherewithal of states and localities to fulfill their expansive roles in a more coercive federal system. At the very least, such initiatives will increasingly put state and local officials on the defensive, forced to justify decisions to continue tax bases abandoned by federal officials or to seek new revenues when preempted from existing tax sources. Intergovernmental tax competition may well intensify in coming years, as federal policymakers facing burgeoning deficits from the baby boom retirement eye states' command of consumption taxation.[23]

—Public disclosure: Federal policies have resorted to the public information tool as a seemingly inexpensive strategy to shame regulated entities, whether they be private businesses or state and local governments, into adopting widely shared federal policy goals.[24] In the Bush era, such strategies were pursued to provide various publics in the state and local sector with leverage in negotiating policy changes consistent with federal goals. Some analysts have concluded that the No Child Left Behind Act will succeed in generating change not through the regulatory "front door" of administrative rule making and oversight but rather through the publication of school performance data for all parents to see. Armed with new information on how their schools stack up against standards, parents may use this information not only to fortify their voice in school decisionmaking but also to inform their decision to possibly exit from their community should scores be better in neighboring school districts.

—Performance models: Although federal agencies have been required to prepare performance plans and metrics for the past twelve years, they have been slow to apply these metrics to grants and other intergovernmental mechanisms. However, such measures became increasingly central approaches for building pressure on the state and local sector to support federal program goals. Both welfare reform and the No Child Left Behind Act illustrate how states or local government providers are increasingly held accountable for performance outcomes experienced by clients in federal programs. As noted by Beryl Radin in chapter 11 of this volume, when performance models are articulated in national legislation and administrative rules, such measures can have a profoundly centralizing impact on intergovernmental programs. Notwithstanding the relatively minor fiscal role played by many programs compared with state and local investments, the assertion of national performance metrics enables federal officials to achieve new influence over the entire intergovernmental service area. Thus though the federal government contributes only 8 percent of the costs of public elementary and secondary education, the No Child Left Behind program articulates performance metrics that go to the heart of curriculum and teaching throughout the nation.

The well-known proclivity of managers to work to measures is accentuated when the federally prescribed metrics become transformed from merely hortatory goal statements to threshold levels that can trigger changes in funding or service provision. Thus the newly restrictive welfare job placement mandates will indeed trigger the loss of a portion of Temporary Assistance for Needy Families funds should states fail to meet the targets. Under the No Child Left Behind Act, the concept of "performance metrics with consequences" has been taken to a new level, as the schools' performance shortfalls are automatically linked to such actions as enabling parents to transfer children to other schools and takeover by the state.

All told, these innovations show that the Bush administration and Congress have not been content to take states and localities as they found them. Rather, these kinds of tools are intentionally designed to challenge state and local leaders and managers by putting public officials on the defensive through new metrics and accountability strategies. Energizing new publics and new providers to vie for at least a share of public service provision under federal programs is a vital part of this new strategy to deconstruct public authority within the state and local sector. The administration's faith-based initiative is an example of national officials' intentionally attempting to shift in-state provider networks to embolden groups that might be expected to offer competing visions for public service provision to existing public bureaucracies. Although not always successful, the administration's effort to empower clients to choose providers under vouchers and to encourage contracting out of social services are other important examples of centralizing federal policy tools' being deployed to reconstruct public administration in state and local governments.

Impact of the Unfunded Mandates Reform Act of 1995

It is notable that these significant federal policy centralization actions occurred despite the existence of the Unfunded Mandates Reform Act of 1995. Passage of this act was made possible by unified state and local lobbying and was seized upon by a new Republican Congress as one of the first planks of its new Contract with America. The reform was greeted with high hopes by those who expected it to signal the dawn of enlightened intergovernmental cooperation and policymaking.

Briefly, UMRA established a new regime for Congress, as well as the executive branch, as it considers legislation defined as unfunded mandates by the law. It strengthens requirements for the CBO to estimate state and local cost and private sector impacts of legislation reported by committees, and it provides a point of order for those intergovernmental mandates exceeding a defined cost threshold or lacking a CBO estimate. The point of order is meant to serve as a vehicle for those concerned about proposed mandates, allowing them to force members to vote separately on the desirability of using a mandate to carry out the goals of the underlying legislation. As such, it is not an impenetrable barrier but more like a speed bump, and it has the potential to embarrass mandate proponents and rally opponents. The unfunded mandate point of order joined a long list of points of order that have been incorporated into the rules of Congress to regulate floor debate and actions on issues ranging from the enforcement of federal budgetary constraints to the prohibition of nongermane amendments.

The actual effect of points of order on congressional behavior can be achieved through several pathways. The first involves the actual raising of points of order by members to stop mandates in their legislative tracks. This pathway has not been particularly productive from the state and local standpoint—a Government Accountability Office report has found that as of March 2004, thirteen points of order had been raised in the House and none in the Senate since the passage of UMRA, and the point of order was sustained only one time, on a 1996 minimum wage vote.[25] The second pathway is created when the CBO cost estimate and the potential for a point of order work as a deterrent, prompting mandate advocates to temper or withdraw their proposals. This certainly has worked in recent years on several notable occasions. In one instance, legislation reported out of the House Ways and

Means Committee would have narrowed the authority of states to impose taxes on businesses that lacked physical nexus in their states.[26] When the CBO estimated annual revenue costs exceeding $3 billion over time, the leadership of the House was persuaded to pull the bill from the calendar.[27] However, this strategy worked only as part of an effective state and local lobbying campaign that adroitly used the CBO estimate to sidetrack the proposed tax preemption.

Notwithstanding this example, the major mandates discussed earlier proceeded in spite of UMRA's web of procedures and information. One obvious reason is that UMRA's coverage is limited, exempting many of the mandates passed in the past five years. Specifically, UMRA primarily covers only statutory direct orders, excluding most grant conditions and preemptions whose fiscal effects fall below the threshold; and statutory direct orders dealing with constitutional rights, prohibition of discrimination, national security, and Social Security are among those excluded from coverage. Moreover, the analytic and procedural requirements do not apply to appropriations bills, floor amendments, or conference reports—those tools of "unorthodox lawmaking" that have become increasingly prevalent in Congress.[28] Among the major mandates discussed here, education reform, homeland security grant conditions, tax base decoupling, elections reform, and welfare reform are among the actions that arguably are not covered by UMRA.

The Politics of Mandates: Toward an Analytic Framework

As the foregoing suggests, UMRA was not able to provide the institutional ballast to prevent surges of nationalizing legislation. The roots of federal mandate and preemptions run deep through the modern political system, and it is unrealistic to expect a procedure to forestall strongly rooted national policy movements involving the intergovernmental system. Indeed, the enactment of UMRA reflected a recognition that the systemic political factors that previously served to institutionalize restraint on the exercise of federal regulatory power over states and localities had become eclipsed by secular shifts in political incentives and national policymaking processes. Yet, as has been discussed, at times federal mandate proposals were stopped or significantly modified, reflecting some continuing forbearance and deference to the state and local sector.

The key analytic project is to understand those factors that shape national decisions on federalism questions. Specifically, what factors influence whether mandates or other forms of coercive federalism will be adopted, modified, or rejected? William Gormley argues that mandates have variable levels of intergovernmental conflict and outcomes, based in part on the magnitude of federal financial support and the range and extent of federal mandates covering particular areas.[29]

The history of mandates over recent decades suggests that several factors have formative influence in determining mandate policy outcomes, reflecting the positions and incentives of federal, state, local, and other political allies as they affect mandates. I have listed the variables below, along with suggested hypotheses linking them to the potential for national policy centralization.

—Federal political cohesion: Federal mandates will tend to increase to the extent that relevant federal officials are unified and mobilized to advance new national goals.

—State and local political cohesion: Federal mandates and other forms of policy centralization will tend to increase if state and local governments are neither united nor effectively mobilized to protect their interests.

—Federal-state policy congruence: Federal mandates will tend to increase to the extent that leading federal and state leaders are in agreement about the substantive goals behind the mandate.

—Alliances: Federal mandates will increase to the extent that state and local governments do not enjoy the support of politically influential interest group or partisan allies.

The cases of federal mandate decisions examined here offer some useful insights on the implications of these variables for the national policy process and our federal system.

Federal Political Cohesion

The cohesiveness and intensity of federal officials for those mandates that passed in recent years were impressive. The presence of unified Republican control over both the presidency and Congress in this period facilitated the passage of mandates to pursue highly partisan agendas. The tax cut agenda of 2001 and the welfare reform reauthorization of 2006 were both driven by deep-seated partisan goals pursued by the Bush administration and conservative Republican leaders in Congress. In at least these cases, strong ideologically based partisan goals trumped any residual support by these party leaders for federalism values. As previous decades have illustrated, the relegation of federalism to a secondary value is itself a nonpartisan phenomenon, reflected by Democrats for certain mandates in health, labor, and environmental areas and by Republicans for business preemption, tax policy, and moral policy goals.

However, partisanship does not account for the entire mandate story since 2001. In fact, some of the most important mandates passed during the Bush era transcended partisan differences and were embraced by broad coalitions that were either truly bipartisan or at least crosspartisan. In these cases, mandates were framed in symbolic and even moral terms that compelled broad support and made opposition politically untenable. Mandated reforms to state and local elections processes enacted under the Help America Vote Act were broadly supported by Republican and Democratic leaders alike in Congress, fearful that they might be blamed for another debacle like the 2000 election on their watch. Homeland security could be placed in this category as well—the perception of crisis prompted leaders of both parties to embrace mandates to protect the very homeland of the nation against potential terrorist attack. Finally, passage of No Child Left Behind was achieved through a broad crosspartisan coalition, as both parties saw significant advantage in championing this new mandate and perceived significant political disadvantages if identified as opposed to such a compelling national goal.

State and Local Political Cohesion

The positioning and cohesion of the state and local sector have played a pivotal, if not surprising, role in the politics of federal mandates. One might expect states, as powerful interest groups represented in Washington, to forcefully argue for their views. However, for a number of reasons, state leaders are often neutralized and even champion particular mandates and preemptions. First, state and local groups are often disarmed by their lack of political cohesion on key policy issues; lacking agreement, they are often unable to articulate positions in national debates.[30] Second, as political leaders, they are sometimes swept away by the compelling political appeal of major federal mandates and preemptions, whether addressing elections reform, education standards, or homeland security requirements. Indeed, with respect to the major mandates enacted from 2001 to 2006, many mandates originate from innovations piloted by state officials themselves. For instance, the roots of No Child Left Behind can be traced to a 1989 conference on education reform, initiated by governors, in Charlottesville, Virginia, followed by formation of the National Education Goals Panel, a state-oriented commission that worked for more than a decade to sustain support for national reforms.

Third, state leaders have come to endorse certain preemptions and mandates to address collective action problems stemming from intergovernmental competition that can undermine states' incentives to assume policy leadership in key areas. Governors and other state leaders have supported mandates in order to put a floor under competition from other states that can undermine their policy initiatives. The Real ID Act, which has drawn the ire of state and local officials for its regulatory intrusiveness and high costs, was born of a voluntary national standards–setting initiative undertaken by state motor vehicle administrators in the prior decade, who recognized that the absence of harmony among state license procedures made the entire system vulnerable to security threats. Ironically, such voluntary national standard initiatives are vulnerable to capture by federal policy officials anxious to respond to national problems and eager to legitimize the solution as a state-based approach. In recent years, progressive or advanced states have come to champion partial preemptions that place a floor on competition among states while allowing advanced states to maintain their policy initiatives.[31]

Paul Manna captures states' positioning dilemmas well in his book on the politics of educational federalism. He suggests that mandates such as No Child Left Behind come about when government officials at both federal and state levels perceive an advantage to engaging the resources, authority, and legitimacy of other levels of government. The tendency for federal officials to engage in this practice is, of course, what gives rise to grants, mandates, and other tools of third-party governance. However, Manna adds that states have similar incentives to "borrow authority" from the federal government to pursue items on their policy agendas that they cannot carry out on their own.[32]

Ironically, in the contemporary environment of nationalized economic, social, cultural, and political forces, the very innovations that states pioneered have helped fuel the nationalization of policy. Far from being cause for celebration, state innovations and differences are cause for alarm and signal the need for further federal action from advocates who want to expand state-initiated policies to the nation as a whole and from business and others who are opposed to these policies. In either case, mandates and preemptions are tools used to either expand or override these policies. Frank Baumgartner and Bryan Jones describe these policy dynamics as "venue shopping," which, they argue, can promote greater policy activism at all levels as advocates and opponents opportunistically find that level of government most hospitable to their position.[33]

This is not to say that states and localities are without influence in the politics of mandating. As key interest groups, they can have an impact when taking cohesive positions and mobilizing their memberships to advance their interests. However, given the substantial ambivalence of state and local officials toward the goals promoted by mandates, I have argued elsewhere, state and local governments achieve their political impact less in the debate over whether to mandate than in the debate over how to mandate.[34] Indeed, under such mandates as No Child Left Behind and the Help America Vote Act, states did gain substantial new federal funds for implementing these complex initiatives and significant regulatory concessions as well. This is partly owing to the relative ease through which state and local governments can agree on the means rather than the ends of mandated programs, as well as the desire of many in Congress to mollify opponents to facilitate passage.

Perhaps more fundamentally, state and local governments gain bargaining leverage when considering implementation issues because the federal government critically relies on them to achieve its policy goals. Simply put, the policy ambition of the federal government far exceeds its administrative, legal, fiscal, and political capacity to implement federal programs, mandates, and preemptions. Accordingly, states and local governments, as well as a wide range of nonprofit and private corporations, are brought in as third parties to carry out federal initiatives through a host of governmental tools, including grants and loans in addition to regulatory tools.[35] The implementation literature has long noted that intergovernmental relations during implementation are characterized more by bargaining than by top-down fiat.[36]

Table 13-1 shows potential outcomes stemming from combinations of two variables—federal and state political cohesion. The classic unfunded mandate outcome can be expected when federal officials are cohesive and states are either divided or not engaged. We might expect mandates to be funded and regulatory flexibility to be provided when states and federal officials are both equally engaged and cohesive. When states are cohesive and federal officials divided or unengaged, a grant or even outright defeat of federal involvement might be expected, much along the lines predicted by Phillip Monypenny, who concludes that federal grants are adopted when national leaders lack sufficient consensus to agree on stronger tools.[37] Finally, lack of cohesion and engagement from both sides can be expected to produce policy gridlock.

The relative cohesion and intensity of federal and state actors helps explain some of the outcomes presented here.[38] In the face of cohesive and engaged federal leadership, the ambivalence and divisions among state officials helped pave the way for the Help America Vote Act, No Child Left Behind, the Real ID Act, and estate tax cuts. The cases of defeated federal proposals illustrate the reverse—cohesive state officials and divided or unengaged federal

Table 13-1. *Impact of Federal and State Cohesion*

| | Federal cohesion | |
State cohesion	High	Low
HIGH	Funded mandate/partial preemption	Grant
LOW	Unfunded mandate/total preemption	Gridlock

officials. A unified state and local campaign was indeed able to defeat such proposals as the protection of methyl tertiary butyl ether producers, the business activity tax, and the administration's proposed capping of the Medicaid program, taking advantage of both federal dissensus and powerful interest group support. Given the complexity of the policy process, it is not surprising that other factors influence outcomes beyond the relative cohesion of each sector. For instance, in the case of welfare reform reauthorization, states not only were cohesive and well mobilized but they also had powerful allies in social advocacy groups and Senate Democrats intent on defeating new work mandates and pressing for higher funding. Nonetheless, the persistence of Bush administration officials and conservative leadership in Congress, along with the adroit use of budget reconciliation to sidestep a Democrat-led filibuster, were instrumental in gaining final passage.

Goal Congruence

The congruence in goals among federal and state or local officials also has a bearing on the potential adoption of mandates and other coercive federalism approaches. Although considerable tension marks the relationships between federal officials and their state and local counterparts, the extent of state and local support for the underlying goals of some of the major mandates passed from 2001 to 2006 is impressive. Broadly speaking, in a society whose economy, culture, and communications have become increasingly nationalized, it is not surprising that state and local officials have become less insulated from and more vulnerable to national values and interests. Institutional developments are partly responsible—a nationalized media and national interest groups that have increasingly colonized state capitols have carried national values to state and local doorsteps.

The tools of cooperative federalism have also helped institutionalize national priorities throughout the intergovernmental system. Federal grant programs have, over time, had a centralizing influence over state and local priorities, as those programs have succeeded in building supportive bureau-cracies and clientele groups that have become powerful advocates for feder-ally funded initiatives within state and local governments. Well-known stud-ies on policy implementation have long pointed to what is known as a "maturation effect," whereby the interests of federal principals and state and local agents converge over time in a professional consensus on strategic direc-tion and program priorities.[39] Most of the five major centralizing actions taken over the period 2001–06 arose from a foundation of support that had been nurtured over the years through cooperative federalism frameworks. Whether it be education's accommodation with federal equity goals, state motor vehicle departments' cooperation in commercial driver's licensure, the largely successful devolution of welfare achieved ten years earlier, or the pre-vious federal efforts to promote voting rights and access, federal programs may have succeeded in institutionalizing support for national goals and inter-ests within state and local governments. Ironically, the familiarity and politi-cal support spawned by these essentially cooperative forerunners may well have paved the way for their more coercive successors.

Interest Group Alliances

The position of key interest groups plays a vital role in mandate outcomes. The major mandates passed since 2001 were often promoted by powerful interest groups in alliance with key congressional and executive political entrepreneurs. Preemption of states' taxation of sales over the Internet, for instance, was spearheaded by a broad business coalition of telecommunica-tions and Internet-based firms that saw an opportunity to throw off the yoke of differing state and local taxation regimes. They were supported by congres-sional entrepreneurs of both parties, such as Democratic senator Ron Wyden from Oregon and Republican senator George Allen from Virginia—both from states whose economies had strong Internet companies.

Conversely, state and local governments realized major victories when they were able to build coalitions with powerful groups opposed to mandate pro-posals. Their successful defeat of President Bush's proposal to reform and cut the Medicaid program benefited from the forceful advocacy of social welfare groups as well as health care providers concerned about the implications of these changes for their bottom lines. Similarly, the alliance of the state and local sector with the environmental movement was pivotal to their success in warding off the proposed preemption of local lawsuits over pollution from methyl tertiary butyl ether contamination.

The Entropy of Mandates

It is likely that the relationships among these variables change over time, with important implications for mandate politics and outcomes. Mandates are often enacted on a wave of enthusiasm, as advocates make a case that is compelling enough to rise to the status of a valence issue, opposition being perceived as politically illegitimate. Anthony Downs writes that many issues are subject to an "issue attention cycle," whereby issues that rise on waves of enthusiasm and alarmed discovery are destined to fall and lose support as concerns over their costs and design problems—which lay politically dormant during their initial adoption—become more apparent and politically salient.[40]

Mandates, too, have a political life cycle that often parallels the issue attention cycle. Mandate proposals, on first blush, tend to highlight the benefits, whereas the costs are difficult to measure or appreciate until regulations are issued, often years after initial passage of legislation. During the initial passage, state and local government officials are prone to being divided, ambivalent, and actually supportive of the purposes, exhibiting low cohesion and high goal congruence—an ideal breeding ground for the propagation of centralizing policies, as noted above. However, these political dynamics are reversed during the implementation cycle. State and local cohesion grows as the costs and program design challenges become more salient to officials throughout the country; not surprisingly, conflict between the goals and priorities of state and local and federal officials heightens at this stage, as well. Thus, for instance, though state and local officials offered little opposition to initial passage of No Child Left Behind, many are now joining forces with teachers unions to mount vigorous protests of the program's standards and constraints, including attempting to gain court injunctions against the program's most onerous mandates.

Thus the politics behind the initial adoption of mandates is centralizing, and the politics of implementation is decentralizing. Although policy analysts would prefer a system in which costs and benefits are considered synoptically, in fact costs are often dealt with separately and serially from benefits as a result. This style of policymaking resembles the politics of speculative augmentation that Charles Jones has found to characterize the development of clean air policy.[41] Under pressure to take bold action in response to public bandwagons, Congress adopts policy that is not firmly grounded in the capability of its implementers. Such a policy produces a lurching attempt to square policy ambition with administrative and fiscal realities, inviting public disillusionment with the policy and even with government itself once the mismatches between policy goals and implementation become apparent.

Conclusions

Federal actions constituting coercive federalism, including mandates, continue to be a significant feature of our government system, relied upon by a diverse range of actors to accomplish a wide variety of policy and political goals. The early years of the twenty-first century continued trends observed in prior decades, breaking new ground in the nationalization and centralization of policy in areas that had heretofore largely been untouched by the instruments of coercive federalism. Intergovernmental tensions and consequences have been accentuated by simultaneous federal actions that both increase intergovernmental fiscal burdens through spending mandates and at the same time limit revenues available to state and local governments to finance these far-flung federal policy initiatives. The combined effects of these initiatives will work together to encumber a greater share of the fiscal commons for national policy initiatives than we have seen in the past.

Notwithstanding the intergovernmental tensions that mandates bring about, many of these initiatives have garnered broad support from both federal and state actors in our system. Policy issues increasingly sweep over federal and state governments alike in waves of enthusiasm that know no political boundaries. In a nationalized media culture, state and national political communities and values have become more integrated, and state and local leaders have become every bit as vulnerable to the same publicly compelling policy stampedes as are national leaders. Jurisdictional boundaries have increasingly become permeable; federal grants have prompted the institutionalization of national values and interests in state governments, while state policy innovations increasingly seed the national agenda with compelling new problem definitions and solutions. Cross-pressured by overlapping allegiances to national values and interests, state and local officials have become uncertain trumpeters of their own prerogatives in the federal system. Federal and state governments perceive an advantage to "borrowing authority" to engage the resources, authority, and legitimacy of other levels of government.[42] In essence, all levels of government are increasingly engaged in an "opportunistic federalism" whereby all actors in the system attempt to use one another to achieve particular policy goals, irrespective of traditional boundaries and authority distributions.[43] Although the Supreme Court has resumed its role in recent times of policing the boundaries, John Kincaid argues that the Court has undergone a "federalism fizzle" in ruling against states on recent preemption cases in the past several years.[44]

As we face such vexing challenges as the baby boom retirement and global economic change, marbleized, networked approaches to governance may in fact be necessary to respond to daunting problems. Whether it be health care costs, climate change, or education, intergovernmental responses will be necessary. In "borrowing authority," however, it matters whether cooperative or coercive federalism tools are engaged. Although perhaps more efficient in responding to insistent national majorities, coercive strategies have the potential to short-circuit the feedback loops in our system, curtailing the potential for policy learning through the accretion of experience gained by state and local governments. And most certainly, such strategies also can work to undercut the ability of our system to accommodate the diversity of our nation and the vitality of our federal system.

Notes

1. John Kincaid, "From Cooperative to Coercive Federalism," *Annals of the American Academy of Political and Social Science* 509 (May 1990): 139–52.

2. U.S. Advisory Commission on Intergovernmental Relations, *Federally Induced Costs Affecting State and Local Governments*, M-193 (Government Printing Office, 1994).

3. U.S. Advisory Commission on Intergovernmental Relations, *Regulatory Federalism: Policy, Progress, Impact, and Reform*, A-95 (GPO, 1984).

4. Paul L. Posner, *The Politics of Unfunded Mandates: Whither Federalism?* (Georgetown University Press, 1998).

5. Ibid.

6. Daniel Judah Elazar, *Constitutional Design and Power-Sharing in the Post-Modern Epoch* (Lanham, Md.: University Press of America, 1991).

7. John C. Fortier and Norman J. Ornstein, "President Bush: Legislative Strategist," in *The George W. Bush Presidency: An Early Assessment*, edited by Fred I. Greenstein, pp. 138–72 (Johns Hopkins University Press, 2003), 139.

8. While not enough to fully cover all incremental costs, federal appropriations for Title I increased by 45 percent in the five years since the passage of NCLB (Office of Management and Budget, *Analytic Perspectives: Budget of the U.S. Government* [2006], p. 102).

9. Paul E. Peterson, Barry G. Rabe, and Kenneth K. Wong, *When Federalism Works* (Brookings, 1986).

10. Ellen Pearlman, "Welfare Workout," *Governing* 20 (November 2006): 54–57.

11. Sarah F. Liebschutz and Daniel J. Palazzolo, "The States and the Help America Vote Act," *Publius: The Journal of Federalism* 35 (Fall 2005): 497–517.

12. Congressional Research Service, *Election Reform: The Help America Vote Act and Issues for Congress,* EBERF4 (June 2004).

13. *Interstate Income Tax Law,* P.L. 86-272.

14. *National Bellas Hess Inc.* v. *Illinois Department of Revenue,* 386 U.S. 753 (1967); *Quill Corporation, Petitioner* v. *North Dakota,* by and through its Tax Commissioner, Heidi Heitkamp, 504 U.S. 298 (1992).

15. Congressional Budget Office, "Cost estimate on HR 3678, Internet Tax Freedom Act Amendments of 2007," October 17, 2007.

16. Paul Posner, "Emergence of Protective Federalism," paper prepared for the annual meeting of the American Political Science Association, Philadelphia, August 27, 2003 (www.allacademic.com/meta/p63473_index.html).

17. Roger Cross, *Driver's License Security Issues,* testimony before the House Subcommittee on Highways and Transit, Committee on Transportation and Infrastructure, 107 Congress, 2 sess., September 5, 2002.

18. *Intelligence Reform and Terrorism Prevention Act of 2004,* P.L. 108-408.

19. *Emergency Supplemental Appropriations Act for Defense, the Global War on Terror, and Tsunami Relief,* P.L. 109-13.

20. National Governors Association, National Conference of State Legislatures, American Association of Motor Vehicles Administrators, *The Real ID Act: National Impact Analysis* (Washington, 2006).

21. *Energy Policy Act of 2005,* H.R. 6.

22. Congressional Budget Office, Cost Estimate, in letter to author, July 11, 2006.

23. National Academy of Public Administration, *Financing Governments in the 21st Century: Intergovernmental Collaboration Can Promote Fiscal and Economic Goals* (Washington, 2006).

24. Janet Weiss, "Public Information," in *The Tools of Government: A Guide to the New Governance,* edited by Lester Salamon (Oxford University Press, 2002), pp. 217–54.

25. U.S. Government Accountability Office, *Unfunded Mandates: Analysis of Reform Act Coverage,* GAO-04-637 (Government Printing Office, May 2004).

26. See *Business Activity Tax Simplification Act of 2005,* H.R. 1956.

27. Congressional Budget Office, Cost estimate, July 11, 2006.

28. Barbara Sinclair, *Unorthodox Lawmaking: New Legislative Processes in the U.S. Congress,* 2nd ed. (Washington: CQ Press, 2000).

29. William T. Gormley Jr., "Money and Mandates: The Politics of Intergovernmental Conflict," *Publius: The Journal of Federalism* 36 (Fall 2006): 523–40.

30. Donald Haider, *When Governments Come to Washington: Governors, Mayors, and Intergovernmental Lobbying* (New York: Free Press, 1974).

31. R. Daniel Kelemen, "A Political Theory of Regulatory Federalism," paper prepared for the annual meeting of the American Political Science Association, Atlanta, Georgia, September 2–5, 1999.

32. Paul Manna, *School's In: Federalism and the National Education Agenda, 1965–2001* (Georgetown University Press, 2006), p. 38.

33. Frank Baumgartner and Bryan Jones, *Agendas and Instability in American Politics* (University of Chicago Press, 1993), p. 217.

34. Posner, *Politics of Unfunded Mandates.*

35. Lester Salamon, ed., *The Tools of Government: A Guide to the New Governance* (Oxford University Press, 2002).

36. Helen Ingram, "Policy Implementation through Bargaining: The Case of Federal Grants in Aid," *Public Policy* 25 (Fall 1977): 499–526.

37. Phillip Monypenny, "Federal Grants-in-Aid to State and Local Governments: A Political Analysis," *National Tax Journal* 13 (March 1960): 1–16.

38. Cohesion is defined as degree of agreement and political mobilization or engagement. At the federal level, it is defined by degree of consensus achieved across parties. Cohesion for state officials is based on positions taken by the leading organizations of state officials.

39. Peterson, Rabe, and Wong, *When Federalism Works.*

40. Anthony Downs, "Up and Down with Ecology: The Issue Attention Cycle," *Public Interest* 28 (Summer 1972): 38–50.

41. Charles O. Jones, *Clean Air: The Policy and Politics of Pollution Control* (University of Pittsburgh Press, 1975).

42. Manna, *School's In.*

43. Timothy J. Conlan, "From Cooperative to Opportunistic Federalism: Reflections on the Half-Century Anniversary of the Commission on Intergovernmental Relations," *Public Administration Review* 66 (September–October 2006): 663–76.

44. John Kincaid, "State-Federal Relations: Federal Dollars Down, Federal Power Up," in *The Book of the States 2006* (Lexington, Ky.: Council of State Governments, 2006), pp. 19–25, 24.

14

Intergovernmental Lobbying:

How Opportunistic Actors Create a Less Structured and Balanced Federal System

TROY E. SMITH

The distribution of power and responsibilities among the federal tiers of U.S. government has changed over time according to different constitutional interpretations and political practices. During America's first century, state governments' powers and responsibilities were protected by a dual-federalism interpretation of the Constitution. During the nation's second century, state governments saw their power and responsibilities diluted as Congress and the Supreme Court reinterpreted the Constitution to promote collaboration between the state and national governments. In this, America's third century, state governments have used political processes to preserve their powers and promote their interests, because they cannot rely on a constitutional division of responsibilities, Congress, or the Supreme Court to preserve specific powers. Some of the most important political processes are evident in Congress, where states lobby to preserve their powers and promote their interests. In these political processes, state governments act like other interest groups vying before Congress for power, federal funds, and protection from undesirable federal intervention. Contemporary state government lobbying often, however, results unexpectedly in the accretion of national power and authority.

Governors are the most likely lobby representing states' interests. They have more lobbying resources and can limit the lobbying activities of most other state officials. This chapter therefore focuses on gubernatorial lobbying. However, much of what is said here about governors also applies to other state officials who are willing to commit time and resources to intergovernmental lobbying.

The Evolution of American Federalism

The nineteenth century's system of dual federalism, with its narrowly interpreted Constitution and division of responsibilities among the federal tiers, gave way in the twentieth century to cooperation and then to process federalism. This transition was made possible by a Supreme Court that, after the Civil War, asserted its right to define the distribution of powers in the federal system and then, failing to clearly define and enforce those boundaries, abandoned the responsibility to the political process in 1985.

In the twentieth century, Congress (with the judiciary's allowance and sometimes invitation) interpreted its constitutional grants of power broadly. In the first half of the century, Congress used the Constitution's general welfare clause as an independent power to tax and spend (*United States* v. *Butler* [1936]), and the interstate commerce clause to regulate the health, safety, and welfare of citizens (*United States* v. *Darby Lumber Company* [1941] and *Wickard* v. *Filburn* [1942]). These were powers once thought reserved to the states. In the second half of the twentieth century, Congress moved from working cooperatively with states in certain policy areas to imposing requirements, restrictions, and limitations on the states. For example, Congress attached conditions to federal grants that often had little to do with the grant's purpose (in the form of crossover sanctions and crosscutting sanctions). Congress also implemented mandates (requiring states to take certain actions) and preemptions (prohibiting states from certain powers or actions).[1]

State governments' control over law and policy eroded as Congress and the judiciary emphasized individuals over state governments. Federal interventions in traditional state areas of authority were often justified to guarantee individual rights denied by state and local governments. Consequently, the judiciary's incorporation of the Bill of Rights and the Warren Court's individual rights revolution emphasized individuals over communities and national oversight over states' police powers. This shift continued as Congress tied program funding to individuals rather than geographic areas.[2] The national government's growing involvement in domestic and local issues did not mean an equal decline in state powers and responsibilities— indeed, state powers and responsibilities often increased as federal programs opened new areas of responsibility for the states—but it did represent a decline in states' autonomy and ability to control their own policies.

As the federal government assumed greater responsibility for more programs and policy areas in the twentieth century, Congress shifted significant control over the substance and intricacies of intergovernmental programs to the federal bureaucracy and the courts.[3] By allowing national preeminence over policymaking, the federal judiciary and Supreme Court, wittingly or not, empowered themselves to define the policy details of congressional programs, thus further displacing state governments.

As Congress and the judiciary supplanted traditional federalism divisions in one area after another, the remaining federalism limits became increasingly difficult to defend. In 1985, in a decision that has not been reversed, the Supreme Court declared that it would no longer adjudicate disputes between the national and state governments but leave it to the political process to resolve them.[4] Despite some limited pro-state rulings in the 1990s that attempted to limit the scope of the commerce clause (for example, *United States* v. *Lopez* [1995], *Printz* v. *United States* [1997]) and to buttress states' sovereign immunity (for example, *Alden* v. *Maine* [1999]), the court's state-friendly federalism rulings stalled after 2002.[5] The *Gonzales* v. *Raich* (2005) decision, which upheld national laws forbidding the possession of marijuana over states' laws allowing its use for medical purposes, reasserted the preeminence of the national government's commerce power over states' police powers, and Justice John Paul Stevens's majority opinion instructing the proponents of medical marijuana to take their case to Congress reaffirmed *Garcia's* doctrine of process federalism. Similarly, the Court significantly restricted states' sovereign immunity rights in a number of 2004 rulings.[6] If state governments are to defend and protect their interests in the intergovernmental system, they need to develop their capacity to participate in and influence the national policymaking process. In many instances, this means state officials or their representatives must lobby the federal government.

Political processes have become an important means of distributing responsibilities between the federal tiers. In the twentieth century, the Supreme Court and certain political practices removed constitutional barriers and authorized other political practices that significantly redistributed power in the national government's favor.[7] The "end of southern exceptionalism"[8] has not reversed this process. How power and responsibilities are to be distributed among America's federal tiers is no longer self-evident from the Constitution but must now be sought in the political processes of America's intergovernmental system.

Three Misleading Assumptions

The federal structure of the United States creates considerable ambiguity and complications in any effort to understand how states communicate with, and try to influence, Congress and national policymaking. Those efforts are often hampered by three misleading assumptions.

The first is that states will work cooperatively to oppose federal incursions on state powers. This assumption is challenged by Mancur Olson's work on collective action.[9] According to Olson, collective actions suffer from three problems: first, as the number of members in a group increases, the group's stated interests and objectives are diluted; second, larger groups impose disproportionate organizational costs; third, in large groups, some members may free ride, that is, they seek to gain the benefits without paying any of the costs or doing any of the work. Efforts to get state officials to agree on a position and work collectively suffer from all three of these problems at both the intrastate and interstate levels.[10] State governments' lack of cohesion, Martha Derthick notes, has provided the federal government opportunities to adopt policies that restrict the states.[11] In light of these findings, state government collective action cannot be assumed.

The second assumption posits that the public favors its state government over the national government. Yet a significant portion of the population feels little attachment to its state or local governments, in large part because growing mobility diminishes people's attachment to a specific geographic location, the nationalization of news gives significantly less attention to local and state issues, and federal funds are increasingly transferred directly to individuals rather than through state governments.[12] Consequently, public loyalty to state governments has declined, reducing state officials' ability to challenge national encroachments and increasing Congress's discretionary powers.

The third assumption conflates "state" as a geographic unit with "state government." Institutional theory teaches that individual interests are shaped in large part by the institutions to which one belongs.[13] Hence, though members of Congress and state government officials may be elected by the same constituents, their different institutions create different policy interests.[14] Members of Congress and state officials, Larry D. Kramer correctly notes, "are rivals, not allies."[15] Preemptions and mandates are one means whereby senators, representatives, and presidents can represent the desires of their constituents while simultaneously impairing state governments' interests. Distinguishing between the political and geographic units reveals that actions often considered state centered may not support state governments' roles or responsibilities in the federal system.[16]

These three assumptions impair our ability to understand the inherent obstacles and difficulties facing state governments when they try to protect and promote their common and collective interests in the federal system. To acknowledge these as assumptions rather than established facts is to recognize that neither collective action, nor public loyalty, nor congressional members' support are inherent features that can be relied on to protect state government interests in the intergovernmental system.

Congress: Institutions, Roles, and Interests

To influence the creation of intergovernmental programs, state officials must work largely through members of Congress, the architects of the intergovernmental system and a "key force" pushing the centralization of power in the national government.[17] State officials, however, have little formal constitutional power they can bring to bear on members of Congress. The institutional powers state officials do have are more often used for partisan, rather than institutional, objectives (reapportionment, for example, could be used more effectively to enhance state institutional interests vis-à-vis Congress). Consequently, state officials must approach Congress on its own turf and terms, using various lobbying strategies to influence public policy. Successful lobbying requires an understanding of how the institutions, roles, and interests of Congress affect what, where, and how members of Congress may be accessed and influenced.

Institutions: Political Parties

Up until the 1960s, political parties were state based, and members of Congress ignored the interests of the state-centered political parties at great peril. State political parties, in many instances, either funded campaigns, decided who would run for Congress on the party's label, or determined the campaign issues the candidates would run on—and sometimes, all three. State and local officials enjoyed considerable power at national and state party conventions, where either the party's presidential or congressional candidates were selected. Many state parties viewed their congressional representatives as "emissaries sent to represent their local party's interests in Washington."[18]

Consequently, state political parties were an important means of state government influence on national policies.[19]

During the 1960s, as candidates decided to run without state or local party support, raised their own campaign funds, and chose their own campaign issues, their reliance on state political parties decreased.[20] The rise of candidate-centered elections appeared to correlate with a decline of American parties.[21] What actually happened, however, was that state and local parties were displaced in congressional races by national party organizations—once dismissed as "politics without power."[22] National party organizations now often recruit candidates, offer campaign advice and expertise, determine the issues and agendas for candidates to run on (for example, the 1994 Contract with America), and direct and focus power, organizational skills, and money to win congressional seats and control national institutions.[23]

The relative importance of national party organizations within Congress has also grown significantly.[24] Unlike earlier eras of decentralized power with individual members of Congress seeking individual programs favored by state and local party organizations, much of the contemporary era features strong party leaders directing interparty fights over omnibus bills containing the majority party's spending and taxing priorities and occasional interparty fights over morality policy. Slim majorities in Congress, tight electoral competition at the polls, and limited federal funds for discretionary programs have increased congressional members' willingness to empower their party leaders to set the agenda, determine the rules governing debate and the content of bills, and manage the party's public relations campaigns in an effort to build public support for the party. Although party leaders lack the power to deny nominations or elections to Congress, and a large, diverse nation creates multiple and conflicting agendas within the same party, the national party organizations have gained significant and effective powers that create important loyalties and commitments among their members.[25] The influence of national political party organizations in congressional campaigns and inside Congress has waxed, while the state and local party organizations' connections to congressional candidates have waned.

Consequently, bonds between members of Congress and state and local officials have weakened considerably.[26] Relationships, camaraderie, and trust between state and national officials are important preconditions for effective lobbying and often develop as candidates for state and national office campaign together.[27] The few remaining institutional connections between congressional and state party officials have been jeopardized by the 2002 Bipartisan Campaign Reform Act, which has further nationalized congressional campaigns. The act requires that any electioneering for national candidates by a state political party must be paid for with "hard money," contributed directly to a candidate's campaign. Consequently, Democratic "coordinated campaigns" and Republican "victory plans," both of which coordinated national and state party organizational and voter mobilization efforts through significant hard and soft money transfers, will most likely be reduced considerably. This will diminish state and local parties' motivation to participate in federal elections.[28] After the 2004 elections, Raymond J. La Raja noted that "political spending in federal elections is now concentrated heavily at the national level."[29] The act advances a four-decade-long trend of separating and distancing state and national officials, which is likely to further diminish the personal bonds between state and national officials essential to exchanging information, constructive collaboration, and lobbying.[30]

Until the 1960s, members of Congress viewed themselves as delegates representing their state and local party organizations. Today, on intergovernmental matters, they are likely to view themselves as trustees with few limitations or punishments for voting contrary to the wishes of their state and local party organizations. Statistical analysis indicates that state political parties today are no longer a significant factor facilitating or impairing gubernatorial lobbying in Washington.[31] Members of Congress and their staff express a willingness to help members of their state party, but they will not risk their own political careers to do so.[32] Today, the role of state political parties in facilitating intergovernmental lobbying appears intermittent, informal, personal, and declining.

Institutions: The House of Representatives and the Senate

State government officials who lobby Congress sometimes find it easier to work with their state's U.S. senators than with members of the House of Representatives. This difference is largely attributable to differences in constituencies, terms of office, and institutional organization. The Senate, however, presents its own unique difficulties impairing state governments' lobbying influence.

State government officials lobbying the House of Representatives must find representatives with sufficient power in the House who are willing to replace their district-oriented perspective for a state-oriented perspective. The hierarchical organization of the House means that power resides in the majority party's leaders, while the rank and file and the minority party have minimal influence. Consequently, state government officials must identify and lobby those representatives who can affect the legislative process. Even then, representatives may not be receptive because their two-year terms of office keep many representatives focused on their district's or national interests rather than their state's interests. "There is little in the current system that pushes them to define issues in statewide terms."[33] Consequently, the potential pressure points available to state government advocates to influence representatives are limited.

Senators tend to be more attentive than representatives to the interests of state government, because senators are less likely than representatives to hold a "safe" seat, and senators represent more diverse constituencies, requiring them to appeal to a broader group to win reelection.[34] Senators also tend to be attentive to the interests of their governors, because governors and senators represent the same constituents and governors are often the most dangerous challengers a senator will face. In addition, senators may welcome state officials' perspectives, because two senators from each state with limited committee assignments cannot monitor or understand every issue being considered by Congress that may affect their state.[35] Individual senators are also often more influential in the legislative process than representatives, owing to the decentralized structure of the Senate and the power of the filibuster. This gives almost every governor access and some means to influence one or two congressional members who can affect bills in Congress.

The nature of intergovernmental data also favors the representation of state interests in the Senate. Because most federal program data are disaggregated by state but not by congressional district, state officials can use these data to demonstrate how proposed programs and amendments will affect a state's citizens. Because the citizens are a senator's constituents, and Congress values representation, senators are very interested in these data. In the 104th Congress (1995–96), Florida's governor Lawton Chiles failed to influence representatives from Florida but succeeded with Florida's senators, because information on the possible consequences of the proposed welfare reform could be determined at the state level but rarely at the district level. When presented with state-level data, Florida's representatives usually claimed that their districts' demography was sufficiently different from the state's that the data did not apply to them. The ability to match data to constituents aids significantly in lobbying campaigns, because it appeals to the congressional member's desire to represent his or her constituents.

Although state officials have certain advantages in lobbying senators, this does not mean that senators are always more receptive to state officials' interests and preferences; and senators are certainly not reliable protectors of state governments' powers and interests.[36] As intended by the founders, senators are not beholden to state governments and may take a national, as opposed to a state, view of issues.[37] Senators may oppose a governor if doing so will prevent a legislative victory that would enhance the governor's reelection prospects and ability to challenge the senator in a future election. Senators who previously served as governor often think they understand the states' perspective and are more likely to challenge the state governments' and governors' arguments. Finally, many senators hold ambitions for higher office and work to expand their constituency beyond the state's borders. Any or all of these factors may impair state governments' ability to influence senators.

Neither representatives nor senators emphasize federalism as a vital and primary concern. State officials in Washington find that members of Congress are more likely to respond to their appeals when a state government's interests can be framed in terms of the member's constituents. In doing so, it is important to note, the interests represented by the state official are not the state government's interests but the state government's understanding of the state populace's interests. Such framing is effective because it appeals to the representative role of members of Congress.

Roles

Congress has two roles: representation and policymaking. Members of Congress place a premium on representation, and they have structured Congress to effectively represent interests rather than to form consistent, coherent, and long-term policies.[38] Examining Congress's role in shaping America's federal system should, therefore, acknowledge Congress's preference for interest representation over consistent, coherent, and long-term policymaking and examine who or what members of Congress represent.

As national political party organizations displaced state political parties, members of Congress shifted from representing the interests of their state party and state governments to representing their constituents, national interest groups (which increasingly provide significant campaign resources), or their national party in hopes of gaining or maintaining majority status. Because Congress values representation over consistent and coherent policymaking, issues that are not well represented before Congress generally receive little attention. Today, no group exists with the primary purpose of defending and promoting federalism. Consequently and not surprisingly, studies find that neither chamber of Congress nor either political party places much value on federalism except as a secondary interest used primarily to embarrass the opposing party's position on a specific issue.[39] Lacking a consistent and vociferous advocate, state governments' general powers and interests have often been underrepresented or neglected in congressional policymaking.

Congress does take its role as a policymaker seriously, especially when policymaking benefits representation. It would be difficult for many incumbents to justify their reelection if they could not demonstrate some effectiveness in proposing, crafting, and passing policy. Yet much of current congressional policymaking is targeted to congressional members' constituents. One area in which members of Congress shape policy to benefit favored interests is in writing earmarks—designating funds to a specific purpose or constituency. Between 1998 and 2005, the number of earmarks increased 667 percent.[40] Although policymaking is what Congress does, omnibus bills, committees subject to party leaders' oversight and control, and limited opportunities to introduce amendments suggest a Congress more intent on representing political parties and favored clientele than on the process of good policymaking.[41]

When budget deficits make national funds scarce, Congress shifts from the pork-barrel politics of disbursing public funds to rewarding rent-seeking behaviors using unfunded mandates, regulatory programs, targeted tax breaks, and public facilitation of private lawsuits for a "preferred clientele."[42] Congressional members seeking support for their bills may also offer supporters "fixes," in the form of exemptions from the proposed policy's rules and regulations. These legislative tactics allow politicians to claim credit, help supporters, and co-opt opponents.

Consequently, both Democratic and Republican members of Congress supported many policies that shifted power and authority from the state and local governments to the national government.[43] Successful intergovernmental lobbyists recognize that though members of Congress desire, and often earnestly work for, clear and coherent policies, such policies are unlikely to pass if they interfere with congressional members' role as representatives.

The past four decades have witnessed a significant shift in how members of Congress represent various interests. Before the 1960s, when state and local political parties were strong factors in congressional elections, members of Congress were likely to be delegates on federalism and intergovernmental affairs and trustees or free agents on other issues. Congressional representation shifted with the decline of state and local political parties and the rise of national party organizations, national interest groups, sunshine laws, and "gotcha" journalism. In the twenty-first century, members of Congress are more likely to be trustees or free agents on federalism and intergovernmental issues and delegates on issues of concern to the national parties and vital interest groups. Consequently, federalism and intergovernmental interests are likely to be neglected or reduced to secondary status behind pressures members of Congress feel to raise campaign funds, gain influential political endorsements, avoid offending the wrong groups, and feed the media without being eaten by it. In this environment, it is no wonder that members of Congress feel more pressure to represent their national parties and favored interest groups than defer to the traditional norms of federalism or carefully craft the intricate details of coherent, consistent, and long-term intergovernmental policies.

Interests

Lobbying often requires recognizing the interests of members of Congress and how and where one can impair or facilitate the accomplishment of those interests. The primary interests of members of Congress, according to Richard Fenno, are reelection, policy, and power in the institution.[44] The influence of state officials often depends on their ability to affect the policy and reelection interests of members of Congress.

These days, the most effective means state officials have of influencing Congress is to provide expertise on the consequences of various policy proposals. State officials' experience with policies gives them expertise Congress may seek in order to structure and implement policies that fulfill its objectives.[45] When Congress rewrote U.S. welfare policy under the Personal Responsibility and Work Opportunity Reconciliation Act of 1996, its members and their staff listened closely to the expertise a few governors had gained while reforming their state's welfare policies (although the governors' influence in 1995–96 owed in no small part to the new Republican majority's inexperience in crafting policy and has declined significantly ever since).[46] Although limited, state governments' best opportunities to influence Congress are through policy expertise and bureaucratic innovation rather than through political parties.

Some state officials, particularly the governor, may be in a position to positively or negatively influence the election or reelection of members of Congress, although the Bipartisan Campaign Reform Act will likely minimize those opportunities. In the past, state officials might have campaigned with a congressional candidate, popular state officials might have endorsed or withheld their endorsement from congressional candidates, and state political parties funneled considerable soft money to congressional candidates' campaigns. All these gave state officials points of access and influence with congressional candidates. As noted above, however, the act's provision prohibiting state political parties from using soft money for national campaigns will have a chilling effect on state officials' role in campaigns for national office, thereby diminishing one pressure point state officials have used to access and influence members of Congress.

Politically popular state officials with access to a bully pulpit may try to pressure members of Congress to address a specific issue by directing media attention to that issue. Former Idaho governor Cecil Andrus referred to this tactic as "rattling the cage" of his congressional delegates.[47] Although such tactics may be successful in the short term, they tend to anger members of Congress and impair future collaboration.

State and local officials may unwittingly influence the elevation to the national level of issues traditionally reserved to the states. State and local campaigns and elections are indicators of which public issues are hot and which are not. Congressional members often adopt state campaigns' successful issues and avoid the issues that failed to move people. Thus congressional candidates may push state issues to the national level if doing so will help their election.

Even in pursuing reelection and public policy, the value of interest representation is consequential. The reelection of members of Congress depends on their responsiveness to the powerful interests at the district, state, and national levels. Policy expertise is most often heeded when it complements a congressional member's favored interests. Structural federalism and the states' reserved powers receive little attention or priority in this system. Members of Congress from both parties justify shifting policy issues from the state to the national arena by claiming the shift better represents their constituents' valued interests. Given that few formal bonds remain connecting members of Congress to their state and local government institutions and parties, for state government officials to influence policymaking at the national level they must connect their interests with the roles and interests of congressional members. As Representative Ed Royce (R-Calif.), speaking as a member of Congress, put it, "We do what state officials ask when it benefits our interests."[48]

Intergovernmental Lobbying

If state government interests are to be reflected in the policies and programs created by Congress, then state officials must monitor the proposals being considered by Congress, analyze how those proposals will affect their state, and communicate their ideas, interests, experiences, and preferences to those members of Congress who can favorably influence the proposed policies in a manner that catches congressional attention. Monitoring, analyzing, and effective communication takes time, energy, and resources, much of which must be invested well before the issues reach Congress.

For example, interpersonal relationships between state and federal officials are vital elements in successful lobbying that are often neglected. Although the values, institutions, and interests of Congress are important, lobbyists should never forget that Congress is composed of individual human beings. The informal and personal relationships state officials develop with members of Congress are vital to influencing Congress.[49] One congressional staffer declared that personal relationships determine who you trust and what information you will accept as trustworthy. Representative Martin Sabo (D-Minn.) has observed that "personal contact is still the key to political influence. In politics, personal relationships are always more important than formal ones."[50] If state officials are going to participate in lobbying national officials, their success will depend on the personal ties they or their deputies develop with federal officials.

Another important variable contributing to state government's lobbying success at the federal level is the level of unity within a state's congressional delegation.[51] Many variables affect unity, but governors can help or hurt this unity through their personal relationships with members of Congress and the way they communicate with their congressional delegation. Similar party affiliation between the governor, representatives, and senators does not guarantee unity, nor does a different party affiliation ensure discord.[52] The Illinois congressional delegation makes a conscious effort to promote unity, meeting regularly with representatives of the governor's staff to inform each other of important issues and decide which issues they can work together to support.

State officials' efforts to influence Congress vary considerably.[53] Some governors rely on their state's congressional delegation to represent and promote the state's interests. This is probably not an effective means of promoting a state government's interests. Studies examining which states receive the most federal aid have found little evidence supporting the hypothesis that Congress-based variables such as committee assignments, seniority, and party loyalty increase a state's share of federal funding.[54] States with an office in Washington are much more effective in the federal aid game.[55] Other studies show a positive relationship between state and local government lobbying efforts and success.[56] In each of these studies, successful lobbying focuses on individual and specific interests rather than state governments' general and collective interests.

Like other individuals, state officials must decide whether to commit their time, energy, and resources to lobbying or instead to free ride on the efforts of other public officials and associations. Unlike most individuals who must rely on interest groups and lobbying associations to access and lobby members of Congress, state officials have almost guaranteed individual access to members of Congress. This means they can lobby on their own or work collectively with others.

Collective Action

Most studies of state lobbying examine collective lobbying by state officials' associations. These associations, such as the National Governors Association and the National Conference of State Legislatures, provide many services to state officials, including monitoring issues Congress is considering and organizing lobbying efforts to shape the proposed policies. These associations may promote federalism values when those values correspond to their members' interests and policy goals, although federalism is not their primary purpose. In the last half of the twentieth century, intergovernmental lobbying was less about policy or the shape of America's federal system than about who would share in the national government's money. Associations of state officials also lobby at times for the nationalization of policy.[57] This undermines the influence of state governments by confirming congressional impressions that state governments are opportunistic lobbyists rather than principled defenders of structural responsibilities.[58] The associations' ad hoc approach to federalism issues reflects the diverse interests of state officials and the values, interests, and organization of Congress.

National associations of state officials serve a vital role in monitoring Congress and organizing state lobbying activities. The issues these organizations can monitor, however, are limited, the positions they take on the issues are restricted by the need for consensus from diverse, ambitious, and fractious politicians, and active participation by state officials is often very limited.[59] The need for broad consensus on policy positions ensures that the positions of most associations will be diluted and intentionally vague, if a position is taken at all. The increasing partisan polarization in Congress has also affected state officials and has at times created irresolvable divisions in these associations.[60] Finally, ambitious state officials seeking higher office may try to use the associations to gain attention and boost their own popularity and election chances.

Although these groups are vital players on many federalism and intergovernmental issues, their participation and influence in Congress is limited. Those state officials who rely solely on national associations to inform them of relevant issues, according to congressional staff, usually communicate their interests to Congress too late in the debates to substantively affect the proposed legislation.[61] Associations, consequently, should be one of many tools used by state officials to promote their interests before Congress; often they are the only tool, and even then, rarely used.

The effectiveness of associations of state officials is limited. Members of Congress and their staff perceive these associations as "a lobby like any other, which seeks federal benefits for its members on favorable terms."[62] David B. Walker suggests that the lobbying efforts of a national association can be effective when the following three conditions are met: the group's members firmly unite; they can show they suffer real fiscal pain; and they can demonstrate they have a better way.[63] It is rare for all these conditions to be present.[64] The 1990s provide only two high-profile success stories of states working collectively to influence national policy: the 1995 Unfunded Mandates Reform Act and Temporary Assistance for Needy Families. However, the former has been repeatedly circumvented, and the latter places new requirements on the states.[65] With the possible exception of the new welfare reform policy, no federal legislation has significantly devolved power to the state governments.

Individual Lobbying

Collective action is the most obvious but not the only means to influence Congress and national policy. Many state government officials lobby members of Congress individually to gain favorable policy and treatment. Almost two-thirds of state governments maintain some type of office in Washington to facilitate communication between federal institutions and the state government. State offices monitor issues in Congress and federal agencies that may affect the state and inform the state's congressional delegation of those issues. They work with public interest groups such as the National Governors Association to promote their state's interests, and they lobby members of Congress and federal agencies on their own.

The exact number of states with a Washington office varies as various states close or open their offices. In February 2007, thirty-four state governments had offices in the nation's capital.[66] A study of why states create offices in Washington has found that the most statistically significant factor was public trust in the federal government, even when qualitative data showed the governor would like to have a Washington office.[67] In many states, maintaining an office in the capital is politically difficult because it is often seen as a wasteful duplication of the congressional delegation's responsibilities. Gubernatorial challengers may target and campaign against a sitting governor's

Washington office.[68] However, studies indicate that state government offices in Washington save or earn states much more money than they cost.[69]

State offices in Washington can organize and prioritize state claims for federal assistance. Because many state government agencies seek assistance from the state's congressional delegation, failure to organize, coordinate, and prioritize these requests may confuse the state's congressional delegation and lead them to focus on low priorities and miss more important items. However, weak governors have a difficult time controlling the messages other elected state officials may communicate to Washington. This can present a significant problem in states with many elected executive officials, all claiming legitimacy to represent their state's interests.

The New York governor's office in Washington is particularly effective in promoting New York's interests. It monitors Congress and federal agencies for bills and regulations that may affect the state. It sends relevant bills and proposed regulations to the state agency responsible for the issue and requests an analysis of how the proposal will affect New York's programs, policies, and federal revenue stream. It also requests possible amendments that would benefit New York's interests. These requests from the governor's Washington office are priority actions in the state agencies. The agency's analysis and proposed amendments are communicated to a member of New York's congressional delegation who is in the best position to positively affect the bill for New York.

Much of the literature on intergovernmental lobbying assumes that states work collectively to promote collective state interests and individually to promote specific state interests. This assumption needs to be rethought, given our understanding of the difficulty of mobilizing political groups and the problems of collective action. Individual lobbying activities receive little scholarly attention and scrutiny, but they can significantly benefit the attentive and active state and affect the larger system of intergovernmental relations between the federal and state governments.

Evidence that states can accomplish many of their intergovernmental objectives without collective participation is found in the lack of participation by the nation's most populous states in the National Governors Association's lobbying activities.[70] As the data in table 14-1 suggest, participation in the association's collective action activities (for example, giving testimony before Congress and meeting with federal officials) declines as a state's population increases.[71] Yet the most populous states have some of the best resources to influence national policy, including the most employees in their Washington offices, better access to Congress owing to their state's large

Table 14-1. *Federal Lobbying Activities by National Governors Association Members, by State's Population, Various Years*

State	Population, 2006 estimated (n)	Washington office employees		Meetings, 1994– 97[a] (n)	Testimonies, 1994– 97[b] (n)	Total meetings and testimonies (n)
		1997	2007			
California	36,457,549	9	8	0	0	0
Texas	23,507,783	15	6	0	0	0
New York	19,306,183	9	6	0	0	0
Florida	18,089,888	7	7	2	0	2
Illinois	12,831,970	8	3	1	0	1
Pennsylvania	12,440,621	7	10[c]	1	0	1
Ohio	11,478,006	5	1	4	0	4
Michigan	10,095,643	4	4	6	4	10
Georgia	9,363,941	0	2	0	1	1
North Carolina	8,856,505	5	5	0	1	1
New Jersey	8,724,560	8	1	1	0	1
Virginia	7,642,884	3	4	0	2	2
Massachusetts	6,437,193	4	5	0	1	1
Washington	6,395,798	2	1	2	1	3
Indiana	6,313,520	1	2	2	0	2
Arizona	6,166,318	0	2	0	1	1
Tennessee	6,038,803	1	0	0	0	0
Missouri	5,842,713	5	0	0	0	0
Maryland	5,615,727	5	1	0	0	0
Wisconsin	5,556,506	4	2	6	0	6
Minnesota	5,167,101	3	3	3	0	3
Colorado	4,753,377	0	0	7	1	8
Alabama	4,599,030	0	0	0	0	0
South Carolina	4,321,249	2	1	1	0	1
Louisiana	4,287,768	0	1	0	0	0
Kentucky	4,206,074	0	1[d]	6	5	11
Oregon	3,700,758	2	1	0	0	0
Oklahoma	3,579,212	0	0	1	0	1
Connecticut	3,504,809	2	2	0	2	2
Iowa	2,982,085	3	4	1	0	1

State	Population, 2006 estimated (n)	Washington office employees		Meetings, 1994–97[a] (n)	Testi-monies, 1994–97[b] (n)	Total meetings and testi-monies (n)
		1997	2007			
Mississippi	2,910,540	0	0	0	0	0
Arkansas	2,810,872	0	1	0	0	0
Kansas	2,764,075	0	1c	0	1	1
Utah	2,550,063	2	0	8	1	9
Nevada	2,495,529	2	2	8	0	8
New Mexico	1,954,599	0	1	0	0	0
West Virginia	1,818,470	0	0	2	1	3
Nebraska	1,768,331	1	0	8	0	8
Idaho	1,466,465	0	0	0	0	0
Maine	1,321,574	0	0	2	0	2
New Hampshire	1,314,895	0	0	1	0	1
Hawaii	1,285,498	1	0	1	0	1
Rhode Island	1,067,610	2	0	0	0	0
Montana	944,632	0	0	0	0	0
Delaware	853,476	2	2	4	1	5
South Dakota	781,919	0	0	0	0	0
Alaska	670,053	6	6	0	2	2
North Dakota	635,867	2	1	0	1	1
Vermont	623,908	0	60c	11	2	13
Wyoming	515,004	0	0	2	1	3

Source: Data from U.S. Census Bureau, Population Division, released December 22, 2006; National Governors Association, *The Governor's Washington Office* (Washington, October 1997), p. 9; Jennifer Jensen, "Filling the Hall of the States: Explaining the Establishment of State Offices in Washington," Ph.D. dissertation, University of North Carolina, Chapel Hill, 2000; National Governors Association, "All Testimonies" (www.nga.org/portal/site/nga/menuitem.8492123c14d1421 a18d81fa6501010a0/?vgnextoid=455c8aaa2ebbff00VgnVCM1000001a01010aRCRD&vgnextfmt= testimony); and interviews by author of staff at the National Governors Association and states' Washington offices.

a. Records after 1997 are not available.

b. Records for 1998 are not available.

c. Contract lobbyist firm.

d. Part-time employee.

congressional delegations, and a higher probability of having their representatives in key positions in the House of Representatives. When governors from populous states (Florida and Michigan) did participate in collective action activities, it was because the governors were committed to realizing policy change and altered their traditional methods of lobbying with the 104th Congress. To the extent that the most populous states are lobbying on Capitol Hill and not working collectively, they withhold their influence from promoting states' collective interests.

The factors that determine when states will work collectively with other states and when they will lobby individually are not known. Two examples suggest that states may work individually when they have a powerful ally in Congress. New York State and New York City received permission to use federal funds from President Bill Clinton's Community Oriented Policing Services program to purchase computers—rather than putting new police officers on the streets, as the program intended—after gaining the support of House Judiciary Committee member Charles Schumer (D-N.Y.). Governor Michael Leavitt (R-Utah) worked with the Senate Judiciary Committee chair, Senator Orrin Hatch (R-Utah), to exempt Utah from the truth-in-sentencing requirements while still receiving federal funds from the program. In both cases, state governments generally opposed the bills' intents, although not vociferously.

These two examples demonstrate that those states with powerful congressional connections may use those connections to gain special exemptions from bills generally opposed by state governments. The remaining states may work collectively to oppose the bills, but without the state or states with powerful congressional connections, their lobbying strength is significantly impaired. The incentive for individual states to lobby for specific benefits and the difficulty of collective action suggest an inherent weakness in relying on state governments to use the political system to safeguard states' general interests.

If state officials choose to participate in intergovernmental lobbying, they must decide whether to lobby collectively or individually. Collective action is difficult to achieve because of the challenge of defining common interests and overcoming the free-rider problem. Individual lobbying does not require coordination with other state officials, does not generate broad opposition, demands less power to succeed, and provides immediate and specific individual state benefits. The temptation to go it alone when a state official has sufficient power is great. Going it alone does not protect general state powers, however, and often results in either explicit or tacit support for placing federal limitations, sanctions, and mandates on other state governments.

Even individual lobbying faces political obstacles that limit state officials' ability to influence the national government. Few state officials are politically strong enough to oppose popular issues such as federal anticrime legislation. For a state official to actively lobby against, or merely express opposition to, a national proposal prohibiting carjacking or rape on the grounds that such responsibilities belong to the states would be to risk alienating a significant portion of the public, for example. In addition, a governor's trips to Washington to lobby on a bill are often viewed by the local press and many citizens as political junkets. A common yearly press story in many states is the number of times the governor has traveled outside the state. Some governors avoid trips to Washington during an election year to minimize the political fallout such trips might generate. These limits on the ability of state officials to participate in the national political process means that state governments' collective and individual positions on certain proposed policies may be meekly expressed—if expressed at all.

Conclusion

Political processes have always played a role in determining how power and responsibilities are allocated among America's levels of federal government. They became the principal means of distributing responsibilities between the federal tiers, and an effective means of promoting individual states' specific interests, at the beginning of the nation's third century. However, states' collective interests are not adequately protected through political processes for two reasons. First, the breakdown of state and local political parties released members of Congress to be free agents on federalism and intergovernmental issues at the same time that national and constituency pressures and concerns bound members of Congress to national party organizations and interest groups that often opposed state governments' collective interests. Second, given the problems of collective action and the nature of the national political process, individual states seeking state-specific benefits are more effective than an association of states seeking to protect the collective interests of those states. The consequence of these two factors is a political process that significantly favors the national government's powers and interests over the state governments' general powers and interests.

State government officials hoping to influence the federal system and national policy must play on Congress's turf and terms. Congress values representation of constituents and interest groups much more than formulating, implementing, and overseeing consistent, coherent, and long-term policies that reflect structural federalism or state governments' needs and interests. Two conclusions flow from this. First, state officials cannot assume their members of Congress will recognize and actively work to protect their state government's interests. Second, state officials lobby most effectively when they can demonstrate a specific proposal benefits (or harms) a congressional member's roles and interests. When the political process is played on Congress's turf and terms, state governments have few effective checks to limit the federal government's accretion of power.

The twenty-first century presents unique challenges for state governments. The looming national budget deficits and debt may lead Congress to shift burdens to the state and local governments through alternative pork-barrel techniques. The business community is aligning in favor of uniform national standards, which will further undermine state governments' powers to define and control their communities' health, safety, morals, and welfare. In responding to these challenges, state governments will need to maintain an active presence in Washington to monitor proposals before Congress that will affect them, to determine how those proposals can be amended to reduce negative consequences, and to persuade powerful members of Congress to stand up for the interests of state governments. It is a weak hope that state government officials will learn to set aside the short-term gains from individual actions and recognize the long-term benefits of collective action for general interests.

The Supreme Court should recognize that political processes provide state governments insufficient protection from federal burdens. The Court should define and enforce the outer boundaries of federalism that preserve the integrity of the separate tiers but refrain from addressing political questions, much as it does in national cases of separation of powers. Without a Supreme Court definition of the outer boundaries of federalism, neither the president, Congress, nor state officials will abide limits on power that interfere with responsiveness and representation. The twenty-first century has already witnessed the breakdown of traditional norms of behavior that once limited the nationalization of power and federal intrusions on state governments, such as the No Child Left Behind Act of 2001, the Help America Vote Act of 2002, the REAL ID Act of 2005, the displacement of popularly approved state health laws for a national police action conveniently labeled as a "war" on drugs, and authorization for the president to overrule a governor and call up National Guard troops.[72] So far, the courts have permitted these encroachments under the theory of process federalism.[73]

The checks of process federalism are inadequate to preserve a federal balance of powers. Under process federalism, neither federal nor state officials are constrained by or willing defenders of structural federalism's boundaries. American federalism appears to have moved into an era of opportunistic federalism, characterized by the pursuit by most actors in the system of "their immediate interests with little regard for the institutional or collective consequences."[74] The consequences of this shift require serious consideration. A number of the questions need attention: Is a national democracy, as facilitated by process federalism, preferable to a division of responsibilities between nation and states? Is the national government's capacity sufficient to adequately represent the diverse interests and assume the responsibilities of the United States? Is Congress's emphasis on representation over clear and coherent policies likely to produce adequate solutions to twenty-first-century problems? Does the pursuit by individual state and federal officials of opportunistic strategies and self-interests rather than shared goals best promote the interests of the nation and the states? In the past, the answers to these questions have often been yes. However, the twenty-first-century problems of terrorism, debt, national capacity, and globalization suggest the need to revisit these questions.

Notes

1. See Martha Derthick, "U.S. Congress," in *Federalism in America: An Encyclopedia,* edited by Joseph R. Marbach, Ellis Katz, and Troy E. Smith (Westport, Conn.: Greenwood Press, 2005), pp. 657–63, 658. For an explanation of why the United States shifted from dual federalism to cooperative federalism, see Kimberley S. Johnson, *Governing the American State: Congress and the New Federalism, 1877–1929* (Princeton University Press, 2007).

2. John W. Kincaid, "Constitutional Federalism: Labor's Role in Displacing Places to Benefit Persons," *PS: Political Science and Politics* 26 (June 1993): 172–77.

3. Donald F. Kettl, "The Maturing of American Federalism," in *The Costs of Federalism,* edited by Robert T. Golembiewski and Aaron Wildavsky (New Brunswick, N.J.: Transaction Books, 1985), pp. 73–88, 77–78; Shep R. Melnick, *Between the Lines: Interpreting Welfare Rights* (Brookings, 1994).

4. *Garcia* v. *San Antonio Transportation Authority,* 469 U.S. 528 (1985).

5. John W. Kincaid, "State-Federal Relations: Defense, Demography, Debt, and Deconstruction as Destiny," in *Book of the States 2005,* vol. 37 (Lexington, Ky.: Council of State Governments, 2005), pp. 25–30.

6. *Tennessee* v. *Lane,* 541 U.S. 509 (2004); *Sabri* v. *United States,* 541 U.S. 600 (2004); *Blakely* v. *Washington,* 542 U.S. 296 (2004). See Kincaid, "State-Federal Relations," p. 29.

In 2006 the court limited *Alden* in *Central Virginia Community College* v. *Katz,* 546 U.S. 356 (2006).

7. See Raoul Blindenbacher and Abigail Ostien, *A Global Dialogue on Federalism,* vol. 2 (Quebec: McGill-Queen's University Press, 2005); Ann O'M. Bowman and George A. Krause, "Power Shift: Measuring Policy Centralization in U.S. Intergovernmental Relations, 1947–1998," *American Politics Research* 31 (May 2003): 301–25; Kincaid, "State-Federal Relations"; David B. Walker, *The Rebirth of Federalism: Slouching toward Washington,* 2nd ed. (New York: Chatham House, 2000).

8. Martha Derthick, "American Federalism: Madison's Middle Ground," *Public Administration Review* 47 (January 1987): 66–74, p. 72.

9. Mancur Olson, *The Logic of Collective Action* (Harvard University Press, 1965).

10. Donald H. Haider, *When Governments Come to Washington: Governors, Mayors, and Intergovernmental Lobbying* (New York: Free Press, 1974); Troy E. Smith, "When States Lobby," Ph.D. dissertation, State University of New York, Albany, 1998.

11. Martha Derthick, *Keeping the Compound Republic: Essays on American Federalism* (Brookings, 2001), pp. 39, 58, 60–61.

12. James Q. Wilson, "City Life and Citizenship," in *Dilemmas of Scale in America's Federal Democracy,* edited by Martha Derthick (Cambridge University Press, 1999), pp. 17–36; Doris A. Graber, "Swiss Cheese Journalism," *State Government News* 36 (July 1993): 19–21; Kincaid, "Constitutional Federalism."

13. James G. March and Johan P. Olsen, *Democratic Governance* (New York: Free Press, 1995).

14. Martha Derthick, "New Players: The Governors and Welfare Reform," *Brookings Review* 14 (Spring 1996): 43–45.

15. Larry D. Kramer, "Putting the Politics Back into the Political Safeguards of Federalism," *Columbia Law Review* 100 (January 2000): 215–93, p. 224.

16. Derthick, *Keeping the Compound Republic,* p. 58.

17. Walker, *Rebirth of Federalism,* p. 27. See also Bowman and Krause, "Power Shift"; Derthick, *Keeping the Compound Republic,* p. 39; William E. Hudson, "The New Federalism Paradox," *Policy Studies Journal* 8 (Summer 1980): 900–06, p. 901; Kettl, "Maturing of American Federalism."

18. Timothy J. Conlan, "Politics and Governance: Conflicting Trends in the 1990s?" *Annals of the American Academy of Political and Social Science* 509 (May 1990): 128–38, p. 130.

19. Morton Grodzins, *The American System: A New View of Government in the United States* (Chicago: Rand McNally, 1966), esp. chap. 10. See also Jesse H. Choper, "The Scope of National Power vis-à-vis the States: The Dispensability of Judicial Review," *Yale Law Journal* 86 (July 1977): 1552–621, p. 1552; Kramer, "Putting the Politics Back into the Political Safeguards of Federalism"; and Herbert Wechsler, "The Political Safeguards of Federalism: The Role of the State in the Composition and Selection of the National Government," *Columbia Law Review* 54 (April 1954): 534–60.

20. The decline in state control over parties occurred during the same period that state

and local groups increased their lobbying activities (Haider, *When Governments Come to Washington,* p. 111). In 1985 the U.S. Advisory Commission on Intergovernmental Relations (*The Transformation in American Politics: Implications for Federalism,* A-106 [Government Printing Office, 1986]) recommended overhauling the party system to grant state officials greater influence in the political process in order to redress the balance between the national and state governments. Those recommendations were not followed. The ACIR analysis in this volume was more important than the recommendations.

21. John J. Coleman, *Party Decline in America: Policy, Politics, and the Fiscal State* (Princeton University Press, 1996); Martin P. Wattenberg, *The Decline of American Political Parties, 1952–1996* (Harvard University Press, 1998).

22. Cornelius Cotter and Bernard Hennessey, *Politics without Power: The National Committees* (New York: Atherton, 1964); Robin Kolodny and David A. Dulio, "Political Party Adaptation in U.S. Congressional Campaigns: Why Political Parties Use Coordinated Expenditures to Hire Political Consultants," *Party Politics* 9 (November 2003): 729–46, p. 731; Steven S. Smith, Jason M. Roberts, and Ryan J. Vander Wielen, *The American Congress,* 4th ed. (Cambridge University Press, 2006), p. 154.

23. Conlan, "Politics and Governance"; Anthony Corrado, *The Election after Reform* (Lanham, Md.: Rowman and Littlefield, 2006); Rachel Gibson and Andrea Rommele, "A Party-Centered Theory of Professionalized Campaigning," *Harvard International Journal of Press/Politics* 6 (Fall 2001): 31–43; Kolodny and Dulio, "Political Party Adaptation"; Alan Rosenthal, "If the Party's Over, Where's All That Noise Coming From?" *State Government* 57, no. 2 (1984): 50–54; Smith, Roberts, and Vander Wielen, *American Congress,* p. 154.

24. John H. Aldrich and David W. Rohde, "The Logic of Conditional Party Government: Revisiting the Electoral Connection," in *Congress Reconsidered,* 7th ed., edited by Lawrence C. Dodd and Bruce I. Oppenheimer (Washington: CQ Press, 2001), pp. 269–92; Gary W. Cox and Matthew D. McCubbins, *Legislative Leviathan: Party Government in the House* (University of California Press, 1993); Richard Fleisher and Jon R. Bond, "Congress and the President in a Partisan Era," in *Polarized Politics: Congress and the President in a Partisan Era,* edited by Jon R. Bond and Richard Fleisher (Washington: CQ Press, 2000), pp. 1–8; and Smith, Roberts, and Vander Wielen, *American Congress,* p. 154.

25. Smith, Roberts, and Vander Wielen, *American Congress,* p. 154.

26. Ibid.

27. Ronald Hrebenar, *Interest Group Politics in America,* 3d ed. (New York: M. E. Sharpe, 1997); Smith, "When States Lobby."

28. Raymond J. La Raja, *Life after Reform: When the Bipartisan Campaign Reform Act Meets Politics* (Lanham, Md.: Rowman and Littlefield, 2003), p. 113.

29. Ibid., p. 11.

30. One possible exception to this is the Bipartisan Campaign Reform Act's Levin funds, which allow state political parties to receive soft money donations up to $10,000 per individual to pay for limited federal election activities, such as voter registration and get-out-the vote efforts. Given the limited activities these funds can finance, their ability to facilitate relationships between federal and state officials appears limited, and few states

showed any serious interest in raising Levin funds in the 2004 election ("A Little-Used Campaign Finance Rule: State and Local Parties Not Warming Up to Levin Funds" [www.publicintegrity.org/partylines/report.aspx?aid=402]; La Raja, *Life after Reform,* p. 6).

31. Jennifer Jensen, "Filling the Hall of the States: Explaining the Establishment of State Offices in Washington," Ph.D. dissertation, University of North Carolina–Chapel Hill, 2000.

32. Interviews conducted by the author. More than 120 interviews of elected and unelected government officials were conducted for this research. Unelected officials were promised anonymity for their participation. The position or political party of an unelected official is identified when relevant.

33. Beryl A. Radin, "California in Washington," in *California Policy Choices,* vol. 6 (University of Southern California School of Public Administration, 1990), p. 294.

34. Representatives' seats tend to be more secure than those of senators because turnover is higher among senators. It is not exactly clear why, but some theories are that the challengers are better at the Senate level, those challengers do a better job of raising campaign money, and senators represent a much more politically diverse constituency.

35. Radin, "California in Washington," p. 294.

36. See Derthick, *Keeping the Compound Republic,* pp. 60–61.

37. Michael J. Malbin, "Congress during the Convention and Ratification," in *The Framing and Ratification of the Constitution,* edited by Leonard W. Levy and Dennis J. Mahoney, pp. 185–208 (New York: Macmillan, 1987).

38. Roger H. Davidson and Walter J. Oleszek, *Congress and Its Members,* 8th ed. (Washington: CQ Press, 2002); Kenneth A. Shepsle, "The Changing Textbook Congress," in *Can the Government Govern?* edited by John E. Chubb and Paul E. Peterson, pp. 238–66 (Brookings, 1989).

39. Paul L. Posner, *The Politics of Unfunded Mandates: Whither Federalism?* (Georgetown University Press, 1998). See Michael R. Malaby and David J. Webber, "Federalism in the 101st Congress," *Publius: The Journal of Federalism* 21 (Summer 1991): 77–92, pp. 84–86.

40. "Why Republicans Can't Cut Spending," Reason Foundation, January 23, 2006 (www.reason.com/news/show/34711.html).

41. Thomas J. Mann and Norman J. Ornstein, *The Broken Branch: How Congress Is Failing America and How to Get It Back on Track* (Oxford University Press, 2006); Kimberley A. Strassel, "It's a Tough Life: The Secret New Way of Earmarks," *Wall Street Journal,* February 9, 2007 (www.opinionjournal.com/columnists/kstrasselpw/?id=110009647); Lyndsey Layton, "In Majority, Democrats Run Hill Much as GOP Did," *Washington Post,* February 18, 2007, p. A4.

42. Pietro S. Nivola, "The New Pork Barrel," *Public Interest* 131 (Spring 1998): 92–104, pp. 93–94; see also Kincaid, "State-Federal Relations."

43. See Kincaid, "State-Federal Relations"; Dale Krane and Heidi Koenig, "The State of American Federalism, 2004: Is Federalism Still a Core Value?" *Publius: The Journal of Federalism* 35 (Winter 2005): 1–42; and Posner, *Politics of Unfunded Mandates.*

44. Richard F. Fenno Jr., *Congressmen in Committees* (Boston: Little, Brown, 1973).

45. Derthick, "New Players," pp. 44–45; Lawrence D. Brown, *New Policies, New Politics: Government's Response to Government's Growth* (Brookings, 1983).

46. Smith, "When States Lobby"; Eliza Newlin Carney, "Power Grab," *National Journal,* April 11, 1998, pp. 798–801; "Why Republicans Can't Cut Spending"; Richard Scheppach, "Turnabout Overdue in State-Federal Relations," Stateline, November 14, 2006 (www.stateline.ord/live/details/story?contentId=157856).

47. Idaho governor Cecil Andrus, telephone conversation with author, July 8, 1996.

48. Ed Royce, U.S. Representative for California's Fortieth District, interview with author, May 8, 1998.

49. Hrebenar, *Interest Group Politics;* see also Richard F. Fenno, *Home Style* (Boston: Little Brown, 1978), p. 24.

50. Quoted in Carol Steinbach, "Calling on Congress: What Some State Legislatures Are Doing to Improve Relations with Federal Lawmakers," *State Legislatures* 10 (February 1984): 17–20.

51. Neil Berch, "Why Do Some States Play the Federal Aid Game Better Than Others?" *American Politics Quarterly Research* 20 (July 1992): 366–77; Daniel J. Elazar, *American Federalism: A View from the States* (New York: Thomas Y. Crowell, 1966).

52. Jensen, "Filling the Hall of the States," pp. 124–25.

53. See Dennis O. Grady, "American Governors and State-Federal Relations: Attitudes and Activities, 1960–1980," *State Government* 57, no. 3 (1984): 106–12; Jensen, "Filling the Hall of the States."

54. See Thomas J. Anton, *American Federalism and Public Policy: How the System Works* (Temple University Press, 1989); Berch, "Why Do Some States"; Fenno, *Home Style;* John A. Ferejohn, *Pork Barrel Politics* (Stanford University Press, 1974); Bruce A. Ray, "Congressional Losers in the U.S. Federal Spending Process," *Legislative Studies Quarterly* 3 (August 1980): 359–72; and Leonard G. Ritt, "Committee Position, Seniority, and the Distribution of Government Expenditures," *Public Policy* 24 (Fall 1976): 463–89.

55. Berch, "Why Do Some States," p. 375; Jensen, "Filling the Hall of the States," pp. 124–25.

56. Anton, *American Federalism and Public Policy;* John E. Oppenheim, "Federal Response to Natural Disasters: A Spatial Political Analysis," Ph.D. dissertation, University of Michigan, 1983; Michael Rich, "Congress, the Bureaucracy, and the Cities: Distributive Politics in the Allocation of the Federal Grants-in-Aid for Community and Economic Development," Ph.D. dissertation, Northwestern University, 1985.

57. Derthick, *Keeping the Compound Republic,* pp. 39, 58, 60–61; Posner, *Politics of Unfunded Mandates;* Smith, "When States Lobby"; Joseph F. Zimmerman, "Interstate Cooperation: The Roles of the State Attorneys General," *Publius: The Journal of Federalism* 28 (Winter 1998): 71–89.

58. This perception is justified in some, but not all, instances of state government appeals for the nationalization of certain issues. Those issues related to the regulation of interstate commerce may require nationalization, but some proposals for nationalization are efforts to shift responsibility and costs to the national government.

59. Kavan Peterson, "On the Record: Kentucky Gov. Paul Patton," Stateline, May 21, 2003 (www.stateline.org/live/printable/story?contentId=15259); Derthick, "New Players," pp. 44–45; Smith, "When States Lobby."

60. Jason White, "Govs to Bush: Fund Mandates," Stateline, February 24, 2003 (www.stateline.org/live/printable/story?contentId=15430).

61. David L. Cingranelli, "State Government Lobbies in the National Political Process," Rockefeller Institute reprint series, no. 12 (1984), p. 125.

62. Derthick, "New Players," p. 45. See also John D. Nugent, "Public Officials' Associations," in *Federalism in America,* edited by Marbach, Katz, and Smith, pp. 518–24.

63. Walker, *Rebirth of Federalism,* p. 325.

64. *Fortune* reports that Washington insiders consider the National Governors Association to be one of the twenty-five most influential groups lobbying Congress. This conclusion may be overstated. The methodology relies merely on professionals' perceptions, raising serious questions about the conclusion. Moreover, there have not been a lot of big issues considered by Congress in the last five years that involved the National Governors Association, and the association has been active on fairly noncontroversial issues that have been approved (Jeffrey H. Birnbaum, "Washington's Power 25," *Fortune,* December 8, 1997, pp. 144–52; Jeffrey H. Birnbaum, "Follow the Money," *Fortune,* December 6, 1999, pp. 207–08).

65. Paul Posner, "Unfunded Mandate Reform: How Is It Working?" *Rockefeller Institute Bulletin* (1998): 35–46.

66. The states having offices or retaining agents in Washington in 2007 were Alaska, Arizona, Arkansas, California, Connecticut, Delaware, Florida, Georgia, Idaho, Illinois, Indiana, Iowa, Kansas, Kentucky, Louisiana, Maryland, Massachusetts, Michigan, Minnesota, Nevada, New Jersey, New Mexico, New York, North Carolina, North Dakota, Ohio, Oregon, Pennsylvania, South Carolina, Texas, Vermont, Virginia, Washington, Wisconsin.

67. Jensen, "Filling the Hall of the States," p. 135.

68. A few governors who targeted the state's Washington office during their gubernatorial campaigns and then closed the office once elected are Frank White (Arkansas), Frank Keating (Oklahoma), and Mike Johanns (Nebraska) (Jensen, "Filling the Hall of States," p. 156). Missouri governor Matt Blunt (R-Mo.) closed the governor's Washington office in 2005 on the basis that it wasted tax payer funds ("2005 State of State Address," January 26, 2005 [www.gov.mo.gov/State_of_the_State_2005.htm]).

69. Berch, "Why Do Some States"; and Jensen, "Filling the Hall of the States," p. 155.

70. See Beverly A. Cigler, "Not Just Another Special Interest: Intergovernmental Representation," in *Interest Group Politics,* edited by Allan J. Cigler and Burdett A. Loomis, 4th ed. (Washington: CQ Press, 1995), pp. 1331–353, p. 1335.

71. Testifying before Congress has been found to be one of the best indicators of group lobbying activity and involvement and influence in the policymaking network. See Edward O. Laumann and David Knoke, *The Organizational State: Social Choice in National Policy Domains* (University of Wisconsin Press, 1987); Allen R. Hays, "Voices for

Urban Housing: Interest Group Action and Advocacy for Social Programs before Congress," paper prepared for the Twentieth Annual Meeting, Urban Affairs Association, Charlotte, North Carolina, April 18–21,1990.

72. *Gonzales* v. *Raich*, 545 U.S. 1 (2005); Kavan Peterson, "Governors Lose in Powers Over National Guard," Stateline, January 12, 2007 (www.stateline.org/live/printable/story?contentId=170453).

73. See, for example, *Gonzales* v. *Raich* (2005).

74. Timothy J. Conlan, "From Cooperative to Opportunistic Federalism: Reflections on the Half-Century Anniversary of the Commission on Intergovernmental Relations," *Public Administration Review* 66 (September–October 2006): 663–76, p. 667. See also chapter 15 of this volume.

15

Conclusion

Managing Complex Problems in a Compound Republic

PAUL L. POSNER AND TIMOTHY J. CONLAN

The chapters in this book illustrate that, as we enter the new century, our federal system remains a central vehicle used by national, state, and local officials to satisfy an ever-expanding range of needs and goals. Whether it be homeland security, health care, education, or environmental policy, national policymakers have increasingly turned to state and local governments as the critical workhorses. State and local governments have stepped up as well, mounting new initiatives to address health, safety, education, and infrastructure needs, much as they have done for decades.

However, although the system is still expected to satisfy existing needs, the new demands placed on it threaten to change the fundamental character of roles and relationships among our nation's governments. The flexibility of state and local governments to satisfy their own unique needs and diverse interests has become encumbered by the growing reach of prodigious and increasingly ambitious national policy goals, which have come to frame the agendas and shape the delivery of programs in an ever-widening number of policy areas. Ironically, many of these national policy issues originated with the state and local sector, but they often get transformed when making the intergovernmental round-trip.

The chapters in this volume show a system coping with the stress of satisfying multiple goals and actors in the face of higher stakes, greater visibility from more stakeholders, and more tension among the often inconsistent objectives pursued in our public programs. Governments at all levels increasingly borrow authority and resources from many different sectors to satisfy increasingly restive publics who want the services that government brings without a large bureaucracy or price tag. The tensions inherent in our intergovernmental system flow from the paradoxical and oft-conflicting expectations we have for our system: we want to promote both accountability for national goals and flexibility for local differences, to maximize outcomes while minimizing costs, to capitalize on the resources and authority of other governments and private actors without losing control and autonomy. Ultimately, these tensions reflect the underlying ambivalence that Americans traditionally maintain toward government, where the contradictory aphorisms "get the government off our backs" and "there ought to be a law" can often be found in the same political speech.

Nationalization of the Policy Agenda

The extension of the federal policy regime to an ever-wider range of issues is premised on the emergence of a broad consensus supporting the nationalization of both problems and solutions. Questions about the legitimacy of the federal role, once among the most contentious issues dividing our party system, have largely been settled. Conservative Republican, moderate Democratic, and liberal Democratic regimes have all affirmed a secular preference for a strong national response to emerging issues through our intergovernmental system. The public, too, has shown little patience with the structural constraints of our traditional federal system, supporting national interventions from community policing to educational accountability.

This secular tendency was put to the test in the administration of George W. Bush. Some anticipated that a conservative Republican administration, led by a former governor and matched with a Republican-controlled Congress for the first time in nearly fifty years, would halt or reverse the historical trajectory of an expanded federal role and increasing intergovernmentalization of domestic governance. Yet the Bush administration consolidated the national policy regime, using the familiar pattern of tapping the state and local sector to advance national goals. Indeed, far from slowing down the nationalization of the policy agenda, the Bush administration, with its

Republican-controlled Congress, accelerated it in several policy domains and further seeded it with new ideas that warranted a federal response.

The institutional erosion of state and local governments' political influence in our system, examined in chapter 14 by Troy Smith, helped set the stage for this nationalization of policy agendas and solutions. Fundamental political forces have eroded the traditional bastions of state and local influence that undergirded our federal system for decades. State and local party organizations declined while national parties gained influence. Individualization of congressional politics further diminished state and local influence in the political system, as did the proliferation of interest groups in Washington after 1960.[1]

Reinforcing these structural changes in the political system have been changes in conservative ideology. Liberals in the United States have been broadly supportive of an active and largely centralizing federal role in the U.S. federal system since the New Deal of the 1930s. This ideological predisposition first centered around issues of economic regulation and social insurance and was reinforced by the civil rights struggles of the 1950s and 1960s and the environmental movement.

Traditional conservatives, in contrast, were once principled advocates of deference to states' rights and a restrained federal role, reflecting a Burkean respect for the value of traditional social and governmental institutions. Since the 1980s, however, the relative influence of such institutional conservatives has waned, as the influence of religiously based social conservatives and libertarian-oriented economic conservatives has expanded. Although these two strains of modern conservatism often differ strongly on issues of social and foreign policy, they share an instrumentalist orientation toward issues of federalism. Rather than observing a consistent position on questions of federal and state roles in the intergovernmental system, their primary commitment is to the values of social or economic conservatism. Hence on issues ranging from federal promotion of school choice and traditional marriage, to federal preemption of state economic regulation and medical marijuana laws, contemporary conservatives are prone to support novel and even aggressive expansions of federal authority vis-à-vis the states to advance their political, economic, or social policy goals.

Other shifts in our political system have contributed to the nationalization of policy agendas and politics. The growth of national media institutions focused on Washington has created a powerful resource for those groups wishing to nationalize problems and issues, as reporters increasingly seek national dimensions or applications for state and local problems or solutions.

The advent of lobbies representing broad, diffuse interests, the so-called public interest groups, has fueled national policy advocacy as many of these groups have settled in Washington rather than the states. Perhaps the most important development in the interest group sector has been the pronounced, but little noticed, shift of business groups from allies of the states to advocates of national regulation by federal agencies. This trend underscores the impact of the nationalization and globalization of the economy on our federal system. As corporations increasingly operate in a global environment, coping with fifty separate state regulatory regimes is seen as a hindrance to economic efficiency and competitiveness.

Consequences for Intergovernmental Management

These forces have given rise to a secular growth in federal programs addressing a wider range of problems and issues over the past five decades. However, this national program response has sidestepped the creation of large new federal bureaucracies. Rather, for the most part, new national policies have used more indirect governance tools to achieve their goals, accompanied by reliance on an ever-widening range of third parties, most notably state and local governments. Simply put, the policy ambitions of federal leaders have far exceeded the federal government's administrative, legal, fiscal, and political capacity. Accordingly, state and local governments, as well as a wide range of nonprofit and private corporations, have been engaged as third parties to carry out federal initiatives through a host of governmental tools, including grants and loans in addition to regulatory tools.[2]

Thus in many respects the federal role has continued to expand by standing on the shoulders of state and local governments, which have solidified their emerging role as the true workhorses of our federal system. While gaining additional federal grant funds, their own fiscal, administrative, and political resources are leveraged in the process. Thus in No Child Left Behind the federal government has sought to steer the entire system of public elementary and secondary education in the direction of parental choice and greater accountability, even as state and local governments provide more than 90 percent of public funding. National homeland security and election reform legislation similarly are premised on the federal government's capacity to harness state and local authority, administrative machinery, and personnel in pursuit of national goals and standards.

In many respects, the expanding federal role in setting the agenda for the intergovernmental system has been a secular force in American government for the past fifty years. However, such policies were often spawned and implemented through the institutions of cooperative federalism. The older cooperative model expanded the federal role at the same time as it strengthened the state and local foundations for that role. Recognizing the growing federal fiduciary and functional interest in a strong state and local sector, the federal government in the cooperative era provided fiscal assistance and capacity building to enhance the vitality and capacity of its state and local partners. State and local governments retained vital bargaining power with national leaders because they could at least threaten to withhold their cooperation, which was so vital for national programs to succeed.[3]

In recent years, we are witnessing a transition away from this supportive and collaborative model to a more coercive, opportunistic model. In contrast with the earlier cooperative model, federal officials are increasingly enticed and pressured to respond to a prodigious agenda of national problems through more centralized and nationalizing policy actions and tools, whether it be mandates or preemptions in various forms. Seemingly no issue of domestic governance, regardless of how small or localized, is off the table for a national policy response. When comprehensive health care reform eluded President Bill Clinton, school uniforms and community policing became popular items in his domestic agenda. Long-standing areas of local control, such as education, have given way to national policy regimes in the face of leaders anxious to prove their policy and political mettle to restive publics. Thus following the 1996 presidential election, Republican elites came to realize that defining themselves as the party whose presidential standard bearer carried the Tenth Amendment in his shirt pocket and whose congressional leaders sought to turn leadership in education back to states and localities was a losing proposition.

Recent centralizing actions succeeded in overturning cooperative federalism frameworks that had evolved over many years. Whether it be tax cooperation through tax base sharing and administration, the Federal Emergency Management Agency's highly partnerial model for emergency preparedness, state and local education's accommodation with federal equity goals, state motor vehicle departments' cooperation in commercial driver's licensure, or the largely successful devolution of welfare achieved ten years earlier, the centralizing actions that have unfolded in the past seven years mark a major turning point toward a more insistent, demanding federal role with uncertain consequences for program performance and finances. Ironically, the familiarity and political support spawned by these relatively cooperative forerunners may very well have paved the way for their more coercive successors.

Intergovernmental tensions and consequences have been accentuated by simultaneous federal actions that both increase intergovernmental fiscal burdens through spending mandates and limit revenues available to state and local governments to finance these far-flung federal policy initiatives. The combined effect of these initiatives will work together to encumber a greater share of the state and local fiscal commons for national policy initiatives than we have seen in the past.

Consequently, while the question of the federal role has been settled in favor of an expansive role for the national government, the framework for intergovernmental management remains unsettled and evolving. Cooperative federalism tended to generate a "picket-fence" form of intergovernmental administration. Intergovernmental relationships flowed up and down through "vertical functional autocracies" that cut across the horizontal governance structures of our multitiered federal system.[4] These functional stovepipes became the channels for federal grants and other forms of cooperative intergovernmental relationships, and they defined the space for intergovernmental bargaining and negotiation. Even as more coercive federal policy instruments were employed in the 1960s, 1970s, and 1980s, professionalized intergovernmental subsystems proved capable of absorbing regulatory shocks and negotiating cooperative intergovernmental relationships if granted sufficient time.[5]

This intergovernmental capacity to manage change is being put to the test by coercive, opportunistic federalism. The changes in political parties, the media, and interest groups discussed earlier have opened up the intergovernmental system to more, and more rapid, exogenous policy changes. Assertive national policies in welfare, education, homeland security, and electoral reform have their roots in crises, events, or political agendas outside of the professional subsystems that have shaped policy and managed implementation in the past. Ironically, many of these policy changes have their roots in individual state and local policy innovations, but they lose their flexibility when formulated as uniform federal policies extended to the entire nation. With more political options for rapid and substantial policy change in our political system, the intergovernmental managers of the future must have an understanding of intergovernmental politics as well as administration.

Moreover, national officials are increasingly less content to take states and localities as they find them. Rather, emerging federal policy tools place public officials on the defensive through privatization and new accountability strategies. Energizing new publics and new providers to vie for at least a share of public service provision under federal programs is a vital part of this new strategy to challenge public authority within the state and local sector. Contracting out, the pursuit of alternative service vehicles such as charter schools, the Bush administration's faith-based initiative, and the pursuit of vouchers are several recent examples wherein public agencies and administrators are being challenged at all levels of government by competing actors and visions for public service provision. Public disclosure has also been deployed to "shame" entities, whether private businesses or state and local governments, to adopt widely shared federal policy goals. Whether it be the publication of school performance data for all parents to see or water quality data in local ratepayers' bills, federal officials have sought to use performance metrics to strengthen the position of advocates for favored programs and policies within state and local governments. These strategies reflect a more insistent federal policy profile, harking back to the "creative federalism" of Lyndon Johnson's Great Society, intent on achieving national goals through or around state and local governments.

Eroding State and Local Foundations

The new federal role, like the old, is premised on the institutional capacities of state and local governments. Certainly, the management capacities and policymaking institutions of state and local governments have been extensively modernized and professionalized during the past five decades. Such governments have come a long way: once derided for being stuck in the horse-and-buggy era, they are now championed as policy and management innovators. Indeed, state and local governments were engaged with performance management and measurement far earlier than the federal government.

But the fiscal and political foundations of that strength may be eroding. The state and local sector itself will be challenged in the future to hold its own in the face of forces that threaten to erode traditional tax bases and legal authorities. Left unaddressed, such erosion may leave federal policymakers in the future borrowing weakness rather than strength.

Financially, a globalized, technological economy is working to gradually undermine the fiscal underpinnings of state and local finance. As Ray Scheppach and Frank Shafroth demonstrate in chapter 4 of this volume, the mainstay of most states' revenue systems—the sales tax—is threatened by the shift to a service-based economy and the rise of the Internet. What is more, the growing mobility of investment, employment, and population constricts other revenue sources, as well, lest high marginal tax rates prompt a race, slide, or shuffle to the bottom. On the spending side, an aging society will place yet additional demands on the state and local sector to finance health care and pensions for their own employees, as well as serving as the fiscal partner for national long-term care for an aging population. Already the states' share of Medicaid has become the largest spending item in their budgets, increasingly crowding out other spending priorities for state and local needs such as infrastructure and higher education. In a 2007 study, the Government Accountability Office concluded that over the next forty years, state and local governments' fiscal outlook will deteriorate, driven in great part by the exponential growth of health care costs.[6]

The nationalization and globalization of the economy have also worked to undermine traditional state and local regulatory roles. As corporations increasingly operate in a global environment, they seek to lessen the burden posed by fifty different state regulatory regimes. This trend is reinforced by trade agreements that have been interpreted by the courts and international bodies as having preemptive effects on state and local laws. The European Union has identified state product labeling and recycled content laws as trade barriers, and foreign investors have challenged state fuel additive and other standards as violating trade agreements.

In the emerging intergovernmental politics of the twenty-first century, the state and local capacity for collective action will become even more critical to promoting their roles in the system and warding off further centralization. Thanks to the erosion of constraints on the federal role at the federal level, the strength of state and local collective action has become more central in defining the boundaries of our federal system. State and local governments' success in warding off federal preemptions and other nationalizing initiatives will be dependent both on their ability to successfully press their claims with federal officials and on their capacity to capture and channel nationalizing pressures through various forms of self-regulation and policy harmonization. A key emerging test for states is whether and how they can accommodate the pressure for national harmonization through state-led national, as opposed to federal, standards-setting initiatives that reflect the differential values and interests of the states while satisfying the requisites of a global economy and national political culture.

Can the state and local sector emulate the business community and adopt voluntary collective standards to address national or global pressures on their own and thereby deflect federal preemptions and mandates? One successful example is the National Association of Insurance Commissioners, which develops model law for state insurance agencies. The Gramm-Leach-Bliley

Act of 1999, reforming federal regulation of the financial services industry, directed this organization to promulgate uniform standards for insurance sales and licensure; if a majority of states did not adopt this code, the federal government would establish a new national instrumentality to provide for uniform insurance laws. Faced with this pressure, thirty-nine states adopted the standards.

However, the prospects are not as clear or encouraging in other areas. For instance, to gain the support of the business community and Congress to tax remote sales through Internet and mail orders, states adopted a homogenized and simplified sales tax framework, but a number of economically important states have so far chosen not to adopt these changes. The capacity of state and local elected officials to act cohesively on the many sensitive and divisive issues facing the nation is notoriously limited. State and local officials sometimes lose sight of their own prerogatives as they are gripped by the same waves of national policy enthusiasms and ideas that sweep over national officeholders. Differences in party affiliations and state economic interests have hampered lobbying and policy harmonization among states in the past, and such natural rivalries will continue to challenge states going forward.

Enduring Strengths

Against this backdrop, the intergovernmental system retains considerable capacity for adaptation and flexibility. In chapter 2, Richard Nathan illustrates how states have sustained and enhanced their long-standing roles as policy laboratories of innovation in our system. In issues as wide ranging as global warming and health care coverage for the uninsured, states have retained their traditional role in our system to serve as policy laboratories. Frustrated by political and policy gridlock at the national level, many groups are finding states to be hospitable and eager champions of new policy ideas and reforms.

The states' record of policy innovation has succeeded in providing them with a stronger voice in shaping the agenda of issues facing the nation. These state-led innovations suggest that the political cohesion that eludes states operating as collective interest groups on the national scene in fact helps fortify the role of individual states as policy innovators and catalysts. The greater cohesion and homogeneity within the states enables them to step out more smartly on politically complex issues that hamstring national leaders beset by gridlock and political polarization. Notwithstanding the growth of state and local interest groups in Washington, the greater cohesion of individual states compared with the federal government remains their most important political asset and a continuing source of vitality in our federal system.

The capacity of our intergovernmental system to pilot and champion policy innovation is found not only in states but in other intergovernmental settings as well. Several chapters discuss the growing role played by regional officials in solving regional problems, especially in environmental policy and homeland security. Barry Rabe's discussion, in chapter 9, of the Regional Greenhouse Gas Initiative pursued by northeastern states is an example of how states are organizing themselves into regional groups to take the lead on an international policy problem in the face of gridlock at the federal level.

Faced with real constraints on the size of the federal government, the continuing need to rely on state and local governments to deliver federal programs can be a strength of our system as well. Although state and local governments have traditionally assumed central roles in grants, even under more coercive instruments such as preemptions, federal officials often have been forced to rely on state and local regulatory regimes to supplement paltry staff levels and to promote greater political support. Partial preemption strategies, for instance, provide states with vital opportunities to exceed federal regulatory standards when participating in federal regulatory enforcement regimes. While perhaps falling short of the cooperative partnerships observed for federal grants, nonetheless the substantial state roles promote a degree of decentralization, thanks to the critical role played by states in implementing federal standards and, in some cases, in promulgating the standards themselves.

In addition to partial preemptions, several other policy and management innovations have sought to improve the balance between federal accountability and state and local flexibility. All have had mixed records of success to date, though arguably each still holds some potential for our federal system. The block grant record is admirably summarized by Carl Stenberg in chapter 12, while Carol and Bill Weissert review recent experience with federal waivers in health care programs. Performance measures, which are attracting the most contemporary attention, have become institutionalized within executive agencies of federal and most state governments. Depending on how they are implemented, such metrics promise to improve the information available for decisionmaking and accountability at each level of government. However, the consequences of their application to intergovernmental management are still controversial. Shelley Metzenbaum argues in chapter 10 that performance-based goals can enhance partnerships by promoting accountability for national goals while providing greater state and local flexibility in determining how such goals will be reached. Beryl Radin, on the other hand, points to the centralizing implications associated with the application of the federal definition of metrics to the entire intergovernmental enterprise, regardless of how small the relative contribution of federal funds may be.

The Future Outlook: Compound Solutions for Complex Problems

Intergovernmental systems are by their nature plagued—and sometimes blessed—by conflicts and competition among the actors. Although cooperation may remain the goal, it often seems elusive as governments jockey for advantage, arguing over the goals of programs as well as the rules of the game. The system is demanding and challenges all actors to juggle their own needs and priorities with those demanded of the broader system. State and local governments are confronted with the challenge of addressing their own unique needs while at the same time assuming stewardship for a growing plate of national priorities. The federal government struggles with the gap between its accountability for compelling national concerns and its relative lack of control over achieving national outcomes. The public is presented with the dilemma of sorting out responsibilities for outcomes with too many cooks in the intergovernmental kitchen. Frank Bane, the first executive director of the Advisory Commission on Intergovernmental Relations, once observed that the only clear virtue of such a system is that "some damn fool at the top can't screw it all up."

In some respects, the boundaries between federal, state, and local governments have become ever more permeable and interdependent over the years. The growing number of national programs in recent years has only accelerated the federal dependence on state and local governments' financial, managerial, and political resources. The framing of the goals for many federal programs, in fact, often originated in state and local policy laboratories. Federal programs, in turn, have prompted the institutionalization of national values and interests in state and local governments. Most national programs have come to be recognized as complex bargains containing ambitious national goals tempered by intergovernmental actors empowered to implement, tailor, and reformulate these objectives to meet the diverse realities of governance in states and communities across the nation. Federal and state governments perceive an advantage to "borrowing authority" to engage the resources, authority, and legitimacy of other levels of government.[7] In essence, all levels of government are increasingly engaged in an "opportunistic federalism" in which all actors in the system attempt to use one another to achieve particular policy goals, irrespective of traditional boundaries and authority distributions.[8]

Such a system is difficult to manage, involves seemingly unpalatable trade-offs to the partners, and can obfuscate real accountability and responsibility for outcomes. It is no wonder that serious efforts were made in the 1980s to sort out and "decongest" the system, with the hope that roles and responsibilities could be clarified and simplified. However, such efforts foundered on the shoals of political opposition, as political actors disagreed about both what should be done and who should do it in such programs as welfare, Medicaid, and food stamps. It became apparent that there was little appetite among federal or state officials to surrender control over programs that economists such as Alice Rivlin asserted should be delivered locally while centralizing welfare and health programs that called for national financing and control.[9]

The lack of appetite for serious reform did not rekindle appreciation for our intergovernmental system, but perhaps it should have. Intergovernmental systems are best suited for policy areas in which there is conflict over the goals and objectives that inhibit the development of purely national programs and wide distribution of the resources and capacities necessary to address particular problems or goals. Ultimately, our intergovernmental system is well suited for many of the wicked problems we face today—problems with contestable definitions and dimensions and no fixed boundaries.

Overcentralized approaches to defining objectives and implementation standards and regimes threaten to undermine the very advantages that intergovernmental systems are designed to promote. In the face of conflict over values and uncertainties over results, intergovernmental systems offer the prospect of adaptability, creativity, and flexibility. Hegemonic programs and accountability systems designed with the interests of only one actor in mind threaten to undermine these values. Policy learning can be compromised as well when the variability across states and localities is not incorporated in policy design and program implementation. Learning can also be compromised when national leaders leap too quickly to adopt state innovations before sufficient time has passed and analysis been performed to judge their effectiveness, a greater risk as the process of vertical policy diffusion has accelerated, fueled by anxious and ambitious political leaders.

The nationalization and centralization of our system most certainly jeopardizes local flexibility and adaptability. But these trends can jeopardize national performance and reputations as well, particularly when national goals depend on state or local partners for implementation. The response to Hurricane Katrina is the latest episode in which national policy officials were caught short by the realties of the intergovernmental system. Success in joint, collaborative policy regimes means that the capacities and values of state and local officials must be a focus of policy design, not assumed away or ignored in the implementation process. The failure to take into account the states' costs and administrative complications flowing from the hardened state driver's license mandate under the 2005 Real ID Act is yet another case in which national performance will be undermined by an overly centralized and coercive policy process. The crucible of crisis, such as Katrina, is often necessary to induce the degree of humility among public officials at all levels that leads to productive and cooperative partnerships.

Given the growing importance of intergovernmental partnerships, it has become more important for leaders at all levels of government to have access to information about best and worst practices in intergovernmental management across many different policy arenas. Ironically, as intergovernmental management has become more critical to national programs, national institutions dedicated to monitoring and evaluating these systems have withered. The Advisory Commission on Intergovernmental Relations disappeared more than twelve years ago, and the Office of Management and Budget abolished its intergovernmental management division many years ago. While the Government Accountability Office and the Congressional Budget Office have retained an intergovernmental analytic capacity, Congress itself has not sustained vital subcommittees with a focus on intergovernmental management. It is left to such organizations as the National Academy of Public Administration to support intergovernmental analysis cutting across programs and interests.

A look ahead to the challenges of the future suggests that intergovernmental management will continue to characterize our nation's approach to future policy problems. Whether addressing homeland security, global warming, or the education of the future workforce, partnership across governments will continue to be the watchword over this century as well. The question is whether we will design and manage intergovernmental partnerships by engaging key intergovernmental actors—not just when things go wrong but in designing programs and policies up front to reflect the real interests and capacities of all parties so critical to successfully addressing complex problems and managing complex systems.

Notes

1. U.S. Advisory Commission on Intergovernmental Relations, *The Transformation in American Politics: Implications for Federalism,* A-106 (Government Printing Office, 1986).

2. Lester Salamon, ed., *The Tools of Government: A Guide to the New Governance* (Oxford University Press, 2002).

3. Martha Derthick, *The Influence of Federal Grants: Public Assistance in Massachusetts* (Harvard University Press, 1970).

4. Harold Seidman, *Politics, Position, and Power*, 5th ed. (Oxford University Press, 1997), p. 149.

5. Paul E. Peterson, Barry Rabe, and Kenneth Wong, *When Federalism Works* (Brookings, 1986).

6. U.S. Government Accountability Office, *State and Local Governments: Persistent Fiscal Challenges Will Likely Emerge within the Next Decade*, GAO-07-1080SP (GPO, July 2007).

7. Paul Manna, *School's In: Federalism and the National Education Agenda, 1965–2001* (Georgetown University Press, 2006).

8. Timothy J. Conlan, "From Cooperative to Opportunistic Federalism: Reflections on the Half-Century Anniversary of the Commission on Intergovernmental Relations," *Public Administration Review* 66 (September–October 2006): 663–76.

9. Alice Rivlin, *Reviving the American Dream: The Economy, the States, and the Federal Government* (Brookings, 1992).

Contributors

Timothy J. Conlan
George Mason University

Jocelyn M. Johnston
American University

Shelley H. Metzenbaum
University of Massachusetts–Boston

Rania Nader
Indiana University

Richard P. Nathan
Nelson A. Rockefeller Institute
of Government

Paul L. Posner
George Mason University

Barry G. Rabe
University of Michigan

Beryl A. Radin
American University

Raymond C. Scheppach
National Governors Association

Frank Shafroth
Office of Representative
Jim Moran

Troy E. Smith
Brigham Young University
at Hawaii

Carl W. Stenberg
University of North Carolina–
Chapel Hill

Carol S. Weissert
Florida State University

William G. Weissert
Florida State University

Charles R. Wise
Ohio State University

Kenneth K. Wong
Brown University

Index

Accountability: block grants and, 143, 246, 251, 255, 272, 273; GPRA measurement and reporting requirements, 245–47; homeland security financial administration, 86–87, 89; intergovernmental performance monitoring and, 243–44, 260; learning leadership and, 210; in NCLB, 107–10, 120; in public education, 103–04, 110, 120; tax system, 64, 66–67; in third-party governments, 249–50; welfare program performance standards: 125

Adams, John, 13

Advisory Commission on Intergovernmental Relations: accomplishments, 4–5; demise, 5; purpose, 4

Affirmative action, 287

Aging of U.S. population: future challenges for government, 1–2, 44, 344–45; implications for health care system, 169; implications for labor force, 44; patterns, 43–44

Aid to Families with Dependent Children, 7, 125, 127, 128, 129, 134, 135, 141, 159, 160, 171–72

Alabama, 111

Alien and sedition laws, 13

Allen, George, 304

Andrus, Cecil, 321

Arizona, 81, 115

Bane, Frank, 348

Barnow, Burt, 255

Batdorff, Meagan, 118

Baumgartner, Frank, 301

Beam, David, 265

Bell, Terrel, 102

Berry, William, 136

Bioregionalism, 177

Bipartisan Campaign Reform Act, 315–16, 320–21

Block grants, 8; accountability issues, 143, 246, 251, 255, 272, 273; buying power, 274; concerns about, 271–72,

278; conditions favoring, 266; congressional attitudes and actions, 267–68; cost savings, 273; data collection and reporting requirements, 265, 271, 275–76; decentralization role, 264, 266, 270, 275, 278; definition and key features, 266; disadvantages, 127; future prospects, 278; lessons from past designs and implementations, 272–78; life cycle, 272–73; local government involvement, 274, 275, 277–78; negotiated performance measures, 255–57; origins and early evolution, 266–67, 268; outcome-focused measurement and, 223–24, 276–77; performance bonus, 254–55; Program Assessment Rating Tool review, 247–49; race-to-the-bottom theory of state benefit designs, 135–36, 272; reauthorization, 272–73; recent proposals, 269–70; recentralization, 273; social welfare programs, 127, 128, 129, 140; spending caps and cost controls, 271; state administrative capacity, 277–78; state funding of gaps in, 274, 278; targeting issues, 274; welfare reform of *1990*s, 268–69. *See also* Community Development Block Grant Program; Temporary Assistance for Needy Families
Bloomberg, Michael, 112
Bowman, Ann, 177
Boyd, Donald, 140
Brandeis, Louis, 209, 263
Bratton, William, 231–32
Bredesen, Phil, 108
Buckley, Jack, 113
Bush (G. H. W.) administration block grants, 268
Bush (G. W.) administration: block grant proposals, 270–71; education policies, 290–91; environmental policies, 178, 181, 199–200; federalism record, 271,

290, 294, 295–97, 299, 300, 339–40; growth of federal mandates, 8; health care policies, 160, 171, 273, 294, 304; homeland security policies, 77, 80–81, 93, 293–94; intergovernmental performance assessment policies, 247–49; political philosophy, 289–90; social welfare policies, 142; tax policy, 71, 292–93. *See also* No Child Left Behind program
Bushweller, Kevin, 111

California, 115, 180–81, 196
Campaign finance reform, 315–16, 320–21
Campbell, Ben Nighthorse, 230–31
Canada, 182, 196
Carbon emission regulation: in California, 180–81; cap-and-trade programs, 182–84; leakage risk, 196–97. *See also* Regional Greenhouse Gas Initiative
Carwile, William, 81
Centers for Disease Control and Prevention 225–26
Centers for Medicare and Medicaid, 170, 250
Chancellor Beacon Academies, 117
Chaos theory, 29
Chernick, Howard, 128
Chertoff, Michael, 79, 94
Chiles, Lawton, 317
Cho, Chung-Lae, 265
Civil War, 37
Clean Air Act, 180, 181, 229–30, 231, 232
Clinton, Hillary Rodham, 275
Clinton administration: education policy, 107, 112–13, 258–59; health care policies, 160, 167–68; intergovernmental decentralization efforts, 265; welfare policies, 125, 140, 268, 273
Coercive/co-optive federalism: cooperation among state to resist, 313; evolution of

federalism, 33–34, 311, 343; in homeland security measures, 293–94; instruments of, 287–88; intergovernmental
management and, 343–44; negative
effects, 307; performance assessment
requirements for states as, 295–96;
public information strategies, 295;
recent trends, 288–89, 290–94, 306;
in tax policy, 295; Unfunded Mandates
Reform Act and, 297–98. *See also*
Federal mandates
Colorado, 130
Commager, Henry Steele, 17
Commerce clause, 46, 311
Community Development Block Grant
Program: funding trends, 268; local
involvement, 274; performance assessment, 276–77; Strengthening America's
Communities Initiative, 251, 270–71;
waivers, 265, 273
Comprehensive Employment and Training
Act, 266
Congress: block grant control, 267–68,
272–73, 278; centralization trends,
288–89; evolution of federalism,
311–12; homeland security initiatives,
79–80, 88, 95; interest representation
role and policymaking, 318–20; intergovernmental management capacity, 4,
5; intergovernmental performance
goals in legislation, 257–58; Medicaid
waivers and, 161–62, 167; obstacles to
social welfare reform, 54–55; recent
block grant proposals, 269–70; representatives' loyalty to state interests,
313–14, 315–16; significance of
national party organizations, 315; state
partisan politics and, 314–15; targets
for intergovernmental lobbying,
316–18; use of points of order,
297–98. *See also* Intergovernmental
lobbying

Conlan, Timothy, 265, 273
Connecticut, 109, 222, 244
Conservative governance: Bush (G. W.)
administration, 289–90, 339; federalism and, 21, 22, 299, 339, 340; governmental growth and, 6, 20–21; welfare policies, 126–27
Constitution, U.S.: evolution of federalism, 311; intergovernmental budget
framework, 45–46; Supreme Court
role in future of federalism, 330; tax
reform considerations, 56
Coolidge administration, 17
Cooperative federalism: characteristics,
32–33, 341–42; governance skills for,
38; structure of intergovernmental relations, 34, 343; tools of, for centralization, 303–04; transition to coercive
federalism, 9, 32, 342, 343

Decentralization: block grants as instrument of decentralization, 8, 264; centralizing trends, 288–89, 290, 339–41;
chaos theory, 29; Clinton administration efforts, 265; devolution and,
264–65; education system, 105; evolution of federal system, 37–38; instruments of federal centralization,
287–88; key features, 264–65; Medicaid waiver effects, 7; performance
measurement effects, 8, 250; recentralization of block grants, 273; regional
initiatives for, 7
Deficit Reduction Act, 126, 140, 142, 171
DeLay, Tom, 294
Department of Health and Human Services, 86, 93, 151, 159, 169, 170, 233,
256, 265, 291
Department of Transportation, 216–17
Derthick, Martha, 313
Devolution: block grants as instrument of,
264, 269, 270, 275, 278; contractual,

138–39; decentralization and, 264; definition, 125; future prospects, 142–43, 278; partial, 264; policy outcomes to date, 135, 140–43, 265; political movement, 264; second-order, 138; welfare reform, 127, 136–43. *See also* Decentralization
Dingell, John, 161
Dirken, Everett, 15
Discretionary grants, 48, 50–53
District of Columbia School Choice Incentive Act, 113–14
Doolittle, Fred, 124, 274
Dual federalism, 14, 32, 38, 310, 311

Earmarks, 319
Earned income tax credit, 129, 133
Economic development: environmental regulation and, 189–90; regional approach, 52–53; state government role in, 18–19
Economy: current forces and trends, 42, 43–44; current intergovernmental budget framework, 45–48; future challenges for states and localities, 344–45; growth of government, 17; implications of global trends for governance, 44–45; influence on federal-state interactions, 6. *See also* Funding for domestic programs; Tax system
Edison Project, 116–17
Education: accountability in, 103–04, 110, 120; centralizing trends, 290–91; charter school movement, 103, 113, 114, 115, 116, 118; current state of reform, 119–20; emergence of performance-based accountability, 107–10; equity promotion, 105–07; evolution of intergovernmental relations and, 35–36; evolution of political beliefs, 102–03; federal discretionary grants, 48; freedom index, 114–15;

funding, 106; grants-in-aid system, 105–07; innovation management, 104, 120; intergovernmental measurement, 220–23; intergovernmental redesign of policy, 104–05; policy challenges, 7; private sector involvement, 116–18; recent innovations in, 103–04; school choice policies, 112–19; school takeover as reform strategy, 110–12; school voucher programs, 113–14, 115; state government innovations, 18; waivers of federal requirements, 160. *See also* No Child Left Behind program
Elazar, Daniel, 185, 288
Election administration, 292
Elementary and Secondary Education Act, 106
Emergency Management Reform Act, 79–80, 82–83, 85, 95
Energy economy: renewable portfolio standards, 179–80. *See also* Global warming; Regional Greenhouse Gas Initiative
Engel, Kirsten, 181
Engler, John, 134, 161, 199, 264
Entitlement programs, 47, 54. *See also specific program*
Environmental protection: evolution of intergovernmental relations and, 34–35; future of regional collaboration, 200–02; geographic patterns of policy innovation, 180–81; methyl tertiary butyl ether contamination, 294, 303, 304–05; regional collaboration for, 177–78; state government innovations, 18
Environmental Protection Agency, 199–200, 231, 232; performance partnerships, 253
Equity in education, 105–06
Establishment clause, 115–16
European Union carbon emission trading, 182–83, 196, 200
Evolutionary theory, 28–29

Federal Emergency Management Agency, 36–37, 79–80, 81, 87

Federal Highway Administration, 218–20, 225

Federalism: cake metaphor, 26, 27; chaos theory in modeling of, 29; conceptual and historical evolution, 6, 13–17, 310, 311–13, 341–43; constitutional law and, 311; current challenges, 338–39; current political salience, 318–19; evolutionary theory of, 28–29; federal role in promoting equity, 105; fiscal, 164; future challenges, 3, 6–7, 9, 42, 330–31, 344; geological models of development of, 30–38; grants as mechanism of federal influence, 212; liberal activism and, 20; misleading assumptions, 313–14; nationalization of policy agenda in recent times, 339–41; natural science metaphors, 28; need for new model of, 48–49; opportunistic, 331, 348–49; political ideology and, 299, 340; rationale, 212; regionalism and, 176–77, 198–200; responsibility for assistance to poor, 124–25; role of metaphors in study of, 26–27; tax system, 57, 58–60, 71; transition to coercive/co-optive system, 33–34. *See also* Coercive/co-optive federalism; Federal-state relationship

Federalist Papers, 14

Federal mandates, 8; in election administration, 292; historical transition to, 33–34; interest group support, 304–05; motivation, 286; new policy instruments, 295–96; in No Child Left Behind, 109, 290; performance measurement requirements, 295–96; political life cycle, 305–06; politics of implementation and outcomes, 298–305, 306–07; Real ID Act as, 294; state and local political support for, 300–03,

306; taxonomy, 286–88; tax policy, 292–93; trends, 286, 306; use of points of order in legislative process, 297–98; in welfare programs, 292

Federal-state relationship: current education reform, 119–20; current environment, 2–3, 339–44; current intergovernmental budget framework, 45–48; current welfare program delivery, 125, 140–41; economic contexts, 6; entitlement program administration, 53–54; federal lobbying by state and local officials, 8–9; financial administration of homeland security, 86–91; game theory, 166; governmental growth process, 6, 15–17, 20–21, 22; in grants system, 228–29; homeland security, future of, 96–98; homeland security planning framework, 81–85; intelligence and information management for homeland security, 91–96; intergovernmental license model, 165–67; large-scale rapid change in, 37–38; liberal activism in state government, 18–20; Medicaid waivers and, 162–67; models of, 6; in No Child Left Behind administration, 119, 290–91; party politics and, 288, 289; performance movement and, 243–45; power relations, 3, 15; promoting equity in education, 105–07; rationale for homeland security coordination, 77–78; reform of discretionary spending, 50–53; regional environmental initiatives, 198–200, 201–02; state role in national initiatives, 2, 3; strategies to enhance performance measurement implementation, 251–61; tax system coordination, 58–60, 61–62, 63–64, 65–71. *See also* Decentralization; Devolution; Federalism; Federal mandates; Intergovernmental performance monitoring and management

Feinstein, Dianne, 199

Fenno, Richard, 320

*Final Report on the 9/11 Commission Rec-
ommendations,* 93

Fire departments: evolution of intergovernmental relations, 36; federal involvement in state and local policymaking, 3

First Amendment, 115–16

Florida, 115, 116, 162–63, 168, 292, 317

Foer, Franklin, 19–20

Food stamp program: current administration, 53; Personal Responsibility and
Work Opportunity Reconciliation Act
and, 138

Fording, Richard, 136

Fossert, James, 162

Foy, Douglas, 191–92

Frank, Barney, 18

Frankfurter, Felix, 176

Frederickson, David, 250

Frederickson, George, 250

Funding for government programs: block
grant distribution patterns, 275; constitutional framework, 45–46; cost savings in block grants, 273; current patterns, 46–48; discretionary grants, 48,
50–53; earmarks, 319; education, 106;
entitlement programs, 47, 53–54; evolution of block grant programs, 267,
269–70; federal-state interactions in
development of, 16–17; fiscal federalism, 164; future challenges, 2; grants-
in-aid, 32–33; health care spending,
1–2, 157, 169; homeland security
administration, 86–91, 97; obstacles to
reform, 54–55; penalties for federal
noncompliance, 229–33; population
aging and, 44; recent block grant proposals, 270–71; social welfare programs, 47–48, 127, 142; state government activism and, 18–19; state
spending, 46; Temporary Assistance for

Needy Families, 127–30; use of points
of order in legislative process, 297–98

Future challenges: aging of population, 1,
44; block grant performance assessment,
276–77; congressional approval of block
grants, 278; education reform, 119–20;
for federal system, 3, 9, 330–31; global
economic changes, 42, 43; intergovernmental homeland security, 96–98; intergovernmental policy development, 306,
349–50; oversight and analysis of intergovernmental system, 3–5; Regional
Greenhouse Gas Initiative, 190–98;
responsiveness of government, 48–49;
social welfare program reform, 54–55;
state governance, 45, 46, 330, 344–46;
tax reform, 63–64, 72

Gais, Thomas, 132, 139, 162

Galbraith, James K., 21

Gas tax, 46, 56, 68

General Revenue Sharing Act, 263–64

Geological models of federal system development, 30–38

Glastris, Paul, 20

Globalization: future challenges, 2, 42,
344; implications for state regulation,
45, 345; implications for tax system,
58, 344; trends, 43

Global warming: carbon cap-and-trade
programs, 182–84; implications for tax
system, 56; Kyoto Protocol and, 178;
regional approaches, 177–78, 179–84;
renewable portfolio standards, 179–80;
state policymaking, 7. *See also* Regional
Greenhouse Gas Initiative

Gokcekus, Omer, 119

Gormley, William, 299

Government Performance and Results Act
(GPRA): concerns about, 272; future
prospects, 276–77; implementation
challenges, 251–52; implications for

federalism, 213; measurement and reporting requirements, 212–13, 245–47, 276; outcomes orientation, 245; Program Assessment Rating Tool and, 245; purpose, 244

GPRA. *See* Government Performance and Results Act

Gramm-Leach-Bliley Act, 345–46

Grants: in cooperative federalism, 32–33; decentralizing effects, 347; education, 105–07; effective design, 224–25, 226–27, 228, 234; to encourage innovation, 226; as incentive to measurement, 225–26, 234; as mechanism of federal influence, 212, 225, 228; performance assessment, 227–28, 246–47; principal-agent relationship in, 228–29; social welfare programs, 127–29. *See also* Block grants

Grasmick, Nancy, 111–12

Great Society programs, 17, 38, 103, 344

Greene, Jay, 114–15

Greve, Michael, 20

Grodzins, Morton, 14, 26, 29, 288

Growth of government: conservative–liberal politics and, 21; federal system and, 6, 15–17, 20–21; intergovernmental coalitions in, 20–21; recent trends in presidential politics, 263; strategies to reduce, 263–64

Gulick, Luther, 15

Hamel, Sonia, 192

Hamilton, Alexander, 13, 14, 57

Hanson, Russell, 136

Hassel, Bryan C., 118

Hatch, Orrin, 328

Hawaii, 115

Head Start, 106

Health care: characteristics of U. S. system, 157; cooperative federalism in, 33; federal goal setting, 214–16, 233; government programs, 47; home and community-based care services, 167–69, 171; international comparisons, 157; obstacles to reform, 157–58; population aging and, 1–2, 44; prospects for reform, 158; spending trends, 1–2, 169, 345; state government innovations, 18, 158. *See also* Medicaid; Medicare

Healthy People initiative, 214–16, 233

Hellerstein, Walter, 57

Help America Vote Act, 292, 300

Hess, Frederick, 118, 119

Highway Safety Act, 230

Hochschild, Jennifer, 108

Holcomb, Pamela, 139

Homeland security: challenges in implementing national system, 6–7, 96–98; current planning framework, 81–85; distribution of block grant funding, 275; evolution of current structure and operations, 78–81; evolution of intergovernmental relations, 36–37; federal involvement in state and local policymaking, 3, 293–94; financial administration, 86–91, 97; intelligence and information management, 91–96, 97, 98; intergovernmental nature of, 77–78; National Incident Management System, 80, 83, 85; National Infrastructure Protection Plan, 82; National Performance Goal, 97; National Preparedness Goal, 82, 84; National Response Plan, 80, 82, 83, 85; rationale for centralization of activities, 78; risk assessment for resource allocation, 88–89

Homeland Security Block Grant Act, 275

Horn, Wade, 291

Housing and Community Development Act, 266

Hurricane Katrina, 77, 79, 81, 82, 84–85, 95, 349

Illinois, 90, 196

Improving America's Schools Act, 107

Ingram, Helen, 164, 165

Ink, Dwight, 4

Intergovernmental lobbying: congressional representative's interests and, 320–23, 329–30; consistency of message, 325; cooperation among states for, 323–24, 325–28, 345–46; need for, 310, 329; partisan politics and, 314–16; personal relationships in, 322; policy development and, 320, 321; skills and knowledge for, 314; state offices in Washington, 324–25; strategies and techniques, 321–23; structure and function of Congress and, 316–18

Intergovernmental performance monitoring and management: accountability goals and, 243–44, 260; accountability in education, 107–10; block grants, 272, 276–77, 347; in coercive federalism, 343–44; complexity of policy issues and, 349; in cooperative federalism, 343; current institutional capacity, 1, 4–5, 350; data sharing, 217; discretionary spending reform, 50–53; education measurement, 220–23; education policy redesign, 104–05; evolution of federalism, 312; federal role, 260; future challenges, 3–4, 306, 349–50; Government Performance and Results Act, 212–13; health care system, 214–15; homeland security planning framework, 81–85; mandates for states, 295–96; Medicaid wavers, 170; need for learning leaders, 209–11; negotiated performance measures, 255–57; obstacles to reform, 348–49; outcomes of performance movement, 347–48; performance goals in legislation, 257–58; performance partnerships, 251–53, 265; practical advantages, 211–12; program waivers, 259–60; purpose, 8; role of metaphors in, 38–39; sensitivity to context and program differences, 261; standard-setting, 258–59, 347; strategies to enhance federal-state relationship, 251; tax system goals, 65–66; tensions inherent in, 243–44, 251–52, 260, 339, 348; third-party perspectives, 244–45, 249–51; tools for, 213, 233, 341; in transportation sector, 218–20; unintended outcomes of interventions, 8; use of goals for, 210–11, 212, 213, 233; use of grants for, 224–29, 234; use of incentives for, 210, 224, 253–55; use of measurement as tool for, 210–11, 212, 213, 217–24, 233–34, 260–61; use of penalties in, 229–33, 234

Intermodal Surface Transportation and Efficiency Act, 230

International Association of Chiefs of Police, 84

International Fuel Tax Agreement, 68

Internet Tax Freedom Act, 61

Jay, John, 14

Job Training and Partnership Act, 259

Johnson administration, 17, 38, 268

Jones, Bryan, 301

Kentucky, 90, 111

Kestenbaum Commission, 4

Key, V. O., 134

Kramer, Larry D., 313–14

Krueger, Gary, 136

Kyoto Protocol, 178, 182

Labor markets: outcomes of welfare programs, 125–26; population aging and, 44

Ladd, Helen, 124

Landis, James, 176

La Raja, Raymond J., 316

Laski, Harold, 15

Learning leaders, intergovernmental: accountability and, 210; role of, 209–10, 211; tools of, 210–11

Leavitt, Michael, 328

Lee, J. Y., 110

Levy, David, 190

Liberal governance: federalism and, 21, 22, 299, 340; governmental growth and, 6, 18–20

Lieberman, Joseph, 183

Lieberman, Robert, 136

Litz, Franz, 192, 201

Lobbying and interest group politics: in centralization trends, 289; nationalization of policy agenda and, 341; opportunistic behavior in federal policymaking, 3, 331; in policy development, 320. *See also* Intergovernmental lobbying

Macmahon, Arthur W., 15

Madison, James, 13–14

Maine, 90

Malanga, Steven, 20

Mandates. *See* Federal mandates

Manna, Paul, 108, 301

Markle Foundation, 94

Martinson, Karin, 139

Maryland, 111

Massachusetts, 112, 162, 163, 191–92

Maternal and Child Health Bureau, 255–57

McCain, John, 183

McGuinn, Patrick, 118, 119

McLure, Charles, 57

Mead, Lawrence, 139–40

Media, nationalization of policy agenda and, 340

Medicaid: federal-state interactions, 18, 53; funding, 47–48, 294; Medicare and, 54; performance measurement and accountability in, 250–51; Personal Responsibility and Work Opportunity Reconciliation Act and, 138; population aging and, 44; purpose, 47; reform strategies, 54; spending trends, 2, 345; waivers. *See* Medicaid waivers

Medicaid waivers, 7, 273; bargaining process, 166, 170; home and community-based care services, 167–69, 171; implications for health care reform, 158; intergovernmental implications, 162–64; as intergovernmental licenses, 164–67, 171; origins, 159; oversight, 170–71; policy tool theory, 164–65; politics of, 158–62; program waivers, 159–60; purpose, 158, 159; renewal, 166, 169–70; significance of, 158, 172–72

Medicare: current administration, 53; Medicaid and, 54; performance measurement and accountability in, 250; purpose, 47; spending trends, 2

Menino, Thomas, 112

Michigan, 112, 115

Minimum wage, 19

Minner, Ruth Ann, 201

Mobile Telecommunications Sourcing Act, 68–69

Monypenny, Phillip, 302

Motorcycle helmet laws, 230–31

Multistate Tax Commission, 68

Nathan, Richard, 139, 274

National Assessment of Educational Progress, 221–22

National Association of Insurance Commissioners, 345–46

National Conference of State Legislatures, 323

National defense: intergovernmental budget framework, 45–46. *See also* Homeland security

National Emergency Management Association, 83–84, 92–93
National Governors Association, 323, 325
National Highway Traffic Safety Administration, 219–20, 226, 230–31
National Incident Management System, 37
National Performance Review, 265
A Nation at Risk, 103, 107, 221–22
NCLB. *See* No Child Left Behind
Neustadt, Richard, 15
Nevins, Allan, 17
New York, 89, 90, 112, 130, 183, 194–95, 328
Nitz, Lawrence, 136
Nixon administration, 266, 268, 288
No Child Left Behind (NCLB) program, 7, 271; accountability features, 107–08, 110, 296; community engagement and, 108–09; data collection and management, 223; distinguishing features, 107, 222; intergovernmental relations in design of, 36, 104, 222–23, 290–91; outcomes, 119, 120, 223; political trends behind, 102–03, 222, 300, 301; public reporting requirements, 108, 295; school choice provisions, 115–16; state resistance to, 244; supplemental service waivers, 109–10; takeover policies, 110; as unfunded mandate, 109, 290; waivers, 160
North Carolina, 219–20

Office of Intergovernmental Affairs, 4
Office of Management and Budget, 4
Office of State and Local Finance, 4
Office of the Director of National Intelligence, 94
Ohio, 90, 115–16
Olmstead v. *L.C.,* 168–69
Olson, Mancur, 313
O'Malley, Martin, 111–12

Omnibus Budget and Reconciliation Act, 167, 256, 264, 267, 268, 273
Omnibus Crime Control and Safe Streets Act, 266, 268
Oregon, 130
Owens, Major, 259

Partnership for Health Act, 266
Pataki, George, 183, 190
Paterson, Paul, 37
Patrick, Deval, 192
Patterson, James T., 17
Pell grants, 48
Penalties, as federal incentives, 229–33, 234
Pennsylvania, 111, 116–17, 195, 197
Pension programs, 17
Performance Assessment Rating Tool, 213, 251–52
Performance partnerships, 251–53, 265
Personal Responsibility and Work Opportunity Reconciliation Act: administrative costs, 139–40; delinked programs, 138; fiscal design, 127–30, 140; innovation in state implementation, 125, 131–32, 140; outcomes, 125–26, 140, 143; reauthorization, 126–27, 142–43; significant features, 124–25, 268; state role in development of, 320; variation in state policies, 131–35, 141. *See also* Temporary Assistance for Needy Families
Peterson, Paul, 141
Phillips, Joshua, 119
Plotnick, Robert, 134
Points of order, 297–98
Policymaking: challenges in education, 7; challenges in national security, 6–7; challenges in welfare reform, 7; congressional representatives' policy interests versus state interests, 313–14; determinants of federal mandate

outcomes, 298–303; federal model, 15–16; feedback model, 301; future challenges, 306; geographic patterns of innovation, 180–81; interest representation versus, 318–20; lobbyist role, 320; mandate politics, 8; Medicaid wavers, 7; policy tools, 164–65; political aspects of Medicaid waivers, 158–62; states as source of innovation in, 18, 120, 131–32, 140, 180–81, 209, 263, 346; state welfare programs, 134–35. *See also* Intergovernmental lobbying

Population ecology, 28

Posner, Paul, 249

Private sector: in centralization trends, 289, 341; decentralization and, 288; educational services, 116–18; performance measurement in third-party government, 249–51; trends in public services delivery, 343–44; in welfare program delivery, 138–39

Program Assessment Rating Tool, 244, 276; block grant analysis, 247–49; future prospects, 276–77; Government Performance and Results Act and, 245

Public infrastructure: future challenges, 2; intergovernmental funding, 46; regional approach to managing, 52–53; state activism, 18. *See also* Transportation

Public perception and understanding: expectations for government, 2; states' rights, 313

Purcell, Bill, 108

Rabe, Barry, 17, 37

Radin, Beryl, 276

Reagan administration, 102; block grant policies, 160, 268, 274, 275; federalism of, 17, 288; health care policies, 167

Real ID Act, 271, 293–94, 301, 350

Regional Greenhouse Gas Initiative: current status, 177–78, 183–84; early reduction credits, 187; economic development and, 189–90; federal policy and, 198–200, 201–02; flexibility in implementation and compliance, 187–89; future challenges, 190–98; goals, 184; implications for future environmental collaborations, 200–02; institutionalization, 193–95; leakage vulnerability, 196–98; operating framework, 184–85; participant characteristics and relationships, 184–85, 194–96; political considerations in policy formulation, 186–87; requirements, 183, 187, 188; secession of members, 191–92; significance of, 184, 190, 347; triggers and safety valves, 18, 187

Regional strategies: accountability, 52–53; bicoastal regionalism, 180–82; carbon cap-and-trade programs, 182–84; consolidation of grants for, 52; current implementation, 200–01; de facto regionalism, 179–80; for environmental protection, 177–78; federal system and, 198–200; future prospects, 200–02; governance models, 176–77; historical and conceptual evolution, 176, 177; innovation in, 347; international collaboration, 181–82; rationale, 176; renewable portfolio standards, 179–80; secession threat, 191. *See also* Regional Greenhouse Gas Initiative

Regulation of business and commerce: evolution in U.S., 17; future challenges for states, 345–46; globalization trends and, 345; state government activism in, 19

Reinventing Government, 265

Religious beliefs, activism in state government and, 19

Rendell, Edward, 195

Renewable portfolio standards, 179–80, 202

Rhode Island, 192

Ridge, Tom, 78, 111, 117

The Rise of the States (Teaford), 15

Rivlin, Alice, 349

Robert Wood Johnson Foundation, 215

Romney, Mitt, 191–92

Roosevelt (F. D.) administration, 17, 37–38

Royce, Ed, 321

Sabo, Martin, 322

Salamon, Lester, 165, 217

Schiavo, Terri, 19

Schneider, Anne, 164

Schneider, Mark, 113

School lunch program, 105, 106

Schram, Sanford, 136

Schume, Charles, 328

Schwarzenegger, Arnold, 196

Seay, Douglas, 277

Seder, Richard C., 111

Seismic events metaphor, 37–38

Sensenbrenner, James, 294

Separation of powers, 15

September *11, 2000,* terrorist attacks, 36, 77, 271, 293

Service economy, 43

Shaw, Clay, 161

Shaw, Greg, 136

Skocpol, Theda, 16–17

Smith, Jeffrey, 255

Snow, John, 71

Social Security Act, 159, 259

Social security system, 47, 53

Social welfare programs and policies, 7; appropriate level of government administration, 124–25; federal role in promoting equity, 105; funding, 47–48; future prospects, 142–43; innovation in, 131–32, 140; institutional culture,

136; outcomes, 133–34; performance measurement requirements for states, 296; race-to-the-bottom theory of state benefit designs, 135–36, 272; racial aspects, 141; recent centralization trends, 291, 296; state government role in development of, 16–17; state waiver applications, 140, 160. *See also* Personal Responsibility and Work Opportunity Reconciliation Act; *specific program*

Soss, Joe, 135

South Carolina, 220

Specialty Crop Block Grant, 269–70

Specter, Arlen, 108

State and Local Housing Flexibility Act, 275

State Children's Health Insurance Program, 159

State government: congressional representatives' support for, 313–14, 315–16; cooperation among states to resist federal expansion, 313, 345–46; evolution of education policies, 103, 108; future challenges, 330, 344–46; global trade policies and, 45, 345; global warming initiatives, 7, 178–79; health care reform prospects, 158; health care spending trends, 2; innovations in policy and governance, 16–17, 18, 120, 131–32, 140, 180–81, 209, 263, 346; liberal activism in, 18–21, 22; networked model, 48–49; politics of federal mandates, 300–03, 306; public infrastructure provision, 46; public loyalty, 313; recent growth of centralized federalism, 288–89; response to global economic trends, 44–45; restraint of federal growth, 21; school takeover as education reform strategy, 110–12; social welfare program designs, 131–36, 141; tax reform rationale, 60–61; tax revenues, 45, 55, 60. *See also* Federalism; Federal mandates; Federal-state relationship; Intergovernmental lobbying; Lobbying and interest group politics; Regional strategies

Street, John, 108

Strengthening America's Communities Initiative, 251, 270–71

Substance Abuse and Mental Health Services Administration, 272

Sullivan, Andrew, 20

Supremacy clause, 56

Tax system: accountability, 64, 66–67; capital mobility and, 56, 58, 344; current revenue and sources, 45, 55, 60; estate taxes, 67, 292–93, 295; excise taxes, 64; federalist principles, 57, 58–60, 71; federal-state coordination, 58–60, 61–62, 63–64, 65–71; future challenges, 2, 45, 63, 72, 344; implications of digital and intangible goods, 45, 55–56, 62–63, 69–70, 304, 346; income tax model of reform, 67–68; multistate coordination model, 68–69; population aging and, 44; recent federal centralization, 292–93, 295; reform goals, 58–60, 63–65, 70; reform rationale, 55–57, 60–61, 71–72; sales tax, 293, 304, 344, 346; shortcomings of current system, 58; sovereignty concerns, 65; state budgeting, 46; Streamlined Sales Tax Project model, 66

Teaford, Jon C., 15

Technology innovation and diffusion: future of federal-state interactions, 49; global economic change, 43; implications for state tax revenues, 45, 55–56; telecommunications, 59

Telecommunications technology, 59

Temporary Assistance for Needy Families, 7, 47–48, 259, 324; current administration, 53; funding, 127–30, 142; future prospects, 142–43; institutional change for service delivery, 136–38; local administration, 138–39, 274; maintenance-of-effort funding, 129; outcomes, 126, 132, 133–34, 291; performance measurement, 296; race-to-the-bottom theory, 135–36; reauthorization, 273, 291; recession effects, 131; significant features, 125, 126, 129–30, 268, 269; state performance bonus, 254–55; work mandates, 291. *See also* Personal Responsibility and Work Opportunity Reconciliation Act

Tenth Amendment, 56, 105

Teske, Paul, 118

Thompson, Tommy, 125, 161, 166

Thurmond, Strom, 18

Title I education grants, 48

Title V block grants, 255–57

Tower, Edward, 119

Trade: future of state-federal relations, 45; global trends, 43, 345

Transportation: funding, 48; information management in intergovernmental relationship, 218–20, 230; motorcycle helmet laws, 230–31; regional collaboration in infrastructure provision, 52. *See also* Public infrastructure

Treverton, Gregory, 93

Tyler, John, 14

Understanding Intergovernmental Relations (Wright), 26

Unemployment insurance and workers' compensation: evolution in U.S., 17

Unfunded Mandates Reform Act, 264, 287–88, 297–98, 324

USA PATRIOT Act, 88, 271

Utah, 90, 115, 163, 244, 328

Vallas, Paul, 108, 117
Vermont, 163
Victory Schools, 116, 117
Vining, Aidan, 254
Virginia Resolutions, 13

Walker, David B., 324
Washington, D.C., 113–14
Weaver, R. Kent, 127, 132
Weimer, David, 254
Weinberger, Mark, 57
Weissert, Carol, 134

West Virginia, 111
Wheare, K. C., 15
White Hat Management, 116
Winters, Richard, 134
Wisconsin, 125, 130, 139–40
Wong, Kenneth, 37
Workforce Investment Act, 257, 259
Wright, Deil, 26, 33, 265
Wyden, Ron, 304

Ziebarth, Todd, 111
Zimmerman, Joseph, 34, 264